JIM ROHWER

ASIA RISING

SIMON & SCHUSTER

New York • London • Toronto • Sydney • Tokyo • Singapore

SIMON & SCHUSTER
Rockefeller Center
1230 Avenue of the Americas
New York, NY 10020

SIMON & SCHUSTER and colophon are registered trademarks
of Simon & Schuster Inc.

Designed by Irving Perkins Associates

Manufactured in the United States of America

10   9   8   7   6   5   4   3   2   1

Library of Congress Cataloging-in-Publication Data
Rohwer, Jim.
   Asia rising / Jim Rohwer.
      p.   cm.
   Includes bibliographical references and index.
   1. East Asia—Economic conditions.   2. Asia, Southeastern—Economic
conditions.   3. South Asia—Economic conditions.   4. Economic history—
1945–   I. Title.
HC460.5.R64   1995
330.95—dc20   95-38488
                                                                      CIP

ISBN 0-684-80752-1

Some passages of this book appeared in different form in articles the author
wrote for *The Economist* between 1990 and 1994. The interview of Lee Kuan Yew
on pages 329–331 is reprinted in its entirety from *The Economist* of June 29, 1991.
The Economist's permission to reprint these passages is gratefully acknowledged.

For my mother
and the memory of my father

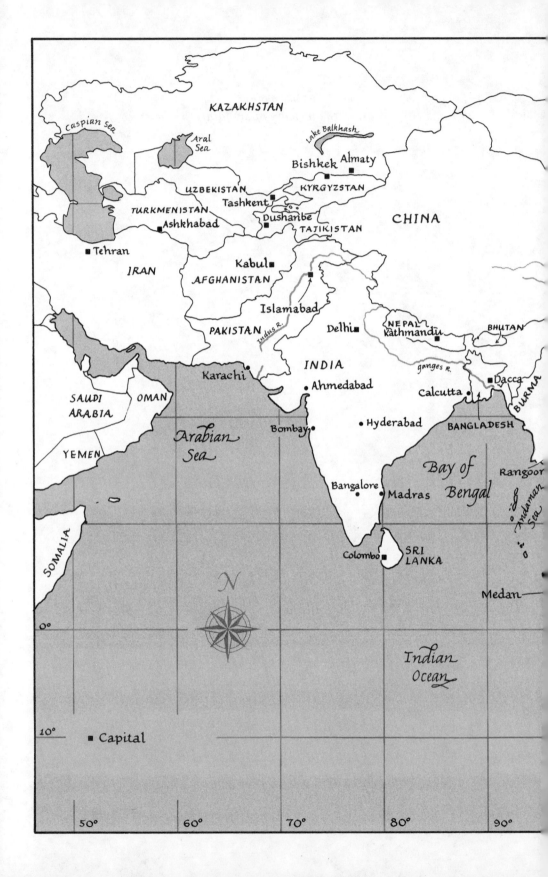

CONTENTS

PART III

MAIN STREET AND WALL STREET IN ASIA

PART IV

POLITICS AND GEOPOLITICS

PROLOGUE: HONG KONG, 1995

I can now permit myself a cigar, and a more leisurely look than I have given in a long time to the view of Hong Kong's teeming harbor that I have from my balcony. I came to Hong Kong only four years ago, but the view has already changed enormously. Thirty or forty apartment buildings have been put up along a mile-long stretch of the road just below mine. A gigantic suspension bridge is going up to the west; it will link Hong Kong's new airport to the city and to the Chinese mainland. Late at night the collection of ships in the harbor, their lights twinkling, still look like varieties of insects skimming swiftly or trundling solemnly across the black water. Yet even I can see that the insects now have far less water to move in: Land reclamation has already reduced the width of the harbor substantially and—who knows?—may one day come close to eliminating it. This is how fast Asia changes. Even now it surprises and excites me. It is going to change the world.

Anybody coming to the nerve center of Asia in, say, 2020 (thirty years after I did) would go not to Hong Kong but to Shanghai. By then Shanghai will be a city of 27 million people, richer than half of Europe's cities and many of America's. It will be the great cultural and industrial center of the Chinese world. It will also be the financial capital of East Asia. Sometime in the first decade of the twenty-first century it will displace Hong Kong as China's main financial-service center and shortly after that surpass Tokyo as the most sophisticated and open financial market in the East Asian time

zone—and thus join the old-timers of London and New York as one
of the indispensable big three of world finance.

Naturally, with Asia as huge as it is in size and population and as
rich as it will then be, the continent will have no one "center":
Asia's economic landscape in 2020 will be dominated by a couple of
dozen megacities that will act as the cultural, financial, and industrial cores of often vast hinterlands. China itself will claim ten of
these, including Taipei, in Taiwan, and Hong Kong, which will still
serve as the banker of southern China and the biggest single intermediary between the overseas Chinese businessmen of Southeast
Asia and China itself.

Northeast Asia will boast several non-Chinese megacities as well.
Seoul, long since the capital of a united Korea, and Vladivostok, the
capital of the Russian Far East, will vie and sometimes cooperate in
the exploitation of Siberia's immense natural wealth, in the industrialization of the region where China, Russia, and Korea meet, and in
the heady, early "Californiazation" of Russia's Pacific coast.

Japan will still have its great conurbations of Tokyo and Osaka,
though by then they will act less as manufacturing centers than as
service nodes linked to and in charge of a huge Japanese network
of manufacturing ventures stretching all the way through East Asia
and Southeast Asia and into the Indian subcontinent. Along the way
this network will pass through the eight or so big urban centers of
Southeast Asia (Manila, Jakarta, Surabaya, Saigon, Bangkok, Kuala
Lumpur, Singapore, and Rangoon) and into India itself, where
Bombay—the financial capital of the whole of South and Central
Asia—will be the first among a half-dozen large cities that dominate
the fast-growing subcontinent.

Not only Asian cities will have been been transformed: In fact, it
is the gradual but relentless lifting of 2 billion rural Asians out
of poverty over the years 1980–2020 that will make possible the
extraordinary boom in consumption and urbanization that has already begun radically to reshape the world economy. The result of
this process in Asia will not be, as it was in America, the creation
of an efficient capital-intensive farm economy in the countryside.
Instead, Asia's countryside will become prized for the recreation it
can offer the well-off—in the same way Western Europe's countryside is valued now, only more so because Asia is even more crowded.

The best example is Bali, the mystical Indonesian island whose
lush volcanic landscape and ancient mix of cultures and religions

long ago started attracting visitors from all over, converting its simple farming folk into smiling fodder for the tourist industry. The religions and the cultures will survive, though as part of a modern society whose people by 2020 will no longer be servants but will instead enjoy incomes as high as those in America in 1995. The place itself will look more like Newport Beach than some timeless land, its homeowners an international mix as prosperous and diverse as those of Carmel or Provence.

I plan to take advantage of all of this. By 2020 I expect to own a house in a district of Shanghai that in imperial days was known as the French Concession (a house bought at the bottom of the market in 1997, when a combination of political worries about workers' riots throughout China and a cyclical collapse in Shanghainese property prices should scare off most outsiders). And I hope to have a weekend place in Bali.

By then I will be past seventy, so you might assume that this is of merely academic interest to me. I think not: I have been told by a palm reader in Burma that I will live for much longer than that. Like many Westerners who came to Asia when it was still mostly poor, I pay more attention to this sort of thing here than I would back home. But then I pay more attention to all sorts of things than I did before I came here. Asia makes you greedy.

AN INVESTOR'S NOTES

Most of you probably doubt that this book's optimistic reasoning about Asia's future is justified. I will explain in a minute what lies behind my reasoning. But suppose for now that I am right and look at the financial consequences of continued Asian success over the next quarter-century. Finance is the right place to begin, because movements in the great asset markets—currencies, commodities, stocks, bonds, and real estate—give the best reflection we have of history's strongest currents.

This is why, first, many Asian currencies will rise in value against those of the rich world. It may seem madness to think today that China's renminbi or India's rupee will rise against the dollar and Deutschemark, let alone (and I would bet even more steeply) against the Japanese yen. Yet look back instead of forward twenty-five years. In 1970, when Japan was generally thought a somewhat backward, high-inflation, and slipshod industrial competitor to the United States, it took 360 yen to buy a dollar. At the yen's mid-1995 high it took just over 80.

Short-term currency movements are hard to fathom, but in the long term a currency's relative value is a comprehensive measure of its country's economic, social, and political strength. When large gaps open and then stay open between two countries' economic growth rates, their productivity growth rates and their ability to generate enough savings to cover their investment needs, you can be sure that the currency of the country on the higher side of these equations will rise against the currency of the country on the lower side. The trend with Asia's currencies has already begun: In the years 1970–95 the Singapore dollar rose sharply against the American dollar. In 1990–95 it rose against every rich-world currency save the yen. Other Asian currencies will follow.

Asia's persistent growth rates, multiplied by its huge populations, make it easy to understand why, second, the prices of commodities like oil, cotton, wheat, and metals will rise in real terms. This will reverse a fifteen-year downward trend that began in the early 1980s and will have big consequences for world income distributions: handsomely raising prices for oil producers, for the efficient grain farmers of America, Argentina, Australia, Ukraine, and the region around Paris, and for the inventors and suppliers of better and cheaper alternatives to old commodities. Liquefied natural gas, for example, of which only Japan bought a significant share in the early 1990s, will enjoy a great boom as an alternative to oil.

Commodity prices will rise in part simply because, with the vast growth of Asian markets, the balance between global supply and demand will tilt. Once countries become very rich, their demand for commodities starts growing more slowly and, for some commodities, eventually goes into an absolute decline (which is why environmentalists should, though almost none do, campaign for the fastest economic growth possible). But countries on their way up are the world's most ravenous consumers of commodities. Exploding car ownership throughout Asia will raise world demand for oil products. Changing Asian diets—in particular the consumption of more meat (which is highly grain-intensive to produce)—will mean a fantastic increase in world demand for grain.

This will combine with shrinking supply in Asia to put even more pressure on commodity prices. China has already become a net oil importer and will permanently remain one. In the first half of the 1990s, China lost more than 1 percent of its farmland to the houses and factories of its rising industrial economy. As early as 1994, for the first time ever, a bowl of rice cost more in China than it did in America. These are the early signs of the unprecedented commodity-price boom that is coming as the biggest numbers in history begin rising into the middle class.

Yet commodity prices will also rise for a financial reason. Rising commodity prices foretell rising inflation. Asia's fast economic growth and its voracious demands for capital will put strong price pressures on the world's financial system.

Hence, third, the high interest rates that the world will be living with for another generation. Despite price pressures that nowadays seem more deflationary than inflationary, the rich world is enduring its highest real interest rates since the first decade of the twentieth century. The long-term rise of Asia will continue and deepen this trend.

There is much talk today about the world's chronic "capital shortage," resulting, it is suggested, from the investment needs of the big swaths of the globe that are suddenly being brought into the modern capitalist economy after having been absent from it for almost a century: China, India, the former Soviet Union, and a resurgent Latin America. Yet the true starting point of high interest rates is the world's dwindling supply of capital—that is, falling savings rates.

In the three decades after 1965 savings rates in the rich countries of Europe and North America were almost halved. Because investment and consumption have not declined (indeed, consumption rates rose), these economies have begun building up debt, both public and private. This adds up. The International Monetary Fund has calculated that each percentage-point rise in global government debt adds 14/100ths of a percentage point to long-term interest rates. Higher government borrowing has accounted for as much as four-fifths of the increase in world real interest rates between 1960 and 1995.

A new Asian card will now come into play. While savings rates were falling in the West during 1970–95, they were rising sharply in East and Southeast Asia. This put Asia's economies as a whole in the unusual position (for poor countries) of not only paying for their own heavy investments but also exporting capital to the West to make up for the rich world's shortfall.

Asia's position will soon begin to change. As incomes rise in Asia past a certain point, savings—both public and household—begin to decline. Taiwan offers an early example. In the 1970s its gross savings rate was around 35 percent of gross domestic product (GDP); in the 1990s, 25 percent; in 1990 its government's total debt equaled 4 percent of GDP and 14 percent of public spending; by 1994 the debt had swollen to the equivalent of 13 percent of GDP and 43 percent of public spending. Throughout Asia, at the same time savings are beginning slowly to shrink, the continent's long-suppressed demands for public investment—for roads, ports, railroads, bridges, sewers, and airports—can no longer be contained.

Because of its anti-welfare mentality, Asia will not let its public finances get into as deep a mess as those of Western countries today. Nor in relative terms, at first, will the slowly growing gap between Asia's savings and investment amount to much alongside the immense government deficits run up in the West, especially the United States. Even so, the post-1995 combination in Asia of slowly falling savings, fast-rising spending on infrastructure, and the continent's growing share of the world economy will increasingly add to the already extreme pressure on capital resources. Asia will thus help keep real interest rates high worldwide for a long time to come.

This development will be connected to another worldwide reversal of fortune in which Asia should play a special role. That explains why, fourth, returns on bonds will rise relative to the returns on equities over the years 1995–2020. This seems baffling at first: For almost the whole of the twentieth century (which, remember, has enjoyed historically low real interest rates) stocks easily outperformed bonds. But it would have been a familiar state of affairs to the financiers of the late nineteenth century, the previous great occasion when vast new regions of the world economy (the Americas and Australia) were opened and built up and the demand for capital was unusually high.

Asia's particular contribution to the world's resurgent bond boom will come in the decade after 1995, when the continent's explosion of infrastructure spending will at last introduce a huge swell of debt securities in a region that has previously relied on equities and bank loans for financing. For those who get their timing right, Asia's entry into bondage will be the investment chance of a lifetime. Those who get it wrong—that is, go in too early—will suffer the same fate as the premature investors in American and Argentinian railway bonds in the nineteenth century: defaults rather than riches.

In view of all this, it is inevitable, fifth, that real-estate prices will also rise in real terms worldwide. They will rise most in Asia, which is anyway more crowded, whose supply of property has long been artificially restricted by governments, and where a cultural preference for tangible assets had already combined as early as 1985–95 with a large pile of amassed savings to send property prices in many Asian cities soaring beyond those anywhere in the West. That is why I am planning to buy my Shanghai house in 1997.

THE ECONOMIC REVOLUTION AND ITS AFTERMATH

If the financial markets behave this way, what will their movements be reporting about Asia's changing place in the world? Their subject is, first and foremost, the continent's dazzling economic performance and its growing economic weight.

In the first third of this book (chapters 1–5) you will be reading more than enough numbers that measure the dimensions of this change and a great deal of explanation about why economies grow in general and why, in particular, the economies of East and Southeast Asia unexpectedly grew faster in the two generations after 1950 than any fairly large economies had ever grown before. Note for now that, if Asia's growth continues even at a somewhat more modest pace for the next quarter-century, the Asian economies (including Japan and India) will by 2020 be bigger than the economies of Europe and the Americas put together.

The (relatively) simple explanation of why this may happen is that, beginning first with Japan in the 1950s and spreading progressively through other East and Southeast Asian countries from the 1960s onward, China from the 1980s onward, and at last India beginning in the 1990s, Asia has been extraordinarily good at putting together the four elements that make for economic growth. Three of these elements are straightforward. First, Asia's workforce has grown fast and puts in long hours. Second, most of East Asia has been extremely good about improving the quality of its workers through education and training. Third, Asian countries have injected unusually large amounts of capital—of machines and equipment—into their economies at an early stage, something which their exceptionally high savings rates have allowed them to finance.

The fourth element of growth—productivity, or the efficiency with which the other three elements are combined—has always been much harder to understand. This is because it sums up many of the deepest influences on the workings of an economy and society: the spread and use of technology, the fit of the society's culture and values with the demands of modern economic life, the country's receptiveness to new ideas and foreign influence. Asia's productivity improved significantly over the years 1950–90, and for reasons the book will explain I think this was mainly because Asian countries were so open to the influence of new ideas of all sorts, especially those from abroad—whether brought to Asia through foreign trade, foreign investment, or foreign technology.

Not many people will instinctively agree with me that Asia has succeeded in large part because of its free-trading mentality (and done worst where that mentality was most absent). But whatever their views on that, most Westerners will probably agree that there are two big questions about Asia: Will it continue to grow as fast as it did in 1970–95, and is the rise of Asia good or bad for the West?

GROWTH SLOWS

My guess is that, around 2000, Asia's economic growth will suddenly slow down.

In part, any such slowdown will be mere optical illusion. All countries, as they successfully develop, move in stages onto slower growth paths. As Japan matured from the 1960s to the 1990s, for instance, its average decennial growth rate fell from 8–9 percent to some 6–7 percent to about 3–4 percent. The miracle economies of East and Southeast Asia have begun following this inevitable trajectory of declining growth. But they started growing later, and to some extent as a group; so when they slow down, also to some extent as a group, it will seem that "Asia" itself has faltered. In fact, as the familiar "miracles" begin to fade, new ones—in some cases, such as Indonesia, much bigger ones—will rise to take their place.

Yet there is a more significant element in the slowdown. The biggest flaw in the success stories of modern Asia—including Japan —has been their failure to develop the transparent and objective public institutions needed to run the more sophisticated societies and economies that their fabulous economic growth is producing (see the last section of this prologue). One aspect of this failure has been the widespread dawdling in most Asian countries over building the infrastructure of a modern economy until circumstances force them to. Much of Asia will be forced into these public investments —which at first result in slower economic growth than equivalent private investments do—towards the end of the century. No country will be more affected than China, which has the continent's most woeful dearth of the physical infrastructure and the public institutions of a twenty-first-century society. As it struggles to build these things, China's growth rate in the decades 2000–2020 will be some 50 percent lower than its growth rate in 1980–2000 will have been.

The impact of all this should not be exaggerated. Early in the 1990s, Asia's growth began feeding off itself in the sense that the trade of Asian countries (including Japan) among themselves became worth more than their trade with the West. The fate of China first, and India in due course, will begin to sway the economic destiny of the whole of Asia (which is why a quarter of the book, chapters 6–9, is devoted to them alone); and as fast-starting China begins to slow down, slow-starting India will begin to speed up. The overall result will be that, while Asia as a whole will not succeed during 1995–2020 in matching its performance of the previous quarter-century and grow more than three times as fast as the West, it nonetheless will grow more than twice as fast as the West. Which still leaves the other fundamental question: Should the West be glad or scared about Asia's rise?

WEST MEETS EAST

When I was writing this book, an American friend of mine in Hong Kong suggested that I call it *The American Houseboy in Asia*. This sums up the nightmare that many Westerners are already beginning to fear as the personal wealth being accumulated in Asia's lightly taxed societies makes it seem as though Asians will soon be the ones on top. The fear is similar to that aroused in the 1980s when suddenly rich Japanese tourists and investors began to troop self-confidently through America and Europe. Like the worries about Japan in the 1980s, the Asia-phobia of the 1990s is hugely misplaced.

The main reason is that for Western economies as a whole, and for huge numbers of Western companies and their workers, the rise in Asia of the biggest middle class in history offers unprecedented moneymaking opportunities. Asia's relatively cheap but often well-educated workforce continues to provide Western, Japanese, and better-off Asian firms with an attractive place to set up factories producing goods for sale in the rich world. But as the years go by, Asia increasingly offers something more tempting: the world's fastest-growing—and often the biggest—markets for the rich world's own products and services.

These opportunities began with light consumer goods; have moved on up the income scale with consumer durables such as refrigerators, televisions, laser-disc players, and air conditioners (and the programming that some of these devices carry, such as movies and music); and continue on to cars, houses, travel, education, and health—eventually the full range of modern middle-class consumption. But more than consumption is involved. Western makers of capital equipment and builders of factories, roads, telecommunications systems, and airports will benefit from the great spurt in Asian investment demand between 1995 and 2005.

On top of all this, Asia is becoming the main growth market for world finance as rich-world bankers fight for the right to channel flows of capital from the world's biggest untapped source of savings, and Western investors flock to the higher returns available in Asia. The details of this business and financial revolution occupy a third of the book (chapters 10–14). The summary is that in the quarter-century after 1995 Asia will account for half the worldwide sales growth in the markets for almost every product and service save the most advanced; and the Western firms that plunge into this robust current of demand will prosper mightily.

Overall, therefore, by the end of the century it will be impossible to claim honestly that the rise of Asia is doing anything but good to the economies and businesses of the West. It will, however, be adding to the damage that modern technology is inflicting on a particular class of workers in the West: the poorly educated. Not even politicians have yet brought themselves to attack the real culprit—technology's generation of ever-faster cycles of economic destruction and creation—so the demagogues among them have begun bashing Asians and Latin Americans instead.

In the case of Asia, at least, the demagogues have an inadvertent point. Technology has already gone a long way towards affecting everyone equally no matter where they are. Among other things, this means that barriers to foreign goods, ideas, and ways of doing things are becoming ever more difficult to maintain. Asia is, numerically, a drop in the flood of change that technology is causing to gush through the West. Yet in the interaction of technology and society, Asia will prove immensely strong: It is far better equipped than America (let alone Europe) to cope with perpetually accelerating change. Economically this means that, because Asia is so competitive, its rise is increasingly adding to the force and speed with which technology has anyway been remaking Western business and society. But there is more to it than that.

STRONG SOCIETIES

Asia will accelerate the shock waves that have already begun to destroy the Western world's assumptions about public policy and social organization. Asia or no, the financial markets have already begun telling countries such as Sweden, Italy, and even America that they are not free to run up debt in perpetuity without paying higher interest rates. In part because of competition from Asia's soundly run economies for the world's savings, this point will be impressed on the West more forcefully.

The main reason the West's public finances are in trouble is a failure to come to grips with the issue of social protection: In Western Europe this has taken the form of the welfare state; in the United States the form of immense intergenerational transfers within the middle class through the Social Security and Medicare programs. The understandable aim of such systems was to create a compassionate society, one in which the government would prevent life's hazards from wantonly striking people down. The result, which started becoming clear as early as the 1960s even without the benefit of Asia's alternative example, has been not only the deterioration of public finances and the paralysis of Western democracy by interest groups but the partial breakdown of the family, of civil society, and of law and order.

More ominous still, social protection is at heart a doctrine of conservatism: It is about guarding people against the destructive effects of change, which in practice means guarding them against change, full stop, since the creative and destructive aspects of it come as a package. As the force of technology has grown, it has become apparent that the only social and political organizations capable of thriving are those based on accepting and adapting to change rather than trying to soften its blow. Countries with big, activist governments will be far less able to cope with the increasing pace of change than those whose main shock absorbers remain smaller units of government and society—particularly the family. Partly thanks to the luck of having developed later, modern Asia's societies are decidedly in the second category. This is the big challenge Asia poses to the West. If the West reacts positively to this challenge and adapts—something that America seems likelier than Europe to do—its inherent strengths will begin telling again in world economic competition. If it resists, it will falter.

You will be glimpsing aspects of the modern Asian model of society and government throughout the book, but particularly in chapter 1 and in the book's last part. The references to Asia's methods are widespread because the subject touches on so many of the qualities that have shaped modern Asia. These include a small role for government, low taxes, little provision for public welfare, the central position of the family relative both to the state and to the individual, a widespread refusal to protect individual companies or people from the blast of competition and technology, openness to the outside world, and a willingness to adapt to new markets and new ways of doing things.

For the past decade these themes have been given their fullest exposition by Lee Kuan Yew, whose words you will find scattered through the book. Mr. Lee, who was Singapore's prime minister from the time of its independence in 1959 until his retirement in 1990, has probably the most lucid and powerful intellect of any English-speaking political leader of the second half of the century. Under his stewardship Singapore has had one of the best records in all of Asia of being lifted from poverty to modern middle-class life.

I suspect that in the early twenty-first century Singapore will nonetheless begin to falter, suffering a far worse slowdown than any of its neighbors. The reason is that its people, used to so much order and authority at home, are finding themselves unable to cope with the turbulence of life and business in the more chaotic countries where Singapore's rising wages and small size are forcing it to make its investments: China, India, Indonesia, and Vietnam. It may prove one of the biggest ironies of modern Asia that Mr. Lee, who has been so eloquent an advocate of the anti-protectionist view of life and society, has left Singapore ill equipped to cope with the twenty-first century. Its citizens have grown too dependent on their government's foresight instead of their own and are too unadventurous.

The stern but overfond father has been too protective of his children.

WEAK INSTITUTIONS

While Asia has a good deal to teach the West about society, it has a lot to learn about the institutions of a modern political and economic system. Asia's worst weakness—and the only flaw that could grievously wound it—is its failure to move beyond the informal and the personal in its ways of doing business, of governing, and of handling relations between states.

That Asia, in the early stage of its development, was free of institutional constraints helped it to grow fast; one reason China zoomed ahead of India at first is that the Chinese were not burdened with the plague of bureaucrats and lawyers that the British colonial system bequeathed India. Likewise, the brilliant early success of the overseas Chinese businessmen has grown in large measure out of the personalized financing and decision-making that formed the backbone of their firms.

Yet at some point—usually around the time economic growth starts to slow down—a more transparent and rule-based system becomes a necessity. The public aspect, whether in the physical shape of a road or railway or in the institutional shape of a set of company accounts that can be read by potential investors from New York as well as Bangkok, claims more attention. It is, for example, starting to become clear that if Asia is ever to produce companies with a global reach, they will have to find some way of institutionalizing management and financial controls that are now made on a mostly personal basis.

In business the compulsion for Asians to change will be blunted by the worldwide destruction of big organizations brought about by shifts in markets and technology—blunted but not eliminated, since the pressure for transparency will rise even while the role of bureaucracy shrinks. In politics Asia will wrestle for a long time with the problem of making governments accountable without allowing them to fall into the Western democratic trap of becoming hostage to special interests. Here, too, the communications revolution will come partly—but again only partly—to the rescue by allowing most local government decisions to be taken by electronic ballot.

In the case of international relations there will not be even a partial respite from the pressure on Asia to create some multilateral framework for allowing its huge and divergent states to live in peace rather than in tense preparedness for war. Lee Kuan Yew has often pointed out that Asia has never had an indigenous balance of power, which is why it is so vital for the American armed forces to stay in East Asia. They alone can preserve the balance that, historically, Asians have never been able to maintain for themselves. If the Americans leave, it will be touch and go whether Asia can create the needed institutions of geopolitical balance in time to save its people from the fate that befell modernizing Europe in the early decades of this century.

So I believe about Asia's future. My beliefs are based on the recent past described in the pages that follow: a past that consists of probably the most amazing and beneficent revolution in history. The reasons why this revolution took place are worth knowing. Had anyone in 1950, roughly the starting point of modern Asia, foreseen even a small part of the story that follows, he would not only have been the wisest of men but, by 1995, also the richest.

PART I

HALF THE
WORLD TURNS

CHAPTER 1

THE MIRACLE

Asia is not going to be civilized after the methods of the West. There is too much Asia and she is too old.

—KIPLING

In the middle of this century it seemed that Asia would not be civilized at all. Practically the whole continent spent the decades 1930–60 in a state of war, revolution, or famine; the really unlucky countries, like China, endured all three. In 1945 Japan, the most advanced country in Asia, lay in ruins, its cities and industry flattened by the American bombing that ended the Pacific war. The Korean War began in 1950 and lasted three years, leaving behind nearly 1 million casualties and a crushed economy and society. The figures for the dead in China were staggering: 10 million Chinese killed during the war with Japan in 1937–45 and another 10 million in the civil war that both preceded and followed the Japanese occupation. China was to lose 40 million more to starvation during Mao Zedong's "Great Leap Forward" in 1958–62 and perhaps 10 million on top of that in the Cultural Revolution of 1966–75.

The casualty list grew longer in the Indochina wars of 1945–80 (which killed a lot of Frenchmen and Americans, too), in guerrilla wars between Communist rebels and non-Communist governments throughout Southeast Asia, and in three wars between India and Pakistan during 1948–71. For good measure, a failed coup in Indonesia in 1965 led to a horrifying bloodbath in which hundreds of thousands of people were slaughtered simply because they were ethnic Chinese; and perhaps 1 million Cambodians, practically the whole of the 15–20 percent of the population with any education, were killed in 1975–78 under the murderous rule of a bunch of Stone Age Communists called the Khmers Rouges.

The common view was that the survivors of all this carnage had a bleak future. In 1960 each Japanese had only one-eighth the dollar income of each American—and Japan, which had been modernizing for almost a century, was the richest place in Asia. South Korea was no richer than Sudan; Taiwan, about as poor as Zaire. Incomes in China and India were barely more than a third as high as Taiwan's. Indeed, in 1960 it might not have seemed altogether insane to bet that Africa would outperform Asia over the next three decades. Observers looking at the straight lines projecting India's population against its grain output foresaw deaths from famine in the scores of millions by the late 1960s. Early in that decade Gunnar Myrdal, a Swede who eventually won a Nobel Prize in economics, was working on a morose 2,200-page book about Asia's prospects, which he found not good because among other things "the epoch of rapidly growing export markets has ended."

Yet at about this dispiriting time a process of export-led economic growth was quietly beginning that over the next thirty years produced in East Asia the fastest rise in incomes, for the biggest number of people, ever seen on earth. In Japan, which had begun growing fast in the 1950s, this took the form of a manufacturing revolution that increased the real income of each Japanese fourfold between 1960 and 1985 and shortly thereafter made Japan the richest country in the world in dollar terms.

In four places that followed in Japan's footsteps with a delay of ten to twenty years—South Korea, Taiwan, Hong Kong, and Singapore—the rise from poverty was every bit as steep, with the size of their economies doubling every eight years during 1960–85 (eightfold in all). Four other countries—Malaysia, Thailand, China, and Indonesia—began hauling themselves out of the dumps in the late 1970s, though one of them (Indonesia) grew at a somewhat more modest pace than the spectacular 8–9 percent a year that all the rest managed. These eight economies were among the world's thirteen most successful at raising real incomes in 1965–90 and in the 1980s grew three times as fast as the rich world (excluding Japan). One measure of the human dimension of their accomplishment is that between 1970 and 1990 the number of desperately poor people in East Asia fell from 400 million to 180 million even while the population of those countries was rising by 425 million—in other words, a net rescue from actual or probable poverty of almost 650 million people, the greatest economic uplifting in history. By 1990 only 10 percent of East Asians were living in what is called absolute poverty, compared with a quarter of Latin Americans, half of black Africans, and half the people on the Indian subcontinent.

Now, with very few exceptions, the rest of Asia has begun imitating the policies that brought such astonishing improvement to East Asia. In 1986, Vietnam followed China's example and began freeing the economy while maintaining tight political control under Communist party rule. By the mid-1990s Vietnam's economic growth was approaching a double-digit rate, inflation was in single figures, and the currency, despite being called the dong, was steady against the dollar. India, which had been Asia's last significant holdout against liberalization and export-driven growth, reversed almost forty-five years of economic policy in 1991 and began to open itself to the outside world and to cut through the world's thickest remaining swaddling of red tape. By mid-decade even North Korea, the most tightly sealed country in the world, was showing some twitches of economic life as it began to experiment with Chinese-like reforms.

The first thirty years of the Asian miracle have already gone a long way towards shifting the world's balance of economic power. Asia's extremely high rates of savings—in East Asia over 30 percent of the value of economic output—has already generated probably the world's biggest pool of investable capital. A hint of its size is suggested by the official reserves held at the end of 1994 by the ten biggest Asian holders of foreign exchange. The reserves of Japan, Taiwan, Singapore, China, Hong Kong, Thailand, Malaysia, India, Indonesia, and the Philippines then added up to some $457 billion —more than 40 percent of the world total.

In the 1980s alone Asia (including Japan) increased its share of world output in dollar terms from 17 percent to 22 percent and its share of manufactured exports from 12 percent to 17 percent. If the size of the world economy is calculated on the basis of what countries actually produce and consume (the jargon for this is "purchasing-power parity," or PPP, a useful trio of initials for later chapters in this book) rather than on what sometimes misleading exchange rates for the dollar suggest they do, Asia's weight is greater still. A

calculation by the International Monetary Fund (IMF, another useful trio of initials) showed that on this basis Asia's share of economic
output in 1990 was 25 percent; that of North America and Western
Europe combined was 46 percent.

And, this decade, Asia has continued to lope ahead. Its momentum is so strong that, by the IMF's guess, Asia's economies taken
together will be half again as big in 2000 as they were in 1993; if so,
they will be getting close to representing 30 percent of world output
even in nominal dollar terms and more than that in PPP terms. The
IMF also reckons that, of the $7.5 trillion (in 1990 dollars) by which
the world economy should grow between 1990 and 2000, half will
be contributed by East Asia alone. The World Bank thinks that Asia
as a whole will also account for half the growth in world trade this
decade. If Asia can outstrip the rest of the world in 1995–2020 more
or less as it did in 1970–95 and thus becomes a largely middle-class
continent, it will then account for more of world output than all the
present-day rich countries together (even putting Japan in the rich
countries' column instead of Asia's) and will have transformed every
business on earth and the hopes of every human for a decent life.

The Carping

Oddly, many people in America and Europe do not see the rise of
Asia for what it is: the greatest, and most thrilling, event of the last
half of this century. Instead of rejoicing that so many people are
now leading lives that are so much better than anyone dreamed
possible only two generations ago, or rubbing their hands at the
chances for ambitious and energetic Westerners that those better
Asian lives will present, the worriers fret that the rise of Asia means
the West—or, at any rate, Western jobs and wages—must fall.

For two reasons these worries are wrongheaded. The first is that
Asia's growth, albeit extraordinary, must be kept in perspective. Paul
Krugman, an economist at Stanford University, has pointed out that
the overwhelming effect of productivity growth in poor countries is
to raise wages there, not to lower them in the rich world. Even the
seemingly large flows of capital in the early 1990s from rich countries to poor count for little in the rich world's economic scales. In
1993 a net $160 billion in capital went from rich countries to poor
countries (some $57 billion of that to Asia). The output of the rich

world—North America, Western Europe, and Japan—amounted to some $18 trillion. Their capital investment at home was $3.5 trillion (or almost seventy times what they invested in Asia); their stock of capital, $60 trillion.

By Mr. Krugman's reckoning, all the capital flows to all the poor countries since the beginning of the 1990s dragged the capital stock of the rich world below the level it would have been at had all that investment been made at home by no more than 0.5 percent, or $300 billion. That translates into a reduction in potential rich-world wages of no more than 0.15 percent. All this compares with a home-grown diversion of capital from productive uses in the United States alone—via the budget deficits the American government has run up since 1980—of more than $3 trillion. Imports of goods from poor countries have probably had as little effect on the rich countries as their own exports of capital. America's imports from the whole of the poor world in the early 1990s amounted to only 1 percent of its gross domestic product (GDP; yet more useful initials, this time measuring the size of the economy).

These static calculations understate the dynamic effect of Asian and other poor-country growth on the West. At the margin, Asian competition is undoubtedly increasing the impact that technological change would anyway have on the West: That, after all, is one of the main aims of trade. But this is more a matter of the distribution of income within a country than it is of the distribution of income between countries, and it has to be handled at home, not abroad.

Another way of looking at the overall effect of Asia's rise, for those of a historical bent, is to recall, as we race towards the end of this century, where Asia stood at its start. By the calculations of Angus Maddison, an economic historian, in 1900, Asia (including Japan) accounted for some 32 percent of the dollar value of gross world product, almost half again as high a share as it has today; North America and Western Europe represented 55 percent, three percentage points *less* than they did ninety years later despite the high Japanese and other East Asian growth rates of 1960–90. Asia is unlikely to surpass its 1900 share of the dollar value of world output before 2010 and even on a PPP basis will have a struggle to make it by 2005. Even then, what is the worry for America and Europe? It would have been batty for the rich to fear Asia in the first decade of this century because it had a third of the world economy, and it will be just as batty in the first decade of the next century.

Indeed, the second (and more compelling) reason not to fear the rise of Asia is that it should be welcomed instead: for the business and other opportunities that its growth is beginning to present and for the extra wealth, and perhaps even happiness through a re-arrangement of social priorities, that it is thereby going to create in the rich world.

By 2000, Asians are expected to account for 3.6 billion of the world's 6.2 billion people. Fully a billion of those Asians—not much less than the entire population of the Americas and Western Europe in 1995—will be living in households with some consumer-spending power; they will be able to buy at least basic goods such as color televisions, refrigerators, and motorbikes. Perhaps 400 million of those consumers—three times as many as in the early 1990s—will have disposable incomes at least equal to the rich-world average today; they will be buying houses, cars, holidays, health care, and education. And if all this consumer spending is to take place, im-mense investments in capital equipment and infrastructure will be needed to make it possible: for a start whole factories, the equip-ment to go in them, power plants, roads, railways, airports, ports, and telecommunications networks. The zooming growth and abso-lute size of Asia's middle class should therefore create some of the biggest business and financial opportunities in history.

The rise of Asia may offer the world more even than that. Since 1500, when China entered its half-millennium of decline, the West has had a monopoly of the world's most powerful current of thought: modernization, the belief that things can be changed, that human consciousness can bend destiny to its will. The totalitarian alternatives to the liberal ideas of progress—communism and fas-cism—were broken either by war, in the case of European fascism and Japanese nationalism, or, in communism's case, by economics. In the next couple of decades Islam may offer another challenge, though it seems bound to be plagued by the identification of so much of its fervor with anti-modernization rather than moderniza-tion.

Asia, or at least the part of Asia under China's cultural sway, might be different. Stuck for centuries in lethargy and conservatism, Asians now believe passionately in modernization—probably more than most Europeans and, to judge by the souring mood in America in the early 1990s, perhaps more than many Americans, too. Asia's civilizations are old and, even under Western colonialism, have remained intact. And, because of their outstanding economic performance since 1980, the developing countries of East Asia are self-confident (in fact, too self-confident). The societies, and in many cases the politics, of East Asia are organized differently from those of the West. If Asians continue to grow rich, they could be in a position to offer the West an example of how to marry fast economic change to social stability and how to reconcile freedom with order.

Even if Asia falls short of providing such a cultural renaissance— and it will be quite an accomplishment if a rich East Asia can avoid succumbing to the same ills that afflict the rich West—it might still offer some pointers about the biggest problem of government faced by the West: one that Westerners are mostly blind to, since they assume (as China did of its own system in 1500) that there is no problem at all, only self-evident virtue. The problem is representative democracy itself, which runs the danger of ceasing to be a vehicle for delivering the services that ordinary people want from government and of becoming instead an instrument for helping strong lobbies pick taxpayers' pockets. This is a danger that developing Asia has been fairly good at avoiding.

THE LAY OF THE LAND

If you think it is impertinent for someone to have written a book about the whole of Asia, you are right. The Asia I have in mind is not the continent of the same name, but it is still so huge and so diverse in climate, culture, wealth, and behavior that a visitor to its different parts could be forgiven for thinking that they lie on different planets.

The Asia that this book is about begins just east of Iran, the last clear outpost of the Middle East, and extends in a broad curve south and east of there to the limit of the Asian landmass (see the map on pages 6–7). It includes the whole of the Indian subcontinent and the islands nearby (such as Sri Lanka), all of Southeast Asia and Indochina (including the Indonesian and Philippine archipelagoes), China and its outriggers (such as Taiwan), and the Korean peninsula. For the most part, it does not include the countries of ex–Soviet Central Asia or Russia's Far East, except as they have dealings with Asia proper (as Vladivostok and Russia's border areas with China and North Korea increasingly do). Likewise, it does not include Australia or New Zealand, even though the fate of these antipodean neighbors increasingly depends on Asia and (in Australia's case especially) they are doing their best to be accepted as Asian; even so, they are still of the West though not in it.

Japan is a special case. Too rich and too idiosyncratic to be wholly Asian, it is at the same time bound more and more to Asia by economic ties as well as by culture and geography. And it is in many ways still the model, for good and ill, of the institutional process of development that its poorer neighbors are beginning to follow. So, in this book, Japan is sometimes part of Asia but mostly—because the big question is whether developing Asia can successfully vault into modernity—it is not: Japan has already made it.

The Asia of this book has some fuzzy border regions. China's Xinjiang Province, for instance, has more in common with the tribe-based Islam of the neighboring ex-Soviet states of Central Asia than it does with the Han Chinese who are its masters. And it would be surprising if the Russian Far East were not one day severed in fact if not by lines on the map from its formal political rulers in Moscow. But what of the core of Asia?

Physically, it is dominated by the Indian subcontinent, which is around half the size of the United States, and by the adjacent vast bulk of China, slightly bigger than America and a little smaller than Canada. Even Asia's smaller fry can be large by the standards of lesser continents: Japan is as big as California or Germany, and Indonesia could accommodate most of the American West. The West would first have to be cut up, though, and then stretched out. Indonesia consists of some thirteen thousand islands strung out in an arc three thousand miles long. Distances in Asia are, in fact, one of the first surprises, and usually an unpleasant one, for a newcomer. A casual glance at a map does not usually lead the inexperienced traveler to the accurate conclusion that it will take as long to fly from Bombay to Singapore as it does to fly across America, and as long to fly on from Singapore to Tokyo as it does to fly from New York to London.

Within this huge area lives an even more unimaginably large concentration of people: 3.3 billion of them in 1995, some 58 percent of the whole world's population. They are not evenly dispersed through Asia's vastness (and, even if they were, the place would still be crowded, since it accounts for only 20 percent of the planet's dry land). California-sized Japan, much of it mountainous and little habitable, nonetheless has almost four times as many people as California. At least four large districts in Hong Kong have probably the highest population densities on earth: more than 400,000 people per square mile, compared with 53,000 in Manhattan.

This is not just a curiosity of city-states: Rural Asia is bursting with people, too. Java, the principal (though by no means the largest) island of Indonesia, has a size of around eighty thousand square miles (roughly the size of Idaho and about half the size of Britain) and a population of some 115 million (compared with 1.1 million in Idaho and 58 million in Britain, or a hundred times as concentrated as Idaho and four times as concentrated as Britain). In Java you are never out of sight of a city, town, or village. This crowding, which is another thing that often makes the newcomer to Asia squirm, has a lot to do with how Asian societies, politics, and economics work—and with the business methods and opportunities that Asia presents.

HISTORY'S BEQUEST

Asia is wealthy not just in people. It is a bewildering amalgam of religions, races, cultures, and languages, of rich and poor, and of the advanced and backward.

Asia's civilizations stretch back as long as four thousand years, in the case of China, and their people do not forget the past. For all their similarities, Vietnamese and Chinese have been fighting off and on for more than two thousand years, as for almost as long have Khmers (Cambodians) and Vietnamese; the antipathy of Koreans and Japanese towards each other goes back at least five hundred years. In the heart of Seoul, South Korea's glossy capital, are replicas of handsome historical buildings—temples and palaces—where explanatory placards remind modern young families on light-hearted Sunday outings how the beastly Japanese invaders burned down the original buildings four hundred years ago. America got over its grudge against the British less than a century after they had burned the White House to the ground in 1814.

There are always pretexts for a fight in Asia. The diversity of religion and language in India—which alone boasts seven major religions and twenty major languages—makes for an explosive cocktail. So does the diversity of race and religion in Southeast Asia.

China, and its cultural offshoots in Japan and Korea, have mostly escaped this tension at home because their populations are so ethnically uniform. But in Southeast Asia the antagonism among Chinese, Indian, and Malay—the Malays are the main ethnic stock in Malaysia, Indonesia, and the Philippines—is intense. The hostility is strengthened, and complicated, by the fact that the Malays of Malaysia and Indonesia are Muslim (as are some of those in the Philippines): not in an implacable Middle Eastern way but still devoutly enough to make them resent even more than they would otherwise do their far richer and rather freewheeling ethnic Chinese compatriots. Fast economic growth has helped muffle the natural grinding between these groups; an economic slowdown would increase it. That the existence of racial and religious antagonism is freely acknowledged in Asia is yet another shock to the first-time Western visitor (especially Americans steeped in liberal disapproval of such atavisms); and it is yet another big gear in the at-first-baffling workings of Asian business and politics.

Modern disparities exist alongside ancient ones; especially in the matter of money. Asia is home not only to the impeccable car factories of Japan and the glimmering skyscrapers of Hong Kong but also to New Guinea tribesmen wearing penis sheaths. The annual income of the average Hong Konger, the richest of Asians outside Japan, is a hundred times that of a Nepalese or a Cambodian, who are the poorest of Asians.

The official figures for the poorest countries need to be read with a skeptical eye: Asia's black-market economies are big, even in fairly well-off places like Taiwan, and visits to supposedly miserable countrysides in Indonesia, China, and even India suggest things cannot be as awful there as the numbers say. Yet however tempered, the figures showing a wide divide between rich and poor are still daunting. Asia already contains probably the biggest concentrations of family wealth in the world, nurtured by the sort of low taxes and high secrecy that Western plutocrats can only dream about; at the same time, it has, mostly in the Indian subcontinent but in large pockets of China and Southeast Asia as well, 65 percent of the whole world's desperately poor people, 730 million Asians in all.

Wealthy societies tend to be sophisticated, and here, too, Asia's range is immense. At one extreme is Hong Kong, which by the early 1990s had evolved into probably the most finely tuned urban society on earth, with a startlingly efficient apparatus for collecting information from Asia, and even farther afield, and disseminating it through the world's most advanced service economy. Even leaving aside, at the other extreme, the small groups of tribes living in nearly Stone Age primitivism in the Irian Jaya jungle or the Himalayan foothills, large numbers of country dwellers in India and Pakistan live in conditions of feudalism unchanged for centuries; and large numbers of Chinese peasants, under arbitrary and tyrannical bureaucratic behavior that their ancient forebears would find familiar.

The gap between rich and poor and advanced and backward in Asia—among countries as well as individuals within countries—is not necessarily a problem, though it would fast become one in most places should economic growth stumble badly. It is already becoming one in China, where the relatively prosperous city dwellers of the coast increasingly find irksome the heavy-handed methods of government that grew out of the Chinese countryside. In rural China these methods may still have a point, but they do not appeal to people who are better acquainted with MTV than with planting rice. This gap, too, is crucial to understanding how Asia works.

To complete this rudely thumbnail sketch of three-fifths of mankind is table 1, on pages 38–39, which sets out some basic comparative facts about the main Asian countries today. Where they find themselves tomorrow will likely be determined by three big forces: the coexistence of old and new in Asia, how very young Asia's population is, and how ruthless its societies are.

OLD AND NEW . . .

Because Asia has risen so far so fast, the old is everywhere found alongside the new. Even in today's Singapore, which is richer than half of Europe and ticks as precisely and pristinely as Frankfurt or Zurich, you still catch an unmistakable whiff of the Asia that J. G. Farrell, a British novelist, described when he wrote, speaking of Singapore just before the Japanese captured it in 1942: "There, too, when you staggered outside into the sweltering night, you would have been able to inhale that incomparable smell of incense, of warm skin, of meat cooking in coconut oil, of honey and frangipani, and hair-oil and lust and sandal-wood and heaven knows what, a perfume like the breath of life itself."

Culturally and socially, as well as sensually, the old Asia has staying

TABLE 1
ASIA AT A GLANCE

	China	India	Hong Kong	Singapore	South Korea	Taiwan
Population (1995 est., millions)	1,202.9	918.2	6.2	3.1	44.8	21.2
Life expectancy	69	61	78	75	71	75
Prevalence of malnutrition (under 5), 1987–92 (%)	21	63	N.A.	N.A.	N.A.	N.A.
Adult literacy (%)	73	48	99+	99+	96	91
Male (%)	83	61	99+	99+	99	96
Female (%)	62	34	99+	99+	93	86
GNP (PPP) (billions of U.S. dollars), 1993	2,803	1,120	134	60	431	N.A.
GNP per capita (PPP) (U.S. dollars, 1993)	2,330	1,220	21,560	19,510	9,630	N.A.
Real GDP (% change year on year)						
75–84	7.5	4.9	8.9	8.0	8.0	8.7
85–94	9.9	5.2	5.7	7.1	8.5	7.5
1994 Gross domestic savings (% GDP)	40.5	22.1	33	48	35.1	26
1994 Gross domestic investment (% GDP)	39.5	22.5	31.1	41.5	36.9	24.1
1994 Government spending (% GDP)	17.5	17.2	16	15	17.7	15.9
1994 Exports (billions of U.S. dollars)	120.2	26.2	151.4	95.8	93.7	92.2
% of GDP	30.9	9.0	114.8	185.8	24.7	38.2
1994 Imports (billions of U.S. dollars)	115.7	28.3	162.3	96.0	96.8	80.3
% of GDP	29.8	9.7	123.1	186.2	25.5	33.3
Foreign exchange reserves (billions of U.S. dollars, end of 1994)	51.6	19.4	49.0	57.9	25.0	92.5

PPP = purchasing-power parity; N.A. = not available.

SOURCES: IMF, *International Financial Statistics* (various monthly issues, 1995); Datastream; Bridge; Asian Development Bank, *Asian Development Outlook 1995* and *1996;* Asian Development Bank, *Key Indicators of Developing Asian and Pacific Countries 1994;* The World Bank, *World Population Projections* 1992–93 edition; The World Bank, *World Development Report 1994; Financial Statistics, Taiwan District, Republic of China* (March

Indonesia	Malaysia	Philippines	Thailand	Bangladesh	Burma	Pakistan	Sri Lanka	Vietnam
194.7	19.6	66.9	60.4	120.7	46	129.1	17.9	74
60	71	65	69	55	60	59	72	67
40	N.A.	34	13	67	32	40	37	N.A.
77	78	90	93	35	81	35	88	89
86	86	91	96	48	90	48	93	94
68	70	89	90	22	72	21	83	84
613	155	179	375	156	N.A.	280	54	N.A.
3,150	7,930	2,670	6,260	1,290	N.A.	2,170	2,890	N.A.
6.6	7.0	3.9	6.9	4.5	6.9	6.0	3.2	N.A.
6.1	6.7	2.2	8.6	4.1	1.5	6.6	4.4	N.A.
38.7	35.6	15.4	37.2	7.1	11.7	18.2	13.6	N.A.
35.5	37.2	25.3	42.9	14.8	12.5	20.1	24.7	19.5
16.7	24.4	18.9	14.9	18.9	8.8	24.7	29.5	29.2
39.5	56.6	13.4	43.8	2.2	0.8	6.7	3.1	3.6
30.9	84.3	21.0	30.6	8.7	N.A.	13.2	N.A.	23.4
31.7	55.2	21.2	53.4	3.9	0.8	8.4	4.7	4.2
24.8	82.2	33.2	37.3	15.0	N.A.	16.5	N.A.	27.3
17.3	26.8	5.9	28.9	3.1	0.4	2.9	2.0	N.A.

1995); *Bank Negara Malaysia Annual Report 1994;* Bank of Thailand, *Monthly Bulletin* (March 1995); *Hong Kong Monthly Digest of Statistics* (May 1995); *Singapore Monthly Digest of Statistics* (March 1995); *Monthly Statistics of South Korea* (February 1995); *Indonesia Monthly Statistics Bulletin* (March 1995); *China Monthly Statistics* (January 1995); Centre for Monitoring Indian Economy, *Monthly Review of the Indian Economy* (April 1995); and *Philippines National Statistics Office Bulletin Board.*

power. A big reason for this is the late start, but now swift pace, of urbanization in the poor countries of Asia. In 1990 only 30 percent of the people in poor Asia lived in cities, compared with 72 percent in Latin America; even Africa, which badly lags Asia in levels of income and industrialization, was more urbanized (35 percent). So the values and habits of rural life have an unusually widespread hold on Asia, and for a transitional decade or two will be influencing the cities as well.

The overall rate of population growth peaked in East Asia and parts of Southeast Asia in the 1960s, in Indonesia in the 1970s, and in the Indian subcontinent in the 1980s. But urban growth rates reach their highest levels later: in Indonesia during the 1980s, India from 1985 to 1995, and China from 1995 to 2005. In historical terms, Asia's urbanization is happening very quickly indeed: in peak periods Asia has had 4.5–5 percent urban population growth a year, compared with 2.1 percent in European countries at their peak in the last half of the nineteenth century.

The result of fast urban growth, usually most obvious after it has begun to slacken, is the creation of gigantic metropolises, of which Asia will have a big share early next century (see below). While it is going on, however, the main consequences of fast urban growth are immense social and environmental strains and the temporary importation into enlarging cities of the ways of thinking and personal ties of the countryside. But this is a two-way street. As Richard Critchfield, an American reporter on village life, has pointed out, by the 1990s migration from farm to city in the poor world had in many places been going on long enough that the values of the cities were being transmitted back to those still left in the countryside.

The transmission belt is kinship and personal acquaintance. Throughout Asia, fresh migrants to cities tend to congregate with each other on the basis of their places of origin in the countryside and of kinship (which usually amounts to the same thing). These ties, and the habits they bring with them, can stretch a long way. As late as the 1980s, overseas Chinese businessmen in Southeast Asia were making decisions about their dealings with each other, and about investment projects in China itself, largely on the ground of which mainland villages their forebears had emigrated from a century before (see chapter 11).

It takes a fair amount of time, too, for modern goods and modern technology to change old beliefs and preferences. It has long been commonplace in the Asian countryside to see villagers in sarongs or in mud houses watching television or, in cities, to see young peasant girls in modest Muslim dress yoking microchips to circuit boards in immaculate electronics factories. This sort of contrast gives significant clues to would-be makers and marketers of consumer goods in Asia (see chapter 12), who need to be aware that, despite the large absolute size of Asia's consuming class, only a very small number of Asians have risen to such high income levels and have so distanced themselves from their traditions that they have entered the global middle class that exists in America, Europe, and to some degree Japan.

But the persistence of the past has deeper consequences than that. At a given level of income, Asians have broken with fewer traditional social norms than their Western counterparts. (Whether that will continue is one of the main topics of chapter 16.) They do not (yet, anyway) get divorced or commit crimes or break with their parents nearly as much as Westerners in similar material circumstances; even richer-than-America Japan had a divorce rate in the mid-1990s that was no more than a third as high as America's. There is no sign that social decay is beginning to eat into Asia at anything like the speed with which it is attacking the West. Whereas in most of the West the rate of illegitimate births has roughly trebled since 1960, in Japan it has stayed almost exactly the same. The enduring strength of Asian families and societies despite furious economic change may be Asia's greatest asset, providing a firm base for thrift, work, educational success, and social stability. The enduring weakness of Asia's public institutions—whether political or corporate—is its greatest liability.

This may sound strange, since so much of Asia is run by authoritarians or even dictators; but their word is not really law, or rather is so only erratically. Lucian Pye, a professor of politics at the Massachusetts Institute of Technology (MIT), has pointed out that for almost all of Asia (Japan partly excepted) the gravest danger has long been not too much government power but too little to prevent disorder, banditry, or even anarchy. In the past few decades, too, Asia's worst political catastrophes, apart from war, have arisen from the breakdown of order: The Indonesian riots of 1965–66 and China's Cultural Revolution are the most obvious examples. Even when power is there to be exercised, its effect can be haphazard, especially in conditions of fevered economic modernization. China's rulers could (just) muster sufficient obedience from the army to mount an assault on the pro-democracy demonstrators in Tiananmen Square in 1989. On the more important matters of restoring the central government's finances and taming the wild demands for credit placed on the banking system in the early 1990s, the leaders in Beijing have had a hard and messy time controlling the willful behavior of China's provincial and local authorities. If, in the words of Laozi, the founder of Daoism, "governing a large state is like boiling a small fish," few Asian governments have the implements for so subtle and delicate an operation.

Among the many implications of this is that Asian nation-states will probably be even less able than their Western counterparts to control the border-smashing tides of technological change and economic integration. None of these nation-states is so fragile that a breakup of ex-Soviet proportions seems likely—not even Indonesia, which, among Asia's big three countries, was the least unified when the modern (post-1950) era began. But already it makes economic sense to think about much of Asia not in terms of countries but of regions: often border-spanning ones such as those of southern China and Hong Kong, Singapore and southern Malaysia and northern Indonesia, and the Koreas and northeast China and southeast Russia; but often, too, city-regions that are the operative economic units lie wholly within a country's borders.

Fast economic growth, long distances, and poor infrastructure have all exaggerated the influence of these internal city-regions. It used to be that a country would have only one main city; now many countries have several. Like the border-spanning regions, city-regions can shrug off much central-government control, except in matters of money supply and foreign-trade policy. But they usually generate their own financial resources and certainly strike their own deals with foreign investors. They should be much on foreign investors' minds; they are where Asian incomes are highest and distribution easiest (see chapter 12). An inkling of the business opportunities that Asia's city-regions will provide is given in table 2, which confines itself to the supercities: the 16 Asian cities that will probably have populations greater than 10 million in the year 2015 (all of which will probably be among the world's twenty-five most populous cities, up from an Asian contingent of seven in 1985).

. . . YOUNG . . .

The second influential fact for Asia's next twenty years—and the most basic reason why today's Asia is full of life, energy, and hope—

TABLE 2
WORLD'S 25 LARGEST CITIES IN 2015

Rank	City	Country	Population (millions) Year 2015	Year 1994
1	Tokyo	Japan	28.7	26.5
2	Bombay	India	27.4	14.5
3	Lagos	Nigeria	24.4	9.7
4	Shanghai	China	23.4	14.7
5	Jakarta	Indonesia	21.2	11.0
6	Sao Paulo	Brazil	20.8	16.1
7	Karachi	Pakistan	20.6	9.5
8	Beijing	China	19.4	12.0
9	Dacca	Bangladesh	19.0	7.4
10	Mexico City	Mexico	18.8	15.5
11	New York	U.S.A.	17.6	16.3
12	Calcutta	India	17.6	11.5
13	Delhi	India	17.6	9.5
14	Tianjin	China	17.0	10.4
15	Manila	Philippines	14.7	9.0
16	Cairo	Egypt	14.5	9.4
17	Los Angeles	U.S.A.	14.3	12.2
18	Seoul	South Korea	13.1	11.5
19	Buenos Aires	Argentina	12.4	10.9
20	Istanbul	Turkey	12.3	7.5
21	Rio de Janeiro	Brazil	11.6	9.8
22	Lahore	Pakistan	10.8	4.9
23	Hyderabad	India	10.7	5.1
24	Osaka	Japan	10.6	10.6
25	Bangkok	Thailand	10.6	6.4

SOURCE: United Nations, *Urban Agglomerations* (1994).　　　　　Asian Cities

is that it is full of young people. Of the 3.3 billion Asians alive in 1995, some 1.7 billion, or around 52 percent, are under the age of twenty-five. Only 35 percent of Americans and 28 percent of Germans are that young.

Over the next twenty years all these 1.7 billion, as many as two-thirds of them literate, will either be in, or will just be entering, their most productive years. One reason Asia performed as spectacularly as it did in 1975–95 is that the billion Asians who were then coursing through their most productive years had been educated well enough that they mostly found jobs of the right sort to harness their energies and help pull the continent's economic growth forward with them.

The bigger bulge of Asians entering their productive years in 1995–2015 will be the continent's last surge of new workers into their productive years before Asia's population begins aging like that of the present-day rich world and its economy necessarily becomes more sedentary along with its middle-aged people. The 1.7 billion will present an even greater opportunity, but also a more perilous risk, than the 1 billion of 1975–95. If Asia's societies educate the class of 1995–2015 well enough and its economies present them with roughly as much chance of appropriate employment as they did the class of 1975–95, Asia will be vaulted fully and firmly into the camp of the global middle class. If they falter, it could create at best surly stagnation and at worst violence and disorder on the scale the 1950s pessimists about Asia shuddered to think about.

. . . AND RUTHLESS TO THE CORE

Whether Asia continues to thrive or begins to stagnate depends on my third and probably most controversial assertion: that East Asia has prospered over the past forty years largely because it has had small, pro-business governments which have refused to offer much public compassion for the unfortunate or improvident. This has been hard on unlucky or feckless individuals, but it has created exceptionally strong and resilient societies and economies. They are likely to stay that way if Asia's governments keep themselves small and maintain their anti-welfare mentality.

This sounds harsh, and it is. Asia's situation arose in part from historical accident. In Western Europe—and (to a lesser degree) in the United States—the Depression, the Second World War and the Cold War led governments to conclude that they must buy national cohesion through income redistribution and such social protections as guaranteed health care. During the Cold War the countries of East Asia were fighting for their lives in a more urgent sense than the West was: The very existence of many of them was directly threatened by military action (as in the cases of South Korea, Taiwan, and

Singapore). Some of them (South Korea, for instance) were literally starving; and all lacked the wherewithal to finance social protections. Their only hope lay in fast economic growth, and they discovered that pro-business, free-market policies provided this. As the countries of East Asia grew from these daunting origins, their debate about the role of government gradually assumed a form that might be described as: Do we put our faith in social engineering or in engineers? Engineers won hands down.

Asia's governments are, as explained a few pages back, surprisingly weak, and even when they are not weak (as they are not in South Korea and Singapore), they are still small. The simplest and single most important measure of a government's size is how much money it spends as a share of GDP. The reason this matters so much is that it can be taken as a proxy of how many decisions are left in the hands of the people who generate national income. The Japanese government's spending as share of GDP, at only 20 percent of gross national product (GNP) in the early 1990s, has until recently been the lowest of that of any member of the rich countries' club, the Organization of Economic Cooperation and Development. (Now that Mexico already is a club member and South Korea shortly will become one, Japan has given up that honor.) Hong Kong, with a GNP per person perhaps a quarter again as large as its colonial master, Britain, has a government that spends less than half as much as a share of GNP than Britain's does. The story is similar for the other better-off Asians, for the rising Asians, and for the poor Asians (though that is par for the course for poor countries everywhere).

The single biggest explanation of the difference in these spending shares is that Asia has rejected the welfare state. By welfare, I do not mean what self-congratulatory Americans of a certain age mean when they denounce welfare. I mean all transfer payments, including the huge ones through Social Security and Medicare, that have not been paid for through funded insurance schemes, not just the scraps thrown to teenage mothers in ghettos. The nature of transfer payments is that they are paid for by taxing current income earners and giving the proceeds to those who did not earn the income. And in every country where transfer payments bulk large in government spending, their beneficiaries are overwhelmingly the middle class. This is what Asia has largely turned away from. Transfer payments in Hong Kong in the early 1990s amounted to no more than 5 percent of government spending. In America they amounted to almost half of federal-government spending, or over 10 percent of GNP.

One of my most eye-popping moments in Asia came during a conversation in Shanghai in 1993 with a high Communist party official who formally had retired but (in the usual Chinese way) was still influential in shaping government policy. I asked him how China was going to handle the socially and politically explosive problem of the wholesale firings that would be needed if state-owned factories were to become competitive. We will have to find ways of satisfying the dismissed workers, he replied, "but we must take care not to make the mistake Europe did in setting up a welfare system that promotes high unemployment."

So much for communism in Asia. If modern-day Asian governments need a motto, it probably comes from Herbert Spencer, a British intellectual of the late nineteenth century, who wrote that "the ultimate result of shielding men from the effects of folly is to fill the world with fools." Asia's consistent ruthlessness in social and economic policy has ensured the absence there of the sort of protection from life's hazards that people (and often businesses) in most rich countries have come to expect. If economies are not sheltered from the ideas and methods of the outside world or from technological change, they run more efficiently. If there are few transfer payments, much more responsibility is thrown onto institutions other than government—particularly onto families. There is nothing misty-eyed about the Asian devotion to family. Parents cultivate their children's abilities, wives stay with lousy husbands, and children remain at their parents' beck and call not because of Confucian pieties but because Asians are too scared of the cruel world to break easily with the only institution that offers them protection from it if things go wrong. Since the peremptory demand of self-preservation pushes families to support those of their members too young or too old to work, they readily save more of their income.

Lower taxes and government spending give the wherewithal for these higher savings. With transfer payments suppressed, the government spending that remains is weighted towards investment: sometimes in hardware such as roads, more significantly in health and education (hence the greater faith in engineers than in social engineers.) In Hong Kong, the most radical of Asian states on these matters, such "people investments" account for half of government spending, compared with a third or less in the West.

The other side of the coin of small government is strong business. Governments making fewer decisions implies companies making more of them—particularly since the lower taxes that accompany smaller governments lead to higher profits and greater accumulations of private wealth. In much of modern Asia, notably Japan and Hong Kong, business has had a greater call on the attention and devotion of society than government has, and a bigger effect on ordinary people's lives. Small government does not mean clean government, as Japan has amply demonstrated, but it does help concentrate the energies of governors on the narrow range of topics where they have something useful to contribute.

Asians have recently been patting themselves on the back over their political, social, and economic arrangements far too enthusiastically. Some Asians seem to believe that they are leaving behind even America, let alone Europe, in the race for the future. This is wrong. America's efficiency, adaptability, and breadth of accomplishment remain unrivaled, and even the best-run and most advanced Asian countries have grave institutional problems to overcome before they can claim to be fully modern. But the Asians have a social-policy advantage which, if they preserve and build on it, will tell heavily in their favor: Their past ruthlessness has left them without the West's excruciating problem of dismantling an unaffordable welfare state that many voters nonetheless depend on. If Asian countries maintain their anti-welfare states for another generation, their abundant economic strengths will come into their own on the world stage. Those strengths, as the next chapter explains, are deep.

CHAPTER 2

HOW EAST ASIA DID IT: THE BASICS

The best way to understand on a human scale just how vast has been the transformation of East Asia wrought by thirty years of the fastest economic growth in history is to talk to someone who was there at the beginning and is still there now. Because the remaking of Asia has been so quick, a lot of such people are around.

One of them is Jack Lau, the head of a Hong Kong holding company called Tomei that has interests in electronics, toys, and finance. Mr. Lau, just turned forty in the early 1990s, was born in mainland China and came to Hong Kong with his parents in the 1950s. They were part of a stream of immigrants that radically re-made Hong Kong in the twenty years after the end of World War II. First came former residents of the territory who had fled to the mainland when the Japanese captured Hong Kong during the war; then, after 1949, Chinese from Shanghai and elsewhere who were escaping the imposition of Communist rule.

The flood of people put the colony under immense strain. In 1945 its population was 600,000. By 1950 it was over 2.2 million. That was bad enough, and worse was to come. Having almost quad-rupled its population in five years, Hong Kong proceeded in the next five years (1951–56) to suffer a shrinkage of one-third in its national income. Almost the whole of the territory's prewar econ-omy had been based on its being a trading intermediary between

China and the outside world. In 1951, in the midst of the Korean War, the United Nations imposed an embargo on militarily useful exports to China, and America banned all trade with the mainland. That year China accounted for 40 percent of Hong Kong's total exports; five years later, the figure was 4 percent.

Hong Kong in the mid-1950s was a land of penury, with many of its residents hungry, ill clothed, and unsheltered. Mr. Lau and his family had food, but they slept on rooftops for three years. In the squatter towns that were home to 750,000 Hong Kongers in the mid-1950s, the average resident had twelve square feet of floor space —or, for a family of five to live in, about as much space as a medium-sized American bathroom. They did not, of course, have bathrooms, and disease was a constant threat. When Mr. Lau's family eventually got a flat in one of the public-housing blocks the Hong Kong government started building in the 1950s, they thought they had reached heaven. These early public-housing flats consisted of two twenty-story or higher columns of private sleeping quarters for families, with communal kitchens and bathrooms sandwiched between the columns on each floor.

Apart from this housing, Hong Kongers in the early postwar decades were given little by their government apart from what they could generate themselves (even primary education was not made wholly cost-free until 1971.) On a scattering of barren overpopulated rocks with no natural resources whatever, what Hong Kongers could generate themselves should by most predictions have been next to nothing. Yet a mere thirty years after the Laus had at last got their public-housing cubicle in the early 1960s, Jack Lau was a multimillionaire, and the average Hong Konger was better off materially than the average resident of any other place on earth save America, Switzerland, Japan, and western Germany.

Stories like Mr. Lau's are so numerous in East Asia that they start seeming trite. South Koreans were even worse off than Hong Kongers thirty-five years ago, ill dressed and shivering in their still war-wracked capital, Seoul. Today the main complaint of Seoul's citizens is that too many people can now afford cars, which clog the roads for the car owners who got there first. An American diplomat recalls that, when he was first posted to Taipei, Taiwan's capital, in 1962, it was a bucolic place with—literally—one traffic light, turned on only when somebody important was passing through town. Now Taipei, like Seoul, endures an ever-worsening crush of traffic jams, while Taiwan itself has become the world's biggest producer of computer monitors and the first or second biggest possessor of foreign-exchange reserves. And so on, first through Singapore, then Kuala Lumpur, and now Bangkok and even Jakarta: where at various times in the past thirty years it seemed Communist guerrillas or abject poverty might destroy whole societies but where today rapidly growing middle classes wrestle with the milder problems of vacations and VCRs.

It is no wonder people like Mr. Lau are optimistic about places like Guangzhou (ex-Canton, the commercial capital of southern China). They see, in the next wave of Asian cities coming to crest, their own hometowns of only twenty years ago—and memories are still vivid after just two decades. Hope and confidence are, for good reason, the most powerful sentiments in mid-1990s Asia. And it is worth keeping in mind the individual aspirations and lives that have been freed over the past thirty years by the unprecedented economic growth whose dissection in this chapter and the next might otherwise seem dry, abstract, and of no consequence. Why East Asia grew so fast and whether the rest of Asia can follow are among the most important matters of public policy in the world.

THE ELEMENTS OF GROWTH

Economic growth is about as little understood as the human mind (with which, in fact, it is intimately linked; see chapter 3). Nobody, for example, can explain why around 1820 the West entered what Angus Maddison, the economic historian mentioned in chapter 1, calls "the capitalist epoch": a 170-year period in which real GDP rose by 2.7 percent a year and real incomes per person by 1.6 percent a year, multiplying output seventyfold and per capita incomes fourteenfold, when in the four centuries before this era the West managed income growth only one-eighth as fast despite considerable technological advance. Nor why, more locally, impressive spurts of growth for a decade or two petered out with no breakthrough to sustained modernization—a fate that befell Russia, the Austro-Hungarian Empire, and much of Latin America in the early part of this century.

Then there is modern East Asia. In general, a country's economic performance in one decade predicts nothing about how well or how poorly it will do in the following ten years. Yet for thirty years, decade in and decade out, seven poor East Asian countries (eight if rich Japan is included) have been among the dozen best-performing economies in the world—a geographical concentration of success so extraordinary that the World Bank guesses there is only one chance in ten thousand that it happened at random. Moreover, in all these countries fast economic growth was accompanied by a fall rather than a rise in income inequality: something almost without precedent in economic history.

Why did this remarkable event happen in East Asia? Despite all the complexities of economic growth, its constituents can be broken down into a mere four categories. These are the quantity of labor (how many people are in the workforce and how many hours they work); the quantity of physical capital (how much land and how many machines, buildings, and bridges are available for the work-force to work with); the quality of labor (how well educated and well trained the workforce is); and—the really difficult category —something that goes by various names but basically means the efficiency with which the inputs of capital and labor are combined. The brief answer to the question of how East Asia succeeded is that it managed to do an unusually good and consistent job at injecting these four elements of growth into its economies. Anyone who wants a longer answer might look at a book published by the World Bank in 1993 called *The East Asian Miracle,* from which most of the facts in the rest of this chapter are drawn.

LABOR

Beginning in the 1970s, the Asian workforce (defined as most peo-ple aged fifteen to sixty-four, with the major exception of house-wives) started growing fast. This was mainly the result of an Asian baby boom that began in some places in the late 1950s and rolled on through various countries on the continent into the 1990s. The workforce boom has followed the pattern of the baby boom with roughly a fifteen-year delay, so the rise in the Asian workforce will probably not begin tailing off until sometime after 2010. And by 2010, according to figures compiled by Andrew Mason and Minja Kim Choe of the East-West Center in Hawaii, the workforces of China and South Korea will be around a quarter bigger than they were in 1990; those of most of the rest of poor Asia—including the already enormous workforces of India and Indonesia—will be half again as big as in 1990. Some workforces (notably those of Bangladesh and Vietnam) will be two-thirds again as big, and the workforce of Pakistan a scary two times larger than it was in 1990.

The quantity of labor available to an economy is not, however, simply a matter of the amount of cannon fodder provided to it by population growth. In some places people work longer hours. In the 1980s the South Korean workweek was some ten hours longer than Japan's and more than fifteen hours longer than West Germany's. Even today, Hong Kongers are extraordinarily hardworking for people with their high level of incomes; most offices still open for a half day on Saturday, and clothing and other shops often stay open until midnight.

Most people assume that there is an inverse link between wealth and working hours—that is, as incomes rise (for both a country and an individual) people work less. That is often true, but not always. It is far from clear that it is a low level of income which drives people to work hard. Surveys in Hong Kong, for instance, suggest that bosses voluntarily work every bit as hard as the employees you might otherwise think were being cruelly exploited. The balance between work and leisure is likelier to be tilted by the material and other rewards that work offers than by a simple preference for leisure over work. In Hong Kong, remember, taxes are extremely low and entrepreneurialism extremely high, both of which make work relatively more attractive there than in other places.

The same seems true of countries as a whole: Workforce growth rates in Asia respond more to opportunities than to levels of poverty. In the best-performing Asian economies, workforce participation rates rose as incomes did in the 1970s and 1980s; this surprised labor economists, who were used to participation rates falling as incomes rose, since children could stay in school longer and old people retire earlier. Conversely, during the 1980s in Asian underachievers such as India, Bangladesh, and Burma, the workforce grew much more slowly than the working-age population because the rewards from work were not tempting.

What this suggests is a complicated relationship between the availability of labor, which is one of the main contributors to economic growth, and the other elements (such as capital) that make labor more productive. A whoosh of working-age people can actually do the opposite of what population pessimists assume. It can give a nice boost to the growth of a poor economy just when it most needs it, subject to a crucial proviso: that the other things are in place to make this bulge of labor productive. Otherwise, glumness is indeed in order.

The success stories of East Asia got this about right. Everywhere in the poor world death rates fell sharply in 1965–90. Unlike most places in the poor world, the fall in death rates in East Asia was followed in very short order by a sharp fall in birthrates, too. So instead of having to cope, as most poor countries did, with a sudden and long-lasting increase in population at a time when other resources were in short supply, East Asia got a sudden but compact burst of population growth. The swift deceleration in the birthrate set off a virtuous circle in which household savings rose, allowing spending on machines and basic education to increase. This provided the last bulge of babies, when they started reaching working age, with the tools they needed to be more productive and the incentives they needed for working harder.

CAPITAL

The more physical capital at the disposal of each worker—capital in the form of roads, machine tools, telephones, computers—the more the workers can produce. The creation of physical capital depends on financial capital: the saving of money by people, companies, and (yes, it can happen) governments that is then, via intermediaries like banks, stock markets, and bond markets, used by others to make physical capital. If the world's capital markets were entirely free, it would not matter where the money was saved and where it was invested; it would naturally flow to where it could earn the highest returns. But capital markets remain highly imperfect, and the lion's share of what a country saves and invests depends on what spare resources it can generate for itself. The countries of East Asia have been phenomenally good at generating capital.

In the mid-1960s the poor East Asian economies were saving only 16 percent of GDP, less than Latin America. By the early 1990s, East Asia, excluding Japan, was saving some 35 percent of GDP, four times as much as the Indian subcontinent and Africa and twice as much as Latin America (and the United States).

Thrift has always been a virtue in East Asia, and modern Asia's governments have built on the two main reasons why. The first reason—the stick of a pro-savings policy—is that governments have been, at best, indifferent to social welfare: If families did not save for hard times by themselves, nobody else would take care of them when misfortune struck. The second reason—which is the carrot—is that the reward for savings (the interest rate given to money that is saved) has been high in Asia, largely because the average rate of interest has been determined by the market.

This is unusual in poor countries, most of which have made the colossal mistake of keeping real interest rates deeply negative. Over fifteen- to twenty-year periods in the 1970s to early 1990s, countries like Mexico, Turkey, and Zambia had real interest rates that were as low as −11 percent to −28 percent a year. In East Asia rates in the formal sector were zero or slightly positive. More important, rates in East Asia's pervasive informal loan markets were strongly positive. Negative interest rates encourage borrowing rather than saving and direct what savings there are to the wrong uses; positive ones encourage more thought about the cost of capital. In some Asian countries very deep thought indeed about the cost of capital was encouraged. In Taiwan until well into the 1980s it was a felony to bounce a check —that is, there were debtors' prisons whose keys were effectively in the creditors' hands. This offered a draconian inducement to both lenders and borrowers (even when they were not intentionally such) to calculate risk accurately.

In more minor ways, too, East Asia's governments created an environment in which saving could flourish. First, they did not make the American mistake of actively penalizing savings: Interest and capital gains were mostly left untaxed, and there was no double taxation of corporate earnings through piling dividend tax on top of corporate income tax. Likewise, there has been no special encouragement given to debt through tax breaks for interest payments by the borrower. Second, East Asia kept its economies on an even keel. Inflation was kept fairly low and did not bounce around too much, which made it easier to plan and to save. Lastly, some institutions were set up—notably postal savings banks in Japan, South Korea, and Taiwan—that made it easy for people, especially in the countryside, who were unacquainted with banks and the like to start saving formally.

East Asia has been investing nearly as much as it saves: almost 35

percent of GDP in 1995, up from 20 percent in 1965. Asia's investment rates in the early 1990s were half again as high as those in
Latin America and Africa. Here, too, government policies have had
an effect. First, governments' own investments have helped to keep
the overall level of investment in these economies high. In most
poor countries in 1980–87, private investment fell as a result of
worldwide recession and debt restructuring. In Latin America and
Africa public investment fell, too, as governments there reduced
spending on roads and so forth in order to maintain previous levels
of spending on current items (like civil-service salaries). In East Asia,
by contrast, public investment rose in these lean years to make up
for weak private investment.

But East Asia's governments also encouraged private investment
in several ways. Tax breaks for certain kinds of favored investment
have been used, and in some countries, notably South Korea, cheap
credit has been directed to favored borrowers through the state-
controlled banking system. In most of East Asia exchange rates and
capital controls have also been used at various times to channel
domestic savings into investments at home when the savers might
really have preferred to invest abroad. Most of all, the trade policies
of the East Asian successes ensured that the prices of capital goods,
especially equipment, relative to those of other goods did not rise
much at a time when they were shooting up in other developing
economies. This meant that investors in East Asia did not have to
pay an increasing amount of money to buy the same amount of
physical capital—so they bought more of it than other countries'
investors did.

The most distinctive feature of East Asia's investment regime,
however, is how much it depended on private business. In the two
decades after 1970 private investment in East Asia accounted on
average for almost two-thirds of total investment; that compares with
roughly a fifty-fifty split in other countries with similar incomes.
Much public-sector investment is both necessary and desirable, producing good returns in itself and, as a by-product, raising returns to
private investment, too. But the lurking danger is that the cost of
public projects will not be judged as ruthlessly as that of private ones
against the returns they are likely to produce. The odds are that an
Asian-style split between public and private investment will impose
more market discipline on both kinds than a fifty-fifty split does.
This is why the recent move by Asian latecomers, such as China and

India, to have more of their infrastructure built with private resources is so encouraging (see chapter 13).

HUMAN CAPITAL

Among the most striking sights for any visitor to an East Asian city
are the hordes of uniformed schoolchildren: On buses and subways,
in the streets, almost everywhere, it seems, at certain times of day,
you run across packs of occasionally mussed but always smartly
dressed boys and girls carrying book bags. No jeans, no scruff, and
no scraggly hair. These are the latest crop of one of modern East
Asia's richest harvests: its unbelievably well educated young people.

Much of East Asia got an educational jump on other poor countries in the 1960s and sped ahead so fast that by the 1980s the
Asian early birds were turning out children who were certainly more
numerate than their counterparts in the rich world and often more
capable of abstract thought of all kinds. By the mid-1960s the four
"dragons"—Hong Kong, Taiwan, Singapore, and South Korea—
had achieved universal primary education; this was a decade or
more ahead of other countries at their income level. Three other
up-and-coming Asian countries—Malaysia, Thailand, and Indonesia
—were also ahead of their (less wealthy) counterparts. By 1987 each
of the dragons also enrolled at least three-quarters of its children in
secondary school. Two of the up-and-comers in 1987 had achieved
universal primary enrollments (Thailand lagged at 95 percent) and
were ahead of their competitors elsewhere in secondary-school enrollments. (Thailand was embarrassingly behind at a mere 28 percent.)

East Asia was well positioned for an educational triumph, and it
took full advantage of the opportunities it had. These opportunities
were provided by its already fast economic growth and the fast deceleration of population growth (both of which in short order trans-
lated education spending as a share of GDP into a comparatively
large absolute sum for each pupil) and by Asia's equal income distributions (which meant more of the poorest families could afford
schooling for their children). But, perhaps uniquely among poor
countries, the East Asians then took advantage of their promising
start by adopting the two most important and most sensible education policies for countries moving up: They concentrated public

spending on primary and secondary education, and they educated girls as widely as boys.

Contrary to popular belief, the East Asian countries did not spend a large share of their GDPs on education: The average for the seven countries mentioned two paragraphs above was 2.5 percent in 1960 and 3.7 percent in 1989. That compares with a developing-country average of 2.2 percent in 1960 and 3.6 percent in 1989; the Asian share in the second year was significantly lower than the share spent that year in black Africa (4.1 percent). The difference is that Asia concentrated its educational firepower on providing basic schooling for all its children, whereas budgets in Latin America and the Indian subcontinent were lavished on universities. One illustrative comparison is offered by Indonesia and Bolivia, which in the late 1980s had roughly the same dollar GDP per person and spent identical shares of 2.3 percent of GDP on education. But their priorities were opposite: Indonesia spent 90 percent of its education budget on primary schools; Bolivia, 40 percent. At the other end of the scale, South Korea spent 10 percent of its education budget on universities in 1985; Venezuela, 43 percent.

Early on in a country's climb to wealth, a Korea-like ratio has two advantages. It increases the productivity of the mass of the workforce, which is what counts in a country whose comparative advantage will temporarily be in light, labor-intensive manufacturing. Second, it does more than anything else to promote income equality, consumer-spending power, and broad support for high-growth economic policies. In a poor country it is only the well-off who go to universities, which makes them a perverse place to spend lots of public money.

A study of Japan by Estelle James, an economist, and Gail Benjamin, an anthropologist, shows to what a ruthless and effective extreme this line of policy can be taken. The Japanese made early education public, universal, and undifferentiated. At each succeeding step of the academic ladder, the public part of education was shrunk in size and made more elite until, at university level, it is tiny. One consequence is a brutally meritocratic selection that populates the public universities with a higher share of poor children than in Brazil or Venezuela while leaving the well-off who could not make the grade to fend for themselves in the private universities.

Another consequence is to increase the value of education to all income slices of the population. Like other aspects of "miraculous" Asia, the fast-rising educational performance of East Asian children can be traced in large part to the simple fact that they work harder than European children and a lot harder than American ones. They get up early (one of the things that first made me realize how massively and energetically Asia is on the move was to see Jakarta's city-center parks at 6:00 A.M. on a Saturday filled with children doing calisthenics before going off to school); they spend longer hours in school, for more weeks of the year, than Western children; and they do more homework in the evening.

They do this throughout East Asia because the meritocratic school systems reward them and their parents for it. Parents, including poor ones, dig into their own pockets to pay for private tutoring outside school hours, since the rewards for success later on are so great. This habit of supplementing public education with private tutoring is well established in South Korea and Japan; in Japan in the early 1990s, two-fifths of children received tutoring before they even started school, and by the time they were teenagers, 70 percent did. The habit is now spreading to China and Indonesia.

Asia's other smart move was to educate girls as much as boys, which has not been the practice in much of the poor world. The first benefit of doing so was that it helped to produce the swift decline in birthrates mentioned earlier: The world over, when girls get more education, they have fewer babies. Second, it gave a big boost to the teaching that mothers were able to give at home to their children both before and after the children started school.

Feminists may wish to skip the rest of this section. A study for the World Bank by Nancy Birdsall and Richard Sabot concludes that instruction at home by mothers seems to have a lot to do with the extremely high test scores East Asian children achieve. The effect is felt throughout primary school but is at its most pronounced in the mathematics test scores of children in kindergarten: Japanese children, who receive a lot of instruction at home (and, by all indications, almost exclusively from their mothers), vastly outperform American children, who are taught little at home.

Japan and South Korea, the two Asian countries that educated their girls the most thoroughly and then most systematically excluded them from the workforce—thus focusing young mothers' skilled energies almost exclusively on their children—are the two countries that had the highest-performing next generation: so high

that by the 1980s South Korean thirteen-year-olds were outper-
forming children from much richer countries on an entire range of
math tests. A similar though less striking pattern appears in Malaysia. In Thailand, by contrast, where girls received reasonably good
educations but (unlike their Japanese and Korean sisters) faced
neither cultural nor formal barriers to working outside the home,
women participated in the labor force far more—indeed as much as
in Scandinavia—and their children, left in the care of less educated
grandparents and other relatives, learned far less.

There is no justification in terms of individual fulfillment for
forcing Japanese or Korean-like subjugation on educated women.
In fact, this presumably has much to do with the growing reluctance
of Japanese women to marry. In 1970 only 18 percent of Japanese
women aged twenty-five to twenty-nine were single, compared with
40 percent in 1990: figures probably not unconnected with another
statistic that shows that once they have a child, only 13 percent of
Japanese women go on working full-time even now. Nor, once
women do start being allowed to function in the workforce on a
more or less equal footing with men, is there any turning back; even
Asia's curmudgeons admit this. But they also regret the loss it entails
for a strongly family based society. Lee Kuan Yew once said that "the
worst mistake we ever made" was to allow well-educated women to
find their way as they would into the workforce.

THAT CERTAIN SOMETHING

The magical element in economic growth, however (and the subject
of chapter 3), is neither the quantity and quality of labor nor physical capital. After a while these items start running out of steam. You
cannot just keep adding people (no matter how well educated) and
capital forever and expect economic growth to continue. The supply
of people dwindles; and in the case of capital, diminishing returns
—slightly less bang for each additional buck—set in, and growth
slows or even comes to a halt. The most spectacular recent example
of this came with the collapse of the Soviet Union. In the years
1960–85 the Soviet Union and the East Asian economies accumulated physical and human capital at about the same rate. But Russia
was using these inputs so inefficiently that, by the end of the Communist experiment, the country's factories were producing finished

goods less valuable than the raw materials that had gone into them. The key for East Asia's long-term future is how efficiently it uses the extra inputs it injects into its economies.

Perhaps the best description of the efficiency with which labor and capital are combined is something called total factor productivity (TFP). This mouthful of jargon has been impossible to measure directly, and so calculations of it are notoriously imprecise. They amount to seeing what is left over after other contributions to economic growth (such as increased physical capital) are subtracted. TFP thus embarrassingly offers anywhere from 0 percent to 70 percent of the statistical explanation for growth. But TFP can still give a rough idea of how well tuned an economic engine is. In rich countries TFP accounts for a third to a half of economic growth. By the World Bank's calculations, around a third of East Asia's growth has been from TFP (an average that masks such extremes as Hong Kong's 56 percent and Malaysia's 13 percent).

This average is extremely high by poor-country standards; only 10 percent of poor countries outside East Asia have rates as high. By the World Bank's reckoning, even if Latin America and Africa had invested as much in machines and people as East Asia (which they did not), their underlying rate of TFP growth in 1960–85 would have been 1 percent, compared with 4 percent for East Asia.

Some people have begun questioning whether the World Bank's calculations are accurate. Alwyn Young, an economist at MIT, reckons that over a twenty-five-year period Singapore's TFP actually fell by 1 percent a year, meaning that more than the whole of its very high output growth in those years came from adding (à la Soviet Union) more and more inputs, first capital and then educated people; efficiency was meanwhile declining. Mr. Young suggests that the rest of the East Asian "miracle" economies, save perhaps Hong Kong, did no better in terms of efficiency than most of the rest of the world: They just threw more capital, physical and human, into the fray.

Whether Mr. Young is right is of huge importance. If Asia's extraordinary quarter century was the economic equivalent of muscle building through steroids, the whole place will slow down quickly, and parts of it could even collapse, as the Soviet Union did (see chapter 4). If not, what has given Asia its efficient edge? A pair of great successes that followed very different policies may point to an answer.

CHAPTER 3

HOW EAST ASIA DID IT: THE ADVANCED COURSE

If, in 1955, you had been forced to identify poor Asia's two likeliest future failures, you would probably have picked Taiwan and South Korea. (You would not have been asked even to consider the pitiful fate that awaited Hong Kong and Singapore.) The Philippines was in great shape, the richest country in Southeast Asia: so rich that in the mid-1950s thousands of Hong Kong Chinese women flocked to Manila to work as maids. (Forty years later the tables had turned, as more than 100,000 Filipinas were working as maids in Hong Kong.) Burma, too, was doing well in 1955, and India, full of promise, democratic politicians, eloquent lawyers, well-trained civil servants, and lots of economists, seemed to have everything going for it. South Korea, meanwhile, was barely functioning again after its war with the North; and Taiwan was little more than an American-bankrolled campground for the Nationalists kicked out of mainland China (temporarily they thought) by Mao's Communists in 1949.

Neither country had much to work with. City-states aside, Taiwan and South Korea respectively had the world's second- and third-highest population densities (after what is now called Bangladesh); both are mountainous, and their population densities on arable land—which is no more than a quarter of the total land in either country—are even higher than that of Bangladesh. Literacy was low: only 13 percent in Korea in 1945, perhaps 25 percent in Taiwan by the end of that decade. Low, too, especially in South Korea, were savings and hence investment. As late as 1962, 80 percent of South Korea's total investment was financed by foreign aid, mainly from the United States. At that time, Communist North Korea, which had inherited the heavy industries built up during the fifty-year Japanese occupation, may well have had higher incomes per head than the South.

Yet after both Taiwan and South Korea had spent the 1950s mostly fumbling their economic chances, in the following three decades they produced two of the best economic performances in Asia, and among the best in the world. Real incomes in Taiwan rose more than sixfold in thirty years, reaching more than $10,000 in 1992. (In 1952 per-capita income in Taiwan had been $67.) South Korea rose a shade faster. Every ten years after 1960, Korea's economy tripled in size, so that it was about twenty-seven times bigger in 1991 than it had been in 1962; real personal incomes went up sevenfold over that period. The sharp rise in incomes led to a steep rise in savings. In the 1950s household savings in Taiwan were 3 percent of GDP, and in Korea in the early 1960s 1–2 percent of GDP. By the 1980s these figures had shot up to around 16 percent in both countries. Overall savings (personal, corporate, and government) were around 35 percent of GDP, which gave the wherewithal for investment on a similar scale. Partly thanks to this investment, the structure of each country's economy was revolutionized. In 1962 farming accounted for 37 percent of the Korean economy; in 1991, the figure was 8 percent; in Taiwan farming fell from around 30 percent to under 4 percent.

Almost uniquely in economic history, Taiwan and South Korea combined extraordinarily fast growth and shocking structural change with increases rather than declines in the equality of income distribution. Rural incomes rose to urban levels and stayed there, and unemployment has been unusually low in both countries. The last time it exceeded 2 percent in Taiwan was 1964, and South Korean unemployment has gone above 4 percent only once since the 1970s. By one common measure of income inequality, Taiwan in the mid-1970s was the most egalitarian place on earth save perhaps for Sweden (and, unlike Sweden, with little income redistribution through the tax system); by the same measure, Korean incomes were more equal than those of America or Japan. Since the mid-1980s, income equality has declined a bit in both Taiwan and South

Korea, probably because the real estate and stock-market asset booms that swept through all of East Asia after 1985 transferred some income as well as wealth to the lucky holders of the assets. Even so, Taiwan and South Korea remain two of the world's most egalitarian societies.

Two Stars in Different Orbits

How did they do it? The feats were accomplished by fairly stern military dictatorships that faced security threats to the very survival of their countries and were bent, above all else, on the development of their economies. This made for a pretty bad environment for civil and political liberties but an excellent one for government decision-making impervious to the wheedling of special-interest lobbies. When Gen. Park Chung Hee took power in South Korea in a 1961 military coup, he vowed to "end starvation"; in general, he spoke with such egalitarian fervor that some American officials were alarmed that they might have a socialist of some sort on their hands. They need not have worried. Invoking a theme that cropped up again in Deng Xiaoping's decommunizing China of the 1980s, Park wrote in his autobiography that "the people of Asia today fear starvation and poverty more than the oppressive duties thrust upon them by totalitarianism"; and, even more to the point: "In human life, economics precedes politics and culture." Both Park and Gen. Chiang Kai-shek, who had run Taiwan since being chased out of China, were flirting not with socialism but with supercapitalism.

In retrospect, it seems clear that both Taiwan and South Korea were doing all they could to maximize the elements of growth described in the preceding chapter. At first, with savings rates relatively low, the money for investment interestingly came from land reform. Here Taiwan and Korea were probably just lucky. Land reform— overthrowing concentrated ownership in the countryside and distributing the expropriated land among those who work it—is pointless before an investible surplus has been built up in the old landlords' hands. The vagaries of war in both Taiwan and Korea had allowed large surpluses to be accumulated in the hands of the old landlords. That accomplished, the external threats faced by the two countries allowed their governments, on grounds of national security, to ram through land nationalizations over the opposition of the old landlords. And this in turn freed a lot of liquid capital for investment by the old landlords in the rising industries of the towns, though more so in Taiwan than in South Korea. On its own account, the government, too, did its part for investment. The great bulk of government spending went for investment (especially in infrastructure) rather than consumption: South Korea's civil-service spending is still unusually low.

In both Taiwan and South Korea the improvement of human capital was given even greater emphasis than the accumulation of physical capital. Spending on education was not particularly high, but as mentioned in chapter 2, it was concentrated first on primary schooling and then on secondary schooling rather than on the fripperies of higher education, for which students good enough often went abroad. Moreover, because of culture (one thing undoubtedly true of the often misdescribed creed of Confucianism is that it values scholarship), relative income equality, and the prospect of fast economic growth—all of which handsomely repaid a family for its investments in its children's education—private spending on schooling was also high. In South Korea in 1990, spending on education, most of which was private, amounted to 10 percent of GDP.

What did Taiwan and Korea do to raise productivity? The principal method was an all-out dash for export-led growth. In the 1950s both Taiwan and South Korea tried to industrialize through the then fashionable process of import substitution, meaning they raised high (sometimes impassable) barriers to certain imports in the hope of nurturing domestic companies that could make the goods instead. In the early 1960s both reversed this process and began relying on exports, particularly manufactured exports, to stimulate growth and remake their industrial structures. The results were stunning. In 1961 the dollar value of South Korea's exports was $45 million; in 1992 it was $76 billion, or roughly seventeen hundred times as high in nominal terms. Even after adjusting for inflation, the rise was spectacular: South Korea's exports grew ninetyfold between 1965 and 1990. Taiwan was slightly more modest: Its exports grew only thirtyfold in real terms between 1965 and 1990. By 1992 Taiwan (with 20 million people) was the world's eleventh biggest exporter; South Korea (with 45 million), the twelfth biggest.

In making their presence felt on the world economic stage, Taiwan and South Korea also radically reshaped their own economies.

In the 1950s manufactured goods made up only a fifth of Taiwan's exports; forty years later they accounted for 95 percent. In both Taiwan and South Korea the shift of exporting from primary products to manufactured ones, and then the amazing rise in the volume of manufactured exports, sped their moves from farming to industry. Their early manufactured exports were labor-intensive goods like textiles and toys, and the rise of these exports greatly boosted labor productivity (and hence wages) and stimulated further investment.

This process of economic upgrading happened in part simply because of what economists call comparative advantage: Selling the things you are efficient at making allows you to acquire more of the things you are less good at making than if you tried to make those things yourself. But, in addition, the productivity increases in export industries that came from exposure to world standards of quality and technology were quickly transmitted through the whole economy thanks to the export firms' demands for intermediate inputs (such as the cloth to make the shirts, or the plastic to make the toys.)

Small and Large

Yet if exports were the motor of growth for both Taiwan and South Korea, the vehicles being driven could hardly have been more different. Taiwan's government did intervene in the economy in several ways, and a surprisingly large—and inefficient—share of industry is still accounted for by government-owned firms (largely in heavy, capital-intensive industries such as shipbuilding and steel): In the late 1980s state-owned firms in Taiwan produced a fifth of industrial output and accounted for 30 percent of capital investment and half of investment in machinery and equipment. But these interventions had fairly mild effects on relative prices, either between Taiwanese and world prices or between prices for different goods within Taiwan; and when an intervention did cause prices to deviate from market levels (e.g., when imports were restricted by quota or tariff), Taiwan was zealous about intervening a second time to counterbalance the distortion (e.g., by giving exporters tax rebates).

South Korea was on another plane entirely. It ran a full-blooded interventionist program of the sort that Japan's bureaucrats had

earlier attempted only a pale sketch of (and then probably not too effectively). The aims of General Park's regime were not in fact much different from those of other command-and-control governments: to develop and mobilize the economy for the sake of national strength (which may be why he sounded suspiciously socialist). Park's genius was to try to accomplish these aims not, as others of his ilk did, by nationalizing businesses or insulating them from the currents of the marketplace, but instead by making strategic decisions about the economy, inducing (or forcing) private firms to follow the strategy and ensuring that they were exposed to the full blast of competition when they did. Another quote from the general captures the Korean paradox: "The fundamental element . . . is the national potential to achieve a completely self-sufficient economy; and exports constitute the leading element for the completion of a self-reliant economy."

This may sound mercantilist—that is, in favor of keeping out imports and building up exports—but it is not. The reason is that anti–import measures are simultaneously anti–export measures: first because they raise the prices of the imported inputs that would-be exporters need for the manufacture of their goods; more important, because they distract might-be exporters by making the protected (and less competitive) home market more profitable than it would otherwise be. To avoid these harmful effects South Korea, like Taiwan, matched every restraint on imports—and there were a lot more of them in Korea—with a countervailing spur to exports.

Similar methods were applied to the Korean domestic economy. One sign of the punctiliousness with which the bureaucracy carried out this balancing act is that, although the Korean economy is riddled with government-ordered distortions, a World Bank study in 1983 found that Korea had one of the least price-distorting regimes in the world. For every tax (or subsidy) there was an opposite and roughly equal subsidy (or penalty).

WHERE CREDIT WAS DUE

Tibor Scitovsky, an economist at Stanford University, has pointed out that for both Taiwan and South Korea the main link between the government's philosophy and the shape of the economy was credit and interest-rate policy. Beginning in the late 1950s, Taiwan

pursued a policy, highly unusual in those days, of letting interest rates rise to "high" levels (i.e., levels where the supply and demand for credit were balanced). This produced high rates of savings and investment, an atomized industrial structure, and equal incomes.

This may seem odd—cheap money, after all, sounds like it must be good for the little guy; in fact, the opposite is true. Cheap money helps borrowers (mostly big firms), hurts savers (mostly individuals), and encourages capital-intensive production, thus cutting employment growth. Along with tight money, Taiwan ran a tight fiscal policy, with a budget surplus every year save one in the quarter century after 1965. The results, in macroeconomic terms, were high savings and more tightly costed, hence more efficient, investment. In industrial terms, tight money led to a large number of small firms that were mostly financed with equity rather than debt. In the early 1980s four-fifths of Taiwan's firms had fewer than twenty employees. And, outside the heavy industries dominated by state-owned firms, there was little or no monopoly power.

South Korea was at the other extreme. Mark Clifford, an American journalist who spent several years covering Korea, has pointed out that, when General Park took power, he distrusted financiers immensely, believing all of them to be speculators and many of them crooks. He seized control of the banks, and for the next thirty years the government ran a careful eye over bank budgets and exercised veto power over the appointment of top bank managers; until the early 1980s its approval was required for each loan of any substantial size.

From 1961 to 1979, South Korea's planners kept interest rates below the market-clearing level and used their control over the banks to direct cheap loans to borrowers that were carrying out the government's strategic aims. The borrowers were export-oriented groups that quickly grew into gigantic family-owned conglomerates called *chaebol*. The government supported their growth through a looser and more erratic monetary policy than Taiwan ran and through heavy foreign borrowing. By 1984 the ten largest *chaebol* absorbed a third of South Korea's total domestic credit; the thirty largest, half of all domestic credit (much of which was, in fact, recycled foreign borrowings by Korean banks). The *chaebol* were debt-laden: By the mid-1980s their ratio of debt to equity had risen to almost five to one (five times the ratio for American industrial firms and more than twice that for Taiwanese firms). And they were almost absurdly diversified: In 1985, Samsung, that year the biggest conglomerate in terms of sales, had under its umbrella thirty-nine companies operating in twenty-six distinct lines of business, including semiconductors, textiles, aerospace, and sugar processing.

The Korean economy became one of the most concentrated in the world (far more so than supposedly monolithic Japan). In 1985 the sales of the two biggest *chaebol* equaled 38 percent of Korea's GNP; those of the ten biggest, 80 percent of GNP. In 1984 the manufacturing value-added of the ten biggest (i.e., their output minus their inputs) amounted to 16 percent of GNP. By 1983 the sales of the top ten *chaebol* totaled some $47 billion, more than six times the sales of Taiwan's top ten groups, even though the Taiwanese economy in those days was almost as big as the South Korean economy. A Korean government survey of twenty-five hundred goods found that in 1988, 21 percent of the country's markets for them were monopolistic and 56 percent oligopolistic.

A tale told by a Samsung executive gives a flavor of the regimental but messianic nature of South Korea's drive to industrialize. In the early 1980s the South was still a military dictatorship (though with a new dictator, since Park had been assassinated in 1979) and still on high alert against the possibility of a sudden attack from the North. Seoul, which is only twenty-five miles from the border with the North, had a strict curfew after midnight. This was a considerable irritation to the capital's businessmen, who are great carousers, and many of whom often ended up having to sleep it off in a jail cell for breaking the curfew. Once, the Samsung executive was being driven home post-curfew after a jolly evening with some colleagues and an American buyer. Stopped at a roadblock, the executive pointed to the American and whispered to the military policeman, "Export promotion." The policeman snapped to attention, saluted smartly, and said, "You are on the nation's business. Proceed."

The most massive effort to wrench the nation's business onto a new strategic path of the government's choosing came with the "Heavy and Chemical Industries" (HCI) plan, which began in 1973. This involved enormous subsidized investments in shipbuilding, petrochemicals, steel, and electronics, imposed on what had until then been mostly a light-industrial base. It was done at huge cost in terms of foreign borrowing, inflation, suppressed savings rates, and inefficient (i.e., low-return) capital investment. It also produced several colossal industrial failures and a macroeconomic imbalance so severe that, a year after the world's second oil-price shock hit in 1979, the government gave up the HCI program and, in the early

1980s, raised interest rates and began pursuing more Taiwan-like policies of letting markets rule in the first instance.

Interestingly, after a few years of administering market medicine to the force-fed industrial system of the 1970s, South Korea found at the end of the 1980s that the HCI program had achieved many of its aims. Korea did have world-class capital-intensive industries that could sometimes give firms from far richer countries a run for their money. Thanks to the years of market-friendly balm in the 1980s, Korea also substantially raised its savings and investment rates, the efficiency of its capital investment, and its productivity growth. On most measures South Korea outperformed Taiwan during the 1980s. But whether getting to this point by the end of the 1980s justified the heavy costs South Korea bore in the 1970s is an open question.

For by the mid-1990s the jury is still out on judging whether Taiwan or South Korea has the better industrial structure or the brighter economic future. Despite efforts by each to graft on some of the strengths of the other, the two economies retain the shape they were given two generations back. Taiwan, too far up the income ladder to avoid the need to innovate for itself now, is reinforcing its earlier habit of setting up R&D (research and development) parks to do the basic high-tech research that individual firms have trouble financing or whose costs they cannot recapture through sales of their own products. Yet Taiwan's entrepreneurs, ingrained with a trader's instinct for a quick profit, still often prefer to move out (to China, say) than up. South Korea, trying to wean the economy from bureaucratic tutelage, finds the weight of its own past heavy. Banks are still burdened with "policy" lending to satisfy past government industrial strategy, and the *chaebol* dominate manufacturing as much as ever. Yet, however different, both Taiwan and South Korea keep growing at rates that are surprisingly high for the amount of extra capital and labor each is injecting every year—so much so that by 2010 each Taiwanese could well have the same income as an American in 1992, and each South Korean the income of a Belgian in 1992. Why are these seeming opposites both doing so well?

GOVERNMENTS AND THEIR PLACE

Ever since it became clear in the late 1970s that Japan had achieved astonishing industrial success, a debate has been growing about

whether the East Asians have got to where they are today by being
apt pupils of the free-market school or instead by being especially
skilled at bringing government intervention successfully to bear on
the economy. The answer is probably both, though when intervention did work, which was not all that often, it did so in special
circumstances and for almost diametrically the opposite reason to
the one for which the somewhat leftish Americans who instinctively
like active government believe it did.

Much of economic growth, and of East Asia's success, is accounted
for by simple injections of capital and labor that are then used
efficiently. It is highly likely that behind this contribution to growth
—and recall that it has accounted for some two-thirds of all growth
in East Asia—lies adherence to well-recognized free-market principles. East Asian governments have tended to allow markets to set the
prices of labor, capital, and goods and to maintain macroeconomic
stability through low inflation, stable and positive real interest rates,
and predictable and export-friendly exchange rates. All of that has
done wonders to raise the level of savings and investment and to
make capital investment efficient.

It is, moreover, no argument against the free-market case to say
that East Asia invested well in physical infrastructure and human
capital. These are, up to a point, common goods that governments
everywhere take responsibility for in at least a financial sense; they
are more akin to policing, a stable currency, and the rule of law
than they are to a true industrial policy. In the crucial matter of
education, in particular, East Asia's governments spent their (fairly
modest) budgets in ways that were not biased in favor of the well-off;
hence, they were less interventionist on this score than most other
governments in the world. And, with both education and infrastructure, private financing and decision-making played a big role alongside that of the government; this helped tie the government's own
spending closely to market measures.

There are plenty of reasons for thinking that the more market-
friendly a government's policies, the better for productivity growth
as well as investment growth. It is, for example, unlikely to be an
accident that Hong Kong has both the world's least interventionist
government and Asia's highest rate of TFP growth.

The ups and downs of Indonesia's capital efficiency and TFP
performance suggest the same thing. Indonesia started on the reform path a bit later than most of its neighbors: only after Sukarno,

the country's bombastic founding father, was stripped of power in 1965–66. Sukarno was very much a product of the grandiose-nationalist mold that had stamped so many Third World leaders of the 1950s. The economic policy his government ran during the "guided economic development" of 1958–65 increasingly shut Indonesia off from the currents of the world economy and brought larger shares of the economy under government control through nationalization and through heavy regulation of private business and investment.

Combined with growing macroeconomic instability (high inflation, balance-of-payments crises, and so on), and indeed political and social instability, too, this policy had "guided" Indonesia straight into a ditch by 1965. In the years since President Suharto, an ex-general, formally took over in 1967, the pattern of Indonesia's economic performance has fit the East Asian bill.

In the late 1960s almost two-thirds of Indonesians were living in absolute poverty; life expectancy was the lowest in East or Southeast Asia, infant mortality among the highest in the world, primary-school enrollment and adult literacy almost as low as India's, and secondary-school enrollment much lower than India's. After a quarter-century of the usual East Asian tonic, when Indonesia's economy grew at an annual rate of more than 6 percent a year, the incidence of terrible poverty had fallen by three-quarters, life expectancy had risen by twenty years, primary schooling was universal, the rate of secondary schooling had almost quintupled, and adult illiteracy had fallen by two-thirds. Savings and investment rates both tripled to roughly 25 percent, and more than half of Indonesia's exports were manufactured goods, compared with the 97 percent of exports that had been oil and primary products only twenty-five years before.

However, the curlicues within this familiar happy pattern are telling: Indonesia has been unusually prone among East Asian countries to sharp changes of policy direction. Amar Bhattacharya, of the World Bank, and Mari Pangestu, an Indonesian economist, reckon that during the Suharto years Indonesia has had five distinct phases of economic policy (and may just have entered a sixth).

During the first period, 1967–73, the government stabilized the economy, liberalized trade, and began deregulating domestic industry. During the heady days of the first oil boom (Indonesia has a lot of oil), 1973–81, the government pretty much kept the macroeconomy on an even keel but, much like South Korea in the same years, began protecting and regulating the economy to favor industries it thought were important. In 1982–85, when prices for its main exports—oil and primary products—fell sharply, Indonesia went even more gung-ho for protection, regulation, government ownership of industry, and import substitution as an industrial policy. In 1985–88, this was reversed: Import barriers were lowered, restraints on foreign investment and private domestic investment were relaxed, and the government began withdrawing from industrial ownership. These reforms accelerated in 1988–93 (but may now be slowing down a bit with the rise to political prominence of a technology minister who is enthusiastic about Korean-like industrial leap-frogging).

TABLE 3
INDONESIA: AGGREGATE EFFICIENCY INDICATORS, 1967–91

	1967–73	1973–81	1982–85	1985–87	1988–91
Rate of return on investment, % per annum (a)	53.4	31.4	13.1	26.0	17.0
Incremental capital output ratio (b)	1.8	2.8	7.8	5.3	3.7
Total factor productivity (c)	2.1	0.9	−2.5	−1.1	2.2

NOTES: (a) Rate of growth of non-oil GDP as a percentage of average investment rate during the period.
   (b) Units of additional capital needed to produce a unit of additional output.
   (c) TFP change is calculated as the difference between rates of growth of value-added and factor inputs (labor and capital); the inputs are weighted by their income shares.
SOURCE: A. Bhattacharya and M. Pangestu, *Indonesia: Development Transformation Since 1965 and the Role of Public Policy* (World Bank, 1992).

The interesting thing about these zigzags, shown in table 3, is that standard measures of both capital efficiency and TFP growth track like clockwork the government's moves towards or away from market-based policies. When the government grew more protectionist and interventionist, efficiency and productivity fell; when it grew less so, they rose. Similar signs show up in South Korea (the HCI program led to a huge fall in capital efficiency) and in Malaysia, where a heavy-industry push in the early 1980s had to be quickly given up because it dragged performance down so fast.

The conclusion that could be drawn from all this, and it is a tempting one, is that East Asian industrial policies were irrelevant at best and often quite harmful; that it was the classically market-friendly policies which supplied all (or in heavily interventionist countries more than all) the lift for these economies during their takeoffs. Amusingly, the case for irrelevance may be at its strongest with Japan, the supposed fount of the "East Asian model of capitalism." One of the best industrial studies of Japan, by an American lawyer named David Friedman, looked at the Japanese machine-tool industry and government attempts to shape it since the 1930s. It found that the machine-tool makers simply ignored the efforts of Ministry of International Trade and Industry (MITI) bureaucrats to restructure the fragmented industry on more concentrated American-like lines. The car and oil industries also shrugged off MITI's importunities.

The Idea of Ideas

Even so, there are reasons for thinking that at least some active government interventions in East Asia have borne fruit. The most convincing of these reasons is an idea of Paul Romer's, an economist at the University of California at Berkeley, about ideas and economic growth.

Ideas are not human capital, the level of which can be thought of as a sign of how well a country is capable of putting ideas into practice. Ideas are the world's pool of existing knowledge—the most efficient sequence, in an example of Mr. Romer's, for sewing twenty pieces of cloth together to make a shirt—and of new knowledge that people tinkering with the processes on an assembly line or with a string of symbols like this sentence come up with.

The main reason the rich world is rich—and why half or more of its economic growth comes from productivity increases—is not because it has physical and human capital in abundance (though that helps) but because it is rich in ideas it knows how to apply. An example from another North American thinker, Jane Jacobs, who writes about cities, suggests why the difference between the stock of capital and the stock of ideas is crucial. After noting that billions in American foreign-aid spending have had little or no effect in raising incomes in many poor countries, Mrs. Jacobs draws a contrast with San Francisco after the earthquake of 1906. San Francisco's physical capital (though little of its human capital) was abolished overnight. The "foreign aid" that then poured into the city from governments, charities, and insurance companies allowed San Francisco to recover quickly and thrive, but "nobody was addled enough to suggest that the Red Cross should therefore go into the business of rushing aid indiscriminately to economically declining or stagnant cities on the ground that this would make them prosper like San Francisco."

It may seem that San Francisco's quick recovery (or that of West Germany or Japan after the Second World War) was simply a matter of its wealth of human capital; but there is much more to it than that. The post-1945 German example gives an indication of why. At the start of the Cold War, East Germany was no poorer in human capital than West Germany, but as the years wore on, it fell further and further behind despite continued large investments in education and training. The East had less physical investment, but not that much less. What it increasingly lacked, however, was contact with the newest ideas and best practices in the West.

In the world described by Mr. Romer, "ideas are the critical input in the production of more valuable human and nonhuman capital." If so, for a poor country ideas have a spectacular virtue. Once they exist anywhere, anybody can acquire them and use them—and, just as important, use them at the same time as everybody else without doing any harm to anyone else (which is not the case with, for example, an office building). These days you not only do not have to reinvent the wheel, you can find out how to make the car and then improve on the carmaking process yourself. This is why countries starting out very far behind the rich world have the chance—if they get things right—to make up ground so fast.

Getting things right means, above all, making an economy as open as possible to foreign influences. In Mr. Romer's view, by far the most common mistake made by poor-country governments is to practice a sort of "neo-mercantilism" of ideas: the belief that a country must "own" some ideas of its own and reap monopoly profits (and technological advancement) from them even if this means restricting the entry of ideas from the rest of the world via trade and foreign investment. This sort of approach—which is what advocates of industrial policy usually have in mind when they argue for active government intervention to support "strategic industries" —is almost invariably disastrous. It makes an economy poorer than it would otherwise be and retards rather than accelerates the acquisition of ideas and their dispersion through the economy.

The clearest recent case of a failed policy of this sort was Brazil's attempt in the 1980s to build a home-grown computer industry through subsidies and a near-total prohibition on the import of

foreign semiconductors and computers. This not only failed miserably to create a computer industry in Brazil but also did grave damage
to other industries, notably cars and aerospace, which fell ever further behind the foreign competition because they were starved of
modern electronics. The evidence is not yet in, but it is likely that
Indonesia's lavish and premature promotion of an aerospace industry this decade will prove another fiasco—not least through its colossal waste of the country's scarce engineering talent.

By Mr. Romer's calculations, the consequences of closing an economy to the ideas embodied in foreign goods and foreign investment
can be catastrophic, far worse even than traditional trade theory
predicts. His studies show that a vast underestimate of the benefits
from either trade or investment occurs when the yardstick being
used fails to take account of the difference between new (improved)
goods, which carry with them the potent brew of new ideas, and
mere extra portions of goods that already exist.

The impact of failing to draw a distinction between old goods and
new can be huge. Mr. Romer reckons that, in a world that has only
old goods, a country imposing a 25 percent tariff suffers a loss of
national income equal to 6.25 percent (though the revenue the
government gets from the tariff can be thought to make up for
some of that). With new goods also available, the loss from the same
tariff zooms to some 50–60 percent of national income.

The story is similar with investment. High accumulation of only
old capital goods quickly leads to declining returns on investment.
But, by Mr. Romer's calculation, if new capital goods are brought in
(and with them the new ideas they embody), the returns to the
economy as a whole from capital-goods investment can rise as more
investment is made and can exceed by a factor of two to three the
private cost of making the investment.

Thus, the surest good policy for a poor country to follow is to do
nothing—that is, to open its doors as wide as possible to foreign
goods and foreign investment and then sit back to watch nature
take its course. But there is a catch. The market for ideas is inevitably
what economists call imperfect. The reason is that, once ideas exist,
it costs almost nothing to replicate them over and over; so, by normal economic standards, their price should be almost zero. But
ideas are usually owned by private firms, which therefore must be
paid what is by definition a monopoly profit if they are to be per-
suaded to part with them.

For society as a whole it is worth paying this monopoly profit because the benefit of introducing new ideas—in terms of employment, wages, productivity, and growth—is higher (usually enormously higher) than the monopoly profit paid to the owner of the ideas. The trouble is that sometimes no one firm will benefit enough from the new ideas to pay for them itself. Thus, pure market-pricing mechanisms may not deliver the incentive needed to get the ideas introduced into an economy in the first place, even though, without the idea, nothing at all of a particular kind of item can be produced no matter how much capital and labor is invested in it. This imperfect-market quirk is what makes limited government intervention potentially beneficial.

In Mr. Romer's terminology, ideas can be used or they can be produced. It is possible even for a very backward country to use the advanced ideas of the West if it allows the owners of those ideas to profit from employing them in that country. The simplest way for a poor country to do this is to encourage multinational companies to set up shop there and start producing goods. Mr. Romer gives the example of Mauritius, a small island in the Indian Ocean which had so bleak a future as it neared independence in the 1960s that the government was urging the country's educated young people to emigrate.

In fact, Mauritius prospered. This happened almost entirely because of the arrival of Hong Kong entrepreneurs who set up clothing factories on the island. They were encouraged to come by the elimination of tariffs on imports of capital goods, unrestricted profit repatriation, a ten-year tax holiday, and centralized wage setting by the government, which made sure wages did not rise too fast and that there were no strikes. This was a clear case of exploitation in both the everyday sense of the word and in the technical economic sense: The workers were paid less than the value of their marginal product. Yet this wicked system caused personal incomes to rise three times faster in Mauritius than they were going up in India and twice as fast as in Sri Lanka and produced full employment on the island by 1988. The reason is that the ideas brought in by the Hong Kongers—about how to run a factory, how to sew the clothes, and how to sell the output—caused a great expansion in investment (both foreign and domestic) and economic growth. The entrepreneurs could be paid the monopoly profits that would induce them to come, and there was still enough left over to raise incomes significantly and generate the domestic expertise for the island's future growth.

As countries move up the income scale, they have to start producing ideas as well as just importing them. And here, too, government intervention of the right sort can play a role. Two of Taiwan's consistent interventions have been to require foreign investors to bring technology with them and to set up research parks where pooled work is done for the myriad small Taiwanese companies that cannot finance it individually. (The research parks, now at world-class high-tech levels, are being created even more frequently these days.) The ideas brought into Taiwan, or generated there, by these methods create more value than is reflected in the pricing of purely private transactions. This is why judicious government intervention can help.

For it to work, though, intervention must satisfy a punishing set of conditions. This is where modern East Asia came into its own. For a complicated mixture of reasons, an unusually high share of the interventions undertaken even by supremely activist governments, such as South Korea's, avoided the mistakes that plague government intervention elsewhere. East Asia's authoritarian governments, single-mindedly dedicated to economic growth as the highest national ambition, rarely succumbed to special pleading from individual beneficiaries of their interventions. When the beneficiaries floundered, they were cut off; when the programs failed (whether in South Korea, Indonesia, or Malaysia), policy was smartly turned around. The aim of intervention was not to protect the beneficiary firms from competition, from foreign influences, or from change itself but to accelerate the impact of all these things as a way of upgrading the firms' abilities. Intervention that provides a spur is very different from the sort that acts as a cushion.

The idea of ideas helps to solve the great puzzle about East Asia: why an apparently wide variety of methods attained similar spectacular results. Hong Kong threw the doors open to foreigners and let domestic producers fend for themselves in every market. Singapore strongly encouraged multinationals to set up shop, though it imposed several restraints on the domestic market. Japan and South Korea were hostile to foreign investment but excellent at listening to market signals from their foreign forays and at buying foreign-technology licenses. China has both exported a lot and welcomed foreign investment. And Taiwan placed technology-transfer conditions on foreign investment, while its thousands of returning entrepreneurs brought with them business practices and technology learned in Silicon Valley.

The common thread running through all this is a willingness, one way or another, to be hooked into the outside world and judged according to its standards. And behind this willingness lies probably the deepest and most important characteristic of modern Asia: its passion for discipline, for change, and for the future. Lee Kuan Yew, Singapore's former prime minister and (since his retirement) something of the philosopher-king of the East Asian way, put it this way in conversations in 1993 and 1994:

Europe is too featherbedded. They took the wrong path. The more you mollycoddle and cosset a society, the less capable they are of adjusting to changes of life. After a while they become soft and a burden to themselves. This idea of your entitlement. Where can you cash this entitlement? Is there a counter up in heaven where you can say, "Look, this chap's not honoring it, now you honor it"?

The one striking difference I find between Central Europe coming out from communism and East Asia is that Central Europe is resentful and bewildered that the Russians have brought this darkness, this blight upon them. They say, "America, Europe, help us." They want to be helped out of this hole.

But in Guangzhou they don't look for a free lift. They say, "These Hong Kongers are doing well, how did they do it? Better find out, catch up with them." Xiamen's the same. They want to catch up with the Taiwanese. There's none of this "Please help me." Instead it's "Please come and do business with me." They do not believe that somebody owes them a living or that they have to be bailed out.

Asians know they've got to make it on their own. Their willingness to endure hardship and to learn to do new things, whatever that may require, is the biggest single advantage that's driving East Asia forward.

The main question now is whether Asia will continue to be driven forward.

CHAPTER 4

HOW LONG CAN THIS KEEP GOING ON?

Growth alone does not make for modernization. To join the rich world means to acquire the ability to grow indefinitely, not by doing more of the same but by moving continuously into ever-higher value-added production. This in turn requires constant improvements in productivity, in economic sophistication, and in the ability to absorb and generate new ideas. Bigger and better inputs of physical and human capital help, but (for reasons suggested in the previous two chapters) they are not enough on their own. In the words of Joseph Schumpeter, the Austrian economist and growth theorist, "Add successively as many mail coaches as you like, you will never get a railway engine thereby."

It is hard to identify much in the way of a purely economic threat to Asia's sustained growth and gradual modernization. In most of Asia, savings and investment rates have been rising in recent years, not falling. The quality of human capital is rising, too. In 1990 six Asian countries produced more than 500,000 university graduates in science and engineering, compared with America's 170,000. China alone graduated 128,000 engineers, twice as many as America. A lot of graduates from American universities are Asians anyway, many of whom eventually return home. For years Taiwan has furnished the biggest single contingent of foreign students in American universities; China is now second. Overall, Asian enrollment in American

universities, 80 percent of it non-Japanese, was more than 200,000
by the early 1990s, up from 20,000 in 1975; and more than three-
quarters of the Asians were studying science or engineering. The
Japanese expect 100,000 of their own university places to be occu-
pied by other Asians in 2000. (The Chinese already have 35,000
university students in Japan.)

In addition to maintaining its high rates of savings and investment
and the quality of its workforce, Asia must master the art of sustained and cost-conscious productivity growth. Much of it already
has. The calculations even of such a skeptic as Alwyn Young, mentioned at the end of chapter 2, show that total-factor-productivity
(TFP) growth—the broadest measure, remember, of economic
efficiency—has been good, if not outstanding, in most of East
Asia; in South Korea and Taiwan it even accelerated during the
1980s.

By contrast, Singapore's exceptionally heavy investment in both
physical and human capital has been accompanied by (even in its
own eyes) disturbingly mediocre productivity growth. This is puz-
zling. In a technical sense, as Mr. Young points out, Singapore's
record of economic growth parallels that of the Soviet Union in the
distant days when the Soviet Union was still growing. If efficiency
actually declines even while more and more inputs are added to an
economy, sooner or later the economy grinds to a halt and then
goes into reverse.

Yet there is something about Singapore, let alone the rest of East
and Southeast Asia, that belies the chilling certitude of this formula.
Even when the Soviet Union's output growth seemed rather cheery
on paper, a cursory look at the gray, gloom-laden, and queue-ridden
everyday life of the Soviet people would not have inspired confidence that this was a country which was about to make a successful
economic takeoff. Conversely, Singapore in the mid-1990s is a well-
groomed, bustling, colorful place chock-full of shops, restaurants,
cars, and tennis courts—in short, of the splendid panoply of modern consumer life—all of it freely available to and widely partaken
of by the mass of the city-state's population. This does not inspire
dread that Singapore's relentlessly rising levels of investment mean
its economy must soon shudder to a Soviet-like halt (an observation
that applies equally to South Korea of the late 1970s and early 1980s,
when people's daily lives were improving remarkably even while the
excessive effort required of the economy by the force-fed industrial-

ization of the 1970s was producing abysmal falls in the efficiency of capital investment).

Even so, the statistics Mr. Young has collected about Singapore are disquieting. In the early 1980s Lee Tsao Yuan, a Singaporean economist (and now an appointed member of Singapore's Parliament), did the original research into Singapore's productivity record that set Mr. Young on the scent. Today Ms. Lee is dubious that Singapore's productivity performance is anywhere near as bad as the numbers seem to say.

First, the possible inaccuracy of the numbers, especially the statistics for Singapore's stocks of inventory and capital, is so gross that they may be saying very little about what is actually happening. Second, Ms. Lee points out that the productivity numbers themselves seem to have started improving in the decade after a mid-1980s recession in the city-state. In 1995 Singapore's central bank calculated that TFP rose by 2 percent a year in 1991–93, and predicted that it would continue doing so for the next several years.

Last, Ms. Lee suggests that Singapore's exceptionally high levels of capital investment—and (for Asia) even more unusually high levels of infrastructure spending on roads and airports and the like —make it possible that the normal assumptions of economic-growth theory do not apply. In particular, Singapore's high infrastructure spending may be dragging down today's productivity-growth figures, even while raising the long-term potential of the economy (precisely opposite to the position of the rest of Asia, which has invested too little in infrastructure during the early stages of growth and may see its productivity performance decline as this shortfall is eventually made up; see chapter 13).

Singapore does, however, face a problem of another sort. Although the city-state's government has conducted an admirably steady macroeconomic policy and has run as free-trading an external policy as anyplace in Asia (save for Hong Kong), it has not been equally open in its conduct of domestic economic and social policy. The government has strong views about social order, which are discussed in more detail in chapter 16, but Singapore is likely to pay an economic price for the stern social control it has exercised for decades. The place lacks the entrepreneurial flair of Hong Kong, Taiwan, or China. This need not be a fatal weakness—look at South Korea—but it leaves Singapore at a disadvantage to some of its neighbors in coping with the growing pace of change that is sweeping through East and Southeast Asia, particularly in places where Singaporean companies are beginning to invest, such as China, Vietnam, and India. The free-spirited Hong Kongers have little trouble coping with chaos, but it discomfits Singaporeans; and in Asia as elsewhere, more rather than less chaos is likely as economies become both more open and more intertwined with one another.

Whatever the truth about Singapore, the future productivity growth (and hence economic growth) of the whole of East Asia depends on one thing above all others. If there is any truth to the main argument of chapter 3—that the key to East Asia's success has been that it was open to change, to the future, and (above all) to the outside world—then the question about how long Asia's growth can persist becomes a simple one. How long can the openness that East Asia has pursued over the past quarter-century persist?

Here much humility is in order. Around 1960 the World Bank made the mistake of offering some long-run predictions about several East Asian countries. The experts came to about the same result as the amateur sizing-up with which chapter 3 began. Among the countries that the World Bank thought would do best were Burma and the Philippines—which, apart from war-wrecked Indochina, have since proven to be East Asia's two biggest failures. The gloomiest futures belonged, naturally, to South Korea and Taiwan.

The stalled economic takeoffs of the past—glaringly in Russia and Latin America early this century—happened because pro-modernization policies were disastrously reversed. With virtually the whole of Asia now having embraced the openness doctrine that the East Asian tigers pioneered, a reversion to protectionism and nationalism does not seem an immediate threat anywhere in Asia. Of course, some reversals of fortune can again be expected. Burma, the Philippines, Vietnam, and (most spectacularly) India may at last be ready for their flowering. Thailand, which has fallen woefully behind the rest of East Asia in education; Hong Kong (see the last sections of this chapter); and South Korea, where the struggle between liberalization and the regimental impulse is going to be terribly complicated by the likely reunification with the Communist North—all will have to struggle to maintain their fine records. Parts of Asia are anyway bound to slow down as they get richer. This inevitably happens as inputs of capital and labor decline and the easy gains from importing already discovered ideas disappear. The step-down is already noticeable among the richest Asians—such as Japan and Taiwan (see chart 1)—and the near-rich will follow.

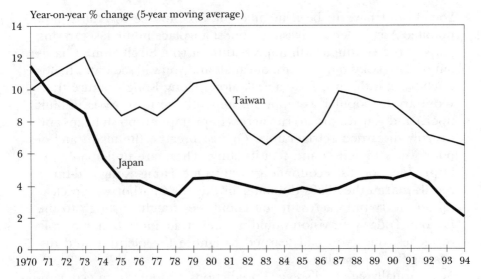

CHART 1
JAPAN AND TAIWAN: REAL GDP GROWTH, 1970–1994

Year-on-year % change (5-year moving average)

SOURCE: Datastream.

Yet, overall, Asia has the chance to continue revolutionizing the world economy through its growth rates multiplied by the size of its population. The main impediments to this happening are likely to be the institutional weaknesses that plague much of Asian corporate and public life. These weaknesses include an opaque and highly personalized system of corporate management, an inefficient financial system that cannot objectively mediate between savers and investors, and a failure to build the infrastructure needed to sustain further economic growth (all discussed in part III of this book). The weaknesses also include unmodernized national political institutions and nonexistent institutions for the maintenance of a geopolitical balance among the countries of East Asia (subjects for part IV). It will take at least a generation, and cost a lot of money and energy, to remedy these shortcomings. The worrying things in the shorter run are physical constraints (i.e., Asia's environmental problems); the fate of Hong Kong, which could set the tone—both institutional and geopolitical—for the whole of Chinese Asia over the next decade; and (discussed in the next chapter) the fate of world free trade.

In Brass, Muck

You do not have to be a member of Greenpeace to realize how polluted Asia is. A casual visit to almost anyplace in the fast-growing parts of the continent will impress this on you. Stroll along what is left of Bangkok's old network of canals and you will see water that is pitch-black with filth. Take a walk along Hong Kong's nature trails (contrary to popular assumption, most of the territory is unbuilt upon) and you are sure to run across impromptu rubbish heaps and casually discarded refrigerators. Or just breathe the air in any of poor Asia's big cities and feel its sting. These are undeniably the by-products of fast economic growth: One Hong Kong old-timer recalls that in the 1950s the water in the city's harbor was so clear that on ferry rides across it you could see straight through to the bottom. Today your vision would not penetrate more than a couple of inches, once you had learned to ignore the plentiful and disgusting flotsam passing by.

It is usually safe to disregard predictions of doom from ecomaniacs, but the rise of Asia does present a special environmental case. The invariable pattern of a poor country entering economic takeoff is that it becomes much more polluted for a couple of decades, after which it is rich enough (and institutionally strong enough) to start spending money and enacting and enforcing laws to clean itself up. Japan, for instance, became badly polluted during its fastest-growth decades of the 1950s and 1960s but then started investing heavily in pollution control. The dramatic result was that despite continued strong economic growth, between 1970 and 1990 sulfur-dioxide emissions fell by more than 80 percent; nitrogen-oxide emissions, by 30 percent; and carbon-monoxide concentrations, by 60 percent.

Yet it is one thing for this process to take place in some relatively (by Asian standards) small countries on the periphery of the continent; it is something else if it happens at roughly the same time in China, India, and Indonesia, which among them will have around 40 percent of the world's population in 2000, crowded onto 11 percent of its dry land. Those who think that this many people cannot quickly industrialize—that, in essence, the great mass of Asia will soon find its economic growth strangled by its polluting by-products—have a point. But the point is about prices, not possibilities.

The impact of China's growth alone will be huge. Already the pressure on China's resources has become intense. Vaclav Smil, a Canadian professor, reckons that soil erosion and the loss of farmland to housing and industries in China's rising cities is reducing arable land by about 0.5 percent a year, in a country that already has one of the world's lowest quantities of farmland per person. The demand for water in northern China has already dried up much of the region's rivers and reservoirs—and no wonder. This northern region produces 40 percent of China's food and half its industrial output but receives only a quarter of the country's rainfall and has access to just 10 percent of its stream runoff. Meanwhile, in the south, flooding along the Yangzi River is a perennial curse, one that China intends to relieve (and, in the process, vastly improve transport and energy supply) by building the world's biggest dam and hydroelectric plant at a place called the Three Gorges. If the dam is actually built, and the government seems intent on it, a lake three hundred miles long will be created at a cost of several billion dollars and the uprooting of perhaps a million people—though probably not until 2010.

Well before then, China's growth will be making itself felt on world markets for all sorts of commodities. Mr. Smil has calculated how much extra productive capacity (or how many extra imports) China will need between 1990 and 2000 if it is to achieve a modest 2 percent annual growth in the per-capita consumption of some basic commodities. In fact, China's annual growth in the per-capita consumption of many of these things was faster than 2 percent in the 1980s; and the 120 million additional Chinese Mr. Smil postulates by 2000 will probably be more like 160 million. So the following paragraph may understate demand.

On Mr. Smil's assumptions, China in 2000 will need an increment of primary energy production equal to the 1990 output of India and Brazil combined. It will need extra coal equal to the 1990 output of India and South Africa combined, extra electricity equal to Brazil's total 1990 output, extra steel equal to Italy's, extra cement and nitrogen equal to Japan's, and extra grain equal to all of Africa's. China will also need extra water equal to Mexico's consumption in 1990. And it will be belching an extra America's worth of particulate emissions into the air and an extra western Germany's worth of sulfur dioxide emissions.

However horrifying (or, depending on your line of business,

mouthwatering) these projections sound, they do not add up to the conclusion that China's growth, or that of other poor Asian countries, must grind to a halt because the resources will not be available to sustain it. For one thing, China's consumption of many of these items simply cannot rise by 2 percent a year per capita. In the case of electricity, for instance, even the most optimistic Chinese planners do not foresee generating capacity rising by more than 15,000–17,000 megawatts a year—admittedly still a huge amount (each year's addition is equal to the entire installed capacity of Switzerland in 1994), but for the decade as a whole only about 60 percent of the figure Mr. Smil mentions.

Second, a fair amount of the projected resource "shortages" in poor Asia is accounted for by mispricing. When prices are below costs, too much of a good is used and not enough is supplied to keep demand and supply in balance. China underprices electricity and, unsurprisingly, uses a lot more of it than countries with more realistic prices. In the early 1990s, Indonesia was spending about $500 million a year on subsidies for home electricity supply to the "poor." In fact, only 4 percent of this subsidy went to the poor, the rest pointlessly to increase electricity consumption by the fairly well off. Irrigation water in Indonesia is almost free of charge and fertilizers are heavily subsidized, and both are overused; the same, on both counts, is true in India. Indonesia even subsidizes the hacking down of its rain forests by charging too little for logging rights and by imposing export taxes on felled timber.

Third, those who have been resources-based pessimists about the world economy have always got it wrong. The real (inflation-adjusted) price of almost every commodity has fallen in the past twenty years, implying that they are in glut, not shortage. The reason for this is not hard to understand. The pessimists tacitly assume that each dollar of GDP represents the consumption of a constant amount of commodity and other resources, so that as GDP rises the consumption of commodities increases by a like amount. In fact, past a certain level of economic development each extra dollar of GDP represents a declining rather than a constant amount of consumption of natural resources. This happens in part because the resources are used with greater efficiency; and in part because, these days, as a rich country gets richer it produces and consumes things that are less resource-intensive.

None of this is to say that, if fast economic growth does spread through much of the Asian landmass for the next generation, it will be an altogether pretty sight. The smoke from huge Indonesian forest fires that in the autumn of 1994 beclouded the skies of Southeast Asia as far away as Kuala Lumpur and Singapore was probably only the first of many bad incidents of large cross-border pollutions. And there seems sure to be a darkening of the industrial pall now hanging over China, which on bad winter days in northern cities can produce air quality anywhere between six and twenty times worse than maximum recommended or actual levels in the West, a fact that already worries China's neighbors rather a lot.

Yet a deterioration in the quality of the physical environment, however regrettable, is entirely compatible with continued fast economic growth. The capacity of people to thrive without much space and with no natural resources is immense, as Hong Kong has triumphantly shown. The crowds of Hong Kong would drive many Americans, who are among the world's most space-rich people, and any nature-lover crazy, but the Hong Kong Chinese live and work in their suffocatingly tight quarters mostly in happiness and tranquillity, each year turning in one of the world's most efficient economic performances. There must, of course, be a hinterland for such places (all of China in Hong Kong's case), but so far there is no sign that the Asian hinterland has shrunk enough to move real commodity prices up at all, let alone enough to start having a serious effect on economic growth or the mix of economic activities.

Another generation of fast Asian growth should start to make these prices move substantially. The International Energy Agency has predicted that world energy demand will be 50 percent higher in 2010 than it was in the mid-1990s and world oil prices 50 percent higher in 2005 than they were a decade earlier; much of the increase in demand will have come from Asia. Even so, there is no solid reason for believing that the world is in any danger of running up against absolute resource limits. Prices will rise, and with them the pattern and perhaps even the pace of Asian economic growth; but Asia's growth will not stop because it has suffocated itself in its own effluents.

The Parable of Hong Kong

Hong Kong has shown what can go right in a small-government, free-market, pro-business society where property rights are secure: that is, just about everything. It is now in danger of showing what can go wrong if some of those conditions are tampered with. If things do go wrong, it will indicate how serious is the risk that strong Asian economic growth will be derailed by institutional weakness, especially in the Chinese part of Asia.

Of all the East Asian success stories, Hong Kong's has been the purest. In the words of Milton Friedman, the Nobel Prize–winning American economist, "If you want to see capitalism at work, go to Hong Kong." There are no controls at all on the flow of capital into and out of the territory, almost no import barriers, few restrictions on foreign companies that want to set up shop there (and, conversely, no official lures to get them to come), and not many restrictions on foreign individuals who want to move there (at least not if they are from other rich countries).

Hong Kong's government has traditionally been so small and hands-offish that the Swiss government seems downright intrusive by comparison. In the mid-1990s, Hong Kong's top marginal income-tax rate was about 15 percent. Government spending has never risen even as high as 20 percent of GDP and is unlikely to do so before at least 2000. The government budget has been in surplus for years, in the early 1990s to the tune of 2–3 percent of GDP; surpluses were so high in 1993 and 1994 that the government red-facedly introduced large tax cuts to try to make its cornucopia more modest. There is no discretion in monetary policy. In 1983, a time of political turmoil between Britain and China over the future of Hong Kong, the government firmly tied its hands by linking Hong Kong's dollar to America's at a fixed rate: This variant of a "currency-board" monetary system means that Hong Kong's monetary policy is as automatic as that of countries on the gold standard a century ago.

There has been some dabbling in interference with the domestic market: an interest-rate cartel designed to keep banks' deposit rates well below their lending rates (it worked; the banks regularly make large profits); and a handful of protected monopolies and oligopolies. Hong Kong has even had one big social-welfare program, set up in the 1950s and 1960s in response to natural disasters (fire and landslides) and riots: Half the population lives in subsidized public housing. In a sense, though, public housing is simply a method for correcting a market failure caused by the government itself. All land in Hong Kong is owned by the government, and it has been extremely sparing over the years in releasing it for development; this has made housing even dearer than geography and the pressure of population would have made it anyway. But by 1994 demands had begun rising from a left-leaning, pro-democracy contingent in the colony's legislature to introduce European frills like compulsory maternity and even paternity leave; and the government itself had taken the potentially dangerous step of proposing a modest but— here is the danger—pay-as-you-go pension scheme. Still, it is indicative of the tone of Hong Kong life that in public even the left-leaning distance themselves from the phrase "welfare state," which has distasteful and even shocking connotations.

Since the government has hardly ever presumed to temper the winds of global competition, Hong Kong's shorn lambs have always been quick to transform themselves into other beasts. People change jobs and even careers as fast as companies change lines of business. The Shanghai textile magnates who fled to Hong Kong with their machinery and factory foremen in the early 1950s quickly created a boom in the colony's textile exports that within a decade had induced rich countries to curb them with trade barriers. The textile magnates swiftly moved into clothes or plastics, especially toys, whose exports rose from HK$100 million worth in 1960 to HK$3 billion worth in 1977. Electronics followed on the heels of toys.

However, the best example of this dizzying process, described by Ronald Findlay and Stanislaw Wellisz, two economists on contract to the World Bank, is the saga of Hong Kong's wig industry. In 1961 Hong Kong had one wig factory. In 1970 the wig industry employed thirty-nine thousand people (5 percent of manufacturing workers) and accounted for 8 percent of Hong Kong's exports. That is when world demand for wigs shifted from those made with human hair (Chinese hair, straight and fine, was the best) to those made with synthetic fibers (which Hong Kong had trouble obtaining); soon after, demand for wigs of every kind dwindled. Seven years after wig making had employed one in every twenty Hong Kong manufacturing workers, it employed precisely fifty-nine workers, or less than one in fifteen thousand. With no unemployment benefits and no retraining support, the former wig workers found their own way to new jobs in toys and electronics. And the wig entrepreneurs? They quickly discovered that wig-making machinery was ideal for scaling fish. In 1971, when the value of Hong Kong's wig exports fell by 44 percent, the territory's economic and export growth barely flickered.

By 1995, Hong Kong's relentless pursuit of its comparative advantage had turned it back into what it had been sixty years before: China's broker with the world, though on a vastly more sophisticated plane than before. As early as 1991, Hong Kong had become the world's most advanced economy in terms of its sectoral distribution of employment: Three-quarters of the workforce was in services, the highest share on earth. The growth has come not in the traditional retail, food, and tourist trades. In the mid-1990s financial and business services accounted for a quarter of Hong Kong's economic growth. By 2000 more Hong Kongers may be working in business and financial services than in manufacturing.

The main service they will be providing is to mediate between China and everybody else. Hong Kong is already the main node of the overseas-Chinese business network (see chapter 11) and of the Western and Japanese multinationals that hope to hook into this network and penetrate China itself. Hong Kong performs the same role, in reverse, for China; and the interpenetration goes deeper than that. By the mid-1990s Hong Kong businesses employed some 3 million factory workers, in twenty-five thousand factories, on the mainland—four times as many manufacturing workers as Hong Kong itself then had. Through its investments in China—which, at some 60 percent of total foreign direct investment in the mainland, made up the biggest single share—Hong Kong was developing lines of business that it had never before taken up, such as electrical goods, tires, and even copper refining. Hong Kong itself was being transformed through a twofold process of foreign investment in the territory. Western, especially American, multinationals arrived with their world-standard management methods and financial muscle; and mainland Chinese companies came with their invaluable home-grown *guanxi* (contacts). Despite the inrush of Westerners, China had, by 1993, outstripped America and Japan to become the biggest investor in Hong Kong.

The economic logic of Hong Kong's modern history is hard to fault—real incomes per person have grown three-and-a-half-fold since 1970 and by the early 1990s Hong Kong had basically no unemployment—and the embrace of China is only the latest extension of this logic. Yet Hong Kong's future depends on which proves to be the more powerful: the advantage of being the principal business and financial entrepôt between China and the rest of the world, or the damage that will be done to the territory's sophisticated social and economic fabric by its being combined with the coarser weave of China.

A Gamble on Democracy

In 1984 the British and Chinese governments signed a treaty called the Joint Declaration that provided for the whole of Hong Kong, parts of which had been a British colony since the 1840s, to be returned to Chinese sovereignty at midnight on June 30, 1997. China promised to preserve Hong Kong's "capitalist way of life" for fifty years. The territory was to have considerable autonomy— "Hong Kong people ruling Hong Kong" was the epigram—under the motherland's general guidance and unalloyed sovereignty: "one country, two systems," in the formulation of Deng Xiaoping, China's top leader. "Elections" to the territory's Legislative Council (Legco) were mentioned, ambiguously, in the Joint Declaration. Talks between Britain and China eventually produced an agreement for a gradual increase in the number of Legco seats filled by regular anyone-can-vote elections from a starting point of eighteen (out of sixty) in 1991 to twenty in 1995 and, in long steps, thirty in 2007.

Hong Kongers remained hopeful throughout most of the 1980s that the peculiar hybrid of "one country, two systems" might actually allow them to go on living their free lives unmolested by China, but their confidence was shattered by the killings of pro-democracy demonstrators that the Chinese government carried out in Beijing's Tiananmen Square in June 1989. As many as a million Hong Kongers went into the streets to launch their own protest against the killings, and when regular Chinese-British talks on Hong Kong's transition resumed a few months later, they did so in an atmosphere of recrimination that grew only more poisoned as the years wore on.

By the mid-1990s all hope of a smooth transition from British to Chinese rule seemed to have been lost. The main reason was the Chinese-British fight that erupted over the question of political reform after the arrival of Chris Patten as (presumably the last) British governor of Hong Kong in 1992. Unlike the mostly donnish diplomats who had preceded him in that post, Mr. Patten was an ebullient and energetic politician who loved the heat of electoral and parliamentary battle. He also had a powerful mind, witty and waspish, which he enjoyed speaking. And he had no experience of (or apparently much taste for) Asia and its ways. On a personal level, in other words, it would have been hard to find someone more temperamentally suited for mutual antipathy with China's stiff, formal, and secretive Communist party bureaucrats.

Mr. Patten's proposal in late 1992 of a set of arrangements for the 1995 Legco elections was a curious piece of policy-making that may yet prove disastrous for Hong Kong. The governor used what was in essence a lawyer's trick of exploiting loopholes as a way of getting out of the spirit of earlier agreements between Britain and China about Legco elections. His aim was to expand to the extent possible (which admittedly was not much) the democratic character and transparency of the system for choosing the indirectly elected members of Legco. The aim itself had obvious virtues. The oddity lay in the attempt so late in the day to wrest concessions on the most sensitive of matters from a negotiating foe that was already in a stronger position than Britain and was getting more powerful with each tick of the clock in the countdown to June 30, 1997.

In July 1994, Mr. Patten's proposals squeaked through a Legco vote and into law, but at a heavy price. China vowed that all the bodies elected in 1995 under these arrangements would be scrapped come 1997. Nuts-and-bolts cooperation between Britain and China having been at a standstill for years, there was now no chance that the hundreds of transitional measures that needed to be taken (such as agreeing on official Chinese-language versions of Hong Kong's laws) would be completed in time.

Nor did the state of affairs on the other side of the border help. Deng Xiaoping, who had made all the big decisions on China's approach to Hong Kong in the 1980s, was powerful enough, and enough of a statesman, to remark a few years ago within earshot of a Hong Kong businessman that it was natural to expect Hong Kong for several years after 1997 to be pro-British in its sentiments and in the way it ran itself. By 1994, however, Deng's health was failing badly, and nobody in the Chinese leadership had the stature or personal security to be so level headed—or, in Communist party terms, soft headed—about Hong Kong.

For decades Hong Kong was a lucky place, in institutional terms perhaps the luckiest on earth: It had all the benefits of democratic politics without any of the politicians. It had civil liberties, economic and social freedoms, a free flow of information, and the rule of law; yet it almost entirely avoided the special-interest politics that tends to plague the kind of government associated with those good things. Now, as it hurtles towards its rendezvous with Chinese destiny, Hong

Kong is nurturing a crop of democratic politicians of its own and at the same time is contemplating something considerably more frightening.

To quote Milton Friedman again, " 'One country, two systems' is from a dream world. One country is one country." There was never any chance that Hong Kong could be sealed off entirely from the mainland's mores after 1997; indeed, with the economic intertwining of Hong Kong and China, that has not proven possible even several years in advance of 1997. A gradual increase in corruption, favoritism, and self-censorship is sure to eat away at the place in the next few years.

That is a tragic lost opportunity for Hong Kong, which, in a somewhat different world, could have been contemplating a secure future as an independent city-state—like Singapore, but in the very first rank of world cities. But this does not mean Hong Kong is in for little more than a slow burial. Few people doubt there will be plenty of money still to be made in Hong Kong for years after 1997; and things could be much better than that. China did agree in the Joint Declaration to leave in place many of the protections of Hong Kong's way of life, particularly the legal system, a separate currency, and free-market economic policies.

My guess is that Mr. Patten's pro-democracy moves, which he justified as a way of securing these other protections, have in fact put them in greater jeopardy. If so, the trade-off made no sense. There is no chance that China, as it is presently constituted, will tolerate a significant degree of political freedom on its soil; but there was a chance that it would not much interfere with other freedoms in Hong Kong if it felt that politics there could be kept under control. Anybody who is realistic about Hong Kong's position —it is inevitably going to be part of China—should realize that these other freedoms are far more precious to it than the shell of a democracy that in this period at least will simply not be allowed to come to life.

Even so, the falling-out between Britain and China is not the end of the matter. The degree to which historical and cultural rancor between Britain and China has infested their debate over Hong Kong should not be underestimated. One Japanese observer thinks that June 30, 1997, is going to prove a politically momentous date in Asia: the end, for all serious purposes, of Western colonialism on the continent, an event that may prove as symbolically important in

Asia as the fall of the Berlin Wall did in Europe. Already Hong Kong Chinese civil servants are building bridges to China with the acquiescence of the British colonial authorities; and other Hong Kong Chinese—not elected but many of them nonetheless good and fair representatives of the interests of the people of Hong Kong —are preparing for an active public role under Chinese rule.

If Hong Kong's civil liberties, property rights, and economic freedoms can still be salvaged—which is possible, though probably only if Hong Kong forswears much of democratic political life for the ten or so years it will take China to loosen up enough to allow it—then the benefits of being China's intermediary with the world could still outweigh the risks of being part of China. Because if Hong Kong can succeed in making of itself the only city on Chinese soil with fully international standards of freedom and contractual obligation, it stands to gain enormously from the great knitting together of Asia's economies that has already begun.

CHAPTER 5

ONE ASIA, NOT TOO DIVISIBLE

Perhaps nothing can give you a better feel for the main force driving Asia than a boat ride in the waters around Hong Kong. At any given time, there are dozens of huge container ships, steaming or at anchor, carrying or getting ready to carry enormous quantities of freight via Hong Kong's eight container terminals. As of 1994, Hong Kong was the world's busiest container port. Among countries, only America and Japan have a total volume of container trade bigger than Hong Kong's, and their economies are, respectively, seventy-five and forty-five times the size of Hong Kong's. The territory's planners guess that its port traffic will have grown by almost 7 percent a year between 1992 and 2011. They reckon that, to keep up, Hong Kong will have to increase its freight-handling capacity each year by the equivalent of one Felixstowe, Britain's biggest port, or almost of one Long Beach, America's third biggest port. Nor is Hong Kong's port the only gigantic one in Asia. Hong Kong's and Singapore's were battling nip-and-tuck through the early 1990s for the distinction of being the world's busiest container port. As early as 1990, six of the world's ten busiest container ports were in East and Southeast Asia. Trade makes Asia's world go round.

This is no surprise, in light either of the general significance of openness for East Asia's economic growth (see chapter 3) or of the volume of East Asia's trade relative to the size of its economies. By the early 1990s trade bulked large enough in the industrializing countries of East and Southeast Asia that its dollar value was equal to that of the whole region's economy. (In smaller places trade was bigger than the national economy: in Singapore, three times as big; in Hong Kong, twice as big). In America in 1992 the ratio of trade to GDP was 16 percent; in Japan, 14 percent; and in Germany, 42 percent—even the German ratio being less than half that of Asia.

East Asians account for a big and rapidly growing share of world trade—and, contrary to the assumption of protectionists in America and Europe, not just of exports. Asians import vast (and increasing) amounts of goods, too. In the six years after 1987, the volume of merchandise imports taken by the fast-rising countries of East and Southeast Asia went up almost two-and-a-half times, bringing them roughly into line with the value of their exports; that compares with import volume growth of less than one and one-half times for America and Japan and one and one-quarter times for Western Europe.

Trade has contributed to a radical shift in the industrial structure of the countries of East and Southeast Asia. Malaysia is a good example of how. In 1970 it exported M$4 billion worth ($1.3 billion worth) of goods; two-thirds of that was accounted for by tin and rubber, 5 percent by oil and gas, and only 15 percent (or M$600 million worth) by manufactured goods. In 1993, Malaysia's exports were worth M$121 billion ($47.1 billion), thirty times as much in nominal terms as they had been worth two decades before. Three-quarters of these imports (M$90 billion worth, or 150 times the figure in 1970) were manufactured goods; 8 percent, oil and gas; 2 percent, rubber; and less than 1 percent, tin.

The modern economy of colonial Malaya—the peninsula was brought under British rule beginning in the 1870s—had been shaped almost entirely by tin mines and rubber plantations (which also substantially reshaped peninsular society through the import of Chinese labor to work the mines and Indian workers to tend the plantations). A mere two decades of very fast growth in manufactured exports overturned the economic structures of the better part of a century. The output of rubber was almost halved in the six years after 1988. In the early 1980s, forty thousand Malaysians were employed producing sixty thousand metric tons of tin a year. Ten years later, only two thousand Malaysians made their living from tin, and output had shrunk to six thousand metric tons. Meanwhile, the output of electronics—which, by the early 1990s, was already large, accounting for over half of all manufactured exports—was rising by more than 30 percent a year.

For all of East and Southeast Asia the years 1970–90 produced an export-led industrial revolution that was the fastest in history. The Basle-based Bank for International Settlements (the central-bankers' bank) has calculated that, if trade flows within a single continental region are stripped out (the reason why is explained below), Asia now supplies more than 40 percent of the world's manufactured exports, compared with 25 percent each for Western Europe and North America; in the early 1970s, Asia's share was only 25 percent.

This has made East and Southeast Asia an industrial powerhouse. On a purchasing-power-parity basis (PPP, as you may remember from chapter 1), East and Southeast Asia accounted for about $300 billion-worth of manufacturing output in 1970 (measured in 1980 dollars and 1980 PPPs). Western Europe produced twice as much, and North America only slightly less than that.

By the mid-1980s, Asia's manufacturing output had caught up with America's and Europe's, and for the past ten years has risen even faster than it did in 1970–85. By the early 1990s, Asia's manufacturing output was worth around $1.4 trillion (again in 1980 dollars and at 1980 PPPs), compared with slightly over $900 billion for Western Europe and slightly under $900 billion for North America. Asia was producing more than 40 percent of the world's manufactured goods; Europe and America, a little more than a quarter each; and Latin America, around 3 percent. It is possible (and likely if India is included) that by 2000 half the world's manufactured goods will be made in Asia.

One way to judge Asia's extraordinary manufacturing achievement is to compare it with that of Latin America in 1970–95. The value of East and Southeast Asia's manufacturing output quintupled in real terms during those years, and their share of (extra-regional) world manufactured exports went up by three-quarters; the value of Latin America's output and its share of exports stayed the same.

Another useful comparison is between Asia's performance outside its own region and that of Western Europe. Like Europe, but for entirely different reasons (see next section), Asia experienced a very fast rise in manufacturing trade within its own region in the years 1970–92; in the early 1970s trade within Asia represented about a third of its total trade, whereas twenty years later it amounted to half. Unlike Europe, though, Asia was also able to continue plugging itself successfully into the outside world. By the early 1990s, Asia's manufacturing trade with countries outside Asia was equivalent to half of its gross regional product. The corresponding figure in Western Europe was only 7 percent of gross regional product (which is why intra-regional manufacturing trade needs to be stripped out of the world figures if you are to get a remotely accurate sense of global performance in the trade of manufactured goods).

It is therefore no surprise that of the three threats to Asia's continued fast growth—its environmental deterioration, its institutional weakness, and trade protectionism in the West—by far the most threatening is the risk that freeish world trade might be stopped. Fortunately, of the three threats this is also the least likely to happen. One reason is that, with the latest GATT (General Agreement on Tariffs and Trade) round ratified by the American Congress late in 1994 and the new trade-promoting World Trade Organization (WTO) having successfully come into being on January 1, 1995, the ability of protectionist-minded politicians to do wholesale damage to the world trading system has diminished.

The power of markets over politics had already been shown by the decision of President Clinton in June 1994 permanently to uncouple China's trade status with the United States from its human-rights performance—a decision that required the president to eat a lot of campaign-rhetoric crow. The common view is that the politics of protectionism is on the rise in America. That may be true in Europe, but it would be surprising if it happened in America. Once the WTO is up and running for a few years, it will be even harder for American politicians to risk the job losses that would be caused to their increasingly influential world exporters by any serious assault on free trade.

THE PACIFIC CENTURY

The second reason why Western protectionism is unlikely to threaten Asia's continued growth is that the continent has built up enough of its own momentum to keep it hurtling forward for a long time. In the 1970s so much of East Asia's economic growth came from its exports to the United States (and, to a lesser degree, to

Western Europe) that Asia's economic cycles followed America's pretty closely. Two decades of quickly growing trade within Asia have weakened the link between the ups and downs of American growth and the pattern of Asian growth.

A weakened link is not an automatic result. Much of intra-Asian trade, especially when it first began growing, was in components of final goods which were eventually sold in the West. By one calculation, as late as 1991, when China had become by far Hong Kong's biggest trading partner because of its assembly work for the territory's companies, more than half of Hong Kong's trade still depended in the end on demand in the United States; most of Hong Kong's China trade involved processing goods for re-export to America. Even so, the big picture is pretty clear. C. H. Kwan, an economist at Nomura Research Institute in Tokyo, has calculated that in the 1970s a 1 percent change, up or down, in America's economic growth rate produced a 1 percent change in the same direction in the growth rate of East Asia outside Japan. After a consistent decennial decline, in the period 1983–92 a 1 percent shift in America's growth rate produced only a 0.3 percent shift in East Asia's.

This came to pass because of an enormous boom in the growth of Asian regional trade in final goods, which in turn was set off by Asia's high economic growth rates and by a rush of foreign direct investment (FDI) stimulated by the opportunities that this growth presented. Chart 2 illustrates what happened to Asian trade flows between 1985 and 1992. Basically, in the mid-1980s America took about a third of Asia's exports (Asia defined here to include Japan); Asians exported roughly another third to each other. By 1992, Asia was the destination for 43 percent of Asian exports, with America the destination for less than 25 percent. In crude terms, by the early 1990s, America depended on Asian markets more than Asia did on America's: A slightly higher share of American exports went to Asia than Asian exports did to America.

The shift happened across the board: Almost every income group among East Asian countries reoriented itself to, well, the Orient. In 1985, Japan's trade with America was $95 billion; its trade with the rest of Asia, $77 billion. In 1992, Japan traded $152 billion worth with America but $177 billion worth with the rest of Asia. In 1985, America accounted for $56 billion worth of the trade of the so-called newly industrializing economies (NIEs)—South Korea, Taiwan, Hong Kong, and Singapore—with the rest of Asia accounting for

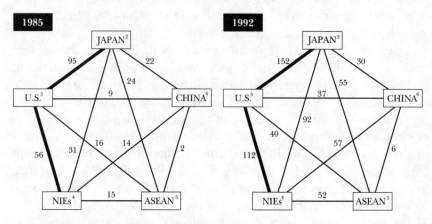

CHART 2
CHANGING TRADE VALUE PATTERNS

Source: Bank of Japan, *Quarterly Bulletin* (February 1994).

Notes: 1. Billions of U.S. dollars. Trade values = exports + imports. Intermediary trade via Hong Kong partially adjusted.
2. Trade values between Japan and other partners excluding China based on Japan statistics.
3. Trade values between U.S. and China/ASEAN based on U.S. statistics.
4. Trade values between NIEs and China/U.S. based on NIEs statistics.
5. Trade values between ASEAN anad NIEs/China based on ASEAN statistics.
6. Trade values between Japan and China based on China statisitics.

$60 billion worth of the NIEs' trade. Seven years later, the value of the NIEs' trade with the rest of Asia was almost twice that of their trade with the United States. The story was similar for the somewhat poorer countries of Southeast Asia. Only China, which at the start of the period already conducted most of its trade with Asia, failed to increase the Asian share much overall (though Asia did start taking a bit more of its exports).

This change has prompted mutterings about a regional "trade bloc" being created in East Asia (or, when combined with high Japanese FDI flows though the region—see below—even talk of a "yen bloc"). Yet it is worth poking a bit beneath the surface. Asia's regional economic links are being forged by a process different from that at work in North America and by one very different from that at work in Europe. North America's three economies have been tied together through the North American Free Trade Agreement (NAFTA), a formal agreement among their three governments entered into in 1994; but business ties among America, Canada, and Mexico were extremely strong anyway, and NAFTA is apparently doing little to hamper trade between its members and the rest of the world.

European integration, too, is government-driven, but in a more extreme way. The formal efforts of the European Community to tighten economic links among its members include not just agreements to reduce trade barriers but also a program for a single currency and a large apparatus of European Community law and bureaucracy that to a degree has displaced the legal and administrative powers of national governments. And the lowering of hurdles within Europe has been accompanied by a raising of barriers to the outside world, or so it appears from the fact that steeply rising "trade intensities" among the countries of Western Europe over the years 1970–90 went hand in hand with sharp declines in the same measure for trade between North America and Europe and between Australia and New Zealand and Europe.

Asia's internal trade has grown without the guidance of regional agreements. The only nods in the direction of a formal regional trading system are vague promises about distant dates. In 1992 the Association of Southeast Asian Nations (ASEAN) committed itself "in principle" to enter into a NAFTA-like arrangement which would (none too originally) be called AFTA; tariffs within AFTA are supposed to be radically reduced by 2004. For the moment, though, statistical tests suggest that ASEAN functions as less of a trade bloc than Asia as a whole or even Pacific Asia does. In late 1994 the members of the world's most awkwardly named international gathering, Asia-Pacific Economic Cooperation (APEC), committed themselves to free trade throughout East Asia and the Pacific, including countries on that ocean's eastern shore such as the United States. But the promise does not fall due for the richer APEC members until 2010; for the rest, in 2020. Another embryonic group, the East Asian Economic Caucus, has not advanced even that far.

Regional trade within East Asia and across the Pacific has instead grown because of GATT-mandated, or even unilateral, tariff cutting, and thanks to the economic links created by the spread of multinational firms throughout the region; in other words, it has grown pretty much along the lines laid down by market forces. The main result of this, as pointed out by Jeffrey Frankel, an economist at the University of California at Berkeley, is that during the 1980s, when the regional trade biases of the European Community and of Western Hemisphere economies were roughly doubling, there was a slight decrease in the regional bias of trade in Pacific Asia.

In view of the large increases in intra-Asian trade described above, how can this be? The main reason is that in the 1980s, East Asia and

Southeast Asia enjoyed such large absolute increases in both output and trade that big natural increases in the share of intra-Asian trade could easily coexist with an open trading regime that did not discriminate against extra-regional trading partners. The natural level of trade between two countries—that is, the level undistorted by tariffs or other forms of protection—depends mainly on three things: how close the two countries are geographically, the size of their economies, and (less significant than the other two items) how rich they are. So, with the East Asian economies physically close to each other and their size and wealth growing quickly throughout the 1980s, their trade with each other was bound to grab an overwhelming share of the increase in their total trade during the decade. There is thus no sign that East Asia is developing a trading "bloc" that excludes anyone else.

Even so, an oddity remains. Asia's trade may have become no more regionally biased during the 1980s, but it started that decade far more regionally biased than either Europe or the Americas. By Mr. Frankel's reckoning, a fairly big share of the intra-regional trade in all three regions cannot be accounted for by factors such as distance and economic size. What, then, might have made East Asia as late as 1980 a more regionally based trading group than either Europe or the Americas? It could not have been any formal trading arrangements (of which there were none) or Japan's influence: The statistics all belie any special role for Japan in knitting East Asia together. It might have had something to do with the dense and border-ignoring business networks of the overseas Chinese scattered throughout East and Southeast Asia (see chapter 10).

Interestingly, Mr. Frankel finds that by far the strongest "natural" trading group in the world is not East Asia but APEC—East and Southeast Asia combined with North America and Australia and New Zealand. This suggests that the dependence of East Asia on America may be just as intense as it ever was. The difference is that, with Asia's increasing economic weight, America's and Asia's need for each other and influence on one another is becoming more mutual. Asia is not going its own way. It just appears to be because it is occupying a bigger piece of the global-trade battleground.

FACTORIES ON THE MOVE

The numbers are much smaller than those for trade, but the flows of foreign direct investment (FDI) into and around Asia may have an even bigger effect on Asia's growth and development. This sounds outlandish. In 1993 the world's total flow of FDI—which means money going directly to build factories or buy buildings, not to buy stocks or bonds—amounted to around $175 billion. That is equal to roughly 5 percent of the value of world exports that year. The flows of FDI into Asian countries was about $50 billion, almost half again as high as the year before (see table 4) and equal to two-thirds of the total amount that went to all poor countries. Even so, that was less than a third of the value of Hong Kong's trade alone.

TABLE 4
FOREIGN DIRECT INVESTMENT TO EAST ASIAN COUNTRIES

(in Billions of U.S. Dollars)

	1985	1986	1987	1988	1989	1990	1991	1992	1993	1994
China	1.7	1.9	2.3	3.2	3.4	3.5	4.4	11.2	27.5	33.8
Indonesia	0.3	0.3	0.4	0.6	0.7	1.1	1.5	1.8	2.0	4.0
Japan	0.6	0.2	1.2	−0.5	−1.1	1.8	1.4	2.7	0.1	0.1
Korea	0.2	0.4	0.6	0.9	0.8	0.7	1.1	0.6	0.5	1.3
Malaysia	0.7	0.5	0.4	0.7	1.7	2.3	4.0	5.2	5.2	5.1
Philippines	—	0.1	0.3	0.9	0.6	0.5	0.5	0.2	0.8	1.7
Singapore	1.0	1.7	2.8	3.7	2.9	5.6	4.9	6.7	6.8	5.5
Thailand	0.2	0.3	0.4	1.1	1.8	2.4	2.0	2.1	1.7	2.2
Taiwan	0.3	0.5	0.7	1.0	2.4	2.3	1.8	1.5	1.2	1.6
Hong Kong	0.3	0.3	0.3	0.3	0.3	0.3	0.2	0.3	0.3	0.3
Vietnam	—	—	—	—	0.2	—	0.7	0.7	1.0	1.4
TOTAL	**5.3**	**6.2**	**9.4**	**11.9**	**13.7**	**20.5**	**22.5**	**33.0**	**47.1**	**57**

SOURCE: Asia-Pacific Economics Group, "Asia-Pacific Profiles," Australian National University, 1995.

Yet FDI reshapes economies and societies far out of proportion to its nominal value. This is why, as chapter 6 explains in some detail, even a country as big as China can be so deeply influenced by the foreign investment that has gone into it. The secret of FDI's power is its ability, even in small amounts, to generate big changes in the industrial structure and technological level of poor countries that receive it, and in their patterns of trade in the future. The main

reason for this, which is the way FDI efficiently transmits new ideas
and technologies, was explained in the example of Mauritius in
chapter 3.

The motor of change in Mauritius was the clothing industry developed on the island by Hong Kong entrepreneurs who had transplanted their factories and technology there. Over time, Mauritius
financed most of the investment in its clothing industry itself; but
the seeds of ideas borne by the (fairly small) FDI with which that
industry was founded eventually sprouted into the whole business.
Whether or not you accept ideas as the cause of this efficient mechanism of transmission, studies by the Bank of Japan have shown that
there are clear correlations between the FDI received by poor Asian
countries and their moves from farming to manufacturing, their
accumulation of capital relative to labor, and the upgrading of their
exports to higher value-added goods.

You can see this process at work in places like Dalian, a port city
of around 3 million people on the Yellow Sea in northeastern China.
Like dozens of other cities in China, Dalian has a development
zone where foreign investors receive various tax and other breaks.
Although in Dalian in the mid-1990s, as in most places in China, the
largest number of foreign-investment projects belonged to Hong
Kong investors, the Japanese came second in number and first in
value. (The Americans were third in number and probably second
in value.) Dalian is familiar to the Japanese: It is located on the
southern tip of Manchuria, which Japan seized in 1931 to kick off
the Pacific war. Yet in Dalian itself Japanese rule was fairly benign.
Japan took over the city, then known as Port Arthur, from the Russians after winning the Russo-Japanese War in 1905, and for the
next forty years treated it and its surroundings as a favorite colony
rather than (like the rest of Manchuria) a conquered province. The
Japanese are welcome again in what was southern Manchuria, and
by 1994 had directed a lot of their foreign investment there: perhaps
a third of Japan's total FDI in China.

In the spring of 1993, Dalian's development zone had barely got
going. Some fifty thousand people worked there, and half of them
lived there. The city's planners are aiming for a million people to
be living in the 190-square-kilometer zone a few years into the next
century. The few industrial parks that were up and running in 1993
looked rather forlorn in the zone's mostly empty vastness, but even
then it was possible to sense what was coming. The full gamut of
industrial investments, from light to very heavy, was under way,

along with the building of a new port intended to have seventy berths when it is finished.

At the light end of the scale were textile factories, such as those of Mitsui Dalian, which had opened three of them in a single week that spring; or Mabuchi Motors, a Japanese maker of micromotors (for raising and lowering car-radio antennas, for example), which in 1993 was in the midst of shifting a whole factory from Taiwan to Dalian. By 1994 a fifth of Mabuchi's total production was accounted for by its Dalian factory.

In a pattern that has been repeated time and again in industrializing Asia over the past forty years, some three-quarters of the shop-floor workers in Dalian's light-industrial factories in 1993 were teenage peasant girls, recruited from the surrounding countryside and prized for their nimble fingers and their docility. There were plenty of higher-tech operations, too. Canon, another Japanese firm, was making cartridges for Hewlett-Packard laser printers, and Toshiba was making compressors, printed circuit boards, and television picture tubes. Farther up the industrial tree were companies like America's Pfizer, which had been making drugs in Dalian since the late 1980s; PPG, which was building a floating-glass plant; and France's Total, which was building an oil refinery and had plans for a petrochemicals plant.

The experience of Toshiba sheds more light on just what this investment process has been accomplishing and how. Toshiba started making black-and-white television tubes in Dalian in the mid-1970s. By the mid-1990s the company had a fifteen-acre Toshiba Park in Dalian, divided into four or five sections, making such items as color-television tubes, rotary compressors for air conditioners and refrigerators, and small motors. Toshiba had found that after a few years' experience workers in its Chinese factories were about 75 percent as productive as Japanese workers but cost a tenth as much. The capacity and quality of many Chinese factories were at or above Japanese levels; in the case of color picture tubes, by the mid-1990s, China's 10-million-a-year capacity was bigger than Japan's (which had fallen from 12–13 million in the late 1980s).

When Toshiba first opened parts-asssembly factories in China, they were wholly owned by the Chinese government; Toshiba simply imported basic technology and outdated equipment and received a fee for running the factories. By the early 1990s it owned most of the factories itself, wholly or in part, and was installing more up-to-date equipment and the best of Toshiba technology. Some of the components being made in China (such as those color picture tubes) were shipped back to Japan for further and finer assembly, but overall there had been a big change since the first wave of Japanese FDI had crashed over East Asia in 1985–89.

Back then the Japanese thought of Malaysia, Thailand, and other Southeast Asian countries as export platforms. Fairly simple components were made there and then shipped back to Japan, or final assembly was done for Japanese goods, which were then exported to America or Europe. By the mid-1990s domestic markets on the Asian mainland were more on Toshiba's mind when it thought about putting factories there. No wonder: Toshiba expects its Asian sales to grow by 10–20 percent a year for the next several years, compared with 3 percent growth in Japan and America and even less than that in Europe. The company was even beginning to think of putting some of the larger plants, whose scale dictates that they must serve continent-wide markets, elsewhere in Asia than Japan.

As all this suggests, FDI flows in Asia have begun to remake the industrial structures of individual Asian countries and the distribution of manufacturing activities among them. Capital equipment (often whole factories) is bulking larger in the exports of richer countries to poorer Asian ones; in return, the quality and sophistication of the (sometimes re-exported) goods produced in part thanks to that capital investment are rising.

The trail of diversification blazed by the world's multinationals is also changing the sources and nature of trade in Asia. The trade of most rich countries contains a large share of what is called intra-firm and intra-industry trade: the former meaning the transfer of goods across borders between different branches of the same firm; the latter meaning both the export and import of, say, cars. Rising shares of intra-firm trade suggest that the role of multinationals and of their technology is expanding; of intra-industry trade, that economies are becoming more closely tied together. Both these kinds of trade have begun accounting for a larger share of Asian trade. But are the multinationals of any one rich country, perhaps the one whose flag bears a rising sun, about to become the overlords of this new Asia?

PRIMI INTER PARES

Japan and America have together always accounted for more than half the FDI going to the NIEs, and in the 1980s Japan was the single biggest FDIor in the poorer countries of Southeast Asia. In 1991, though, the NIEs surpassed Japan as investors in Southeast Asia; and the overseas Chinese (who are scattered throughout Southeast Asia though their investment money is usually channeled through Hong Kong or Taiwan) have far outstripped everybody else in investing in China. That is something. In 1994, China received around $34 billion in FDI: more than half the Asian total, a fifth of the world total, and not much less than the amount invested in the United States.

Even so, since the mid-1980s Japan has been the biggest foreign investor in the rest of Asia. It probably wishes it had gone into Asia in an even bigger way: A survey by Mitsubishi Research Institute in the early 1990s found that 80 percent of Japanese direct investments in Asia had become profitable within two years of their being made, compared with 20 percent in America. Another survey, conducted by three Japanese government agencies and reported in a periodical called the *China Analyst* in 1995, showed that since 1985 the recurring profit margins of the Asian subsidiaries of Japanese manufacturers have always been higher than those of Japanese subsidiaries in Europe or America: In 1994 the margins in Asia were 4 percent, in America 0 and in Europe − 1 percent. Asia's obvious attractions to Japanese investors, and their increasing involvement there, have made many people wonder whether an FDI-based "yen bloc " or, for those with a bit of historical flourish, even a "Greater East Asian Co-Prosperity Sphere" along 1930s lines (though peacefully imposed), was in the making.

For the moment that is improbable, though with the mid-1990s shift in relative values between the yen and dollar it is starting to become more likely. First the history. Japan was the biggest source of FDI for Asia from the mid-1980s—when the first sharp rise in the value of the yen began forcing some of its factories offshore—through the early 1990s. But there are several reasons for questioning how overwhelming or persistent this trend will be. For one thing, Japan accounted on average for no more than 35 percent of the total FDI flows into the poorer countries of East Asia during this period (see chart 3a on page 108). Important, yes; dominant, no. The figures are even less impressive when Japanese FDI is looked at as a share of overall capital spending in these countries: It then falls, usually deeply, into single digits (see chart 3b).

Second, Japan's investments in Asia—like its FDI elsewhere and indeed its manufacturing prowess in general—are heavily concen-

CHART 3a
ORIGIN OF FOREIGN DIRECT INVESTMENT
GOING TO EAST ASIAN NATIONS (1987–91)

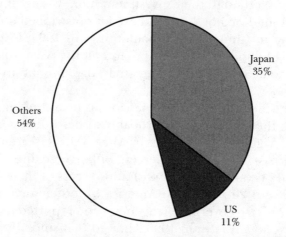

Japan
35%

Others
54%

US
11%

SOURCE: E. Graham and N. Anzai, "Is Japanese Direct Investment Creating an Asian Economic Bloc?" *Columbia Journal of World Business* (Fall 1994).

CHART 3b
FOREIGN DIRECT INVESTMENT AS PERCENTAGE OF
GROSS DOMESTIC FIXED CAPITAL FORMATION, 1987–91,
IN SELECTED EAST ASIAN COUNTRIES

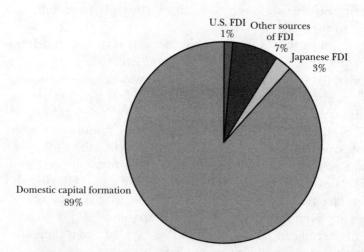

U.S. FDI
1%

Other sources
of FDI
7%

Japanese FDI
3%

Domestic capital formation
89%

SOURCE: E. Graham and N. Anzai, "Is Japanese Direct Investment Creating an Asian Economic Bloc?" *Columbia Journal of World Business* (Fall 1994).

trated in two lines of business: electronics and cars and car parts. Edward Graham and Naoko Anzai, of the Institute for International Economics in Washington, D.C., have calculated that in 1991 electronics accounted for almost 40 percent of the sales of Japanese subsidiaries in East Asia; cars and car parts, for another quarter.

In cars especially Japan's investments may have serious implications for the future of the global business. Kenneth Courtis, Deutsche Bank's Tokyo-based strategist for Asia, reckons that two-thirds of the worldwide increase in car sales this decade will have come from Asia outside Japan. He thinks that some twelve to sixteen factories, each with a capacity of 200,000 cars, will be built in Asia in the 1990s and that ten of them will be Japanese. Unless their American and European competitors act fast to redress the balance—and by the mid-1990s they had begun trying, especially in China, India, and (to a lesser degree) Indonesia—Japan's Asian push could deliver a strong advantage to Japanese car companies in an industry that is increasingly globalized and in which fast rises in volume can deeply affect profits.

But in most other lines of business Japanese firms do not boast such a head start in Asia. Strong domestic competitors exist everywhere, and other Asian multinationals, especially from the transnational network of the overseas Chinese and from South Korea (see chapters 10 and 11), are increasingly stretching their operations into countries where they compete directly with the Japanese.

However, the strongest challenge of all to Japanese dominance of Asia's industrial landscape comes from American firms. Until the mid-1980s, American multinationals had a bigger stock of FDI in Asia than their Japanese counterparts and, beginning in 1989, American flows of FDI quickly started catching up again with Japanese levels—they rose from 20 percent of Japanese flows in 1989 to almost two-thirds in 1992. It is possible that by 1994–95, American and Japanese firms were investing about the same amounts in Asia (see chart 4 on page 110). Moreover, American FDI in Asia may have packed more punch than the overall numbers suggest. America's FDI flows to Asia in the late 1980s and early 1990s grew more slowly than its flows to other parts of the world. But the overseas capital spending of American firms—the money spent on things like factories and equipment that actually churn out the products— grew twice as fast in Asia during those years as it did elsewhere in the world.

Nonetheless, the collapse of the dollar against the yen in the first

CHART 4

**RATIO OF U.S. TO JAPANESE FLOWS AND STOCKS
OF FDI TO EAST ASIAN NATIONS (EXCLUDING JAPAN), 1987–92**

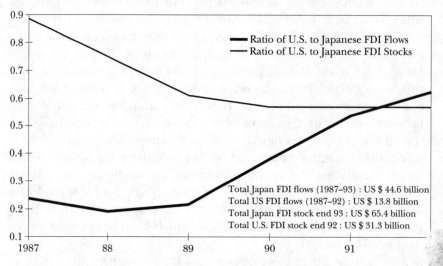

SOURCE: E. Graham and N. Anzai, "Is Japanese Direct Investment Creating an Asian Economic Bloc?"
Columbia Journal of World Business (Fall 1994).

half of 1995 shows how hard it is going to be for American firms to keep up with their Japanese counterparts in investing in Asia. Even in the Japanese financial year 1994–95—before the yen began soaring extraordinarily—Japan's flows of FDI into Asia reached almost $10 billion, a quarter of Japan's total FDI flows (still well behind the 40-plus percent that went into America that year). But the $41 billion total of FDI flows from Japan that year was still below the peak of $50-plus billion Japan sent out in 1990, and with the stronger yen Japanese FDI is likely to surpass that earlier record in 1996 and 1997; for the profitability reasons mentioned above, an even higher share of this increased FDI flow than before will probably go to Asia. The weaker dollar that makes Asia a more attractive destination for Japanese firms conversely makes it a less attractive one for American firms. It will take an exceptional effort of will on the part of the Americans to put more FDI money into a continent where exchange rates are telling them to stay away but long-term business logic is telling them to plunge in.

Still, the Americans do not face as daunting a climb as the Europeans. European firms in 1985 had a stock of FDI in Asia equal to only about 75 percent of the stock of either America or Japan. Despite declarations by many European firms that they now realized how significant Asia was, Europe's FDI flows to Asia over the following five years were almost 10 percent lower than those of American firms and more than 10 percent lower than those of Japanese firms —leaving Europe farther behind than when it started.

Many things lie behind Europe's lagging performance in Asia (some of them are discussed in chapter 10), but the most damaging has been the inward-looking turn taken by European economic policies since 1980. In the same way that taxes on imports act as drags on exports, a "trade-diverting" bloc of the sort that European integration seems to have fostered encourages firms to stay at home rather than venture out. With Asia growing bigger by the year in the world economy and its own market-driven and "trade-creating" bloc being knit closer together, this is no time for investors to shy away. Especially not if Asia's two giants, China and India, can now follow the relative tiddlers of East Asia into dazzling and sustained wealth creation.

PART II

THE FATE OF TWO GIANTS

CHAPTER 6

CHINA'S TRIUMPHS...

It was around 1500 that Europe overtook China as the world's most advanced civilization. For centuries—maybe forever—before then, Chinese science and technology and China's productivity and incomes were the world's best. Over the following five hundred years, while the West grew rich and strong, China first lay torpid and then, for most of the twentieth century, was convulsed by revolution, war, famine, Communist tyranny, and a decade of anarchy called the Cultural Revolution. After so much humiliation, disorder, and misery, in 1979 the Chinese government abruptly began an experiment of almost unbelievable audacity: the attempt to make China, within just a couple of generations, a full member of the modern world—rich, powerful, and again, at last, on top.

If this experiment succeeds, and the obstacles to its doing so are formidable, it will probably have the biggest single influence on the political and economic shape of the world in the first half of the twenty-first century. The simplest reason for this is the size of China's population.

In 1995, China was home to about 1.2 billion people, a little more than a fifth of all mankind. Population projections are pretty worthless (childbearing habits change too quickly and unpredictably), but in the early 1990s the World Bank guessed that in 2010 China would have more than 1.4 billion people, by 2025 almost 1.6 billion, and by 2050 nearly 1.8 billion—still 18 percent of the world's population. Spread over so many people, even comparatively modest personal incomes are magnified into stupendous na-

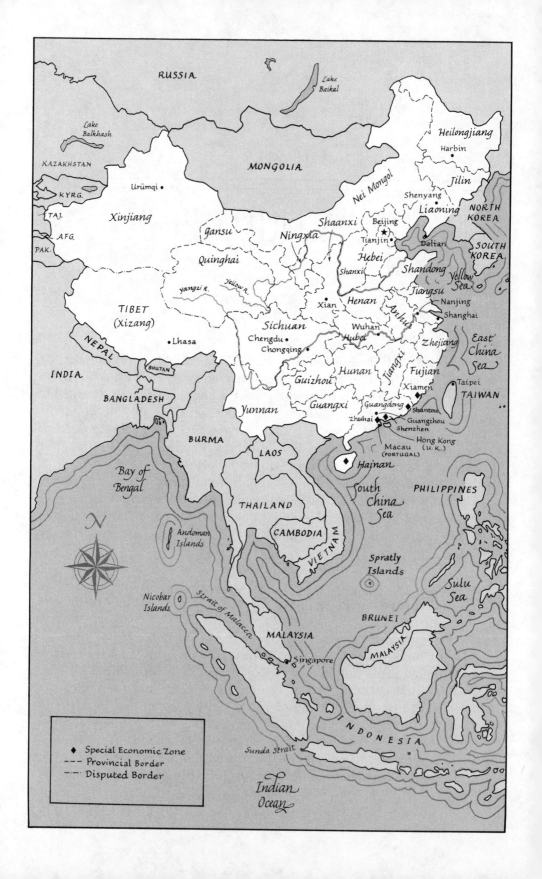

tional economies. If in 2025 China has managed to raise the income of the average Chinese to the level enjoyed by the average Taiwanese in the mid-1990s (a hard but by no means impossible feat), China's economy will be not only by far the biggest in the world—almost half again as big as America's—but equal to some 75–80 percent of the then size of the economies of the United States, Japan, and Western Europe put together. This would radically change the world's economic, business, and financial life.

And not just that. China will not follow the modern Japanese model of economic strength combined with political puniness on the world stage. Japan, for all its post-1945 economic success, has still not recovered from the national crippling that America inflicted on it in the Pacific war and the military occupation that followed. Japan remains what one Singaporean calls a "neutered power," rich, modern, but incapable of asserting itself politically among other powers.

Not China. China emerged ruined from the harrowing decades of the 1930s and 1940s, from war with and occupation by imperial Japan and civil war between its own Communists and Nationalists. But the ruin was only material, not psychological. True, China's rulers have old scores they want to settle with the Western colonial powers that brought the Qing dynasty to its knees in the nineteenth century—especially with Britain, which can conveniently be berated over Hong Kong during the last two years of its stewardship of that territory before it reverts to China in 1997. But apart from that, China is self-confident; it is aware of its powers, both political and military, and has no hesitation about deploying them. When, in 1992–93, China was irritated by French sales of fighter jets to Taiwan, it put the diplomatic and commercial screws on France until the French gave way completely in 1994: France not only renounced future arms sales to Taiwan but even made sure, during a visit to France that year by China's president, that pro-democracy campaigners were not allowed to mount a demonstration that might inconvenience him.

Even so, China's self-confidence has not so far meant a great deal to the world at large. China is, for now, still poor, and its concerns are mostly local. Whatever its quarrels with the United States, France, and Britain, China has never wielded its veto in the UN Security Council to prevent the Western powers from intervening as they deemed necessary in places like the Middle East (the war against Iraq in 1990–91 to roll back its invasion of Kuwait) or the Balkans (the Bosnian mess of 1992–95). Nor, despite America's occasional squabbles with China over such matters as Chinese missile and nuclear-technology sales to Pakistan and some Middle Eastern countries, has a serious rupture over any global issue ever come close.

Yet China's relative poverty and its obsession with economic growth will not last forever. China has had nuclear weapons since the mid-1960s. By the mid-1990s it also had a strapping, and modernizing, conventional military establishment. David Shambaugh, a British scholar, has calculated that the Chinese government's military budget rose by half in real terms between 1988 and 1994, reaching $7 billion in the later year—still, despite the swift rise, a modest sum by world standards. But the Chinese army enjoys far greater revenues from outside the official government budget—from factories, commercial ventures (the People's Liberation Army seems especially fond of joint ventures with foreigners operating luxury hotels in China), local-government budgets, and overseas arms sales. Mr. Shambaugh reckons that in 1993 the army's off-budget revenues amounted to $38 billion. So China's total military spending by the mid-1990s could have been some $45 billion a year, the world's third-biggest after America's and Japan's. Once China is able to turn more of its energy and attention to geopolitical matters, it will have considerable weight not only on the Asian balance of power but on that of the whole world.

A no-longer-poor, self-assured, and militarily strong China in, say, 2010–2020 will pose a particularly ticklish challenge to the West (in practice mostly to America) for another reason. Chinese civilization is both the world's oldest and by far Asia's most pervasive and strongest. Alongside Islam, it is the only plausible challenger in the next couple of decades to the liberal democratic values that have become identified with the rich societies of the West. Many thoughtful people believe that, as a model for the world, only Islam offers any real alternative to Western values, that East Asian authoritarianism, which often masks as a peculiar "modern" Confucianism, is nothing more than a self-serving creed concocted by East Asian authoritarians to justify their own grip on power and that it will have no more staying power than the present generation of East Asian authoritarians do.

I am not so sure about that, as chapter 16 will explain. In any event, China itself (if it is still going strong by the second decade of the twenty-first century) is highly unlikely to be a liberal democratic society. It will be authoritarian, though less crudely so than now, and illiberal. Assuming that what is by then the world's biggest economy is guided by social and political principles as much at odds as these would be with those of the tolerant West, there is going to be a lot of friction between the two camps.

These are the broad implications of a successful Chinese experiment in reform. What if it fails? The rest of the world might assume it would have a bit less to worry about. It has, after all, had centuries of practice in coping with a China that cannot influence events far beyond its borders. But for East Asia, and increasingly for everybody else as Asia's economic weight grows, the consequences could be serious, even disastrous—not least because of the immense tide of refugees that likely would be released upon the whole world. An economically faltering China would spoil the prospects for growth in what is otherwise the world's most promising region; a dismembered China would not be a quiet one. A serious imbalance of power in Asia (and an unstable China will almost by definition cause one) would suck a reluctant America into an attempt, perhaps bloody, to perform a rebalancing act.

But so far the Chinese experiment in economic reform has been a success—a vastly more spectacular one than anyone dreamed it would be when it began.

WHAT DENG WROUGHT

The true awakening of China began not, as many people suppose, with the dramatic moment on October 1, 1949, when a victorious Mao Zedong, proclaiming the People's Republic of China, told a cheering crowd in Beijing's Tiananmen Square that "the 475 million people of China have now stood up." It came almost thirty years later, during what sounds like a snoozer: the third plenary session of the Eleventh Central Committee of the Communist party of China. This meeting was held in December 1978, just over two years after Mao's death. The session agreed to the radical proposals of Deng Xiaoping, Mao's longtime comrade in arms and recent ideological foe, that the Chinese economy, until then enslaved to Stalinist principles of central planning, state ownership, and import substitution, should be reformed and opened up to the outside world.

Deng is going to be one of the harder twentieth-century figures for historians to come to grips with. Henry Kissinger, taking an instant dislike to the pint-sized party hack, called him "a nasty little man." Lee Kuan Yew detected instead in the battle-hardened Sichuanese peasant turned revolutionary both an unmatched understanding of China and an instinct for the right way to introduce his ancient homeland to modernity; Lee unhesitatingly calls Deng "a great man."

Both views have some truth to them. By all accounts Deng was happy and well balanced, with none of the hang-ups of personality or family resentment that led Mao to his turbulent emotional life of three or four wives and his old-age debauchery and self-indulgence. Deng was a lifelong family man, surrounded in his old age by children, grandchildren, and great-grandchildren. He was also unimaginative and unbending in his attachment to the Communist party of China (though not to communism itself); and, like most of the early leaders of modern Asia, utterly ruthless about the protection of his own political power.

For most people in the West, Deng's memory will be forever blotted with the blood of the peaceful pro-democracy demonstrators killed on his orders in and around Tiananmen Square on June 4, 1989. Deng's own memory ran deeper. It ran to a time, in the 1930s and 1940s, when for him and his comrades it was kill or be killed for the sake of the party's authority and China's integrity and when, in China as a whole, at least 20 million people perished from the fighting between China and Japan and among the Chinese themselves.

It ran also to Mao's "Great Leap Forward" of 1958–62, a disastrous anti-market policy, opposed by Deng, which caused the death by starvation of perhaps 40 million Chinese—almost as many people as were killed worldwide in World War II. And it ran to Mao's appalling Cultural Revolution of 1966–75, when another 10 million or so Chinese died and a couple of hundred million had their lives torn to pieces, including Deng, whose son was permanently crippled by falling from a fourth-story window after being tortured by Red Guards and who himself was consigned to menial work in a machine-tool shop in Jiangxi province in the middle of nowhere.

It is unlikely that anyone will ever know for sure what led Deng to change China as he did. As early as the 1950s he had begun hectoring Mao to retain family farming in China; and he always had the understanding of ordinary life that made foreign dignitaries like Mr. Kissinger undervalue him, especially alongside the visionary Mao and Zhou Enlai, Mao's elegant lieutenant.

My guess is that Deng's reformist instincts were crystallized during the Cultural Revolution by his own experience of the impersonal forces of history (and of their personal consequences) and that this led him to his reform proposals of December 1978. He was not alone. The Cultural Revolution instantly and persistently imposed an unimaginable—by Western standards—horror of lawlessness and insecurity on a fifth of mankind. It also created, as I will explain in the next chapter, a generation of talented people who may be the largest group ever put into such a position to change their country for the better—because they were forced to endure the worst their country had to offer of poverty and deprivation, swiftly followed by advanced-degree programs in American universities.

In Deng's own case, the Cultural Revolution liberated him to pursue the heretical policies he had always been partial to. As the next section explains, these reforms were pragmatic and ad hoc rather than studied, as you would expect of reforms fashioned by a revolutionary and prisoner. I suspect that it is for these reforms and their beneficent effects on the fate of hundreds of millions of people, rather than for the blood of thousands of people undoubtedly on his hands from Tiananmen and earlier atrocities, that Deng will in the end be mostly remembered.

Whether or not China's reform experiment persists for another generation or collapses, the Dengist reforms of 1979–94 brought about probably the biggest single improvement in human welfare anywhere at any time. During this decade and a half China's real economic growth averaged 9 percent a year, a rate that doubles the size of the economy in less than eight years. By 2000, barring disaster, China's economy should be eight times bigger than it was when Deng began his reforms in 1979: a record that would equal the performance of Japan, South Korea, and Taiwan during their fastest quarter-centuries of economic growth.

Already, the Chinese have enjoyed an extraordinary rise in living standards. Deng's reforms began in the countryside, where 80 percent of Chinese then lived. In the following six years grain output grew by a third, cotton production almost trebled, and fruit production went up by half. Real farm incomes almost trebled in eight years.

It is likely that in 1978 around 250 million Chinese—a quarter of the population then—were living in what international organizations call "absolute poverty" (i.e., they were wearing rags and starving). By 1985, when the farming reforms were largely completed, the number of absolutely poor Chinese was 100 million, less than 10 percent of the population. Half an America, an entire Japan, maybe two Germanies—that many people were lifted out of poverty during China's first half decade of reform.

The rise in the living standard of the average Chinese was just as sharp. Between 1978 and 1991 grain consumption went up by 20 percent; seafood consumption doubled; pork consumption went up two and one half times; egg consumption, more than three times; poultry consumption, four times. By 1994 there were ninety color televisions for each hundred urban Chinese households, more than nine times as many as at the beginning of the 1980s.

A visitor to China in late 1978 would have found a drab and regimented country in which city dwellers lived on a monotonous diet of rice and noodles, virtually all wore the same boring baggy dark blue clothes, there was no entertainment to speak of and no shops except government-owned ones selling "goods" of execrable quality and design. Every neighborhood was peppered with busybody informants who made sure that no misbehavior, however devoid of political significance, went unreported. And anyone foolish enough to make unauthorized contact with the few foreigners who were then in China would quickly have felt the full weight of the public-security apparatus.

By the mid-1990s the whole of China was only a generation behind its East Asian neighbors. Such indicators of well-being as infant mortality, life expectancy, and the composition of the average Chinese diet rose during the 1980s uncannily in line with their movements in Taiwan in the 1960s (see charts 5a and 5b).

The enlivening of China was at its most visible and spectacular in the cities, suburbs, and surrounding farmland along the country's coast—a region of some 350 million people stretching from Guangzhou (ex-Canton) in the south to Shanghai and Nanjing in the east and on north to Tianjin and Dalian. Restaurants and nightclubs teemed late into evenings that, unlike fifteen years before, glowed with neon and bustled with traffic instead of being sunk in empty darkness. Color and variety had come in abundance to people's

CHART 5a
PER CAPITA ANNUAL CONSUMPTION OF FOODGRAIN:
CHINA (1977–90) AND TAIWAN (1955–68)

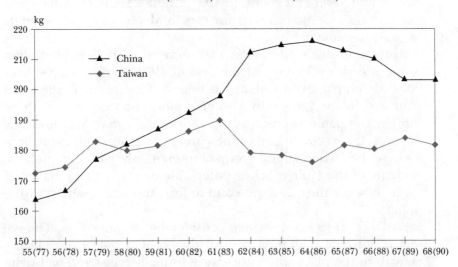

SOURCE: "How Rich Is China: Evidence from the Food Economy," Ma Guonan and Ross Garnaut, Working Papers in Trade and Development, Research School of Pacific Studies, Australian National University (1992).

NOTE: Parentheses show year for China.

CHART 5b
PER CAPITA ANNUAL CONSUMPTION OF RED MEAT:
CHINA (1977–90) AND TAIWAN (1955–68)

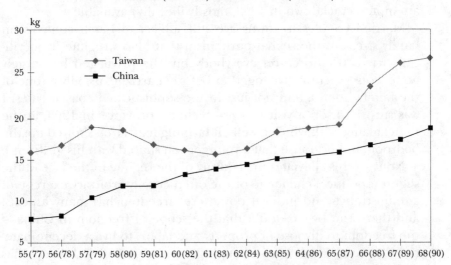

SOURCE: "How Rich Is China: Evidence from the Food Economy," Ma Guonan and Ross Garnaut, Working Papers in Trade and Development, Research School of Pacific Studies, Australian National University (1992).

NOTE: Parentheses show year for China.

dress, some of it as sleek and designer-labeled as any found in Hong Kong. Consumer sales throughout China were brisk, and not just of clothes and lower-end goods: In 1993, China was the second-biggest market (after Germany itself) for cars in Mercedes-Benz's S range, its top-of-the-line models.

By the mid-1990s, China was a far more cosmopolitan place than it had ever been before. At the end of 1994 there were just over 200,000 companies in China that were at least partly funded and managed by foreigners. In Shanghai alone in 1992 two or three foreign companies were opening offices each day. And not only were foreigners coming in; Chinese were going out. Chinese nationals were the second-largest group of foreign-university and graduate students in the United States (after Taiwanese); a like number of Chinese, some thirty-five thousand to forty thousand, were studying in Japan.

Social controls had loosened considerably in other ways. The system of internal migration control that kept people from moving away from the place where they were formally registered had virtually collapsed by the mid-1990s. Mention neighborhood spies to a young Chinese and you are met with a look of incomprehension: They are now practically unknown. Papers and magazines are tightly supervised for their political content but have a pretty free rein on other subjects; and satellite television is widely (though, after an attempted crackdown in 1993, mostly illegally) available.

Married couples in towns are still subject to harsh controls on family size, but the sexual puritanism that Mao's regime hypocritically tried to enforce on everybody but the privileged has largely gone. Young people live together before marriage, usually in one of the family homes, and not just in the sophisticated coastal cities. I was surprised, on a visit to rural Sichuan province in 1993, at the nonchalance with which a well-off farming matriarch showed me the bedroom in her house that a younger son shared with his girlfriend.

None of this alleviates the tyranny of the regime in the face of the slightest political challenge or the often cruelly arbitrary exercise of administrative and judicial power. Yet freedom has many aspects, and there can be no doubt that the scope of freedom in China— the freedom to dispose of property and labor, to live a decent material life if you work hard enough, to make personal choices—has expanded enormously. China has undergone a revolution since 1978: one of the greatest, and mostly for the good, of any on earth this century. How did it happen?

CROSSING THE RIVER BY FEELING THE STONES UNDERFOOT

Unlike the later Communist reform programs in Eastern Europe and Russia, the reforms begun in China late in 1978 were not designed by Harvard professors; they were animated more by instinct than theory and were experimental, gradual, and piecemeal. Neither the destination nor the route was thought out in advance. The heading of this section is one Chinese metaphor for this process and probably the most accurate description of it. A more famous phrase of Deng Xiaoping's sums up the pragmatic spirit of the reforms: "It doesn't matter whether a cat is black or white as long as it catches mice." Unsurprisingly, this method (if that is the right word for it) has produced an often incomprehensible mishmash of policies, practices, and regional variations. Yet for a country of China's size, diversity, and administrative backwardness it may well have been the best way. It is not so different in practice, after all, from the federal solution that the United States had hit upon two hundred years before for running a continent-sized country.

The first reason why the Deng reforms succeeded as well as they did is that China set out from a fairly good starting point. Because China had spent less than thirty years under communism when it began to extricate itself (compared with the Soviet Union's seventy-plus years), commercial habits were still strong. Moreover, unlike both Eastern Europe and Russia, China had never developed a powerful apparatus of central planning; hence, decentralized decision-making and resource allocation were still operating to some extent. And, unlike the European ex-Communist countries, China began its reforms in a state of rough macroeconomic balance. The country had been shattered by the Cultural Revolution, but the government's budget was in balance, the currency was sound, prices were stable, and there was practically no foreign debt. This created a solid launchpad for radical change.

The second big advantage with which China began its reforms was a surprisingly robust economy at the grassroots. The official statistics say that in the years 1965–80—roughly the period of the Cultural Revolution and its aftershocks—China's economy grew at the astonishing real rate of 6.4 percent a year. Even today Chinese statistics are highly unreliable; those collected during the chaos of the Cultural Revolution are far likelier to be fabrications than calculations. Nonetheless, such cross-checking of economic activity as can be done by looking at physical output and consumption has always suggested that Chinese incomes are substantially higher than the official figures say, and that the natural rate of Chinese economic growth is very high by international standards. What this means is that China's government has a wide margin of error. Even when the leadership perpetrates something as stupid as the Cultural Revolution, the Chinese people have unsuspected material resources to draw on, and the Chinese economy keeps plowing ahead.

On reflection, it is not so hard to see why this is so. For reasons explained in chapter 2, much of an economy's potential growth is accounted for by how much that economy saves and invests. Communist China's savings and investment rates have always been among the world's highest; for decades both have been upwards of 30 percent of GDP. Even used inefficiently, capital of those dimensions can generate a lot of economic growth for a long time.

Another striking feature of modern China—and the other big contributor to economic growth—is how many people work and how hard they work. More than 60 percent of China's population is in the workforce, compared with just over 40 percent in Indonesia and under 40 percent in India; and no more than a fifth of that huge gap can be accounted for by the fact that the populations of India and Indonesia are younger than China's. Except in the big state-owned factories, where sloth is often the rule, it is rare to see much idleness in China. Observers have been struck by this for some time. In the 1960s, when he was the American ambassador to India, John Kenneth Galbraith visited China and wrote:

> I once estimated that you could cross the whole of Madras [in southern India] from the airport to the American consulate and not see more than 10 people in each 100 employed or moving in any visibly purposeful way. The rest were unemployed or anyhow not working. Here [in Guangzhou, southern China], children apart, the corresponding proportion of purposeful people is about 90%.

How China had managed, on the eve of Deng's reforms, to create what amounted to full employment outside the state sector is a matter of much debate; but it meant that, when the seeds of reform did come to be scattered, they fell on fallow ground.

FARMERS FIRST

The conditions were favorable to reform, and the early steps of reform could hardly have been more surefooted. At the beginning, Deng's reforms had two main parts: making the family, instead of the commune, the main economic unit in China's countryside; and opening China to the outside world—to foreign trade, foreign investment, and foreign ideas. The farm reforms, which produced immediate and spectacular results, were a work of political genius whose accomplishments were nonetheless short-lived. The opening up, which had few results at the time, was a piece of long-range strategy that has made economic reform in China irreversible.

The logic of freeing farming first was powerful and would have been instinctively compelling in a country, still 80 percent rural, whose leadership had come to power thirty to forty years before on a tide of peasant discontent and many of whose top leaders (like Deng) were themselves of peasant background. The natural bent of these men was strengthened by their painful experience of Mao's Great Leap Backward and its lesson in the folly of collectivized agriculture.

The "household responsibility system" introduced in 1979 in essence abolished collective farming in China. Henceforth, each farming family was responsible for its own output (and income), on land that it at first borrowed and eventually was allowed to "lease" for fifteen or more years (i.e., in effect, to own). The share of crops that had to be handed over to the state distribution network gradually declined, as did the range of crops over whose prices the government exercised any control. Just as important, the government sharply raised the procurement price—at first by 22 percent—for the share of the harvest that had to be delivered to the state.

The results were breathtaking. For the next five years farm output rose by 8–10 percent a year, ending in a record grain harvest in 1984 of 407 million tons: a third bigger than the 1978 crop and one that remained unsurpassed until 1990. Peasants' net real incomes rose even faster. Between 1978 and 1984 they grew by almost 18 percent a year.

This meant that the real incomes of more than three-quarters of China's population—or of some 800 million people—were multiplied almost two and a half times in just six years, the fastest widespread increase in wealth ever. The lives of city dwellers, too, improved immediately (though much less dramatically) through the quality and variety of the diet available to them. They had to pay more, though government subsisides cushioned the transition, but their ample savings made this fairly painless.

Thus, in political terms, the constituency for reform in China was secured quickly, easily, and almost universally. The economic implications of the early reforms were at least as encouraging. Everybody realizes that if a country is to escape from poverty, its farms must generate a surplus of savings and people that can be used by the rising industries of the towns for their wealth-creating growth. The wrong method of generating rural surpluses—adopted by such diverse regimes as those of Stalin in the Soviet Union of the 1930s, the dictators of modern black Africa, who have ruined that continent, feudalist Latin American oligarchs, and India's woolly democratic socialists—is artificially to suppress farm prices and incomes and direct the surplus into industrial projects chosen by the government. Deng's initial reforms did the opposite. They put a lot of investment money into the hands of farmers, who began an industrial revolution of their own.

DOWN OFF THE FARM

China's attempts at industrial reform have never had the unalloyed success of the early farming reforms. In farming, China had the advantage over the Soviet Union and Eastern Europe of being less developed: Even communism had only temporarily ruffled the ancient structures of Chinese peasant life, and far more of the Chinese economy was accounted for by farming. For farming, there was a quick and cheap fix with a high payoff: Just liberate the peasants and they would do the rest.

For reasons that will be explained in more detail in the last section of this chapter, industrial reform has been a more daunting proposition. Industries had come to be owned and controlled almost entirely by the state; they have large capital assets, like factories and equipment, that cannot simply be subdivided among factory workers as plots of land were among peasants; they are concentrated in the politically sensitive cities; and doing anything radical with them would more immediately call into question the role of the Communist party. Even so, the Deng reforms launched a pincer movement against the state-owned industries that has made them jump. One arm of the pincers, described in the next section, is the foreign business influence let in by Deng's open-door policy. The other has been created by the stunning rise in China's non-state industries, especially those in the countryside.

Like much else in Chinese reform, the distinction between the state-owned and "private" sectors of industry is unclear. China has six levels of government, of which the top two are the central government and provincial governments. Firms owned by either of these governments are called state-owned. These firms—often behemoths in coal, steel, and other heavy industries—on average have records of productivity and profitability as dismal as any turned in by Soviet factories in their day. When Deng's reforms began in the late 1970s, China's state-owned firms accounted for about 80 percent of industrial output. Their output continued to increase in absolute terms throughout the 1980s, but the growth of non-state industries was so fast that by 1992 they produced more than the state-owned firms did. It is likely that by 2000 the non-state sector will account for upwards of two-thirds of China's industrial output; of China's total economy (agriculture has long been entirely out of the state's hands, as are many service businesses), the state-owned firms may well account for less than a fifth by 2000.

Yet the companies that are so quickly supplanting China's state-owned firms are not, for the most part, companies that a Westerner would easily recognize as "private." Thoroughly private firms do exist. China has "individual businesses" (family-owned firms employing no more than seven people) and "other enterprises": family firms with more than seven employees, foreign companies, and joint ventures (between a foreign and a Chinese firm or between a state-owned firm and a private one). Private firms' share of China's industrial output grew more than tenfold between 1980 and 1992, but in overall terms it still does not amount to much more than 10 percent.

The spectacular growth in China's non-state industry has come from elsewhere: from what the Chinese call "collectives." These include a form of ownership familiar (though insignificant) in the West: rural and urban cooperatives, which are controlled by their workers. But the biggest share of the credit for China's new industrial revolution can be claimed by another kind of collective. These are firms under the control of lower-level governments. In cities these firms are called district or neighborhood enterprises; in the countryside they are township and village enterprises, or TVEs. The city enterprises have done well enough, but the TVEs have succeeded beyond belief.

In 1980 the TVEs (or their predecessors, the old Maoist commune and brigade enterprises) amounted to some 1.5 million units, employing less than 30 million people and producing 10 percent of industrial output. By 1992 there were some 20 million TVEs, employing 100 million people (almost as many as the state-owned firms) and producing 27 percent of industrial output. During the first fifteen years of reform their output grew by 30 percent a year on average; their exports during the last half of the 1980s, by 65 percent a year. By the early 1990s, TVEs accounted for more than a quarter of China's exports (with another quarter coming from foreign-owned or foreign joint-venture firms). Rural China has been transformed. In 1978 farming represented 70 percent of rural output; by the mid-1990s farming contributed less to rural output than industry did.

The unprecedented industrial miracle created by the TVEs is little understood, and the bewildering variety of forms that these outfits take is no help to understanding. Some function in effect as partnerships; some local governments act as holding companies for the TVEs under their control; and in other places local bureaucrats take an active hand in managing them.

The TVE bestiary includes some very odd specimens. On a visit to rural Sichuan in 1993, I was taken to a TVE that specializes in making reinforcing bars for construction work. This was no humble work shed. Its managers said it had eighteen thousand employees and was the biggest TVE in the province. Its plants covered acres of ground. Two electric-arc blast furnaces were up and running, and a third had been ordered.

The enterprise had been set up in 1984 by its present head, who, when we met him, was a chubby and energetic forty-year-old. He had been exiled to Sichuan from the east coast during the Cultural Revolution, and after it was over he decided to stay on. He got the blessing of the township to set up a small metalworking shop with an initial capitalization of 20,000 yuan (about $2,350 at the 1994 rate of exchange) and twenty or so employees. Financed from its own cash flow and through bank and private loans, the firm had exploded in less than a decade to its present size and now was beginning to dabble in joint ventures: one, with a Hong Kong partner, for real-estate development; another, with a Singaporean partner, for making metal window frames.

We met several directors in the boardroom and asked: "Who owns this company?" The question, which provoked several minutes of lively debate among the directors, was obviously incomprehensible to them. We heard elaborate descriptions of who did what in the company and the role played by the township officials; but we never came close to an answer to the simple question about ownership. What seemed clear was that the founder called all the shots in the company and was by far the most powerful figure in the town. China is developing a class of entrepreneurs who would be instantly recognizable to American robber barons or Victorian mill owners—with the glaring difference that, with property rights over the TVEs as yet entirely undefined, there is for now no telling who would inherit the wealth or the direction of the enterprise.

The absence of enforceable property rights makes the outstanding performance of the TVEs even more inexplicable. Leaving that aside, however, the business conditions in which the TVEs have operated are what you would expect of firms that have shown themselves to be so efficient. They have been thrown entirely onto the market, especially the market for finance.

When the TVEs started growing fast, only 10 percent of retail sales of Chinese state-owned firms were at prices fixed by the market rather than by planners. The TVEs, by contrast, have always faced market prices for both their inputs and their products. Likewise, workers in the TVEs had none of the job security or lavish welfare benefits that state-owned firms provided to their counterparts. The TVEs have also had to operate in a cutthroat competitive environment in China, with no protection from other producers; much of their growth has anyway come from exports, where they have had to compete not just against each other and against China's subsidized state-owned enterprises but against the whole world. Last, and perhaps most significant, the TVEs have been financed at market, instead of subsidized, rates of interest. This has forced them into a continuous cost-cutting search for the best ways to invest and produce.

In the end, the TVEs may prove to have been only a curious transitional arrangement for Chinese industry on its way to a market economy. There are signs (see chapter 7) that the bureaucratic control which in the early days of the TVEs' growth did not harm them may now be hampering their evolution toward big capital-intensive firms. In any event they are facing a rising challenge from China's pure-blooded private sector. Although private firms in total still account for only a third as much industrial output as the TVEs, for the past decade they have easily outstripped the already amazing growth rates of their rural cousins. Foreign investors in China have a lot to do with this.

THE BRACING WIND THROUGH THE OPEN DOOR

Early in 1979, Deng Xiaoping paid a visit to the United States, the first by a top Chinese leader since the founding of Communist China thirty years before. Despite his blunt warning to President Jimmy Carter that the Soviet Union was a "hotbed of war" and that this was no time for America to let down its guard—a message Mr. Carter's pro-detente administration was disinclined to believe—the visit was generally considered a success. It confirmed China as the first Communist country that America could do business with (both figuratively and literally). Yet it did not seem a particularly weighty visit to Americans. The only thing to stick in anyone's mind was the hilarious image of the diminutive Deng wearing (or rather being overwhelmed from above by) a ten-gallon hat while he was attending a rodeo in Houston.

In China the effect of Deng's trip was both profound and electrifying. The overwhelming majority of Chinese had lived for at least a couple of decades with almost no unfiltered word of what went on beyond China's borders; and until President Nixon's trip to China in 1972, America had figured high in the mainland's official demonology. Yet there was China's supreme leader, shown repeatedly on Chinese television and described thoroughly in Chinese newspapers, being best of pals with the United States and doing so against a backdrop of American wealth of a scale and breadth that must have amazed any Chinese who was following the story.

Deng had ordered that his trip be painstakingly covered by Chinese television. In one segment he was being shown around a Ford factory in Atlanta by the company's chairman. On Chinese television the announcer was explaining how much the average worker at this Ford plant was paid: more than fifty times a Chinese car worker's salary. Singapore's Lee Kuan Yew thinks this was deliberate: So shocking a fact, launched from the "evil seat of iniquity" by China's supreme leader, was Deng's dramatic first shot in a campaign to open Chinese minds so wide to the outside world that the country could never be closed again.

The reaching out that followed was in many ways even bolder than the farming reforms, though the opening up of China did not deliver nearly so swift and sharp a whack to the economy. It was a rejection of one of the main propositions of Chinese policymaking for hundreds of years (or roughly since China started going downhill): that China was the center of the world and had nothing to learn from barbarians. It was also a rejection of Mao's (and communism's) creed of self-sufficiency; China would now ally firmly with its East Asian neighbors in believing that outward-oriented trade and investment policies were the surest spur to economic development.

When the foreign-trade reforms began after 1978, China's economy was one of the world's most isolated, with a tiny share of world trade; commodities, especially oil, accounted for most of its exports. Foreign trade and foreign exchange were under the monopolistic control of a central-government ministry, which used the overvalued currency to support the import-substitution policies of the central plan. The inflow of foreign direct investment was less than $300 million a year.

Since then the nominal dollar value of China's foreign trade has grown by 16 percent a year (see table 5 on page 134). In 1992, China became the world's tenth-biggest exporter, behind only advanced industrial economies. Its share of world exports that year was about 2.5 percent, almost three times its share in 1978 (which means that China's trade was growing three times faster than world trade as a whole); and 80 percent of those exports were manufactured goods (rather than commodities like oil or grain), more than twice the share in 1978.

Over the same years China was flooded with foreign direct investment (FDI). The amount that foreigners were investing each year in Chinese factories, land, and so on rose gradually from hundreds of millions of dollars in the late 1970s and early 1980s to $1–$2 billion in the mid-1980s and $3–$4 billion in the late 1980s and early 1990s. Then came the explosion: $11 billion of FDI in 1992, $28 billion in 1993, and $34 billion in 1994, vastly inflated figures no doubt (because much of the FDI was in fact mainland money

TABLE 5
CHINA'S FOREIGN TRADE, 1978–94

	Total Exports*	% Change Year on Year	Total Imports*	% Change Year on Year	Trade Balance*	Total Trade*	% of World Trade	Foreign Direct Investment*
1978	10.0	20.0	10.2	41.1	−0.3	20.2	0.9	
1979	13.6	26.3	14.3	29.6	−0.7	27.9		
1980	18.1	28.1	18.3	23.0	−0.2	36.4	0.9	
1981	21.6	35.5	19.6	23.1	1.8	41.3		
1982	21.1	12.8	17.3	−12.3	3.8	38.5		
1983	20.7	−2.0	19.6	12.0	1.1	40.3		0.9
1984	23.9	15.4	24.3	24.1	−0.4	46.2		1.4
1985	25.1	5.0	39.4	62.0	−14.2	84.5	0.9	2.0
1986	25.8	2.6	39.8	1.2	−14.1	65.6		2.2
1987	34.7	34.9	39.8	0.0	−5.1	74.5		2.8
1988	41.1	18.2	46.4	16.5	−5.3	87.4		3.7
1989	43.2	5.3	48.8	5.3	−5.6	92.1		3.8
1990	51.5	19.2	42.4	−13.3	9.2	93.9	1.6	3.8
1991	58.9	14.4	50.2	18.5	8.7	109.1		4.7
1992	69.6	18.1	64.4	28.3	5.2	134.0	2.2	11.3
1993	75.7	6.8	86.3	34.1	−10.7	162.0	2.5 (a)	25.8
1994	119.8	58.2	105.1	21.8	14.7	224.9		34.0

* (Billions of U.S. Dollars)

NOTE (a) Estimated. Data from 1978–81 are from Department of Trade; otherwise from BOP.
SOURCE: State Statistical Bureau, *Chinese Statistical Abstract 1993*, 101; New China News Agency, *People's Daily*, 10 January 1994, "China Foreign Trade Increases to Reach $195.7 Billion"; *China Daily Business Weekly*, 3 January 1994, "China to Slow Down GDP Growth" and IMF, *International Financial Statistics* (*Year Book* and June 1995).

that had been recycled abroad for tax reasons) but still by far the highest for any poor country. How did China get its foreign trade and investment to grow so fast?

SOUTHERN BELLE

China's foreign-trade reforms followed the experimental, gradualist, and regional pattern of its other economic reforms. In 1980 the government designated four "special economic zones" (SEZs) on China's southern coast: three in Guangdong Province, next to Hong Kong; and one in Fujian Province, across the strait from Taiwan. These laboratories had the advantages of being isolated from much of the rest of the country (in case things went badly wrong) and linked by ties of blood and geography to the two greatest concentrations of overseas Chinese business experience and wealth (see chapter 10). Foreign companies investing in the SEZs were given tax privileges, exemption from many of the laws and regulations that stifled industries elsewhere in urban China, and the right to keep much of the hard-currency earnings they generated.

In Guangdong—or more precisely in the Pearl River delta of southern Guangdong, in and around the province's three SEZs—yet another economic miracle followed. Guangdong as a whole grew very fast (its real GDP growth in the fifteen years after 1978 averaged 13 percent a year), but not significantly faster than the provinces of Fujian and Shandong (both of which also had a lot of foreign investment) or even Jiangsu or Zhejiang (whose fast growth depended much more on their rich mix of TVEs). During the 1980s the economy of much of the Pearl River delta was growing at an average annual rate of 20 percent. The SEZs themselves grew by more than 30 percent a year, a rate that doubles an economy's size in less than three years and multiplies it eight-and-a-half-fold in eight years. Shenzhen, the biggest of the Guangdong SEZs and the one that abuts Hong Kong, was mostly farmland in 1978; by the mid-1990s it was an industrial city of 3–4 million, in appearance almost indistinguishable from northern Hong Kong and with the highest incomes in China.

Hong Kong, indeed, did for Guangdong exactly what Deng had hoped when he launched the SEZ experiment. Even today, most Hong Kongers are no more than two generations removed from China, and the vast bulk of their immigrant forebears were Cantonese speakers from Guangdong whose ties with the province had been suspended, not severed, by the closed-door policy of Maoist China. When, after 1978, it became possible to restore those ties, Hong Kong's commercially acute businessmen wasted no time in taking advantage of the cheap labor (Guangdong's wage rates during the 1980s were about a tenth those of Hong Kong) and cheap land to be found just across the border. Within fifteen years virtually the whole of Hong Kong's manufacturing employment had been shifted north of the border—the conventional guess is that, by 1993, Hong Kong businesses employed 3 million factory workers in Guangdong—leaving the British colony's economy the most service-intensive on earth. And in the early 1990s Hong Kong's low-level service jobs began following in the footsteps of the factory jobs as banks, airlines, and other big service companies moved clerical jobs to Guangdong.

Foreign trade and investment have been the main engine of Guangdong's growth. In the fifteen years after 1978 the nominal value of Guangdong's exports grew by almost 30 percent a year, half again as high a rate as for China as a whole, and in 1990 Guangdong accounted for almost a fifth of China's total exports. During the 1980s almost two-fifths of Guangdong's economic growth was accounted for by the growth of its exports; that is twice the share for China as a whole. Guangdong also claims the lion's share of foreign direct investment in China: in 1991 the province got almost 70 percent of the foreign investment made in all of China by Hong Kong and Macau and more than 40 percent of all foreign investment made in China that year. Guangdong's economy and society have been revolutionized. By the early 1990s fully private businesses in Guangdong had more capital than state-owned and collective (including TVE) businesses put together. And by the mid-1990s the upgrading of Guangdong's skills had reached the point where Hong Kong companies in such customer-sensitive businesses as hotels felt able to start replacing Hong Kong managers in Guangdong with local ones.

Unsurprisingly, the SEZ experiment was extended to other parts of China. In 1984, fourteen cities were made "open coastal cities." In 1988, Guangdong was made a "comprehensive reform experiment zone," which gave it an official nod and wink to become a market economy in all but name. The same year, the whole of Hainan island in the South China Sea was made an SEZ. But by the early 1990s the official process of opening up seemed all too slow. Hundreds of local governments began setting up their own foreign-investment zones, modeled on the SEZs; they evaded censure from higher authorities by using such transparent ruses as not calling their zones "zones." Bowing to reality, the central government in 1992 extended versions of pro-foreign-business regimes to every provincial capital, to thirteen cities along China's land borders, and to ten cities along the Yangzi River (where six huge development zones were also set up). By the mid-1990s the main challenge for the government was to find the places on the map that were not "special." The best course, though it had not yet been taken as of 1995, would be to apply a single trade and investment regime to the whole country.

Of course, not all of China can be transformed by foreign trade and investment with the speed and comprehensiveness that Guang-dong was. But the influence of foreign business has been spreading relentlessly. Until the early 1990s by far the largest share of this investment, around three-quarters, came from Hong Kong and Tai-wan. Although very welcome, this first wave of foreign investment had one weakness. The Chinese businessmen of Hong Kong and Southeast Asia, and to a lesser degree those of Taiwan, are traders by nature; they see an opening and grab it without much thought for either strategy or the long term. Or, as one observer has re-marked, a long-term investment for a Hong Kong businessman is one that has not turned a profit within twenty minutes.

In the early days of China's reawakening, that was fine; if the country is to develop continuously over decades, it will not be. China needs technology transfer, the upgrading of skills, instruction in modern management, and vast quantities of capital. These things can come only from investors who are willing to dig in for the long haul.

IN FOR THE DURATION

Such people have never been entirely absent in reformist China. Babcock & Wilcox, for example, a Canadian engineering company, has had a joint venture in Beijing since 1986 making utility and industrial boilers. This is not a small venture; the one plant now builds more utility boilers each year than are made in the entire United States. As the years have gone by, the quality of the Chinese engineers and managers has risen quickly. The venture's two hun-dred Chinese engineers, all university graduates, are qualified to the standards of the American Society of Mechanical Engineers; by 1994 they had attained what an expatriate manager calls "the low end of world standards"—a lot more competent than they had been five years before. More and more of the design work is being done not at the company's boilermaker headquarters in Ohio but in Beijing. The expatriate manager says that by 1994 the Beijing plant's labor productivity was around one-third of North American levels (though with far less capital for each worker than in North America). The Chinese engineers were costing no more than $100 a month, com-pared with a top wage cost for an engineer in America of $2,500 a month.

This sort of long-term foreign investment is growing fast. One

sign is the sharp rise in Japanese and South Korean investment in
1993–94. Another is the recent entry into China of a new breed of
overseas Chinese investor, of whom one of the most thoughtful
examples is Hong Kong's Ronnie Chan.

Mr. Chan, who runs a big property-development company called
Hang Lung that is listed on the Hong Kong stock market, also
runs private direct investments through an unlisted company called
Morningside. He began investing seriously in China only in 1992,
after he had decided that the reforms were "pervasive and irreversible." Most Hong Kong Chinese, he says, "just use their nose" when
investing in China. His view is that the same sort of business analysis
used to sift investment opportunities in Europe and America must
be applied in China. China has to be approached systematically
because "it is a vast place, with vast resources and tremendous
opportunities—like North America at the turn of the 20th
century."

Mr. Chan looks for investments in businesses that have a chance
of lasting for twenty-five to thirty years. So he does not count on the
continuation of China's present high tariffs when he evaluates a
business. He avoids labor-intensive companies because labor does
not remain cheap for long. He also stays away from high-tech industries (because China is not really going to have high technology for
another generation) and from anything with short product cycles,
such as consumer goods. He looks at a business's competitiveness
in both home and export markets. He likes "small stuff in small
places."

Which, in fact, is often not so small after all. Mr. Chan's projects
tend to be largish medium-tech capital-equipment and intermedi-
ate-goods industries. One example is printing presses, which in the
mid-1990s could be produced in China at 20–30 percent of the cost
in the West but with almost the same quality. Another example is
high-quality paper, a market that has been growing by 25 percent a
year and in which China's costs are about 60 percent of those of the
rest of the world. Interestingly, Mr. Chan's investments have so far
been entirely in state-owned firms because they have better technology, more capital assets, and more of a management structure than
TVEs.

In terms of staffing, Mr. Chan does not believe in using many
foreigners for operations in the mainland. In 1994 he had only two
(one a Taiwanese, the other an American of Chinese descent who is

fluent in Mandarin and Shanghainese). The locals understand the market, the way business is done in China, and (no small matter) Chinese accounting practices.

Yet these remarks of Mr. Chan's point to the single biggest problem for foreign investors in China (and indeed the single biggest problem in general for China's future): the country's pervasive institutional weakness. One longtime observer of foreign businesses in China notes that, while it is fine to use local staff in mainland operations, the managers at the top have to be expatriates: The mainland workforce has not yet developed the habits or learned the practices of modern management. And the fact that only locals are able to penetrate the organization and fathom the accounts of Chinese companies merely confirms how opaque and arbitrary are the methods with which these firms are run. Until that changes, China is not going to attract the best that the most advanced companies of the rich world have to offer.

CHAPTER 7

...AND CHINA'S PROBLEMS

Crossing the river by feeling the stones has carried China amazingly far—to just about the point where the current is at its swiftest and most treacherous. If China is now about to be thrown off balance, the trouble is likely to come from one or more of three places. The first is the state-owned firms, which the government still shies away from reforming outright. The second danger is macroeconomic instability, the risk that inflation will get out of hand. The third is social breakdown and political instability.

They are all connected, in the sense that each has a direct influence on the others and, more significantly, because they all grow out of the same weakness in China's reforms: their failure to begin building the institutions needed to control and regulate a modern society.

By the mid-1990s China was roughly halfway through a process of reform-by-competition: competition among Chinese firms (state-owned, township and village enterprises—TVEs—and foreign-funded ventures), between these firms and their rivals on world markets, between regions, between the various arms of the central government and the Communist party, and between different tiers of government. The speed and willy-nilly quality of this dash for market has done China a world of good. It has created a fair amount of economic and personal freedom, whereas before there was very little; it has sharply raised the efficiency of Chinese firms and of the Chinese economy, and it has enormously increased the material well-being of the average Chinese.

In the process, however, the old methods of social and economic control have become enfeebled a lot faster than modern methods have grown up to take their place. On a visit to China in 1993, Milton Friedman remarked that China had "both too much government and too little": too much of the useless or harmful stuff from the command-economy past; and too little of the new (the rule of law and modern tools of fiscal and monetary management) to prevent the country's competitive exuberance from destroying China through disorder. The danger is at its greatest while the reformed and unreformed parts of the Chinese economy are of about the same size, as they will be for the rest of this decade and maybe for a few years into the new century. My guess is that China will succeed, though not without some hair-raising crises and reversals before it does.

DANCES WITH DINOSAURS

China's state-owned firms still tower over the industrial landscape. With perhaps 110 million workers by the mid-1990s (less than the employment accounted for by the non-state industrial firms) and less than half of industrial output, they are not the overwhelming presence they were when the reforms began. Yet the state firms still hog perhaps three-quarters of industrial assets and a vast majority of China's technological skills and dominate political calculations in the most sensitive parts of urban China. They also are the worm at the core of China's macroeconomic management.

Chinese state-owned firms were created in the 1950s and copied lock, stock, and barrel from their Soviet models. Such firms everywhere have tended to be among the worst industrial enterprises ever formed. In the Soviet bloc, just before communism's collapse there, the stage had been reached where a fair chunk of industry was producing not goods but bads, meaning that the raw materials entering the factory gate were actually worth more than the finished products coming out the other end. This is why industrial production in the ex–Soviet Union collapsed so precipitously when communism suddenly fell.

Things in China's state sector are not as bad, but they are still pretty awful. The reasons why state-owned firms in Communist countries perform so appallingly (as they do in most places; see chapter 8, on India) have been best described by Janos Kornai, a Hungarian-born economist at Harvard. State-owned firms are geared to the bureaucrats who give them orders rather than to the customers who buy from them, to output rather than profit, to the social welfare of their employees rather than to efficiency. Market signals become even more muffled because the "soft budget constraint" given to a firm by the state banking system ensures that loss makers, no matter how hopeless, continue to be financed so that jobs are not jeopardized. Lacking profitability as a guide to the right levels of investment and output, state-owned firms feel an insatiable "investment hunger."

China's state enterprises have acted largely according to script. Throughout the 1980s, when the economy was exploding with growth, the losses of the state-owned firms rose. Nor, during the first fifteen years of reform, were the welfare functions of state firms much cut away. The firms' workers still expect the "plantation" (the word is actually used) to provide them and their families with housing, education, and health care.

In the recovery of 1992–94 from the downturn of 1989–91, the output of state firms grew more slowly than that of the economy as a whole and far more slowly than that of the non-state sector. In 1992 alone, when the economy grew by 13 percent the government officially admitted that a third of state enterprises were in the red; the true share may have been twice that. One estimate, reported by Harry Broadman of the World Bank, is that in 1992 the losses of state firms were equal to a stunning 3 percent of GDP. Meanwhile, during the robust recovery of 1992–93 the state firms were increasing their inventories (meaning they were producing goods that nobody wanted even though demand in the economy was rising fast) as well as their credit demands on each other, on the state banks, and on the government budget. The single biggest contributor to the inflation that menacingly plagued China in 1993–94 was excess capital investment, almost entirely accounted for by state firms.

STRAWS OF HOPE

China is attempting to handle reform of the state firms with the same gradual approach that it has used to such good effect elsewhere in the economy. A bankruptcy law was enacted in 1986 and by the early 1990s was starting to be used (though very sparingly). "Corporatization"—separating the directors and managers of state firms from the bureaucrats who control them—is being tried out. So, too, and more promisingly, is part-privatization, through share flotations on China's own stock markets or foreign ones (especially those in Hong Kong and New York).

All this has done a lot more good than it seems at first glance. For one thing, the losses of the state sector are concentrated in a few industries and regions. Thomas Rawski, an economist at the University of Pittsburgh, has calculated that in 1989 almost 40 percent of state-firm losses were accounted for by two industries, coal and oil. The reason was simple: The government was ordering them to sell their output at prices well below cost. Another 11 percent of the losses in 1989 came from the defense industry. Overall, says the IMF, in the early 1990s as much as 70 percent of state-firm losses each year were "policy-induced," meaning that they were caused by government interference (such as price controls) rather than the state firms' own failings.

Indeed, scattered evidence from the late 1980s and early 1990s suggests that, despite the artificial government-imposed burdens they bear, many state firms have responded in the same way as other parts of the economy to the sharp spur of competition from the TVEs and foreign trade and investment: They have become more efficient. In pre-Deng China the productivity of the state firms was nil or often negative, just like that of their Soviet counterparts. As the reforms gathered speed, however, the total factor productivity (TFP) of state firms began rising. During the 1980s, Mr. Rawski calculates, TFP growth averaged almost 2.5 percent a year—less than half the rate of the non-state firms but still a sharp improvement on the earlier performance of the state firms.

Other signs point to a decline in monopoly power and an equalization of returns across regions, industries, and companies. Barry Naughton, an economist at the University of California at San Diego, has calculated that profitability in state and non-state firms alike has declined as their productivity has risen. Returns in the state and non-state sector have been converging. And the range of profit rates across industries also has been narrowing: from 7–98 percent in 1980 to 8–23 percent in 1989. All of this means that the state firms, too, have been infected by China's general improvement in economic efficiency.

Behind this change in the market behavior of the state firms lies a quiet shift in the incentives that the system gives to the firms and their managers. In pre-1978 China, as in Eastern Europe and the Soviet Union, there was no reason whatever for state firms to increase their profits. Increased profits did not lead to a rise in the retained earnings of the firm. The government simply helped itself to the extra income, leaving the firm with nothing to show for its extra effort.

As the government's direct control over state-firm finances weakened during the 1980s, the incentives changed. More and more, a rise in profits led to a rise in retained earnings. The workers would have been in favor of profit-seeking, since the era of Maoist wage equality had given way to bonus-linked pay, and bonuses rose almost in lockstep with retained earnings. But what reason was there for state-firm managers to look to the market rather than to bureaucrats for their orders?

The bad reason is that, as government supervision of the state firms declined, the firms' managers had many more opportunities for looting the earnings of the firms for their own personal Hong Kong or Hainan bank accounts and letting the state make good any resulting "losses." The more encouraging reason is that the government seems consciously to have been pushing state-firm managers to tie their own interests to the firm's market performance.

An intriguing survey of eight hundred state-owned firms by Mr. Naughton and some of his colleagues found that the ministries supervising the firms had begun to evaluate and reward their managers on commercial rather than political grounds. Top managers had to sign management contracts specifying performance targets; they were often required to post a hefty performance bond, averaging half a year's salary. Their pay was positively linked to growth in sales and profits. Towards the end of the 1980s the government increasingly began to auction top managerial positions. Bidders were allowed to take a look at the firm's accounts. The bids were judged on how much profit they promised to hand over to the supervising ministry, their business plan, how much of retained earnings they agreed to reinvest in the firm, and so on.

The government has also begun experimenting with measures to deal with the most sensitive by-product of any substantial rationalization of the state firms: the effect on the workforce. A conservative estimate is that a "mere" 20 percent of the state firms' workers—or 20 million–plus people—are surplus to the firms' business needs. Even if they could be smoothly reabsorbed into other jobs (which is improbable, since they will be the worst of a generally slack workforce and will be competing with the millions of rural migrants already pouring into China's cities), another complication would have to be taken care of. Recall that the state firms are as much welfare societies for their workers as they are business enterprises. Being thrown out of work means not just losing your job; it may also mean losing your family's apartment and health care, your child's schooling and your pension.

The government's hope is that the reabsorption problem can be made manageable by the growth of service businesses in the cities. Services were artificially suppressed in Mao's day (only manufacturing was considered "real"), so there is plenty of scope for them, and employment in them, to grow. Thus far, this conversion has generally taken the form of a de facto privatization of service businesses attached to the industrial enterprise; surplus factory hands are prodded to take over, say, a restaurant previously owned by the factory and run it on commercial lines.

A few stabs have also been made at trying to separate social security from the operations of the state firms. In 1992 the government began putting workers on labor contracts that spelled out their duties and benefits; instead of being, in effect, a permanent "citizen" of the firm, a worker became a contract employee subject to discipline and even dismissal. The government set up unemployment insurance and job-retraining schemes to make factory closures something that could be contemplated (in theory, anyway); it claimed that by the end of 1993, 79 million workers were covered by unemployment insurance. Retirement funds to pay for pensions have been set up in most cities by municipal governments (notably in Shanghai, where contributions equal to 5 percent of a worker's wage are paid by both the firm and the worker) and by twelve provincial governments. And attempts to create a housing market

have begun with sharp increases in rents and the establishment in
some cities of housing-finance funds.

These are promising beginnings, but they are no more than that.
By every measure—productivity, profitability, return on assets—China's state firms remain on average vastly inferior to the non-state
firms. Yet for better or worse the Chinese government has little
stomach for tackling the economic problem of the state firms
head-on (i.e., through quick and widespread privatization); the political and social risks seem too great. One Chinese economist who
was a top government adviser during the strongly reformist years of
the late 1980s says that the leadership has committed itself to a
policy of "peaceful coexistence": of state firms with non-state ones;
and of the small and medium-size state firms that can be successfully
reformed with the medium and large ones—numbering perhaps no
more than a thousand of the hundred thousand state firms in existence in 1995—that will always remain a public burden but will
never be put to death.

Optimists can point to the modernization of Taiwan's economy
as proof that such an approach can work. Lawrence Lau, an economist at Stanford, says that in 1952 around 55 percent of Taiwan's
value-added in manufacturing and 90 percent of industrial assets
were accounted for by state-owned firms. By the early 1990s, Taiwan's state firms owned only 20 percent of industrial assets and
accounted for only 10 percent of manufactured exports. Taiwan
accomplished this transformation with virtually no privatization and
little shock to the economy; it simply allowed the non-state firms
gradually to surround and engulf the state sector by growing faster.
That might be feasible in China, too, except for one thing: By the
mid-1990s industrial efficiency was improving much more slowly
than a crisis of macroeconomic instability seemed to be building.
Unless China regains its macroeconomic balance, time is in danger
of running out for its policy of industrial gradualism.

In the Balance

Ever since the reforms began, China has been prey to economic
cycles of growing severity. Nothing new about that. Japan suffered
from the same stop-go syndrome in the 1950s and 1960s, when its
powerful economy was being built on fast growth and highish inflation. The difference is that Japan maintained fairly strict macroeco-

nomic disciplines—low budget deficits and tight money and credit —during its stop-go era; China started out that way in 1978, but it has become more lax ever since. It is unclear how long China's savers will continue to bail out the government.

There has been a common pattern, pointed out by the IMF, in each of the four economic cycles that reformist China has been through up until the mid-1990s. (A fifth is likely to start in 1996.) Each of the cycles began (in 1979, 1984, 1986, and 1991, respectively) with a burst of economic reform that led to a jump in economic activity, especially industrial investment; to an expansion in money supply and credit to support the increased demand; then to eventual shortages in the supply of inputs such as raw materials; and lastly to a financial crisis of rising prices or dwindling foreign-exchange reserves (often both), which the government at last extinguished by crashing the economy through high interest rates, credit quotas, and administrative orders forbidding excessive capital investment by state-owned firms. The fire-dousing phase has usually been accompanied by a partial reversal of economic reforms and an invigoration of the political conservatives in the leadership. (It is in such a phase that the Tiananmen Square demonstrations and then crackdown took place in 1989.)

These wild swings in economic performance are undesirable, but they would be tolerable if each successive cycle were not at its top bringing China into a more precarious state of financial imbalance. Table 6 shows that there has been a relentless rise in the Chinese

TABLE 6

COMPONENTS OF CHINA'S CONSOLIDATED GOVERNMENT DEFICIT
1987–93

Components of the deficit (as % of GDP)	1987	1988	1989	1990	1991	1992	1993
Budget deficit*	2.2	2.4	2.3	2.1	2.4	2.5	2.1
PBC lending to banks for policy loans	1.3	4.0	4.2	4.3	3.3	3.3	6.8
Consolidated government deficit	3.5	6.4	6.5	6.3	5.7	5.8	8.9

NOTE* This is the deficit of government at all levels calculated according to IMF rather than Chinese standards.
SOURCE: The World Bank, China: Country Economic Memorandum, "Macroeconomic Stability in a Decentralized Economy" (October 26, 1994).

government's budget deficit since the reforms began. The "real" deficit—meaning what has to be financed through the government's printing presses or through borrowing—rose in 1993 to some 9 percent of GDP. (The American government deficit that so exercised many people in the 1980s and 1990s was in the range of 2–4 percent of GNP.) Even an economy churning out the growth rates China's does eventually has a reckoning when government finances deteriorate as much as this.

A lot of China's trouble is the inevitable result of its ongoing escape from commmunism. Communist governments finance themselves not so much by collecting taxes as by helping themselves to the profits of the industrial firms that they own. In a full-fledged Communist system, these profits are plump: The prices of inputs like raw materials and farm goods are kept low, and the prices of finished industrial goods are set high. The profits go into blocked accounts in the state banking system to which only the government has access.

As reform gets under way, this comfortable fiscal arrangement collapses. In China's case, the early radical farm reforms reversed the cheap provision of farm produce to the cities; to forestall any political trouble in the cities as a result, the government filled the breach with costly subsidies to urban consumers. Then, with the unanticipated rise of the TVEs and the carefully planned price reforms for state-owned industrial firms, the profits of the state firms disappeared: first, because the blast of competition reduced the profit margins of all industrial firms, whoever owned them; and second, because artificial price protection for the state-owned firms was gradually being lifted. Government revenues dwindled alongside state-firm profits. In the late 1970s, all the levels of China's government together had revenues equal to some 35 percent of GNP; by the early 1990s that had shrunk to 16 percent.

These statistics, like most in China, are slippery. As the 1990s wore on, governments in China extracted an increasing share of their revenues "off-budget"—that is, not through the normal fiscal system but, for example, through new businesses they went into. Nonetheless, the finances of China's central government also took a blow from the rising power of China's provincial and local governments.

In the pre-reform days, provincial and local authorities collected government revenue and sent it all to the central government in Beijing. The center then handed back a share of it to the provinces in accordance with the investment and other goals set forth in the national economic plan. Beginning in 1980, various forms of revenue sharing between the central and local governments were introduced. In theory, the sums collected locally were to be divided into three piles: local, central, and shared, with (at first) 80 percent of the shared pile going to the central government. In practice, this quickly became an almost medieval system of tax farming in which the revenue-raising power of the state was turned over to local barons who haggled endlessly with their putative lords in Beijing over just how much of the money they were willing to hand on. (The same happened at the other end of the scale, too, with yearly bargains being struck between enterprises and revenue collectors over how much the firms would have to shell out to satisfy the local government.)

By the late 1980s a "fiscal contract system" was in place that provided for six different kinds of revenue sharing and, in general, a more generous deal for the localities. Unsurprisingly, this arrangement proved no more stable than any of its predecessors. When, in 1990, after three years of experimenting with fiscal contracts, the central government tried to rationalize their operation, it met with such fierce resistance from the provinces that it has had to limp on ever since with the "experimental" regime. By the early 1990s locally collected tax revenue had declined to about 15 percent as a share of GNP, compared with 27 percent in 1979; and of that 15 percent only a third went to the central government.

BANKING ON TROUBLE

Along with the erosion of the government's fiscal position during the 1980s and early 1990s came a parallel decline in the health of the financial system. Part of this was visible on the government's own books: With budgetary revenues lower than spending, as they have been every year of the reform period, the government has to make up the shortfall either by printing money, borrowing it (e.g., through issuing bonds), or both. The larger share of the financing gap has been disguised by the government shoving it onto the books of the state banking system.

Recall that in pre-reform days the financial surplus generated by state-owned firms flowed into bank accounts that the government then helped itself to. The reverse has occurred in the reform era. As the state firms have gone into the red, they have responded financially in two ways. The first is not to pay their suppliers (usually other state-owned firms); this creates a cascade of defaults among state firms. These "triangular debts"—which, by early 1995, had reached some $70 billion—have to be settled somehow, either directly by the government taking them off the enterprises' hands or indirectly through bank loans. And bank borrowing is in any event the second (and more significant) way by which state firms cover their losses.

Before 1978, China had only one bank, the People's Bank of China (PBOC), which acted as nothing more than the government's cashier. Gradual reforms of the banking system went some way towards turning the PBOC into a simulacrum of a central bank, with responsibility for money supply and interbank lending. Four "specialized" banks were created for agricultural, construction, and industrial and commercial lending, and to handle foreign-exchange and international business. So, too, arose "comprehensive" banks (which tend to operate the way Western banks do) and "non-bank financial institutions," which are even more free of regulation.

Yet the vast bulk of bank assets are under the control of state-owned banks that dance to the tune of government policy, or rather to the tunes, because as you would expect in decentralizing China, several different levels of government have their own ideas about what the banks should be doing. Look, for example, at the PBOC itself. In 1979 this bank had 300,000 employees and 15,000 branches; after vigorous slimming, it now has some 130,000 employees and more than 2,000 branches. Each branch often has a couple of competing sets of masters: its formal superiors at PBOC headquarters in Beijing and the local party and government bosses. Even a direct order from Beijing (to reduce lending, say) will often be evaded or quietly countermanded by local officials who want to keep the financial taps open.

Besides, the center's own signals frequently conflict. A significant share of the specialized banks' lending is made for reasons of "policy," not sound credit risk. Among other government "policies" is one which holds, in effect, that no state firm will be deprived of credit if this would make the firm go bust and throw its workers onto the street. So the losses of state-owned firms usually are financed by bank loans for working capital. Nobody knows the exact figure, but finance ministry officials in Beijing guess that by the mid-1990s some 20–30 percent of bank loans to state-owned firms were bad. This is the "soft budget constraint" in action: in industrial terms, no pressure on the state firms to mend their ways; in financial terms, a growing pile of debt either directly on the government's books or, in lightly veiled form, on the books of the government-owned banks.

With the government's real deficit having now reached almost 10 percent of GNP, the question is why China has not long since suffered a financial catastrophe (probably hyperinflation). The answer lies in a characteristically Chinese piece of practicality. As soon as the farm reforms began in 1979, the farmers were thrown almost entirely onto the market: Farm prices were brought up to market levels, but farmers had to pay for their own investment capital, which for the most part was not made available at subsidized rates through the state banking system. Faced with this hard-budget constraint, the farmers quickly improved their productivity and began to save money for future investment out of their cash flow by depositing it in state banks. The same pattern was repeated beginning in the mid-1980s by the TVEs and by other firms and individuals without access to cheap government-bank credit. There was an extraordinary rise in the relative amount of money in the economy: Broad money (cash and bank deposits) as a share of China's GNP leaped from just over a quarter in 1978 to more than 100 percent by the early 1990s. This "financial deepening" produced by the savings of China's superefficient non-state sector rescued the government from the potentially disastrous consequences of its own profligacy.

The practicality lay in the government's realization that, if people were to keep their assets in a form that the government could get its hands on (mainly in bank accounts but also in state bonds), they could not for the most part be forced to but had to be induced to through positive real interest rates. So, guided by the market, the government has shown no hesitation about raising deposit interest rates to whatever level required to attract savings. In times of high inflation (such as 1988–89 and 1994–95) the government indexed deposit rates to counteract the discouraging effect of price rises on would-be savers.

Yet this market-based fix, however sensible, cannot work indefinitely. There is a cumulative cost in economic inefficiency: The more money the government pours down the state-enterprise ratholes or allows to be diverted to speculative investments in real estate and the like by local governments, the more starved are the projects such as roads, ports, railways, and schools that China needs to sustain its growth (and to ease the bottlenecks that themselves add to inflation). The more worrying limit on the use of private savings to finance public waste is that sooner or later people stop wanting to hold any more money in the bank unless the interest paid on it becomes fabulously high; they would rather have motorbikes, cars, gold, anything but a bigger bank account.

This limit may be a lot closer than Chinese officials think. By the mid-1990s the ratio of China's broad money supply to the size of its economy was around 105 percent. In 1990 in Japan, which has a vastly richer and more mature economy than China, the ratio was not all that much bigger: only about 125 percent. And when people decline to deposit any more money in banks—whether because they are afraid future inflation will eat it up or because they just have enough cash, thank you—the switch out of deposits can happen very quickly. If China has not by then made a good start on getting its public finances under control, it could suddenly face a financial crisis of huge dimensions.

It seemed in late 1993 and early 1994 that this point had not been lost on the government. A big Communist party Central Committee meeting in November 1993 produced an economic-reform document perhaps unique in the annals of bombastic Communist writing. It set out in plain language, and without rhetorical bows to the usual gallery of stale ideological idols, a plan for corporatizing the state firms, subjecting them to market disciplines, and slowly privatizing them; a fiscal reform to rid China of its patchwork of taxes and foreign-investment regulations and to ensure a steadier source of revenue for the central and local governments; and a reform of the banking system to make the PBOC a true central bank and to separate "policy" from commercial lending in the other banks. In January 1994, China's different foreign-exchange rates were unified (with a view eventually to making the yuan fully convertible into other currencies), and a value-added tax was introduced to rationalize the tax system. These measures amounted to at least a good start in the gigantic task of reforming and modernizing China's fiscal and financial systems.

Yet it was not a good time, either politically or in terms of the business cycle, to follow through on radical reform. Throughout 1994 execution of the fiscal reforms was patchy, and macroeco-

nomic policy zigzagged every few months. At last, towards the end
of 1994, a consistent squeeze was put on the economy; and by mid-
1995 the signs that the economy was sharply slowing were unmistakable. China seemed to have achieved a correction of its economic
overheating without a crash on the order of the one that took place
in 1988–89. Yet against the background of the deathwatch for Deng
Xiaoping, whose health worsened yet further during the first half of
1995, economic policymaking was buffeted by political struggles.
Social and political instability had joined inflation as a threat to
China's reforms.

PEASANTS UNDER HEEL

Nowhere does the gap between China's past and future yawn wider
than in the matter of social and political control. However chaotic
and corrupt economic life often is in China, most of the economy is
subject to the rough-and-ready discipline of market forces, and at
least a semblance of order emerges. Even in the precarious case of
macroeconomic control the government can still, when it is determined to slow the economy, use its remaining administrative powers
over the state banks and state firms and the indirect tools of monetary policy to get a grip on the country. It is not an elegant combination of methods, but it gets the job done.

Social and political order is more problematic. The rise of a rudimentary sort of pluralism in China, with its dispersion of power both
geographically and institutionally, has had the welcome result of
making the Chinese more free, but at the unwelcome cost of greater
arbitrariness, inconsistency, and corruption in the running of the
country. The Communist party probably has a lot more life in it
than outsiders assume (see the next section but one), but if it is to
regain its grip on China in the coming years, it needs to build some
more modern institutions of control—not multiparty democracy
but instruments to make it easier to supervise officials and make
them accountable. The most crucial of these instruments, as will be
explained in a later section of this chapter, is a rule of law.

In the mid-1990s, China's leaders would not put it that way. Their
eye rests instead on the troubling consequences of Beijing's slipping
power, not yet on how it might sensibly be restored. They focus on
two problems (both of which are indeed worrying): first, disparities

between the different regions of China and the vast movements of population to which these income differences give rise; and second, the conflict between China's regions and localities and the central government.

On the first point, income inequalities are growing both between the prosperous southern and eastern coasts and the interior and between different people living in the same places. Partly because of this and partly because of rising labor productivity thanks to the reforms, people are beginning to move around China in large numbers in search of a better life. The "floating population"—some of whom can be seen camping out in the vicinity of the Guangzhou railway station and others of whom have set up more permanent (and huge) illegal squatter towns on the outskirts of Beijing, Shanghai, and other big cities—is already thought to number 50–100 million. This movement is changing the face of China. The government reckoned that in 1994 alone 50 new cities sprang up in China, bringing the overall total to 620 (of which 35 had populations of more than a million).

The army of migrant labor has a huge potential pool of recruits to draw on. The official guess is that China's farming workforce of some 440 million includes anywhere from 120 million to 200 million people whose services are not really needed on the farms. With rural life in such flux, it is no surprise to find that crime and corruption in the countryside are increasing even faster than they are in the cities. Few foreigners traveling outside the cities fail to return with tales of highway robbery dressed up as toll collection. And by the mid-1990s one of the biggest worries of party officials in Beijing was how corrupt and cruel in their exactions lower-level officials in the countryside had become.

One of the main causes of all this can be explained, though not corrected, easily. The early success of the reforms sprang in large measure from the government's willingness to raise farm-procurement prices sharply at the same time it freed farmers to organize their own production. For a time, in other words, China avoided the common Third World mistake of sucking dry the farmers to pamper the city dwellers. Thus, in 1979–84 real farm incomes grew by an amazing 18 percent a year.

But once the reformers turned their attention to industry, farm incomes suffered. They grew by less than 2.5 percent a year in 1985–88 and by barely over 2 percent a year in 1989–93. The numbers in poverty (still mostly a rural curse) stayed roughly constant after 1985, in unhappy contrast to their sharp fall over the five previous years. The discrepancy between city and farm incomes began to widen again. By the late 1980s the average ratio was two and a half to one, much more extreme than in Indonesia or even Bangladesh.

Government policies are partly to blame and can be changed (though they seem sure not to be except as part of a wholesale reform of China's tax system and of the state firms). Keith Griffin, an economist at the University of California at Riverside, and three of his colleagues calculated that in the late 1980s farmers made an average net transfer of 2 percent of their incomes to central and local governments. But city households received an average net subsidy from the government that amounted to 39 percent of their total income, a subsidy so large that it equaled 95 percent of a rural household's entire disposable income.

Yet even if China's government were not playing Robin Hood in reverse, a severe structural problem between farms and cities would have to be dealt with. It is everywhere and always true that as economies grow and develop, farm employment falls, often precipitously. The only place the surplus labor can go is first into industry and later into service businesses. In the TVEs, China has had a golden opportunity to build labor-absorbing industries not just in already clogged cities but in a multitude of clusters fairly close to where farm labor was being released. Through much of the 1980s this is in fact what happened. In the years 1978–85, TVE employment rose by 16 percent a year; in 1986–88, by a further 11 percent a year. But then, in 1989–93, the compound rate of TVE employment growth fell to just over 3 percent a year.

The encouraging first reason is that since the TVEs operate in a purely market economy, their efficiency has been rising and, thus, their absorption of new labor falling. The sinister second reason, which some of China's best young policy advisers have been fretting about, is that the TVEs' potential to evolve into big, powerful, and higher-tech companies is being stunted by the interference of local bureaucrats. The suspicion of the worriers is that, whereas in the early days of the TVEs the interests of the bureaucrats coincided with those of the enterprises themselves in building up cash flow and profits, the bureaucratic interest now lies in perks such as Japanese cars. The interest of the TVEs now lies in expanding and upgrading themselves into industrial powerhouses that would, not incidentally, be in a position to ignore the demands of the local bureaucrats.

THE NON-DANGERS OF DISINTEGRATION

Local bureaucrats run rampant are the core of the problem of China's dwindling central authority. Many people cast this problem as a conflict between the ambitions of Chinese regional powers, such as provinces, and the writ laid down in Beijing. Glancing at the fate of the Soviet Union (and at China's own history), they foresee attempted secessions or even civil war. A long paper written in 1993 by two Chinese academics, which argued strongly for a constitutional tidying up that would return much authority to the central government, made the chilling point that the only modern country where central-government revenues fell as sharply as they have in China was Yugoslavia just before it disintegrated.

Although the tidying up is fully justified, the alarmist tone is not. I think that, with the vital exception of mineral-rich Xinjiang in China's northwest (where the local Muslims, quietly backed by their co-religionists in ex-Soviet Central Asia, loathe the Han Chinese) and the heartrending but insignificant exception of Tibet, it is unlikely that there will be any serious move to dismember China politically. Ethnic divisions are absent (92 percent of Chinese citizens are ethnic Hans), the army would shoot to kill on this subject, and few local leaders will think it worth the trouble.

Indeed, far from being destabilizing, the drainage of power from Beijing to the provinces is in many ways encouraging the growth of market and other kinds of freedoms in China. Jimmy Lai, an outspoken Hong Kong entrepreneur who made his fortune with a Hong Kong-based Asia-wide chain of casual clothing stores called Giordano, tells the story of what happened when the central government tried to clamp down on Giordano's shops in China in 1994.

Although at that point Mr. Lai still owned the biggest single block of Giordano's equity and sat on the company's board, he had turned his day-to-day attentions to publishing—in particular to his racy gossip weekly, *Next Magazine*. For one of its issues Mr. Lai wrote a signed editorial which included a personal insult to Li Peng, China's prime minister, that was rude even by the lax standards of Hong Kong's tabloid press. Giordano's Beijing shop was promptly shut down and, according to Mr. Lai, the State Council (China's cabinet) issued a secret directive to the provincial authorities to follow suit with any Giordano outlets in their jurisdiction. Yet although Mr. Lai felt compelled shortly after this to retire from Giordano's board (and still cannot get a visa to visit China), the Beijing directive to harass Giordano fell on deaf ears. Mr. Lai says the authorities in Guangdong, the province where Giordano does most of its business, quickly passed the word that the company had nothing to fear there. Not long afterwards the Beijing authorities asked Mr. Lai to reopen the Beijing shop. (He refused.) He is so unafraid of the wrath of the Beijing government that in mid-1995 he started a daily tabloid newspaper in Hong Kong that, it is safe to say, will not have kind things to say about China's government even after Hong Kong reverts to Chinese sovereignty in 1997.

There are two reasons the provinces can get away with such quiet disobedience, and both reasons have their good and bad sides. The first, discussed above (see page 149), is that the central government has fewer fiscal resources than the provinces; this is nice for decentralization of power but bad for the country's macroeconomic health. The second reason is that local bureaucrats are hooked on business.

Another story, this one involving a taxi ride in an inland city, shows how mixed good and bad are in the matter of bureaucrat-as-entrepreneur.

The taxi displayed characters on its door indicating that it was a private cab. When asked how his business was doing, the driver replied that the taxi was not his—he was a mere employee—but belonged to the chief of police. The driver said this had its advantages. The chief had told him that, if ever he was stopped in the cab by public security for any reason, he should tell the cops that this was the chief's taxi and they should mind their own business.

The happy side to this story is what it says about the commitment of practically the entire Chinese state to market economics (provided the apparatus gets something out of it). There is no going back on a policy that expands wealth the way China's market opening has done.

The disturbing side is what the story says about the depth to which corrupt interests have their claws sunk into public administration. The true crisis of the center's loss of power, reflected in local administrative drags on the TVEs, uncontrolled government spending, and impudent assertions of local power over peasants, is a general loss of order in China. This price was worth paying to establish a thriving market economy in China, but it could now seriously interfere with China's efforts to achieve stable long-term growth. Can the Communist party do anything about it?

THE PARTY ON THE PRECIPICE

As Deng Xiaoping grew more and more frail in the autumn of 1994 and the spring of 1995, observers of China and people who make money there became more and more exercised by the question of how the succession at the top of the Communist party would play out. They need not have lost so much sleep over it. The more serious issue for China's stability and future growth is not who triumphs in the power games at the top of the party but instead how strong its institutions are down below.

One of the best accounts of how China's Communist party works is a paper written by Yan Huai, a one-time official in the party's organization department who went into exile after the Tiananmen Square crackdown in 1989. Mr. Yan describes an organization in which the contest for supreme power is a cruel affair, conspiratorial and paranoid. It is also tempestuous and unstable, with unpredictable changes in both political atmosphere and personnel. Deng himself was disgraced and then clawed his way back into power three times. Mr. Yan calculated that in the years 1949–92, on average half of the members of each Politburo Standing Committee (the highest party body) were deposed. When the changes happen, they come like a thunderclap. Then, just as swiftly, it is back to business as usual for the party apparatus.

The party has been able to recover quickly from any leadership turmoil because it has been so effective at extending its tentacles into every part of Chinese life and at rewarding its agents in the party itself, in the government, and in the army. At the end of 1994 the party had 55 million members; it is testimony to the party's continued clout (if only in delivering perks to its members) that it gained a net 2 million members in each of the previous two years. The party exercises control through a highly centralized and intrusive system of supervision that extends from Beijing to the smallest and most remote townships, that penetrates the organs of party and government, barracks and factories, and schools and neighborhoods. The party, says Mr. Yan, is "an omnipresent, omniscient, crisscrossed, interwoven force controlling the entire system of political organization."

The loyalty of government employees is assured not just by the party's watchful eye but also by a centralized system of ranking, privileges, and controls that closely follows—indeed improves upon—the two-thousand-year-old methods of the Chinese imperial bureaucracy. Even religious orders have been absorbed: "The Buddhist abbot is ranked at the department level and the Buddhist monk is ranked at the section level." The loyalty of army officers (who in any event have been trained for generations to obey the party's dictates) and of their men is further guaranteed by material benefits and growing military budgets. The loyalty of ordinary citizens is not needed. Only their obedience is, and the party still deploys ample measures of police-state force to secure that.

Although more of this elaborate system of control undoubtedly remains intact than outsiders can readily credit, it is also true that fifteen years of reform have substantially softened its totalitarian rigor. In many ways this is, of course, a welcome advance not only because it has already widened the scope of personal freedom in China but also because it points to a more pluralist political life in the future. As Mr. Yan points out, the normal progression for a revolutionary regime confronted by political opponents is to move from shooting them to jailing them to exiling them to tolerating them; and it is not too much to expect of China that the phase of tolerance will be reached in the next ten years. Even so, the loosening of totalitarian control has had its bad side: the government's inability, described in the previous section, to enforce discipline not on people at large but on its own agents. Will the party be able to re-learn this art in a more modern form?

TRUST AND COMPETENCE

The trick will not be easy. China's leaders face two big challenges in trying to govern: The first might be called the challenge of legitimacy; the second, the challenge of execution.

Legitimacy revolves around the question whether Communist party rule needs to have an ideological or spiritual element to it—a belief, beyond mere material improvement, that people want to live by, even if not necessarily to die for. The party has long since lost the idealistic convictions with which it took power: They were shattered (along with the party's structure itself) in the Cultural Revolution, then swept cleanly into oblivion by the "to get rich is glorious" spirit of the years of reform. This lack of an ideological compass has increasingly worried some members of the party, particularly as the Deng succession drew near. By the autumn of 1994 the party's search for something to live by had reached a faintly ridiculous phase: The heirs of Marx and Mao sponsored a high-level conference in Beijing to celebrate the 2,545th anniversary of the birth of Confucius, the authoritarian-feudalist sage of ancient China whose teachings the Communists had come into power vowing to expunge forever.

The party's guardians of thought also could not have been pleased by signs that ordinary Chinese were finding their own ways to fill the spiritual vacuum. Throughout the early 1990s, Christianity was growing markedly in strength, finding converts everywhere, but especially in the freer southern part of China; even by an official reckoning, China had 10 million Protestants alone in 1994, compared with a million in 1949. Yet it does not follow that because people undoubtedly need another dimension to their lives than just getting richer, it is the job of politicians to provide it.

Since at least 1991, when the conclusion Deng drew from the collapse of the Soviet Union was that China must speed up its economic reforms rather than reverse them, the party's implicit assumption has been that its hold on power depended on one thing: whether it could continue to deliver rising prosperity. Many people, among them Mr. Yan, think that is entirely right. The Communist party, he says, took power on the basis of promises that it would make the material lives of workers and peasants better, and that is still the test of its legitimacy. And if China's rulers are casting around for East Asian precedents on this question, they have a strong one in Japan. The Liberal Democratic party that ruled Japan uninterruptedly from 1955 to 1993 delivered some of the best government in the post-1945 world, although throughout its decades in power the party was corrupt, self-serving, and devoid of any ideas except winning the next election and profiting from office. The pragmatic view of what matters on this score is stated by Gordon Wu, a Hong Kong businessman who has built several infrastructure projects in

China: "Under [Maoist] self-reliance there was a lot of blah, blah, blah and no color TV; under the open-door policy they have color TV and are moving on to air conditioning."

Respect for the Communist party also arises from the fact that, for now, it alone stands between China and grave disorder. The frightening thing about China—in particular contrast to Japan at a similar stage of economic development thirty to forty years ago—is how few social stabilizers there are apart from brute force. Russia has shown over the past decade that the legacy of centuries of absolutism can be at least partly dissipated in fairly short order (though how long it will be until non-despotic stability takes root there is an open question). But in China there has been virtually none of the social and institutional development to make an alternative to Communist party rule plausible. Dissidents, intellectuals, even the embryonic trade unions, offer no organized force that could even begin to manage a country with China's immense size and problems. One Shanghai journalist, jailed for six months after the Tiananmen Square killings, says the alternative to the party is not democracy; it is the army, the secret police, or warlordism. And it stands to reason that in a country whose worst modern horrors (most recently the Cultural Revolution) have arisen from too little order, not too much, most people still prefer tough party control to the risks of the abyss.

The package of much-improved living standards and fear of disorder seems, for now anyway, to have won for the party at least a suspension of popular judgment and perhaps even more than that. Huang Yasheng, who teaches at the University of Michigan, has reported the results of a careful survey of Chinese public opinion carried out in 1990—a year and a half after the Tiananmen Square killings—by two American academics. They found that almost 60 percent of those surveyed thought that the government treated its citizens fairly.

Yet even if it enjoys more tolerance from ordinary Chinese than almost any Westerner can imagine, China's Communist party still faces a daunting second challenge: how to execute a modernization of its authority in the radically changed China of the mid-1990s. It is clear to almost everybody that the old methods are rusted beyond rescue, but new ones capable of working in an economy equally balanced between state-run and free-market are hard to fashion.

The people who are going to try—the forward-looking (and often foreign-educated) technocrats in their forties and fifties who control the middling heights of the Chinese bureaucracy—have several models to draw on. Although Chinese officials express their highest admiration for Singapore's combination of tight political control and free-market but government-guided economics, this (for them) ideal can only be a dream. As Singaporeans themselves point out, running a city-state of 3 million people is rather different from running a half-continent of 1.2 billion. Perhaps the best example for China is the slow decompression by which Taiwan's Kuomintang, which shares the Communist party's Leninist heritage, over a fifteen-year period built up some internal party democracy and introduced a bit of accountability and pluralism into the island's lower-level government, all the while maintaining strict national political controls.

The irony for China's leaders is that decompression might be the easier part; finding new methods of control could be harder. Already a fair amount of surprisingly lively democracy has been introduced at lower levels of party and government. By 1993 local and even provincial parties were occasionally refusing to accept candidates proposed by the authorities in Beijing for posts in their areas; in a couple of cases this happened even with governorships.

More significantly, in 1987 China enacted a law that almost nobody outside the country has heard of. It permits China's villages, where most Chinese still live, to experiment with choosing their own mayors and ruling councils. The elections have spread to 80 percent of China's villages, with some 4.2 million village officials now having been elected by the people rather than appointed by the party. Election methods vary widely, but many villages have settled on anyone-can-vote elections by secret ballot to choose their leaders. Moreover, these leaders have powers over affairs that matter more to China's rural majority than the grand politics of Beijing does: issues like schools, roads, and tax collection.

Yet however encouraging such developments, they can lead to a more stable and open political order in China only if they are accompanied by a reassertion of central authority over matters that need nationwide compliance. By the mid-1990s a group of "neo-authoritarians," who curiously were being portrayed in the press as wicked conservatives, were offering some good ideas. These were based on such themes as uniform national rules for taxation and investment regulation; a constitutional revision to shore up the central government's finances and clean up the division of powers and responsibilities between the central and local governments; and, to promote more income equality between regions and forestall further fragmentation of the market, national allocations of money for infrastructure spending.

Cleaner lines of authority will not in themselves be enough to bring renegade local powers under tighter control. The worst failure of the later Deng years (though admittedly one with an extremely long pedigree in China) was that nothing was done to try to switch the fount of power away from individual prestige and towards the government or even party offices that people occupy. In a broader sense the doing of business through *guanxi,* or personal connections, must change if China is to take full advantage of what all foreign investors, and not just those of the overseas Chinese diaspora, have to offer.

Indeed, even the overseas Chinese have become fed up. Chinese officials got the shock of their lives in late 1994 when Li Ka-shing, Hong Kong's most famous businessman and long a chum of China's top leaders, gave a public speech in Hong Kong in which he lashed out at the mainland government for its failure to give investors "the long-term, stable policies" they needed if they were to continue doing business there. Mr. Li's speech came when thunderclouds had begun gathering as a result of unpaid debts to foreign lenders and investors—probably worth billions of dollars—that state-owned firms were refusing to honor. Foreign-investment pressure for a more transparent regulatory regime is bound to rise. The party's only real hope of shoring up its authority, with foreigners and Chinese alike, is to begin depersonalizing public business in China, especially by tying the hands of bureaucrats through explicit (and court-enforceable) laws, first on banking and other commercial subjects and later on matters that affect individuals.

Moves in this direction have already begun, and they will pick up speed as China increases its population of lawyers from fifty thousand in 1993 to two hundred thousand in 2000. But what real chance is there that the Communist party, which came to power and has thrived on the basis of arbitrary authority, will quietly surrender many of the main instruments through which its control has been exercised: the state industrial firms, the financial system, the unchecked extra-legality? More of a chance than that list suggests. For one thing, China's continued race to a market economy will stumble without such changes. For another, they need not threaten (and may actually enhance) the party's political power, though not its other kinds of power. Mr. Yan, for example, thinks that party control of state firms and banks is not essential to its undisputed political mastery, provided it owns a big enough business empire to finance itself comfortably (as Taiwan's Kuomintang did). Even in the touchy case of the rule of law, China's neo-authoritarians can again take comfort from their beloved Singapore, where a transparent and uncorrupt legal system and widely respected property rights have not only allowed a vigorous market economy to flourish but have posed no threat to the ruling party's political control.

Hope Racing Fear

With a list of problems this intimidating and the risk of a sudden crisis (say, of finance) so high, it might seem that the logical view of China's prospects is one of gloom. It is not. The reasons for this are many and include the momentum that fifteen years of reform have built up and China's pervasive passion for improvement. But three reasons stand out above all others.

The first, and least known, is that China has an abundance of talented people whose views, abilities, and motivations have been shaped by a uniquely bracing combination of experiences. There are literally millions of relatively privileged Chinese who as teenagers or young adults endured the hell of the Cultural Revolution, in many cases wasting years in the depths of rural China without schooling or health care; who then received crash university educations, often at the best schools in the United States; and who are now working abroad or in China itself as bankers, businessmen, and even bureaucrats.

These people, now in early middle age, have an intimate personal knowledge, as Mao and Deng did, of the lowest and broadest reaches of Chinese society. But they also have knowledge, and in many cases personal experience, of the most advanced parts of the modern world. And, thanks to their having been plunged into the cauldron of the Cultural Revolution, they are steely, ambitious, focused, and driven. They are also, for the most part, intensely patriotic (even those who for now are abroad), with a vivid recollection of how catastrophic China can be when disorder grips it. These are the people who will gradually take over the running of China during the next two decades.

They will make for a generation of leaders with qualities and strengths unparalleled in China's history—and perhaps the world's. The nearest equivalent may have been the generation of Americans who fought in World War II and returned to lead the United States in 1950–90. But by mid-century America was a rich country with abundant human resources; and however valuable the contribution of the wartime generation, it did not have as enormous an impact on America as the Cultural Revolution generation is going to have on China.

Second, even before that generation takes over, China's government will enjoy a large margin of error. Recall how much the Chinese save and invest compared to other people and how hard they work. Even the colossal follies of Mao's day could not stop these advantages from telling in positive economic growth rates and even, as the Cultural Revolution wound down, rising productivity. Today's government has less raw power than Mao's did, but it is already a much better government than his was and is unlikely to make mistakes so crippling that China's advantages could not more than make up for them.

The third reason for optimism is that China's leaders have committed themselves to economic development as the paramount aim of government and party policy. It is irrelevant if (as is likely) they have not done so for the most altruistic of motives. The endless and fruitless speculation over the policy consequences of who might come out on top in any post-Deng succession struggle is also mostly irrelevant. In 1977, only a few months after the fall of the Gang of Four, Norman Macrae, then *The Economist*'s deputy editor, wrote that what was in store for China was "an end to boring ideology, and a drive for economic growth," and that it did not make any difference whether the new man carrying out this policy "will be named Ping or Pong or Deng." The same is true today.

In conversations in 1992 and 1994, Singapore's Lee Kuan Yew offered a somewhat more considered explanation of why this is so:

> These are not ordinary people, you know. They are products of a very self-conscious civilization—self-conscious because they know they once did it and now they are out of the race, and they must get back into the race. . . .

Anyway, it's no longer a question of what the leaders want. If the leaders don't bring progress and prosperity to replace backwardness and poverty, there will be a revolution in China, a real one in which armies will change sides and will shoot ministers. That's part of Chinese tradition.

The people now know that it's the system that is at fault. They see the Taiwanese. Look at them bringing all their gifts to relatives. They look at Hong Kong. If people in Singapore can make it and people in China cannot, then it has to be the stupidity of the Soviet system that Mao adopted. Then let's get rid of it.

Ever since 1978, the Chinese leadership has been prepared to throw overboard any person, policy, or belief that threatened to damage the drive for economic development. I see no reason why that will change. My guess is that if China's leaders are to hew to their overriding aim, they will be forced to create a non-Communist party of China (CPC) that progressively establishes more transparent and sophisticated methods of social and economic control, but that this non-CPC will still have a good generation's worth of authoritarian political life left in it after such reforms.

The institution building and regional widening of progress that will be needed for the next stage of China's reforms will, however, likely slow its economic growth over the course of the next decade to only about two-thirds of what it was in 1978–91: say, a steadier 6–7 percent a year. That would be to China's long-term good. An adolescent pace of life, one without rules or heed, is exhilarating; but it needs to be given up in time.

CHAPTER 8

INDIA: THE TORTOISE IN ITS SHELL

Even the most casual traveler in Asia senses at once how unalike China and India are. Set against China's near unity of language and ethnicity and its basic irreligiosity are India's junglelike profusion of peoples (genetically intermingled and uncountably diverse), twenty major languages (of which fifteen are recognized in the Constitution), and seven major religions (many of them—especially Islam and Hinduism—so mutually antipathetic that their members occasionally slaughter each other by the hundreds). China is a dictatorship with tight controls on the press; India, a well-established political democracy with a no-holds-barred free press (though a lot more is made of this than it deserves in a society half of whose people still cannot read a word). China's moneymaking frenzy and its enthusiasm for markets contrast with India's sometimes puritanical and sometimes mystical disdain for business and with its slow coversion to pro-market reforms. And, to the bafflement of India's Western friends and the chagrin of Indians themselves, China has done a far better job than India at improving the lives of its people in the fifty-odd years since India won independence and China had its Communist revolution.

It may seem, in fact, only thanks to an accident of geography that you are reading about these two giants in the same book. Yet their destinies are more entangled than that. Because they are big neigh-

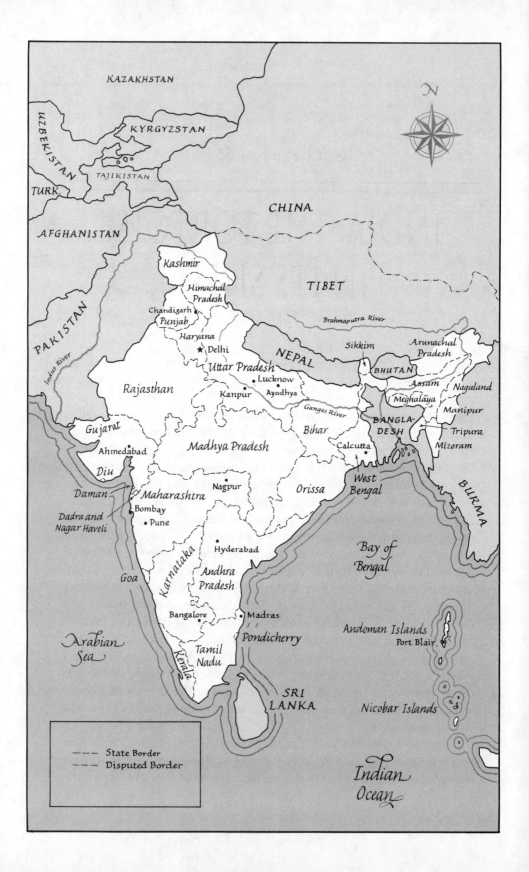

bors with big armed forces, they have to take geopolitical account of each other. They fought a border war in the Himalayas in 1962, and, although their relations are now peaceful, if both continue to grow powerful they could within a generation be jostling each other for position and influence in Southeast Asia and the seas that touch on it; already the Chinese navy has port rights in Burma, which has borders with both India and China.

The economic ties between India and China are also beginning to strengthen, another instance of (and in part due to) the growing commercial web that is drawing all of Asia closer together. On a visit to southern India in 1994, I saw a storage yard where hundreds of whole, uprooted teak trees were stacked. It turned out that these trees were from Burma, whose magnificent teak forests must (if my small glimpse was anything to go by) be disappearing faster than even pessimists fear; and the presence of the felled trees in India was one element in a booming triangular trade: Through twin towns on either side of the Indian-Burmese border pass (from Burma) teak for use in India and heroin for transshipment through Calcutta to far-flung destinations; and (from India) Western luxury items like German beer and scotch whiskey for border shoppers and, for the domestic Burmese market and on-shipment to China, Indian medicines (India is one of the world's biggest bulk-drug producers), car parts, textiles, and chemicals.

At a higher level, too, China's experience is making an imprint on India. Both giants were, in their modern form, born at the same time as the Cold War, and both sided with the Soviet Union against the United States in economic organization and foreign policy. Despite India's greater political affinity with America, it was China that first pushed away Russia as a geopolitical ally and then as an economic paragon. It was China that (understandably) first gravitated to the East Asian model of economic development. But as the 1980s wore on into the 1990s, thoughtful Indians began speaking more and more about what the Chinese-based economies of East Asia had accomplished; and, in a moment of economic crisis in 1991, India consciously began copying the spirit of what had been done to its east.

Any outsider trying to reckon with Asia as a whole needs to keep an eye on both China and India at the same time. One reason is sheer population. At the end of 1994 there were some 900 million Indians, compared with 1.2 billion Chinese; but Indians are reproducing themselves at around twice the rate of Chinese, and if that continues, by 2025 there will be 1.4 billion Indians compared with 1.6 billion Chinese—together about 35 percent of the world's population. Even if by then Indian incomes are still well behind Chinese incomes, India will be by far the world's second-biggest market for most products.

More significantly, India is a particularly useful complement to China because the two are so different. Until their economies become vastly more integrated, the business cycles of the two will continue to move (as they do now) mostly independently. Moreover, India's strengths are China's weaknesses, and vice versa. China moves faster than India but is also more unstable. China has too little law and bureaucracy; India, too much. China faces its crucial test in developing an institutional structure to sustain a modern market economy. India has that skeleton in place but so far lacks the dynamism and market-friendly policies that have given China so much economic energy.

In this hare-and-tortoise contest it is a good idea to place bets on both beasts. Singapore's government, for one, has explicitly recognized this: It has plunged into the development of China, in particular sponsoring a brand-new and self-contained industrial township on the outskirts of Suzhou, a city in eastern China near Shanghai; but it also deliberately reached out to India in 1994 to promote Singaporean investment in Bangalore, a southern city that is India's high-tech capital. It is a healthy diversification that others would do well to follow.

THE LOST DECADES AND THEIR CONSEQUENCES

Yet in the spring of 1991 it was hard to see why the rest of the world should trouble itself with India at all. The country was an economic wreck. Two minor spasms of reform, one in the late 1970s under Indira Gandhi's prime ministership and the other in the mid-1980s under Rajiv Gandhi, her son, had done almost nothing to improve the efficiency of the most comprehensively regulated and isolated economy outside the Soviet bloc. For years prior to the springtime reckoning of 1991, India had managed to sustain its (modest) level of economic growth only through borrowing abroad. Even before political stalemate in 1990–91 and a general collapse of confidence had reduced the country's foreign-exchange reserves to only about $1 billion in May 1991 (enough to pay for about twenty days' worth of imports), India had become a place to avoid for the world's businessmen. Noisy rows with multinationals like Coca-Cola and IBM, both of which were ejected from India in 1977, were only the most prominent symbols of how unwelcome foreign investors were to India and how unappealing India was to them. For a few years before the crisis, flows of foreign direct investment (FDI) averaged a trifling $100 million a year—less than one-fiftieth of the amount China attracted in 1991.

The human and material damage done to India by the economic policies it followed until 1991 is staggering. By practically every measure, India performed not only below its potential but embarrassingly badly compared with almost every country save those in black Africa and a few other basket cases. In the 1970s, India's economy grew by an average of 3.7 percent a year, less than half China's rate (7.9 percent); in the 1980s it managed 5.8 percent, but China grew by 10.4 percent a year that decade. In terms of GNP per person (which is what counts for rising incomes) India lagged even farther behind China.

Table 7 is drawn from a comparative study of China and India published in 1995 by *Business China,* a newsletter put out by the Economist Intelligence Unit in Hong Kong. The study paints a devastating portrait, of which the table gives a glimpse, of the depth and breadth of India's relative failure. It has been so complete that, to have any hope at all about India's future in comparison with China's, you have to make an enormous leap of faith that the relative performance of the two countries over the past forty-five years will be largely reversed over the next twenty-five.

India miserably let down its people both in the overall quality of life it was able to deliver and in reducing the worst poverty. The standard-of-living indicators in table 7 tell part of the story: From similar starting points in the 1960s, China had so far outstripped India by the late 1980s and early 1990s that India was well behind on every score. Worse yet was the fate of the poorest Indians. By the World Bank's count, China had about 130 million people living in absolute poverty in 1990 (without even enough food), some 11 percent of its population. The same year, there were almost 450 million absolutely poor Indians—more than half of India's population (a worse incidence of poverty than even black Africa

TABLE 7
CHINA AND INDIA: STANDARDS OF LIVING

	China	India
Population (millions)	1,203	918
Life expectancy	69	61
Infant mortality (per 1,000 births)	31	79
Adult literacy (%)	73	48
Population growth (annual %)	1.2	1.9
Consumer durables ownership (% households)		
Bicycle	81	49
Color TV	40	5.7
Refrigerator	25	4.2
Electric iron	22	14
Daily calorie intake	2,730	2,243

Economics	China	India
1992 GNP per capita (PPP, U.S. dollars)	1,910	1,210
1992 GNP per capita (U.S. dollars)	470	310
1980–92 Average GDP annual growth (%)	9.1	5.2
1980–92 Average GDP per capita annual growth (%)	7.6	3
1994 CPI (year-on-year %)	21.7	11.1
1993 Gross savings (% GDP)	35.8	24.2
1993 Gross domestic investment (% GDP)	42.1	20.4

Foreign Sector	China	India
1980–92 Exports (annual average % growth)	11.9	5.9
1980–92 Imports (annual average % growth)	9.2	1.9
Trade (% world trade)	2.9	0.6
Foreign direct investment		
1991 Actual inflow (billions of U.S. dollars)	4.4	0.2
1992 Actual inflow (billions of U.S. dollars)	11.2	0.3
1993 Actual inflow (billions of U.S dollars)	27.5	0.6
1994 Actual inflow (billions of U.S. dollars)	34.0	0.7
1994 Foreign debt (billions of U.S. dollars)	83.5	73
1994 Foreign-exchange reserves		
(billions of U.S. dollars)	52.9	19.7
1993 Debt-service ratio (%)	13	29

Infrastructure	China	India
Per capita electricity consumption (kwh)	643	270
Telephones		
Installed telephone lines (millions)	26	6.8
Lines per 100 people	2.3	0.8
Planned installed line capacity in 2000 (millions)	100	20

1993 Road freight (% total domestic freight)	75	60
1993 Rail freight** (billion-ton-kilometers)	1,158	254
1993 Port throughput (millions of tons)	678	180

Note **: freight tons carried times distance traveled

Agriculture	**China**	**India**
Cultivated land per capita (hectares)	0.08	0.2
Fertilizer consumption (kilograms per hectare)	307	75.2
1993 Foodgrain production (millions of tons)	456	182
1992 Yields, by agricultural crops (hundreds of kilograms per hectare)		
Rice (paddy)	58.1	26.1
Wheat (paddy)	33	24
Cotton (lint)	6.8	2.7
Groundnut (in shell)	21	9.5

SOURCE: Economist Intelligence Unit, *Business China* (Summer 1995).

had) and almost 40 percent of the whole world's absolutely poor people.

How can it possibly have happened that, despite the Great Leap Backward in 1958–62, the Cultural Revolution, and widespread lawlessness and tyranny, China's authoritarian government has delivered far greater benefits to the average Chinese than India's fairly stable and democratically elected governments have delivered to the average Indian? The short answer is that by and large China's government has followed policies which, because they rely in a rough-and-ready way on the market to set prices and allocate resources, spread the benefits of economic growth pretty widely through the society. In India, by contrast, despite decades of lip service to the principles of equality and socialism, the country's rulers have acted almost entirely at the behest of special-interest lobbies representing the better-off.

In education, for instance, India lavishes relatively large sums on universities, while leaving the rural poor to fend for themselves for primary schooling. On average, Indian governments at all levels spend 60 percent of their budgets on salaries for civil servants (who earn far more than the average Indian, especially in the countryside), while stinting on the infrastructure and services that would benefit society at large. The system of industrial licensing and regulation and trade protectionism described later in this chapter has had the similar effect of enriching certain companies and their pampered workforces at the expense of firms and people without political clout.

Such perversity runs the gamut of the Indian economy, but it has done its worst damage in the countryside. Like all poor countries, China and India have been—and largely remain—rural societies. What happens in the countryside determines much of their economic performance and social well-being. China, especially in the stage of the early Dengist reforms, has been far better than India at designing policies that favor the rural masses.

In the half-decade or so after 1978, China freed its farmers to produce for the market. Farm incomes trebled, creating for the first time appreciable consumer purchasing power in the countryside and, in addition, a vast pool of savings to finance rural industrialization through the township and village enterprises (see chapter 6). By contrast, India's farms stagnated. Large subsidies for fertilizer, electricity, and water went not to the poor but to the relatively well-off in the countryside. Meanwhile, the terms of trade were loaded against agriculture and in favor of (already richer) consumers in the towns; government-procurement prices for rice, wheat, and sugar were below the cost of production (there will be more about all this in chapter 9). Through this underpricing of agricultural output, savings were in effect forcibly extracted from the countryside to finance the government-led industrialization of the towns.

An example from the *Business China* study shows that this was mainly a failure of policy in India rather than something—such as the weather, soil quality, or cultural differences—over which governments had little or no control. From the early 1980s to the early 1990s food-grain production in India rose on average by 2.8 percent a year. But in West Bengal, a poor state in easternmost India, the rate of increase was 5.9 percent a year, over a third again as fast as the rate of increase in the richest farming states in India, Punjab and Haryana. The reason is that since 1977 West Bengal has been ruled by a Communist party that, to the extent it could at state level, copied the Chinese methods of agricultural reform and village-level decision making. (Interestingly, in newly reformist India, West Bengal is one of the states most enthusiastically bidding for FDI.)

India-wide, however, agricultural performance has been dismal. Farm output, which more than anything else determines how well or how badly most people in poor countries live, rose in India in the 1970s and 1980s by only 2.1 percent a year; that compared with a rise of almost 6 percent in Sri Lanka, almost 5 percent in Malaysia, and almost 4 percent in Indonesia and Burma. As table 7 shows,

China's yields per hectare of rice, cotton, and peanuts were higher in 1978 than India's in 1992; and China, whose agricultural efficiency was already well ahead of India's in 1978, widened the performance gap over the next fifteen years. By 1992, China's yields of rice, wheat, cotton, and peanuts were approaching, or had already exceeded, comparable yields in the United States; and they were two to three times India's yields for rice, cotton, and peanuts and 40 percent higher than India's yields for wheat.

Despite (or rather, as explained above, because of) India's high fertilizer subsidies, China applied four times as much fertilizer per hectare of cultivated land as India did in 1993. And despite having 75 percent more cultivated land than China did that year (and two and a half times as much cultivated land per person), India produced only 40 percent as much food grain as China. In raw terms, in other words, each hectare of Chinese farmland was producing almost five times as much grain as each hectare of Indian farmland.

India's industrial growth has lagged even more than agricultural growth. In the 1960s its industrial output rose 5.5 percent a year— about half the rate in neighboring Pakistan, less than half the rate in Thailand, and a third the rate in South Korea. In the 1970s, India did even worse compared with its Asian neighbors and although its performance picked up in relative terms in the 1980s, this owed everything to an increase in capital and labor and less than nothing to an increase in productivity. The best study of Indian manufacturing productivity, by an Indian economist named Isher Ahluwalia, showed that between 1960 and 1985 total factor productivity in manufacturing fell by an average of 0.4 percent a year.

India's relative economic inefficiency has been reflected in the size of its markets and the relative opportunities for foreign businesses. The gushing talk in the mid-1990s about India's huge "middle class" is mostly hot air. According to the *Business China* study, almost every consumer market in China is vastly bigger than its Indian counterpart; for instance, 40 percent of Chinese households owned color TVs in 1993, compared with 6 percent of Indian households in 1992.

In the mid-1990s only about 3.5 million Indian households had annual incomes above $2,500. A Gallup survey of China in 1994 showed that the average income of the 7 million households in just three (though the richest three) Chinese cities—Guangzhou,

Shanghai, and Beijing—was between $1,500 and $2,000. Because
Indian households have on average half again as many members as
Chinese households (six versus four), it is a fair bet that, just before
India's economic reforms had had a chance to take hold, these
three Chinese cities boasted more per capita spending power in
similarly "middle-class" households than the whole of India did. It
is therefore not too surprising that although Nestlé, the Swiss food
group, set up its first factories in China only in 1989, a quarter-
century after its first ones in India, by 1995 it had the same revenues
in the two countries; or that Carrier, an American air-conditioner
maker that set up shop in both China and India in 1987 with like-size
injections of capital, by 1995 had five times the revenues from China
that it had from India.

The most bizarre twist to the horrifying story of India's lost decades is that by the late 1980s much of India's ruling elite was
complacent, thinking that under their stewardship India had done
rather well. The "Hindu rate of growth"—a chilling phrase coined
by an Indian economist to describe the 3 percent annual GNP
growth that was all India could expect in the long run—had, after
all, been nearly doubled during the 1980s. Even the rumblings of
history seemed no more than an object of curiosity to the men
running India, like a passing electrical storm on the horizon. In a
private conversation in 1990, V. P. Singh, then India's prime minister, shrugged his shoulders when I asked whether the revolutionary
events in the Soviet Union and Eastern Europe were not causing
India to rethink its inward-looking and central-planning approach.
Mr. Singh, a decent and intelligent (though unadventurous) man
who, as finance minister in the mid-1980s, had designed the tinkering economic reforms of that day, said that he personally thought
the events in Russia were of great significance but that there was
little consciousness of them or impact from them in India. India's
politicians, he went on, were mere servants of the people, and Indian economic reform would have to proceed at a slow pace.

Within a year history had made itself felt even in India. In the
realm of ideas, the collapse of state planning in Russia and the rush
to market in such formerly interventionist economies as those of
Latin America left the defenders of India's system almost alone. And
on the practical plane the Soviet Union's disintegration destroyed
the biggest single market for India's exports; Iraq's invasion of Kuwait and the war that followed deprived India of $2 billion worth of

foreign-exchange remittances from the Indians who were sent packing from their jobs in the Gulf; and India's overstretched international borrowing of the 1980s could no longer be sustained. In June 1991, Indians saw on their televisions symbolically devastating shots of gold bullion being trucked from the vaults of the central bank for eventual shipment to the Bank of England to secure a loan for India; the last thing a traditional Indian family parts with before catastrophe overwhelms it is its gold. Some still say that this footage was shown deliberately by India's new government to prepare people for what came next. Whether that is true or not, India's new leaders were readying the wrecking ball for central planning's last great edifice.

PLANNED IN HELL

The system they set out to demolish was unbelievable. It was designed in mid-century according to the advanced theories of economic development then most fashionable in the West ("India's misfortune," as Jagdish Bhagwati, an Indian-born economist, has written, "was to have brilliant economists"); and the theories were put into execution with a thoroughness that did the Indian bureaucracy proud.

The main ideas behind this system (which could be characterized as Soviet communism minus the violence but plus private property) were that India's scarce, investable resources needed to be directed to their socially most productive uses (including poverty alleviation and industrialization) and that only the government could be trusted to deploy capital efficiently to these ends—not the Indian market and certainly not the exploitative international market for goods and capital. The three main pillars of the system were a high degree of direct government ownership of industry (and later entire government ownership of banks); a high degree of government regulation of privately owned industrial businesses; and the screwing down of foreign trade (later just imports) and foreign investment to the lowest possible level. After 1978, China grew by letting competition flourish; before 1991, India tried to grow by eliminating as much of it as possible because it was "wasteful."

Government ownership of industrial enterprises in India was the most extensive in the non-Communist world. Several lines of business were designated "core industries," in which only government-owned firms would be allowed to operate. These included not just defense industries and atomic energy but also railways, airlines and aircraft building, electricity generation and distribution, coal, iron and steel, and heavy machinery. Two waves of bank nationalization, in 1969 and 1977, added virtually the whole of the financial system to the government's quiver of businesses.

By 1991 government and the industries it owned employed 71 percent of the nearly 27 million people who worked in the "organized sector" (basically, outfits employing at least ten people), and state-owned industrial firms had almost twice as much fixed capital as private firms. In the two decades after 1970 government employment grew by an average of 2.9 percent a year, more than three times as fast as the private sector's 0.8 percent a year. State workers were paid, on average, twice what their private-sector counterparts earned; total compensation for railway workers (1.6 million of them) was on average two and a half times India's average family income; for bank employees (more than 900,000), four and a half times. Nor did the state firms use these pricey inputs at all efficiently. The state industrial firms' return on capital employed varied in the derisory range of 2–2.5 percent in the years 1990–92—and did that well only because of "administrative pricing" in the oil sector. If the state oil firms were excluded, the return on capital in the state firms would have been negative.

The fact that the "commanding heights" of industry which India's government took over were both sweeping in their breadth and miraculous in their inefficiency had several bad consequences for the economy, two of them devastating. First, the state firms have put a big dent in India's public finances. In 1992 almost half of the state-owned firms were in the red, with an aggregate loss of more than $1 billion. Government money is drained by both direct subsidies and hidden ones. (In 1991 about 30 percent of the capital investment in state-owned heavy industry was financed not by these businesses but by taxpayers.) Second, many of the state industries are so basic to the economy—transport, energy, steel—that their inefficiencies are transmitted to the rest of the economy through high prices, bad products, and poor services.

What of the private industrial firms? An Indian Kafka would be needed to do justice to this subject. The government set up a system that required industrial firms to obtain a government-granted license before they could set up a production line, add another, move the line, or convert it to making an even slightly different product (because of technological change, for instance, or shifting market demand). The private firms loved this system; it guaranteed them profits without the need for thought, innovation, or worry about new competitors. For the economy and the consumer, it was a disaster.

To the basic licensing requirements, which applied to all industrial firms, were added special bundles of red tape. Big firms had to get clearance from an "anti-monopoly" regulator before they could even apply for one of the industrial licenses; they often waited as long as two or three years for this clearance. Small firms had their own "protections," which stopped anyone else from making the products reserved to them but also punished them if they had the audacity to succeed and grow too big.

Lastly, anybody still tempted to set up a business was assured that, no matter how much money it lost, the business could not legally be shut down without the consent of its entire workforce. "Sick units," as would-be bankrupts are officially called, numbered almost 225,000 in 1991; their bank loans amounted to almost 110 billion rupees (or over $4 billion at the then rate of exchange). Bankruptcy was unheard of, mergers almost impossible to carry off. Some of the sick were palmed off on a government agency. Of the rest, most were abandoned in fact if not officially. Their owners simply walked away, having stripped what assets they could, leaving their still formally employed workers to fend for themselves.

The natural third complement to government ownership of the biggest industries and tight regulation of the rest was sharp vigilance to make sure that foreigners did not undo the government's good work by bringing in unneeded products or diverting needed resources. Imports were curtailed as much as possible. Imports of consumer goods were flatly outlawed; capital and intermediate goods faced a pallisade of licensing restrictions. Anything that made it through these quantitative restrictions was burdened with some of the world's highest tariffs: over 100 percent on every kind of good, reaching as high as 400 percent on some. FDI was minimized through a licensing regime even more draconian than that imposed on Indian firms. (Foreign portfolio investment in Indian stocks was simply not allowed.) By 1990, India was less tied to the world economy—in terms of exports, imports, foreign investment, and technology transfer—than virtually any other country in Asia.

This comprehensive anti-competitive system brought India a staggering amount of exactly the waste that its idealistic architects had intended it to avoid. India wanted to promote industrialization, but its share of world value-added in manufacturing declined so fast that India fell from being the world's eighth-biggest industrial power in 1955 to only the sixteenth biggest in 1973. It has since fallen further: In 1970, South Korea, a small country with a population around one-twentieth the size of India's, boasted manufacturing value-added equal to 25 percent of India's; in 1981 it was equal to 60 percent. This meant that each Korean was producing around twelve times as much as each Indian in 1981.

Moreover, the very instrument of the planners' dreams—the Indian civil service—was irremediably tarnished by the use to which they put it. The licenses, conditions, and other restraints were in many cases granted or withheld not automatically but at the sole discretion of the individual bureaucrats in charge of them. It is no wonder that the relatively clean Indian civil service of the 1950s— Jawaharlal Nehru, then prime minister, had an official jailed for two years for accepting a gift of six bottles of whiskey—had by 1991 become as venal as any in Asia.

CHAPTER 9

INDIA: THE TORTOISE SETS OUT

In the years since July 1991, India has gradually dismantled significant parts of its central-planning apparatus. There was no immediate explosion of wealth creation, as there had been in China after the first Dengist reforms, but by the mid-1990s the Indian economy was shuddering on the launch pad. Provided the government can come to grips over the next few years with its unmet challenges—many of them strikingly like those now facing China—there is no reason why India cannot, in its stately way, take off. If it does, the July 1991 revolution of P. V. Narasimha Rao and Manmohan Singh may come to seem as momentous as the December 1978 revolution of Deng Xiaoping.

Messrs. Rao and Singh were an improbable pair of revolutionaries. Mr. Rao was a lifelong hack of the ruling Congress party, an institution less totalitarian but no less venomous and corrupt than China's Communist party. He became prime minister in June 1991 by an accident of death: Rajiv Gandhi, himself prime minister in the mid-1980s and the son and political heir of Indira Gandhi, another prime minister and the molder of the modern Congress party, had been assassinated by a bomb in May during the general-election campaign. Mr. Rao, a cautious and inoffensive timeserver with heart trouble, seemed to the Congress barons like the perfect stopgap. Mr. Singh, an immaculately bearded and beturbaned Sikh whom

Mr. Rao appointed finance minister, was an academic economist who had worked at the World Bank. In the early 1970s he had written a book pointing out that India's anti-foreign bias was harmful, but he had otherwise been a supporter of the central-planning regime. He had, indeed, served in high posts in several Indian governments that had staunchly backed—and even added to—the very system the Rao government set out to dismantle.

India's macroeconomic crisis of 1990–91 would not, in fact, have left whatever government took power in mid-1991 any choice but reform. But India's overseas creditors—the IMF, commercial bankers, and "non-resident Indians" (NRIs)—would probably have demanded no more than macroeconomic adjustments (changes in the government budget and the foreign-trade and foreign-exchange regime) to resume lending. To the surprise of almost every "expert" observer (I got it completely wrong, too), Mr. Singh's emergency budget of July 1991 instead launched a direct assault on the grotesque microeconomic distortions, especially the industrial-licensing system, that were the ultimate cause of the budgetary problems. Steadfastly backed by Mr. Rao, Mr. Singh gradually whittled away at the central-planning system over the next few years. By 1995 a half-miracle of policy conversion had been accomplished.

THE DOOR CRACKS OPEN

Here, in decreasing order of radicalism, is what has been done:

Licensing and Other Regulations. In 1991 the requirements for Indian companies to get government permission before they set up, shifted, or abolished production lines were eliminated for all but eighteen industries, though the still-restricted production of "items of elitist consumption" (that old puritanism again) included such potentially big industries as cars, consumer durables, and consumer electronics. But even those restrictions were wiped out in 1994. In connection with the near abolition of "the license raj," as it had come to be known, the powers of the special anti-monopoly body were curtailed so that it would begin to operate as a normal antitrust agency and no longer block competition via entry, expansion, or mergers in industries with a few dominant firms.

Out the window entirely went the Controller of Capital Issues, which had possessed the magisterial power to tell firms what price they could issue their stocks and bonds at. Joining this anachronism in banishment was a provision that had required bank loans to private firms to include a clause allowing the loan to be compulsorily converted into equity at the lender's whim. (And remember that all banks are owned by the state.) By the end of 1994 most bank lending and deposit rates had been deregulated, and there were just three lending rates (compared with fifty in pre-reform days). Even the protections and privileges of the politically sensitive "small-scale" sector had been narrowed.

Foreign Trade and Investment. Most quantitative restrictions on imports have been removed—except, predictably, for wicked consumer goods like watches and televisions, which can be brought in only as part of a traveler's hand baggage. Tariffs had been cut by 1995 to a maximum of 65 percent (down from the 400 percent of pre-reform days), with the declared goal of an average tariff of 25 percent. Foreigners making direct investments in some high-tech industries and in power generation are allowed to own 100 percent of the businesses. In other businesses, foreigners can own 51 percent of a joint venture and use their own brand names (forbidden before); and "one-stop shopping" for foreign-investment approval is supposed to be assured through a single government agency. By 1995 foreign-investment funds (though not yet foreign individuals) could buy and sell shares listed on Indian stock markets; and Indian firms were allowed to raise money on the international capital markets. The rupee has been made fully convertible on the current account (i.e., in connection with foreign trade); convertibility on the capital account is expected well before 2000.

State-Owned Firms. The dozens of "core industries" reserved for state-owned companies were reduced to eight, and, even in these still-reserved fields, loopholes through which private participation could slip opened up quickly (particularly in oil exploration). A privatization program was set up, with thirty-one state-owned firms on the list by 1994; but the government was willing to sell no more than 49 percent even of these middling firms and nothing at all of state-sector blockbusters, such as railways and telecommunications. In 1994 the government undertook a cautious experiment that let a few private banks begin limited operations. There would, however, be a serious threat to the deposit base of the costly and inefficient state-owned banks if a private banking free-for-all were allowed.

Tax Reform. In addition to the cuts in tariffs, personal and corporate income tax rates have been lowered. Customs and excise-tax regulations were simplified, and collection procedures were speeded up; both changes should prove a boon to industrial efficiency and put a damper on corruption.

In the first couple of years of reform, when the government had to restore some balance to its own books and to India's external account and bring price rises under control, the economy hardly grew at all in real terms; manufacturing output actually shrank in 1991–93. But by 1995 real economic growth had reached 6 percent (and was accelerating), and industrial output was going up by 8 percent a year. The dollar value of exports rose by more than 20 percent in 1994, and by the end of that year the country's foreign-exchange reserves, which had scraped bottom in mid-1991 at little more than $1 billion, were brimming with more than $20 billion. India's ironic problem was that foreign confidence was so high that too much money was pouring in, making it hard to keep the rupee and the money supply from rising too far.

A change in mood was evident earlier than the change in fortunes. The Bombay stock market doubled in 1991, then madly redoubled in the first three months of 1992 before a financial scandal knocked some sense into it. Evidence of the Western-like consumerism that so horrified the socialists of Nehru's day sprouted quickly, often in the shape of foreign brands like Pepsi (or, a matter of some importance to India's chattering classes, scotch whiskey) that had until recently been banned. Commercial loosening seemed to overlap with other kinds: By 1994, Bombay casually boasted huge billboards advertising not machine tools or chemical dyes (the typical Soviet-era fare) but instead "Kama Sutra scented condoms."

Competition was allowed to make its magic felt in previously desolate fields. Air passengers, who had long had no choice but to throw themselves on the surly and incompetent mercies of Indian Airlines, the state-owned monopoly carrier on domestic routes, suddenly had privately owned competitors vying for their business. They could not believe their eyes when presented with clean aircraft that often ran on schedule, alcoholic drinks and decent food on board, and cheerful service delivered by crisply dressed staff who went so far as to give the customers questionnaires asking what could be improved. This competition no doubt contributed something to the appointment, in late 1994, of a new private-sector chairman for Indian Airlines and its sister international carrier, Air India, and moves in 1995 to begin privatizing the two carriers.

Many of the travelers Indian Airlines could once abuse with impunity were businessmen on their way to Delhi, an indispensable pilgrimage during the license raj. With far less need nowadays for a central-government bureaucrat's okay (though see below), business travelers are likelier to be found on their way to Bombay, India's financial capital, or to regional economic centers like Bangalore, Madras, Hyderabad, Ahmadabad, or even Communist-run but now foreign investment seeking Calcutta, the capital of West Bengal (see chapter 8). By 1994, Bombay had also developed the sort of mesmeric attraction for foreign bankers and investors that Beijing and Shanghai had begun to hold for them a couple of years earlier. The bankers had a lot of new foreign cash to work with. Foreign investment in India (in equities as well as factories), which had been only $100 million in 1991, reached some $6.5 billion in the 1994–95 financial year. Indian companies, which had until 1992 been forbidden to raise money in the international capital markets, raised more than $2.4 billion in the 1993–94 financial year alone.

Yet might these enthusiastic foreigners not be jumping the gun? In 1995, when China's reforms were seventeen years old, India's had just turned four. Already, India's government was showing signs of shying away from the decisions that will be needed if the economy's promising new start is to become a long-distance run.

TRAHISON DES CLERCS

A big initial problem has been bringing the spirit of the reformist moves at the top to bear on the humdrum administration of the government below. By every account, the "bonfire of the licences" has so far done nothing whatever to reduce the burden of paperwork on business and little even to cut back on the bureaucratic approvals needed before a project can go ahead. The reason the paperwork mountain still towers so high is that, although central-government approval for an investment is usually no longer required, all the form filling and form filing that used to accompany an application still must be done.

The more serious matter of continued bureaucratic veto power arises mainly from India's federal system. Each Indian state mimics the old central-government apparatus of control, although the licenses required by the states tend more towards the practical (sewage and telephone connections) than towards upholding the decrees of the economic planners. Yet the power of the states, and of politics, to derail the central government's reform plans can be large, as was shown in August 1995 when a new opposition government in Maharashtra canceled a Delhi-blessed $2.8 billion power project to be built by Enron, a Texas company.

On a more mundane level of obstruction, a survey by the Confederation of Indian Industry found that a power-plant project requires an average of seventeen approvals by nineteen different government agencies. Hong Kong investors in southern China say that the elapsed time from the moment they take a decision to build, say, a toy factory to the moment the dolls start rolling out the door can be as brief as three months. Indians say that a minimum of eighteen months would be required in their country—and that reckons without the formidable blocking powers of the Indian courts. In 1992 the central government's telecommunications ministry awarded licenses to private consortiums to set up mobile phone systems in India's four biggest cities. Two years later, the courts were still deliberating on the legal challenges of the losing bidders.

This sort of thing, however uneconomic, is more of a nuisance than a threat to the whole future of the reforms and may in any event mostly pass away of its own accord as India's various states vie with each other to attract foreign investment. Yet serious threats do exist. Many of them will sound familiar after the description in chapter 7 of what China is now facing.

India's government is doing far too many of the things it should not be doing, including employing too many civil servants, running industrial enterprises that ought to be privately owned, and giving subsidies to people who do not need them. This is playing havoc with the government's own finances, hence jeopardizing macroeconomic stability and also reducing the government's ability to do the things it ought to be doing: mostly, educating children and building infrastructure. And the failure to do so exposes Indian politics even more to its greatest hazards: caste and religious strife.

The stakes for getting the next stage of reform right are even higher in India than in China. On the negative side, India's late start, worse poverty, and lower savings rate (in the low twenties versus China's mid-30s) leave India with less room for maneuver when it makes mistakes. But it stands to gain more, too. Because of India's relative institutional sophistication, every instance of good government policy there has more leverage to produce consistent and widespread results than it does in fragmented and anarchic China. This is the tortoise's hidden strength.

WHERE THE ROADBLOCKS LIE

As in China, the foremost problem in India's government and the industrial firms that it owns is too many workers; but the problem is even more severe in India. First, by some measures—though conspicuously not the share of industrial output accounted for by the state sector, which is much higher in China—India's economy is today more socialist than China's. Because of the very fast growth of Chinese non-state firms over the past fifteen years, China's state-owned industrial firms employ no more than 40 percent of the industrial workforce; the rest work in firms that face the full blast of the market. In India's "organized sector" (firms employing more than ten workers), 70 percent of the workers get their paychecks from the government. The shares are even higher in such politically crucial "Hindi belt" states as Uttar Pradesh (81 percent), Bihar (82 percent) and Madhya Pradesh (86 percent). And even leaving aside civil servants, more than 55 percent of the organized sector's workforce is in government-owned firms.

Second, India's government has so far shown even less stomach than China's for a fight with its workers. Both India's civil service and its state-firm workforce are heavily unionized. Despite the regulation pruning that India's reforms have introduced, not one civil servant is known to have been thrown out of work as a result. Workers in state-owned firms, especially the railways and the banks, are as militant as they are well paid. One good story about the lengths to which state workers believe their entitlements run is told by Jagdish Bhagwati, the economist mentioned in chapter 8. Workers of one "sick" firm, which had been shut down as a going concern but was still obliged by law to continue meeting its payroll, demanded not only their hourly wage but also the overtime they would probably have received had the firm continued doing business. Another firm, Scooters India in Lucknow, still pays the wages of three thousand workers although it has not made a scooter in ten years.

The government's unwillingness to countenance job losses extends even to privately owned industrial firms; hence, the steadfast refusal to let bankrupt firms formally go bust. An "exit" policy has been promised for years but has never made its entrance. Meanwhile, the drag on the economy worsens: Between 1976 and 1991 the number of firms on the government's official sick list (including a few state-owned firms but mostly private ones) increased by an average of 23 percent a year; the nominal value of their dud bank loans, by 17 percent a year.

But at least in the private sector competition can make up for some of these inefficiencies. Continued overmanning in the state-owned firms spreads the mischief much wider. It forces the government to go slowly in allowing private firms to compete with state monopolies, even though this opening up is part of the stated reform program. And it makes the government's halting privatization efforts that much more cautious. Not only does the government have to reckon with the state firms' unions as lobbyists and their workers as voters; it has to contend with the clamor of politicians for whom jobs at all levels of the state-owned firms have become a lucrative form of patronage. The clamor is especially loud in Hindi-belt states like those mentioned earlier, where state-owned firms overwhelmingly dominate the formal economy and where national elections are won and lost.

FINANCIAL FOLLIES

From the inefficient and overmanned state firms, with their soft-budget constraints, to the state banks (all banks were nationalized in the 1970s), the path of government deficits runs in India much as it does in China and with the same debilitating effect on public finances. India's banks have the added burden on their productivity and income of the most obstreperous and best-paid class of workers in India. But the serious financial drain on the banks has come from the demands the government grew accustomed to placing on them. One sign of how serious is that in the mid-1990s, when the spreads between deposit and lending rates were eight to nine percentage points (one of the highest in the world), few banks were in profit.

To finance its deficit, the Indian government began requiring banks to hold low-yielding government debt in an amount equal at one time to as much as 38.5 percent of their deposits. That ratio was steadily reduced during the early 1990s, hitting 25 percent in 1993. Moreover, the government stopped using below-market loans from the banks as a way to finance its deficit (it increasingly does this, like the American government, by issuing bonds in the open market); but even the reduced bondholding requirement narrows the scope for banks to manage their assets, and the effects of the past below-market loans linger on bank balance sheets. So does India's version of China's "policy loans." A survey of fifty big banks showed that of the loans they made between 1977 and 1990, 41 percent went to government-favored borrowers like farmers, 15 percent to state-owned firms, and another 2 percent to government departments. Guesses vary, but anywhere from 20 percent to 50 percent of bank balance sheets may be in the red.

That is a hidden financial burden on the government. (Just how burdensome became less hidden in 1994–95, when the banks got government re-capitalization aid of 57 billion rupees [$1.8 billion], with another 56 billion rupees' worth scheduled for 1995–96.) The government's own budget deficit is in the open; and it is big. In earlier decades India's government, like China's, was fiscally conservative. It ran small budget deficits, or even surpluses, and in keeping with its overall policy of self-sufficiency, borrowed little overseas. This changed in the 1980s, and by the time of India's macroeconomic crisis of 1990–91 the budget deficit had grown to 9 percent of GDP. This fell to around 6 percent in each of the following two years but by 1994 had climbed back up to 7.5 percent and was still over 6.5 percent the following year. The only saving grace is that India is nowhere near as close as China to the financial brink: Its tools of monetary management are far more sophisticated, and it has used them to lower inflation from 12–13 percent in the early 1990s to single digits in 1995. In 1994 the government agreed with the central bank that it would gradually cut back on—and by 1997 entirely stop—monetizing the deficit (i.e., printing money—and hence adding to inflation—to pay for the deficit). Even so, the chasm between revenue and spending poses a big threat in the long run.

Part of the reason the deficit proved hard to control was fast-rising interest payments on the government's fast-swelling debt and the need to bail out state-firm losses amounting to some 40 billion rupees. But the root of the problem is government subsidies.

Central-government subsidies in the 1993–94 financial year amounted to almost 130 billion rupees, more than half again as much as the government had predicted; subsidies from the states added another 84 billion rupees. In all, subsidies accounted for more than 10 percent of total government spending and 20 percent of current spending. And despite repeated annual promises that subsidies will be sharply cut back, they continue to grow. Subsidies in the 1994–95 financial year were marginally higher than in the previous year, even though the central government had predicted that its own subsidies would decline by a quarter.

Almost 85 percent of central-government subsidies (and more of the state ones) are food-related. The central government subsidizes the food of middle-class city dwellers and the fertilizers used by middle-class farmers; the states provide the same farmers with cheap electricity (indeed, often free, since some 20 percent of the power delivered by state electricity boards is simply stolen) and cheap water.

The damage this inflicts on public finances, bad though it is, is not the worst of its effects. One problem, as mentioned in chapter 8, is the deleterious impact of subsidies on agricultural productivity and income distribution (both between countryside and city and between rich and poor in the countryside). This effect has been aggravated by the government's food-procurement policies, which have forced farmers to sell grain to the state at below-market, and sometimes below-cost, prices. To enforce the nonmarket in grain, the government at times has gone so far as to restrict transfers of grain even between adjacent rural districts; as of the mid-1990s it still forbids interstate transfers without a permit.

Worse yet, the perverted largesse of subsidies has starved the government of the wherewithal for the sort of capital spending that would have raised economic growth for the whole of society and benefited the poor most of all: investment in primary education, health care, and rural infrastructure.

With a majority of adults (and two-thirds of women) illiterate in 1990, India can ill afford to be spending less than ten dollars a person on education each year and putting up with primary-school attendance rates of 60 percent. Education spending in total amounted to 3 percent of GDP in 1993. This was already far below the shares spent by successful East Asian countries, and in the following two years India's education spending actually declined in after-inflation terms, sinking to less than 2 percent of GDP in 1995. Moreover, India's spending—unlike, for example, that of Indonesia, which has almost universal primary education—is weighted heavily in favor of higher education rather than basic schooling (more treats for the better-off).

The story is similar for spending on health care (lots of big hospitals used by the better-off, few clinics for the rural poor) and for rural infrastructure. Spending on things like roads and irrigation systems is the best way to improve the productivity and market access of the poorest farmers (who are usually landless laborers). Most agricultural spending is funneled through state-government budgets, and in the 1980s current spending by the states on subsidies, which is second only to spending on civil-service salaries, rose by 17 percent a year in nominal terms, whereas capital spending—what pays for the roads and waterworks—rose by only 9 percent a year (after inflation, hardly at all).

Dwindling supplies of government money for infrastructure investment have broader and even more ominous implications for the economy as a whole. Between 1992 and 1995 overall infrastructure spending fell in real terms, and this was responsible for much of the decline in India's real stock of capital over those years. As foreign money flows in, some of this lost ground will be made up. But nothing affects future economic growth as much as capital formation in the present, and India's government needs to find some way of increasing its own contribution if the economic machine is not to begin grinding down.

PROFANE AND SACRED

As if all that were not enough, the government's success or failure at getting the economy moving will have a lot to do with how dangerous religious and caste politics prove to be in coming years. Much of the occasional violence and instability that make India seem a frightening place wears a religious mask. In September 1947, just after British India was divided into India and Pakistan, 5 million refugees went on the move to get to the right side of the border (meaning the side where a majority of their co-religionists were); in formerly united Punjab, as many as 500,000 of those who found themselves on the wrong side of the new border at the wrong time were killed in mutual massacres of Sikhs, Hindus, and Muslims.

There have been religious or ethnic outbursts ever since. Guerrilla campaigns were carried out during the 1980s and 1990s in Punjab (Sikh versus Hindu) and Kashmir (Hindu versus Muslim). Tribal rebellions by Nagas and Mizos flared in northeastern India throughout the 1980s, and the migration over the past decade of some 10 million (Muslim) Bangladeshis into West Bengal and the Indian interior beyond has raised Hindu-Muslim tensions further. The most prominent (and potentially the most dangerous) communal incidents were the assassination of Indira Gandhi in 1984 by her Sikh bodyguard and the subsequent Sikh-Hindu riots in Delhi that killed thousands; and the 1992 destruction of a disused mosque at Ayodhya by Hindus in which hundreds died.

There is less irrational fanaticism behind this violence than meets the eye. Because so much of economic activity in India has been under government sway, and so many good jobs in the gift of political patrons, political intrigue has been a useful tool for extracting a share of the spoils; and with religious-based politics enjoying a growing audience, religious-based economic claims are being made more loudly.

From the biggest single religious divide in India, that between the upper-caste Hindus (of whom there are some 525 million) and the Muslims (110 million), has sprung the strongest recent challenge to the formally secular rule of the Congress party. Many political analysts in India think that but for the assassination of Rajiv Gandhi near the end of the 1991 general-election campaign, which scared a lot of voters back into the arms of the Congress party, the Bharatiya Janata party (BJP), which is openly Hindu nationalist, would have won. The BJP has respectable front men, but in their shadow lurk some pretty unsavory (not to say proto-fascist) characters.

The party, whose strength grew throughout the 1980s, stands for the values of the small-shopkeeping class of the Hindi belt. Hence, the BJP favors economic reform insofar as its stands for deregulation of the domestic economy but is against liberal rules for foreign investment (it was a BJP government in Maharashtra that canceled the Enron project in 1995; see page 186). The nationalist strain is reinforced by professed disgust with corruption and by vague resentment of special rules (on marriage, for instance) that have been granted to Muslims. This message has a surprisingly strong appeal even to the internationalized yuppies of India's northern cities, who might be expected to realize that Muslims, outnumbered by Hindus more than five to one and with significantly lower average incomes and educations, do not pose a grave threat to Hindu existence; and that, if foreigners are not allowed into India, it will mean the perpetuation of the old game of seeking wealth through politics and patronage rather than market performance.

By the mid-1990s, both Congress and the BJP were beginning to lose ground over the older, deeper, and even more sinister antagonisms of the caste system. Hindu in origin, the ideas and practices of caste have penetrated throughout Indian society. These ideas and practices are a disgrace. They thrive on minute classifications of people, based solely on their parentage, which in extreme but all-too-common cases dictate whom people can marry and what sorts of work they can do. True to form, the Congress party applied its (justifiable) indignation to this problem and came up with a remedy that worsens the disease. It began setting aside university places and government jobs for outcastes (those previously considered too contemptible even to make it into the caste system).

A few decades of slow economic growth had made such sinecures even more valuable by the late 1980s; pressure from the lower castes rose for more set-asides, with the upper castes resisting more. The government of V. P. Singh fell on account of this issue in 1990. In 1993 and 1994 pro-quota parties gathering votes from lower-caste Hindus and Muslims alike began beating both the Congress party and the BJP in state elections in the populous Hindi belt, which gives reformers in the central government yet another headache: If people are convinced that wealth flows mainly from patronage and that it is their turn at the public trough, it will be hard to convince them of the virtues of patronage-busting liberalization.

SUNLIGHT AND SHADOW

Can India's government break through these entrenched obstacles to reform? One optimist is P. Chidambaram: a Harvard Business School graduate, a scion of one of India's richest big-business families, and commerce minister in the Rao government until he fell foul of some pretty silly charges in a financial scandal. In 1995, Mr. Rao returned the commerce portfolio to him, thus again zipping his mouth shut with ministerial responsibility. But sitting as a private citizen in a Delhi house in the spring of 1993, Mr. Chidambaram made a staccato series of points about India's reforms.

The revolution of ideas, he said, has already been achieved, with the intellectual respectability of Nehruvian socialism forever shattered. So what the progress of reform now depends on is men in office who have the will to break through the usual political barriers. The rent seekers—those who profit from manipulating the regulatory system—will fight this, but they can be overcome. Another external crisis could give the oomph needed to vanquish them, or better yet, the growth of a critical mass of reformers in the parliamentary Congress party.

The way to create that mass, said Mr. Chidambaram, is to speed up reform and do some highly visible things to distribute the gains widely among the population. First, immediately strip $3 billion out of government spending on subsidies and state firms and put it into schools and hospitals. Second, identify no more than five lines of infrastructure for the government to take a leading role in promoting and open the rest to private control. Third, throw the state governments into a competitive race for an "exit" policy (how to let firms go bust and fire workers), with the winners getting to keep the extra revenue and the fruits of higher growth. To land seaborne freight in India, for instance, costs 150 percent as much as in next-door Sri Lanka; let India's ports compete to bring the cost down. Fourth, launch a "big-bang" privatization of state-owned firms, which is the only way to spread ownership of their shares widely, make their managers accountable, and stop their losses. Fifth, investment must rise, and the only realistic way of doing this is to get savings to rise first. An extra ten percentage points should be added over the next five years to India's 22–23 percent gross savings rate by following Japan's post-1945 practice of eliminating tax and inflation biases against savings and introducing some incentives for it.

Mr. Chidambaram said that Congress, for all its faults, remains the only party remotely capable of carrying out such a program. It has a formal political structure, even its bad parliamentary members have a grasp of what is involved in governing, and it is capable of absorbing new ideas. It also, occasionally and uniquely in India, is able to stand up to special-interest pressures. The lower-caste contenders are not even parties. As for the BJP, it not only poses demagogic dangers but has no depth of talent and no coherent economic philosophy. Its city-trader mentality prevents it from understanding either the global economy or the aspirations of the poor in India's south and west (outside the Hindi belt). The BJP hates foreign investment, but, said Mr. Chidambaram, it is Pepsi and Kellogg that pay Indian farmers world prices for their products, not the subsidized middle classes of India's towns and cities.

It is, of course, almost entirely under Congress party governments that the foundations of the economic system Mr. Chidambaram wants to tear down were laid and elaborately built upon. And an altogether more somber view of India's ability to break free of this past comes from Mohan Guruswamy, a southern Indian businessman who is well connected with all the national parties. Mr. Guruswamy says that India is plagued with what political theorists call a "soft state," meaning governments incapable of making hard decisions. Democracy has an outstanding virtue in India: It is the only form of political organization supple enough to accommodate the extraordinary diversity of Indian society. India's only authoritarian experiment—Indira Gandhi's strong-woman rule of the late 1970s—quickly failed. And the best that could be expected of a "successful" period of authoritarian rule is that India would break up, with the parts that are capable of racing ahead (Punjab, Gujarat, Bombay, and a few places in the south) freed to do so.

Yet the usual weaknesses of democracy—timidity and the power of special-interest lobbies—are at their most acute in India. Mr. Guruswamy notes that democracy has in fact done little to reduce the power of India's ruling classes, whether in the still-feudal countryside or among officials, who, even after the start of reform, for the most part still "enjoy power," most visibly by having a hundred or more petitioners perpetually waiting outside their offices for an audience. Voting has become a sham, with a smaller share of people casting ballots and those who do tending to vote along lines of religion or caste (which did not used to happen). This is only natural when politicians respond mainly to fund-raisers and lobbyists seeking to secure or expand their share of the public purse.

Because of all this, almost everything connected with the state runs badly. The rule of law, which looks good on paper, offers no counterweight in reality. How could it when litigants resort to the courts mostly to delay decisions? By Mr. Guruswamy's reckoning, the million cases on the Supreme Court's docket in the early 1990s will take 325 years to clear. The only institution not to have become infected with the rent-seeking virus, he says, is the Indian army, which is disciplined, relatively clean, scrupulously nonsectarian, and clear in its purposes—which absolutely do not include getting involved in running the country. As for the political parties, the BJP does pose the threat of populist demagogy and, anyway, is no less corrupt than the Congress party, and Congress, though more capable, is too self-serving to pursue radical reform: At party conferences, cabalistic meetings about Central Committee posts regularly outdraw the finance minister.

Appealing (and attainable) though the Chidambaram view is, I suspect it is not going to be realized as quickly as he would like. On the other hand, by 2000 many of the obstacles described by Mr. Guruswamy may have begun wearing away. Even a modest continuation of reform for the next few years should release forces of change from below that will make the acceleration to a breakthrough inevitable. Those forces have already built up more than most people realize.

PERCOLATING UP

Because the worst feature of Indian socialism was how little it did to improve the lot of the really poor—meaning that income inequalities actually widened—India's mediocre economic performance over forty-five years was not as lousy as the countrywide numbers suggest at improving the lives of everybody else. As one Indian observer puts it, half the people have done terribly but the other half not badly at all. The improvement for the lucky (or rather favored) half has been accelerating. MARG, a market-research firm in Bombay, figures that real GDP per capita for these people rose as much in the thirteen years after 1977 as it had in the thirty years before. With the partial opening of the early 1990s adding its push, the structures of Indian society and business are fast being transformed.

The potential for social change is high because those with anything at all have more than the official statistics say they do. Estimates of the size of India's black-market economy vary anywhere between 20 percent and 50 percent of official GNP. Then, too, purchasing power is higher than dollar GNP figures would suggest. In the countryside, for example, few people pay rent; owning their own hovels, they have more to spend on bicycles. It is thought that on a purchasing-power-parity basis average Indian GNP per person was around $1,000 in the mid 1990s—some three times larger than dollar GNP per person.

Economic change has come fastest in the cities, especially those most exposed to the world beyond India. None has been more exposed than Bombay. This city of 13 million, India's financial and commercial capital, has always been money-conscious—to a degree where what passes for entertainment there would not do so many other places in the world, even including Hong Kong. Since 1958, a lawyer and tax expert named N. A. Palkhivala has given annual lectures on the latest Indian government budget. His 1994 talk, which lasted several hours, drew an overflow crowd of fifty thousand to Bombay's Brabourne cricket stadium.

Thanks to the post-1991 reforms, Bombay has been rocketed out of the orbit of Indian cost structures and into that of the advanced East Asian metropolises. Multinationals in both business and finance poured into Bombay and began bidding up the prices of the relatively few services that were of international quality. Between 1993 and 1994 office and home rents in neighborhoods that expatriates would venture into rose 75–100 percent in dollar terms. The selling price per square foot of office space in the best area of Bombay rose around sevenfold in rupee terms between 1988 and 1994, reaching around $800—not much less than in Hong Kong; by some reckonings, in 1995 office space in Bombay was the most expensive in the world. Salaries went the same way. Branch managers of local financial companies on annual salaries of $12,000 were being hired away by foreign financial firms for $40,000. If the top forty Indian industrial firms started paying managerial salaries in this sort of range, said one credit analyst, it would literally wipe out their profits.

A little farther away all this seemed nonsensical, as it might well prove to be with the next bursting of the financial bubble. Businessmen said that as of 1994 highly skilled labor in places like Bangalore (strong in computer software) and Hyderabad (drugs, electronic engineering, and automation) was still a bargain by world standards. The head of the Indian operation of Glaxo, a British drug company, reckoned he could still hire a good research scientist for 200,000 rupees (not quite $7,000) a year; a head of R&D would fetch compensation, including an apartment and car, of $15,000–$20,000. In both cases the figure in the West would have been ten times as high. Roughly the same ratio (which also seems to prevail in China) applies for electrical, electronic, and pneumatic engineers. This may help explain why large numbers of Indian engineers and doctors have left for the West, especially America, and why Western companies make such heavy use, via satellite links, of the talents of Indian software writers who have stayed put in Bangalore.

India's secondary centers are hardly stagnating. The population of Hyderabad, a dirty, chaotic, and bursting city that is now India's fifth most populous (with some 4.5 million people in 1994), grew by 220 percent in the 1970s and 270 percent in the 1980s—the fastest rates of growth for any big city in India. In the spring of 1994 water was supplied for residential use in Hyderabad for one hour a day; in the summer it was one hour every other day. But government decrepitude was matched by private vigor. At a fair clip, professors were leaving nearby government research labs in defense electronics and pharmaceuticals to set up companies in industrial parks on the city's outskirts (or interim outskirts, until new shantytowns surround them). At a less elevated level, the already packed roads were becoming ever more immobilized by the five thousand new vehicles— from scooters to trucks—that Hyderabad was registering each month.

The appetite of regional centers far smaller than Hyderabad for modern products and services, especially financial ones, is growing fast. By 1994 more than 20 million Indians owned shares in companies listed on the country's nineteen stock markets; as early as 1992, 16 percent of India's total stock-market capitalization was held by mutual funds. Uday Kotak, the head of Kotak Mahindra, a broad Bombay-based financial firm that got its start in consumer finance, says that by 1994 the firm was extending its consumer-finance operations ever farther afield to meet demands for car, consumer-durable, and retail finance. Car buyers tended to be mostly entrepreneurs of small and medium-sized firms, together with a scattering of professionals but few salaried employees. By 1994, Kotak Mahindra had consumer-finance branches in places as small as Kolhapur (population 450,000). Its retail-finance services (like department-store credit), marketed through six thousand to seven thousand sub-agents for the Tata and other big business groups, reached people in places a lot more remote than that.

COUNTRY MATTERS

For the countryside, too, is being shaken up. Hyderabad's population has been swelling so fast in part because people have been leaving the parched and unproductive land around it. Yet economic betterment and outside influences have been reaching even forlorn places like that. Migration is one cause. The early successes of the "green revolution" in Punjab (much aided by the fine system of canals that the British had left behind) raised incomes there until every village could afford electricity and tractors. The wealth spread to the states of Uttar Pradesh, Gujarat, Haryana, and Karnataka. By the early 1980s farmworkers from Bihar began arriving in Punjab, where average incomes were more than fifty times higher, to take casual work. A decade later Biharis made up eighty-five percent of the workforce in Punjab's small bicycle factories. Punjabis in turn started heading for Bombay to drive and then own taxis.

Not all the migrants have been of such modest means. Formerly rural parts of the southern state of Kerala are being turned into retirement suburbs for Indians who went to the Persian Gulf to work in the oil fields and have returned with (relative) fortunes to their homeland. More exalted still is the return of professional Indians from America and Europe. In eerie reminiscence of the Chinese pattern, "non-resident Indians" (NRIs) who want to buy a place in the motherland are now numerous enough to warrant property developers putting up smart "villas" behind guarded walls in the countryside near most big cities, including several developments within fifty miles of Hyderabad, in areas the poor are deserting for the city. Private hospitals have been built in rural areas of the states of Andhra Pradesh and Tamil Nadu by NRI doctors who think there is now enough demand from well-off Indians to support world-class medical care in India itself. (And, as in China, more and more of the less well off, too, are turning to private providers of health care and primary and secondary education as state-provided services break down.)

But the single biggest influence on the changing views of ordinary Indians has been the rise of television, particularly satellite TV. In no other country nearly so poor (not even TV-rich China) has television had such an impact. In the early 1990s at least 200 million Indians watched television on an average day. Even four-fifths of villagers had access to television (usually through communal watching). That would not have mattered so much had TV remained the state monopoly it was in the late 1980s, when India had some of the most boring (and advertisement-free) television in the world. Satellite TV changed that. By 1993, India had at least sixty thousand cable-TV operators (most feeding no more than a few dozen subscribers and often stealing the signals to do it). Hong Kong–based Star-TV was being seen by perhaps 20 million households; Zee TV, in Bombay, did the Hindi-language programming for Star, then began investing in its own cable networks. Even the state channels responded to this racy fare, improving and spicing up their programs. In the early 1990s some 70 percent of total Indian advertising spending went for television ads.

Advertisers have a lot of customers to sell to even in rural India. In the early 1990s three-quarters of Indians still lived in the countryside, in some 550,000 villages. Poor though Indian peasants are on average, their economic sophistication varies widely. Only a third are thought to be wholly outside the money economy, with about 40 percent wholly in and the rest in between. Those with more than subsistence amounts of cash are so numerous—more than 300 million—that the absolute size of rural markets for many products is becoming bigger than that of city markets. In 1984 only 28 percent of the packaged goods sold in India were bought in the countryside; by 1989 the share was 37 percent, and it has already surpassed half for many categories such as detergents, hand soap, and packaged tea. For all the rest, rural sales will account for more than half well before the century is out.

Part of the reason for such shifts is that as city dwellers get richer they start substituting purchases of, say, quartz wristwatches for those of mechanical wristwatches, or of VCRs for radios, leaving it to the hicks to buy the less sophisticated products. But rural purchasing power is also rising quickly: A survey by India's National Council of Applied Economic Research (NCAER) found that in 1984 rural families spent 87 percent of their budgets on necessities (food, clothing, shelter); by the early 1990s that share was down to 67 percent. The NCAER's most recent consumer survey, conducted in 1992–93, suggests that the growth of wealth in the countryside is accelerating and widening. The better-off sort of farmer is now in the league to buy VCRs and cars. Washing machines, unheard of in the countryside a decade before, were owned by one in ten rural households in 1992. And low-income rural people—though (obviously) still well above the threshold of absolute poverty—accounted for 18 percent of the sales throughout India of lipstick, 20 percent of face cream, and 33 percent of nail polish.

The atomized nature of rural markets requires some clever thinking about marketing (see chapter 12): Hindustan Lever, which sells modest consumer goods like soap and packaged tea, has found that only just over a tenth of India's villages can sustain one of its outlets. But provided they have adequate incomes and the infrastructure (like paved roads) to support a distribution system, rural consumers at a given level of disposable income buy almost exactly what their urban counterparts do—largely, says S. M. Datta, the chairman of Hindustan Lever, thanks to the revolution in aspirations that television, with its (to non-Indians) dreadful soap operas and snazzy commercials, has brought to the countryside.

NEW BOARD FOR THE BUSINESS GAME

To go with an already changing society, the post-1991 reforms have started to bring about a big shake-up in Indian business.

Unsurprisingly, the economic-policy follies of 1950–90 distorted Indian business in some fairly grotesque ways. The industrial structure itself was warped: The "anti-monopoly" law, reinforced by the effective ban on foreign competition, encouraged the creation of big, high-wage, capital-intensive businesses; the reservation of some eight hundred lines of business for small firms simultaneously encouraged uneconomically small units. One result is that, unlike China, which has a healthy number of strong medium-sized businesses in medium-tech capital-goods industries, India has a weak mid-sized range of industrial firms. Another result is a loopy distribution of capital and labor: Indian steel plants with twenty times the workforce employed at a plant with the same output in South Korea; and, at the other extreme, a 5,000-metric-ton-capacity filament-yarn factory in India, when comparable South Korean plants have a capacity of 500,000 metric tons.

Some odd "business" skills were rewarded, and destructive forms of corporate governance encouraged. Almost no Indian companies bothered doing business abroad, since profits in the domestic market were artificially plump. This alone would have guaranteed a failure to hone management to world standards, but other effects were worse. The licensing system put a premium on the cultivation of political and bureaucratic contacts (hence all those trips to Delhi) and on monopolistic gamesmanship: Companies would often diversify into lines of business in which they had no interest, simply to preempt a competitor's access to a license.

The capital structure imposed on firms by government regulation resulted in a separation—almost always morally hazardous and occasionally downright corrupting—between the interests of the owner-managers and those of the other shareholders and of the enterprise itself. Like most of the rising big businesses throughout Asia (see chapter 10), Indian firms are young enough still to be dominated by the families that founded them. But in the family firms of the overseas Chinese (and to a slightly lesser extent of the South Koreans), the owner-managers are also the biggest shareholders. What is good for the firm is good for them. In India, by contrast, the family that founded and generally runs a firm rarely owns a majority of the shares.

Many of the shares are publicly held—nothing extraordinary about that. But in the normal case most of the shares, and almost always the biggest single concentration of shares, are held by government-controlled bodies. The largest firms were built up in close cooperation with the government, which took a keen interest in pointing them in the right direction; the government also took big slices of equity in them, through the holdings of state-owned industrial firms, state-owned financial firms, and occasionally even ministries.

Even when the government did not take the direct approach in acquiring a stake, it could always do so through the banking system. Recall that in pre-reform days every bank loan to a private company contained a clause allowing the state-owned bank to convert the loan into equity in the borrower whenever it felt like it. Thus, all too often the controlling family's main aims have not included the maximization of capital appreciation and dividends (since it gets little financial benefit out of that) but have included keeping the government's board representatives quiet (since the family thereby retains management control). At best this makes for inefficiency and divided loyalties; at worst for the looting of the firm (e.g., through phony transfer pricing with strictly family owned parts of the group or by inflating the book value of assets far above their real cost and pocketing the difference.)

Some of these old structures were changing even before the reforms began. As elsewhere in Asia, the aging and passing away of the founding generation had begun opening the way to the rise of professional managers bearing American MBAs and computer spreadsheets and to the rationalization and sometimes the breakup of diverse industrial groups along family fault lines. The reforms have helped push this along.

Many industrialists, even those who favored the reforms as a matter of principle, were scared that two generations of protection had made Indian business so flabby that as many as a quarter of the top two hundred companies would be in trouble once they were hit by foreign competition. This proved far too gloomy a view, but fear made for a good tonic. Firms began cutting costs—sometimes even labor costs in cooperation with unions that themselves had taken fright—and started to do serious budgeting and project planning. Without the perverse spur of the licensing system, the big groups have begun taking a careful look at which of their industries actually make business sense and voluntarily selling off those that do not. Joint ventures with foreign firms have increased sharply, especially in investment banking. The blossoming of the capital markets has made owner-managers more sensitive to the interests of the new shareholders (and of the firm itself).

It is unlikely that before 2000 many Indian firms are going to follow their overseas-Chinese and South Korean counterparts in expanding outside their home market; it will take that long for most of them to iron out the kinks in their domestic operations and make sure they are taking full advantage of India itself. But many of them are quickly being made efficient enough to compete abroad when the time comes. They will have their hands full. Asia has begun swarming with businessmen, and business opportunities, of all kinds.

PART III

MAIN STREET AND WALL STREET IN ASIA

CHAPTER 10

THE BUSINESS ROSTER: THE WEST, JAPAN, AND KOREA

A firm is a social organism. Everywhere it is a reflection—and a product—of the society and economy in which it operates, the level of technology, the specific characteristics of its line of business, and the markets where it tries to make money. Business in Asia is an especially complicated affair because, as earlier chapters have pointed out, the continent embraces astonishing diversity in all these respects. This part of the book tries to make sense of that diversity by describing, in this chapter and the next, the main corporate contenders, classified roughly by national origin, for business in the region; and in the later three chapters—on consumer markets, infrastructure, and finance—the main kinds of Asian markets in which those contenders will be striving to win. But it may help to begin with a more general view of how business and finance in Asia fit into the deeper currents that are shaping the continent's future.

Three overlapping issues, aspects of each of which you will find throughout this part of the book, will shape the evolution of Asian business and finance over the next generation. The first question is the nature of the business: Is it technology-intensive or not, and is it geared more to manufacturing or to marketing? Second, does the organization grow out of the Western, the Japanese, the Korean, or the Chinese tradition? Third, how are Asian firms and Asian systems going to cope with the biggest single challenge to Asia—the weakness of its institutions—as the continent enters the next phase of its modernization?

On the first point, Asia is no different from anywhere else on earth in being subject to the iron laws of technological progress. In many industries—essentially those that have been around for a long time, such as textiles, toys, and shoes—there is still a hand-me-down character to the transfer of capital equipment and technology from richer to poorer countries. In the more advanced industries this is becoming increasingly rare in relation both to the factories making the products and to the products themselves. Motorola's chip-making plant and Toshiba's color-television-tube plant in China are as advanced as any such plants in the rich world. And (an example discussed in chapter 12) Unilever markets its most up-to-date detergents in Irian Jaya almost as soon as it sells them in Amsterdam.

This matters because technological progress is simultaneously making possible uniform global production, and in some cases (like Coke) uniform goods; but also extremely fine differentiation of products whose appeal depends a lot on local tastes (which will matter most in fields like music and television). The combination of world-class manufacturing and delivery with narrow segmentation of markets will have an especially large effect in poor countries like those of Asia, where cultural differences remain much stronger than in, say, the United States. It will, moreover, affect a firm's policies on staffing and promotion. Toshiba does not, for example, need Chinese managers for its factories on the mainland, which produce goods that are going to be shipped all over the world for sale. But Toshiba will certainly need to hire and promote mainland Chinese managers when it starts marketing in China in a big way.

Second, as this chapter and the next will explain, the firms vying with each other for business in Asia—and eventually on a global scale—have radically different backgrounds and strengths and will need to improve themselves in very different ways as Asia bulks larger on the world business stage. The firms of the Chinese diaspora, based in the megacities of East Asia (including those along coastal China itself), are family-run businesses with superb speed of decision-making but deep organizational incompetence. This makes them excellent in industries where decisions need to be taken quickly and can be taken informally and often by one man (such as, traditionally, shipping or property); but not very good at performing in places where personal connections are absent or in industries that demand a high degree of organization (such as carmaking).

Japanese firms are usually the exact reverse of the overseas Chinese firm. They are slow to decide but excellent at collecting information from throughout the organization and at mass execution of a strategy; this is why they are strong at sophisticated manufacturing like cars and electronic hardware. South Korea's big firms partake of both Japanese and Chinese influence: They were founded by entrepreneurs and are run, usually autocratically, by the heirs of the founding family. Yet, like Japanese (and unlike Chinese) firms, they command the organizational loyalty of their workers and can run a managerially and logistically complicated business.

Western (especially American) firms tend to have more balance among their strengths than any of their Asian competitors. They are especially good at inventiveness and initiative. Once mature, they are not so good at leaping on opportunities the way the Chinese do or at executing mass manufacturing, as the Japanese and Koreans do. The Americans also tend to have trouble with Asia's informal and personal (and often corrupt) ways of doing business. One of the most interesting events in world business over the next generation will be to see how all these camps learn from each other.

The third and probably widest-ranging question is how Asian firms, and indeed Asian countries, are going to cope with the demands that modernization will place on them to create more transparent and predictable institutions. One side of this question is how successfully Asian firms (especially Chinese ones) will be able to adjust themselves to a more sophisticated business setting in Asia itself and to operations outside Asia. Another side to the question is broader still. Infrastructure and finance (discussed in chapters 13 and 14) are not only business opportunities but also whole fields of business and social organization where Asia's institutional weaknesses have been at their most crippling. Correcting them over the next generation will take a great deal of skill and perhaps cost Asia a few percentage points of economic growth.

The transformation of Asian business is, in the next decade or two, also going to catapult onto international markets a host of impressive Asian firms of which not one Western businessman in a hundred will yet have heard. The overwhelming majority of business in each Asian country, as everywhere else in the world, is conducted by local firms; most of them are small, and although many of them have trading interests in the outside world, few have investment interests there. This does not mean that the non-Japanese and non-Korean countries of Asia are devoid of multinationals; several Asian multinationals exist, many of substantial size even in global terms. The curiosity is that almost none has significant operations outside Asia; they are only regional multinationals. This, as will become clear, is a result of managerial rather than financial constraints.

Although they may at present be uncosmopolitan, Asia's local firms are often extremely strong or even dominant on their home ground. As Asia's economic weight in the world gets relatively bigger, many of these firms will use their homegrown advantages to expand to global size. Some of these new stars will come from India now that its many potentially great but until now regulation-warped big firms are knocked into shape by real competition. Others may come from Malay firms in Malaysia and Indonesia. The richest blind lode of corporate giants surely exists in China itself: I would guess mainly among medium-tech capital-goods firms, many without yet even an English-language name, in which well-connected foreign direct investors are quietly taking stakes. It may be 2005 before any of these unknown firms pops to the surface. Whoever identifies them early and accurately stands to be richer fifteen years hence than anyone bright and lucky enough to have had the chance to invest in Microsoft in 1980.

Meanwhile, transnational business in Asia is going to be dominated by the three groups of firms mentioned above, which are always in hot competition not only with themselves but with rising local business powers as well. The first of these groups contains the multinationals of the West: Europe and America. The second consists of Asia's familiar multinationals: those of Japan and, behind them (though still the first serious business contenders to emerge in Asia outside Japan or greater China), the conglomerates of South Korea. The third group is the least familiar in the West but nonetheless one of the most potent business tribes in the world: the network of the overseas Chinese, who are the subject of the next chapter.

Rich Man's Challenge

By 1993 the stock of Japanese, American, and European foreign direct investment (FDI) in Asia was some $130 billion and rising by around 10 percent a year. Trade between the rich world and Asia amounted to more than $500 billion. And Asia received net capital inflows from the rich world of some $60 billion. The increasing flows of goods, services, equipment, and money between the rich world and Asia have called forth a flood of companies and managers to service the economic links that these flows represent. In both 1991 and 1992 more than twelve hundred Japanese companies made new direct investments in the rest of Asia; and by 1993, Hong Kong alone was home to the Asian headquarters of some seven hundred multinational firms. How well are the rich world's companies succeeding at running their Asian businesses?

Mike Morris, a Manila-based business consultant with a firm called the Marketing Partnership, says that rich-world multinationals in Asia fall into three categories. Those doing best are the ones that have understood the many requirements—some of them mutually hard to reconcile—for building a successful regional operation in Asia. The essence of the challenge is to combine the sophisticated systems and methods of control used in the multinational's rich-world operations with an accurate sense of how to accommodate Asia's diverse cultural peculiarities—which deeply affect the firm in its dealings with governments, its own employees, and its customers.

This may sound like nothing more than "think global, act local," the formula coined by Ken Ohmae, a Japanese business thinker. But it is an especially hard trick to perform in Asia because of the immense variety of cultures in which a truly transnational firm has to operate there. In Mr. Morris's view, no multinational has yet made a full-blown success of this, in part because regional managers have not gone far enough towards seeing themselves (or being allowed by their home offices to act) as strategists rather than as mere executives. Some multinationals have done well at exploiting individual country markets in Asia but not at tying their Asian operations together; Mr. Morris counts Unilever, an Anglo-Dutch food and soap group, in this column. Others, like McDonald's, are ahead at imposing universal systems but have not successfully worked out how to accommodate the full range of Asian cultural variety (e.g., the partiality of the mainland Chinese consumer to chicken rather than hamburgers).

Still, all these are well ahead of the competition in Mr. Morris's second category. The second-tier multinationals have been hesitant about creating a new model of organization that better reflects the rapidly growing size of Asia's markets and their unusual complexities. They have also tended to prune their Asian operations at the first blush of red ink. This makes them highly vulnerable to the assertive efforts of both local companies and category 1 multinationals to grab market share.

The third category comprises Mr. Morris's "no-hopers": Western firms that try to deal with Asia the way their forebears did in the early post-1945 years. They simply do not take account of the modern (i.e., post-1980) size and sophistication of Asian markets and act as little more than agents or importers for distant foreign parents. European firms, in Mr. Morris's view, are disproportionately represented in this category.

EUROSCLEROSIS EAST

The charge that the much maligned Europeans are nowhere in Asia, and heading backwards from there, at first glance seems absurd. Asia is full of European firms doing a top-notch job: Unilever throughout Asia in detergents, cosmetics, and food; France's Danone (formerly BSN) and Switzerland's Nestlé in food; France's Carrefour and Holland's Makro in retailing; Swiss-based ABB Asea Brown Boveri and Anglo-French GEC-Alsthom in engineering; Germany's Volkswagen and Mercedes-Benz in cars and Wella in shampoos and the like; Britain's ICI and Germany's Hoechst in chemicals; Switzerland's Ciba-Geigy in drugs; and France's Alcatel, Sweden's Ericsson, and Germany's Siemens in telecoms. By 1993, moreover, much of European business—and especially German business—had woken up to Asia's potential and was pressing Europe's governments to do what they could to help. For what it is worth, a European Union summit in late 1994 added its voice to the national calls for a European business push into Asia.

Yet the figures are fairly unambiguous, as is the low regard in which European firms are held by people doing business in Asia. Although Europe seems to be holding its own in shares of trade between the rich world and Asia it has, as noted in chapter 5, been losing ground in the share of rich-world FDI in Asia. (And South Korean FDI in Asia has been growing much faster, though from a tiny base, than all the rich world's FDI.) Philippe Lasserre, a professor at INSEAD, a business school just outside Paris, has calculated that from the late 1970s to the late 1980s, in only two of ten East Asian countries did European firms increase their share of both trade and investment.

The Europeans can take no comfort from the thought that they may be making up some of this lost ground by the quality of their performance in Asia. The *Far Eastern Economic Review,* a Hong Kong-based weekly owned by Dow Jones, runs an annual survey of the opinions of managers and professionals throughout Asia about the "corporate leadership" qualities of companies doing business in the region. In the 1995 version of this survey the multinationals category (from which Japanese and South Korean companies, counted as locals, are excluded) puts only one European company, Switzerland's Nestlé, among the top ten, after Coca-Cola, Motorola, McDonald's, and Microsoft; only five Europeans make the top twenty, the other fifteen being American.

Few European firms are expecting any improvement in their standing in Asia. An INSEAD survey of more than a hundred European chief executives in the mid-1980s found that on average they thought 5 percent or less of their worldwide sales by 1990 would be accounted for by Asia—a preposterously low figure for a region that represented more than a quarter of world purchasing power that year. The seeming resignation of European business to a minor role in Asia is the more astonishing because, according to another survey of European business leaders, this one carried out in 1994 by British-based Harris Research, three-quarters of Europe's top business leaders think that China and Southeast Asia offer the best potential for manufacturing investment in the world (with over a quarter saying Western Europe offered the worst potential); and 45 percent think China and Southeast Asia will be economically the world's most powerful region by 2010 (with again over a quarter saying Western Europe will suffer the greatest economic decline of any region).

Powerful sentiments, you would think, in favor of a big European investment drive into Asia. Yet by the mid-1990s there was no sign of this materializing. Indeed, even one of the greatest of the European Union's semi-Asian boondoggles—a big stipend for young European businesspeople to enjoy a year or two in Japan learning Japanese and Japanese customs for free—sometimes does not have enough applicants to eat up its budget.

Mr. Lasserre puts the blame for European apathy about Asia on several things. One, mentioned in chapter 5, is the inward pull that the rise of an apparently trade-diverting European Union has had on European companies. A second is the belief of European managers that political risk in Asia is too high in relation to the rather distant rewards. The third reason is the ease, familiarity, and accessibility of other markets, especially America.

The tepidness with which, despite their fine words about Asia's importance, many European companies regard their Asian prospects is reflected in their internal organization. Mr. Lasserre found that Asia has no "voice" at board level and that few in top management have any experience of Asia. Because business in Asia is much less predictable, and the numbers less provable, than in Europe or America, the deck is stacked against Asian units of European firms in their planning and budgeting exercises. And, at the level of personnel, Asian experience is of little or negative help for the career advancement of expatriate managers, while at the same time local Asian staff feel they have no upward path within the firm. In sum, far too many European firms have not felt driven to stake a claim in Asia. These are all weaknesses that the successful multinationals in Asia—European and otherwise—have managed to avoid.

The Western firms that have best avoided these pitfalls are those of the United States. The reason is that American firms are the best placed for putting together the elements of Mr. Morris's elusive "amalgam" of business virtues for operating in Asia. They have depth of capital, strong internal corporate systems, and the (for Asia) invaluable potential, nurtured in their nation-of-immigrants homeland, of being able to deal with a multiplicity of cultures.

How Some Do It

Of Asia's three culturally sensitive actors identified by Mr. Morris—governments and local firms, workers, and consumers—consumers get a chapter of their own (chapter 12). This section and the next are about the successes of Western firms, mostly American ones, at coping with Asia's other two main business actors: managers and employees; and governments and local business allies.

The first task of a multinational doing serious business in Asia is to work out where to put the boss of the Asian operation. It sounds simple but is not. In the early 1990s the head of the Asia business of Fluor Daniel, a construction company headquartered in Irvine, California, was based not in Asia but in Irvine, California. As explained by Dick Corano, then the man in charge of Asia for Fluor, "Asia is a ten-hour square, anyway, and this way I can have a close relationship with headquarters." It is true that, if you have operations throughout Asia, the long-range air travel required means there is no particularly good place to put a regional headquarters.

The answer is bound to be easier for some kinds of business than for others. Single-product businesses in which each sale is large and national markets are not enormously different—engineering and infrastructure projects, say, or oil exploration—are at the less complicated end of the managerial spectrum. Del Williamson, who in 1994 was running GE Industrial and Power Systems Asia out of Hong Kong, answered to the head of General Electric's power systems division at its world headquarters in Schenectady, New York, but that was the only link between the Hong Kong business and headquarters. Some standards were set centrally—new product requirements, for instance, or global strategy—but Mr. Williamson and his staff made all the commercial decisions for the Asian business themselves. No one in Schenectady had anything to say about marketing, sales, or service in Asia. Mr. Williamson's guess was that, in all, perhaps six people at the Schenectady headquarters had any influence at all on the profitability of the Asian operation.

Most others do not enjoy such spare and clean lines of organization. In the mid-1990s, Unilever ran its Asian businesses on a geographic basis, with their chiefs (there were two, one for East Asia and the other for the Indian subcontinent) based in London and holding seats on the Unilever board of directors. (Recall Mr. Lasserre's criticism of many European firms for not providing a board voice for Asia.) But Unilever also had product divisions (e.g., for detergents or cosmetics), and the regional groups consulted with them as well as calling on centralized operations, such as research and development, for help. A lot of meetings were also necessary between headquarters staff and the local businesses in individual Asian countries. The local companies were given targets for sales, profit, and so on, which varied depending on the strategic aim (if the aim was to build market share, profits would be lower); they were then left pretty much on their own to hit the targets.

Probably the most crucial local decision is about staffing: How many expatriates do you ship out from the West, and how many locals do you hire and promote? The question becomes even more vexed when the demands of corporate culture are added to the complications of national culture.

The question is especially significant in Asia because personal ties and loyalties matter so much there. Tam Chung Ding, who in the mid-1990s was running Motorola's Asian semiconductor business from Hong Kong, points out that engineering students with whom he was in college in the late 1970s were now running the chip divisions of South Korean conglomerates. The old connections make it easier for him to sell to these firms or negotiate collaborative deals with them. Mr. Tam reckons that Western firms do best by growing their Asian business fairly deliberately and staffing it with locals from the very beginning. This both shows a commitment to the local market and builds the loyalties of people with the right skills and connections.

The depth and breadth of personal attachments can run surprisingly far. When asked what Fluor Daniel's special strengths are in Asia, both the head of the Asian operations, Dick Corano, and the head of the firm, Les McCraw, mentioned the number of construction workers and engineers trained by the firm in the four decades it has been in Asia: some fifteen thousand South Koreans and ten thousand Indonesians. Fluor has found that many of those it has trained eventually come to join the company; and, even if they do not, their earlier tie to Fluor makes cross-border projects and joint ventures with their new firms much easier to arrange.

Mr. Williamson of GE Power Systems pointed out that some way must be found to bring in and promote local people but at the same time inculcate them with the firm's values and culture. By 1994, GE Power's Asian business employed two hundred professionals, 60 percent of them Americans and the rest Asians. Limits on promotion opportunities were not much of an obstacle to integrating locals; the good project jobs increasingly are found in Asia rather than on GE's home ground. But GE takes care systematically to drum into its local recruits the methods and beliefs by which the company is run.

The astute use of Asian talent can work wonders for a multinational's Asian business. American International Group (AIG) is America's most profitable big insurer. It is also the biggest foreign insurance company in most of East Asia—and may be America's most Asian firm in terms of the way it works (meaning the family and personal connections it values), the attitudes and nationalities of the people who run it, and where it gets its business.

Indeed, AIG is Asian by birth, having been founded in Shanghai in 1919 by a young Californian named Cornelius Starr and transplanted to New York only in 1939, when war left Starr no other choice. Even in Shanghai, Starr had defied colonial prejudice to hire and promote Chinese managers. Edmund Tse, who today runs AIG's Asian life business out of Hong Kong, is the son of the Chinese manager of AIG's Shanghai office in Starr's day.

The firm's commitment to Asia never flagged and, as soon as war and politics permitted, it reentered every Asian country it could (most recently its birthplace, where a new Shanghai office was opened in 1993). As you might expect, it has had little trouble anywhere finding and promoting local talent: AIG's worldwide investment business is in the hands of Filipinos who came out of its Manila operation. The whole firm's culture is so pervaded by Asian attitudes and methods that it is pointless to worry about any conflict between the firm's views and those of the Asians who work in it.

Perhaps no multinational besides AIG has been as enthusiastic about promoting Asians as Citicorp. The New York-based bank has been in Asia even longer than AIG, having opened a trade-finance business in various Asian ports in 1902. Its familiarity with Asia and its banking power—it dominates the (often restricted) foreign-bank markets for corporate finance and consumer banking throughout Asia—have allowed it to attract Asian stars to its staff. By 1995, Citicorp's Asian consumer banking was run out of Singapore by an Indian, and corporate and government finance were run out of Singapore by a Pakistani. Of the twenty-one managers reporting to the Indian, ten were Asians. The movement upwards for Asians does not stop with Asia. Both the Singapore executives were among Citicorp's fifteen executive vice presidents (then two steps from the top); one of the bank's five vice chairmen (one step from the top) was Chinese. That would be inconceivable in a Japanese bank, which is one reason why American firms have such a marvelous chance in Asia.

The Hunt for Allies

The same thing that makes the cultivation of Asian staff important for a Western multinational—the significance of personal links and loyalties in Asia—also makes it important to pick the right local partners and to deal in the right way with whatever government has a say in what the firm is trying to do.

The choice of a local partner can mean life or death for a foreign firm. In 1993 I asked an executive of Nissan, Japan's second biggest carmaker, about his company's prospects in the rising market of Indonesia. He shrugged his shoulders, more or less admitting that Indonesia seemed lost. Nissan had a market share there of 1 percent, less than that of the minnow Daihatsu. The reason: "We linked up with the wrong guy."

Sadly, it is an easy mistake to make, and in business surroundings as opaque as those of Asia there are no good ways of avoiding it— except perhaps patience. One Western publishing firm that has decided to go into China is doing almost nothing for the first few years but quietly lining up joint-venture partners in far-flung parts of the country.

It sounds maddening, not to mention expensive, but going it alone is not really an alternative either. Even a firm as well established in Asia, and in as relatively uniform an industry, as Fluor Daniel almost always tries to hook up with a local joint-venture partner. Expertise is one reason, the ferocity of competition (in Fluor Daniel's case from well-capitalized Japanese and South Korean engineering firms) another reason, since the right partner can mean the needed edge in a strenuously contested deal. Even Coca-Cola, when it decided to take its plunge into China, sought out a local heavyweight. Robert Kuok, a Hong Kong–based Malaysian with some of the best contacts in China (he got his start in the mainland by winning the lucrative rights to import sugar), agreed to invest $100 million in Coke's Chinese bottling plants.

The next stage in Western-Asian cooperation is likely to be more elaborate. Already American companies in natural-resource and capital-goods businesses are looking for Asian partners as a way into Asian markets and are being told that share swaps—in which the American and Asian firms would simultaneously acquire chunks of each other—are the only method the would-be Asian partner will consider. The Asians believe it is the right structure for building trust. Some pioneering transpacific mergers may be on their way, though as yet they exist merely on investment bankers' drawing boards.

Governments are harder to deal with than joint-venture partners —they do, after all, tend to be monopolies—but winning their trust can be rewarding. There are few places in Asia where governments do not exert a sway over business that would flabbergast Western businessmen who have no experience of the place. Even a swashbuckler like Rupert Murdoch found himself, after he had taken over Star-TV, a pan-Asian satellite network, in 1993, making pilgrimages to places like Malaysia to assure local politicians that Star would not begin broadcasting the sort of Western trash they disapproved of.

Franchises, licenses, and public-procurement power have reaped many a business group a magnificent monopoly harvest in Asia. Examples can be found throughout the continent: the Kuomintang (KMT)-owned or KMT-controlled companies of Taiwan; the telecommunications and natural-resources concessionaires of the Philippines; the timber, cement, and clove-cigarette concessionaries of Indonesia; army-linked business groups in Thailand and ruling-party-linked businesses in Malaysia; and India's grand business houses, which for decades had a mutually parasitic relationship with the government thanks to its tightly regulated and protectionist economic regime. Even in free-trading Hong Kong and Singapore, government connections (and often in Singapore outright government ownership) have given a big boost to politically favored firms, although such firms in both city-states have been held to strict performance standards by world prices and practices. As Asia becomes richer, deregulation and privatization are beginning slowly to dilute the political element in business life (and will help force changes in the traditional methods of Asian family-firm management; see later sections). But this process has not gone far in most of the continent; and it has not even begun in China, the Asian country whose government the West's multinationals have been most eager to propitiate in the 1990s.

Before AIG became the first foreign insurer allowed to do business in China since the revolution, the company spent a decade cultivating both the Chinese central government and Shanghai officials: Both were particularly impressed by the commitment shown by AIG's $50 million investment in Shanghai's posh Portman hotel, apartment, and office complex in the late 1980s. Alcatel, a French firm that is the world's biggest maker of telephone switches, found itself on the right side of the Chinese government more by accident. Along with several other foreign switch makers, Alcatel had begun selling to China in the mid-1980s. But, alone among the competition, Alcatel invested in a switch-making factory in China. When the Tiananmen Square killings took place in 1989, everyone else scampered; Alcatel, because of its factory, stayed put. By the time the others began returning in the early 1990s, Alcatel was well ahead in the race for government contracts thanks to the long-term view of China's prospects that it took (or rather was given).

China is by no means unique in this. In his rise to the top, Robert Kuok, Coca-Cola's Chinese partner, performed significant services for the government of Malaysia—where, in the 1960s, he tried to rescue the state-owned airline and at government request set up a shipping line—as well as for those of the Philippines and China. The failure to negotiate such political minefields successfully can be costly. In 1994, Makro Taiwan—a joint venture involving Makro, a Dutch retailer, Thailand's Charoen Pokphand, and a local Taiwanese partner—had two of its highly successful discount stores shut down by local officials. Makro Taiwan was a victim not just of envious retail rivals but of its own failure to be on the right side of both the Kuomintang-controlled Taiwanese government and opposition-controlled local governments.

Yet in China the complexity of business-government relations demands particular care. Stephen Shaw and Johannes Meier, business consultants with McKinsey's Hong Kong office, have described a two-step process of alliance building for foreign investors in China. In the first stage the foreigners find a joint-venture partner to do business with, relying on the Chinese company, a state-owned firm, to smooth the way with sales, distribution, and government contacts. In the second stage the foreigners often bypass or downgrade relations with the Chinese firm, making an alliance instead directly with the firm's supervising bureau or ministry and using the bureau's contacts and its own to set up a controlled distribution and sales network.

One Western firm that has understood the density of the networking required for a successful Asian business is France's Danone (which until recently was called BSN). The firm got a slow start in Asia compared with rivals such as Nestlé, Unilever, and Nabisco, but it has grown well through joint ventures and acquisitions. It began with a joint venture with Japan's Ajinomoto to sell yogurt and moved on through five joint ventures in China, the latest (in 1994) a deal with the Shanghai city government for the production of eighteen thousand metric tons of soy sauce a year. Meanwhile, Danone acquired a stake in Britannia Industries, one of Asia's biggest biscuit producers, from Nabisco in 1989 (a stake converted to full ownership in 1994) and in 1992 bought Amoy, China's oldest and biggest food company, decamped since 1949 to Hong Kong (and now run, perhaps not incidentally, by a Chinese national who spent ten years in France). Along the way, Danone took a stake in Peregrine International (as did Chicago's Pritzker family—of Hyatt hotels—who run one of Asia's biggest trading companies out of Tokyo). Peregrine International is a privately owned holding company that is the principal shareholder in Peregrine Investments, a Hong Kong–based investment bank with excellent connections throughout the region, especially among ethnic Chinese.

JAPAN, LEADING BUT WORRIED

For the moment, Japanese companies in general are on firmer ground in Asia than their Western competitors. In part this is because two sharp rises in the value of the yen since 1985 have strongly concentrated Japanese corporate minds on the need to shift factories away from Japan itself, which is the most expensive manufacturing site on earth. The second (and more significant) round of corporate departures from Japan, which began in the early 1990s, has included not only giants like Toshiba and Matsushita, experienced in Asian production since at least the mid-1980s, but also small and medium-sized suppliers of parts and capital goods to the giants.

Decade-old fears in Japan that its manufacturing base is being ''hollowed out'' by the migration of its factories are much exaggerated. But the process of moving offshore does seem sure to help push Japanese business in the direction it ought anyway to be going at home—towards higher-value-added production. And the modest uprooting of Japanese small and midsize manufacturers will have a bigger impact, in terms of technology transfer and the balance of trade in capital goods and parts, on the places the factories are being transferred to. Those places are overwhelmingly in Asia: the destination for more than three-quarters of the smallish companies that moved factories out of Japan in 1993.

Japanese firms in the early 1990s were also more focused than others on Asia because they had gone through one of those monolithic but swift changes of attitude and strategy for which corporate Japan is famous. The harbinger of this was the decision of Yaohan, a provincially based Japanese department store chain, to move its world headquarters to Hong Kong in 1990, at a time when most multinationals had sharply pulled back from China after the Tiananmen Square killings of June 1989 and when Hong Kong itself was reeling from a lack of self-confidence about its future. But Kazuo Wada, Yaohan's chairman, reckoned that the future belonged not to Japan but to Asia, and especially China.

Within a few years, with Japan's own economy (temporarily) buckling, Yaohan was thought by other Japanese firms to be "the dream company," envied for the fact that, as one Japanese businessman put it, "its internationalization didn't even include Tokyo, it went straight from Shuzuoka to Asia." By 1993, in the depths of Japan's recession, one of the arguments advanced by the Ministry of Finance for supporting Japanese banks with bad balance sheets was that "the Chinese [meaning the overseas Chinese] are outinvesting us in Asia."

The result of corporate Japan's plunge into Asia was that, by the mid-1990s, as Mr. Morris puts it, "the anatomy of Japan Inc. was very deeply embedded" in much of East and Southeast Asia (save, glaringly, China). Even so, Japanese firms remain weak in the cultural dimension. They are unparalleled at securing information and incorporating it into their systems; but adapting to local circumstance is another matter. Yotaro Kobayashi, the chairman of Fuji Xerox, the Japanese subsidiary of the American information-technology firm, says that American multinationals in Asia have a sturdy capital structure and have been deft at forming strategic alliances to take advantage of local expertise. They are also trying to cultivate and promote Western-trained Asians to run their Asian operations.

Mr. Kobayashi thinks that, as of the mid-1990s, Sony, Matsushita, and Bridgestone had been the most successful Japanese companies at trying to take on the coloration of local Asian markets; but even they were not hiring and promoting locally (in contrast, for example, to Japanese transplants in America and Britain, which had been reasonably good at localizing themselves). Mr. Kobayashi's own company had a profitable joint venture in Thailand, but it had taken it a long time to find a Thai to promote to the top job. Thais still feel safer with local companies. And if a Thai is going to join a multinational, companies of Japanese origin still come well down the preferred list, even though by 1993 Japan had three times as much FDI in Thailand as America did; language and culture bar Thais from the top.

That will change. As Mr. Kobayashi sees it, Japan's push into Asia is going to force internationalization on Japanese companies far more than their investment in the West ever did. The uniformity and apartness in which Japanese firms are still steeped will have to give way if they are to have a strong Asian presence. Japan alone does not have the managerial manpower to run global or regional operations when a region of Asia's complexity grows to form a large part of the business. Jobs for Asians even at Japanese headquarters in Tokyo will begin to open up.

KOREA'S NEW PUSH

For the companies that are most persistently dogging Japan's heels, the conglomerates of South Korea, a different sort of corporate revolution may be in prospect—one which, if it succeeds, could make the Koreans more formidable contenders in Asia than they now appear.

Korean industry, sharply prodded by the Korean government, has always been audacious, whipping itself forward into industries such as semiconductors, shipbuilding, and cars that it probably had no business entering at the stage of development it had by then attained. It has been no less audacious in its moves abroad. Hyundai, one of the two biggest South Korean conglomerates (*chaebol*), began sending huge construction teams abroad in the 1960s to build runways, camps, and so on for the American army in South Vietnam; by the 1970s it was sending even larger teams to the Middle East for the grand civil engineering projects on which the Arab and Iranian regimes there were spending billions of petrodollars. Over the next few years Hyundai and a few other *chaebol* may well be carrying out the more daring and much more expensive work of digging out or chopping down the riches of Siberia's as yet unplundered natural resources.

But the bigger effort of the *chaebol* in the rest of Asia will come in manufacturing and heavy industry, particularly in China (though once North Korea opens up it may prove a stronger rival even than China for the *chaebol's* attentions). Since the mid-1980s the outward orientation of South Korean business has swung sharply away from the United States, which in 1985 took 36 percent of Korea's exports but by the mid-1990s less than a quarter, and towards the rising countries of Asia, which as early as 1992 had doubled their share of South Korean exports from the 13 percent they claimed in 1985 and had surpassed America as the South's biggest export market. South Korean FDI flows have followed on the heels of the shift in trade, and Korean conglomerates are now busy setting up factories in developing Asia.

The South Koreans have trained most of their corporate firepower on the Chinese market. Until the end of the 1980s, South Korea's economic relations with China were scarcely better developed than their diplomatic relations, which did not exist. The end of the Cold War and the eventual collapse of the Soviet Union opened the way for the South to reach out to both Russia and China, which for forty years had stoutly backed Communist North Korea in its fights with the South. The South's skillful Nordpolitik brought striking economic results in China. In 1989, South Korea's trade with China, all of it unofficial, was worth a few hundred million dollars. By 1993 China was South Korea's third-biggest trading partner: That year, trade between the two amounted to $14.5 billion (including goods transshipped through Hong Kong), and the South Korean government expects this figure to double by 1997. By the end of 1993, South Korea was still a bit player on China's FDI stage, but within a year projects were under way or agreements had been signed for multi-billion-dollar Korean investments on the mainland in oil refining, cement, glass, car parts, telephone switches, and television picture tubes and other electronic goods.

All this was unleashed by diplomacy between the South and China; and with relations between North and South Korea still extremely delicate, politics features strongly in the South's economic cultivation of China. But so does business. Both as a market and a manufacturing site, China has deep attractions for the *chaebol*. And China's obedient, ambitious, and cheap factory workforce is perfectly suited for the regimented management methods that the Korean conglomerates developed to such impressive effect back home but, with the coming of democracy to South Korea, can no longer use there. (Though, again, once North Korea and its even more disciplined—and cheaper—workforce become available for the South's factories, a lot of them will go there instead of to China.)

Yet if the *chaebol* are to establish themselves as a significant business force throughout Asia, they are going to have to reshape a lot of their traditional management and organizational systems. The management structures of the *chaebol* tend to be hugely different from those of their Japanese counterparts. The Korean conglomerates were mostly founded forty-odd years ago by entrepreneurs, and in many ways they are in essence a family-run entrepreneurial business grown huge on the back of a rigid bureaucratic structure. Such a structure—albeit Chinese in spirit—creates difficulties of its own for non-Chinese firms trying to compete in the Chinese parts of Asia. But the bigger problem for the *chaebol* is that much of Korean business strategy, and indeed most of the industries in which the big Korean firms concentrate, duplicate the strategy and lines of emphasis of their Japanese competitors.

The *chaebol* have shown that a lot can be accomplished even in export markets by following in the footsteps of Japanese competitors, but with a few years' delay. This is why South Korean firms get such a strong boost when, as happened in 1985–87 and then again in 1993–95, the Japanese yen rises sharply against the dollar but the Korean won does not. But it is also why in the late 1980s, when Korea's currency advantage against the yen evaporated, its firms suffered a bad loss of export market share to the Japanese: Without a big price difference, Korean goods were not up to the Japanese competition. Herculean efforts of work and capital accumulation cannot, in the long run, sustain the South Koreans in head-to-head business battles with the Japanese in any market—and certainly not in Asia now that Japanese firms have thrown themselves wholeheartedly into production there. The Koreans have to become more sophisticated.

The managers of the *chaebol* realize this, and the successful ones are likely to follow Samsung in trying to do something about it. Samsung, which each year disputes with Hyundai for pride of place as South Korea's biggest conglomerate, was well embarked by the mid-1990s on a restructuring program intended to make the firm

competitive as a worldwide multinational—and that, in the view
of its chairman, Lee Kun Hee, meant competitive on quality. The
program included a reduction by half in the number of firms in the
group, a sharp focusing of lines of management and lines of business (the biggest gamble of which is a new $5 billion foray into
carmaking), and decentralizing decision-making powers in the once
unbendingly hierarchical group. Managers are to be rotated abroad
in large numbers for periods of as long as a year so they can develop
a sense of local markets and cultures.

Carrying out this strategy successfully will not be easy. Even so, in
late 1994, around the same time that the South Korean government
at last gave Samsung permission to go into the carmaking business
in competition with the country's three existing carmakers, the company also signed a deal with China that envisioned a $3 billion
investment over a twenty-year period in electronics production in
Tianjin and announced another large manufacturing investment in
Thailand (as well as a new electronics complex in northeast England). If a new sort of *chaebol* really is being born, it could give
Japan Inc. a run for its money in Asia. But the main international
focuses of Samsung and the other Korean conglomerates are, just
like those of their Japanese exemplars and competitors, cars and
electronics. So if the Koreans are to succeed in Asia, they will have
to go through changes just like those the Japanese face, only even
more wrenching because they are starting out well behind the Japanese. And everybody is starting out behind the masters of Asia's and
indeed the world's greatest business network: the overseas Chinese.

CHAPTER 11

THE BUSINESS ROSTER: THE *HUA CH'IAO*

If you are in Saigon, it is worth visiting Cholon, the old Chinese district of the city. Despite the departure of many of Vietnam's ethnic Chinese as a result of war and expulsions, Cholon remains overwhelmingly Chinese. It is also a commercial center of remarkable density and variety. In 1992 the official figure for Vietnam's annual GNP per head was a miserable $220, about the same as Burundi's. Yet Cholon is packed with shops selling goods of all kinds: soap, toothpaste, clothes, shoes, food both fresh and packaged, soft drinks and whiskey, refrigerators, televisions, gold bars and coins, ceramic bathtubs, toilets and tiles (and stainless-steel and brass fixtures to go with them), motorbikes, engines, engine parts, and construction materials.

Some of this is for the retail trade, but much of it is wholesale: Cholon is the warehouse for all of Indochina. Its wholesalers are professional smugglers in cahoots with the Vietnamese army. Through a sophisticated underground network of suppliers—even when the American embargo on trade with Vietnam was still in force there was no problem buying Stanley power tools, John Deere tractors, American Standard toilet bowls, or Kohler boat motors in Cholon—the wholesalers procure goods from around the world. They sell these goods to retailers through informal distribution channels that span Indochina and reach into southwestern China.

An international financial system to support all this trading has its representatives in Cholon as well. It is possible for someone to deposit a large sum with a gold shop there one day and for a relative or business associate to withdraw the equivalent sum from an affiliated gold shop in Bangkok, Hong Kong, or Taipei a day or two later.

Cholon is one knot—a vivid and primitive one but typical nonetheless—in a business net that blankets much of Asia and stretches rather more thinly around the whole world. The net has been woven by people commonly known in Asia as the overseas Chinese: ethnic Chinese living outside China. The overseas Chinese overwhelmingly dominate business throughout Southeast Asia and East Asia, save for Korea and Japan. They also have been the biggest single external force in the economic development of China itself since 1978, accounting until at least the mid-1990s for three-quarters of the foreign direct investment (FDI) that poured into the mainland each year.

By 1995 there were 55–60 million overseas Chinese. Half of them lived in Taiwan (21 million) or Hong Kong (6 million), both of which are almost entirely Chinese. (No need to worry about Chinese government dogma that these places are part of China; for business purposes they are not.) In only one other place, Singapore, do they account for more than half the population (75 percent there, or 2.1 million). Everywhere else in Southeast Asia, and in the other countries (mostly in the West) through which they are sprinkled, the overseas Chinese are a minority: usually a tiny one, politically powerless, often resented and sometimes reviled and persecuted.

Yet they are one of the powerhouses of the world economy. In the mid-1990s, Taiwan, Hong Kong, and Singapore were among the top fifteen trading countries in the world. Elsewhere in Southeast Asia, the small numbers of overseas Chinese belie their extraordinary grip on local economies. Guesses about their financial strength are naturally imprecise, but here are a few: In Indonesia the overseas Chinese make up 4 percent of the population but in the early 1990s controlled seventeen of the twenty-five biggest business groups; one Indonesian investment banker reckoned that 80 percent of bank loans were to Chinese companies. In Thailand (10 percent Chinese) more than ninety of the hundred wealthiest business families are ethnic Chinese. They dominate Bangkok, which is considerably richer than the rest of Thailand; and by one estimate from the mid-1970s ethnic Chinese owned 90 percent of Thai commercial and manufacturing assets and half of Thai bank capital.

In the Philippines (less than 1 percent Chinese) Chinese-owned companies accounted for two-thirds of the sales of the sixty-seven biggest commercial outfits in the late 1980s, and since then rising Chinese firms have begun challenging the dominance of the old Spanish and army-linked firms in property and heavy industry. Even in Malaysia, where the Malay-run government has been trying for twenty-five years to reduce Chinese economic clout, the Chinese still control far more of the economy than their third of the population would entitle them to on numbers alone. A huge part of the East Asian miracle has been a miracle of ethnic Chinese business.

For a laugh, a few stabs have been made at trying to estimate the economic and financial power of "Greater China": the combination of the three places in Asia dominated by the overseas Chinese—Taiwan, Hong Kong, and Singapore—and China itself (a fair combination in view of the tightening economic and financial bonds between them; see below). The World Bank has guessed that Greater China's GDP in 1990 was $2.5 trillion (calculated on a purchasing-power-parity—PPP—basis), already ahead of Japan ($2.1 trillion) and almost half the American figure of $5.4 trillion.

The Bank's guess is that Greater China's economy by 2002 will be a whisker bigger than America's, twice as big as Japan's, and more than three times the size of Germany's. Greater China's economy would be bigger still if you thought of it as "Super Greater China" and added in the three-quarters of the output of Indonesia, the Philippines, Thailand, and Malaysia that is probably under Chinese commercial control. This would make the "Chinese economic pole" bigger than Greater China by perhaps $500–$600 billion in PPP terms in 1990: or half again as big as Japan's economy and more than half the size of America's that year.

On firmer ground, in 1992 Greater China had trade worth $640 billion, more than the value of Japan's trade and closing in on Germany's. The three overseas-Chinese havens in 1993 were the source of some $25 billion of the FDI that flowed into all Asian countries that year—or almost half. And by the end of 1994 the foreign-exchange reserves of the three added up to $200 billion, compared with $126 billion for Japan's. Add in China's reserves of $52 billion and the total for Greater China equaled almost a quarter of world foreign-exchange reserves at the end of 1994. No wonder the World Bank speculates that Greater China makes for a "pole" of economic growth with powers of attraction in the same league as those of America, Japan, and Germany.

As the foreign-exchange reserves suggest, the Chinese sphere's economic weight rests on sturdy financial pillars. Savings rates in the Chinese parts of Asia were in the range of 25–45 percent of GDP, with most places in the middle of the range. Accumulation is high, taxes are low, and the result is one of the world's biggest pools of investable capital. The Asian Development Bank has guessed that by 1998 retained earnings (corporate savings) in Asia will equal some $1.2 trillion, up from $700 billion in 1993; the vast majority of this cash will be in overseas Chinese hands. In the early 1990s the ready cash of individuals in Taiwan alone—household bank deposits, holdings of gold, and deposits in the underground financial system—were worth some $500–$750 billion. Towards the end of the 1990s the private cash holdings of the overseas Chinese should easily exceed $3 trillion.

THE SOJOURNERS' LIFE

The Cantonese name for the overseas Chinese is *nanyang hua ch'iao*. *Nanyang* means "the southern ocean," or South China Sea. (Remember that China was once called the Middle Kingdom, roughly meaning the center of the universe; the sea to its south was the only southern sea worth mentioning.) The character *hua* means "Chinese," and *ch'iao* is a sojourner. The Chinese diaspora was created over a period of six hundred years—overwhelmingly in the decades 1890–1920—by the emigration of successive waves of people, mostly from southern China and across the southern ocean to the countries of Southeast Asia into what was thought would be a temporary exile (hence, sojourner).

Gordon Redding, a business professor at the University of Hong Kong, has described the conditions both in their homeland and in their places of exile that shaped the social and business life of the overseas Chinese. Until the middle of this century the emigrants were almost always peasants, forced out of China mainly by economic pressure and steeped in the traditions of village life—a life of subsistence that always ran the risk of falling into destitution. Hard work and the accumulation of wealth were high virtues. And the social unit that counted above all others—so much so that the others might almost as well not have existed—was the family, the keystone of Confucian society and the source of what little physical security there was: "the first and last resort," in Mr. Redding's words, "and for most the only resort." Not for the Chinese the American social glue of law, government, and public ideals or the Japanese loyalty to organization or even nation. Within the Chinese family there was personal acquaintance, trust, and mutual obligation; outside it, mistrust and indifference.

The conditions of the Chinese diaspora only reinforced what had been true in China itself. The emigrants were continually deposited in places or under circumstances (as in Hong Kong and Taiwan after 1949) where they felt besieged. As recently as 1960, ninety thousand ethnic Chinese fled Indonesia over a three-month period in fear for their lives; and after race riots in 1969, Malaysia passed laws that discriminated against Chinese in the contest for university places and required Malaysian companies (including Chinese-owned firms) to transfer 30 percent of their ownership to Malays over a twenty-year period.

Remnants of the official anti-Chinese discrimination of the past still exist—notably in Malaysia's now modified pro-Malay affirmative-action laws and (less seriously) in Indonesia's old ban on the public display of Chinese characters—but for the most part the overseas Chinese of Southeast Asia are formally treated as full citizens of their countries. Yet ethnic awareness and ethnic tension persist. Even in Thailand, where the Chinese bear Thai names and mostly do not speak Chinese and where their assimilation (often through intermarriage) has gone furthest, everyone knows which families are of Chinese descent and roughly how Chinese they are.

If this sounds familiar from something in European history, it should: As early as the seventeenth-century European travelers in Southeast Asia were describing the Chinese there as "Jew-like." One way that such rich but politically vulnerable minorities can protect themselves is by making mutually beneficial bargains with those in power. Joint ventures between Chinese businesses and government enterprises, ruling parties, military interests, and presidents' families are common throughout Southeast Asia.

However, the main response of the overseas Chinese has been to avoid government and its nuisances (especially taxation) as much as possible. Except for Singapore, which has an especially intrusive government, this has been as true of the places where the Chinese are in a majority as of those where they have been in a minority. The upshot has been a decentralized business structure boasting a

large number of secretive and strikingly uniform family-owned firms
spread throughout East and Southeast Asia. The firms cooperate
smoothly and informally with each other, often across national borders, which, for these purposes, might as well not exist.

The building block of the overseas Chinese business system is,
naturally, the family firm. Even in companies listed on stock markets, the founding family's control and accumulation of capital are
principal aims; lines of authority are drawn to serve these aims. This,
says Mr. Redding, accounts for the typical Chinese firm's power
structure, in which ownership, managerial control, and the family
itself overlap to the point of being indistinguishable. It also explains
the obsession with bringing younger family members into the firm:
They can be expected to safeguard the family's interests.

To this day the sense of obligation remains strong. Heirs who
have become doctors or physicists in America are summoned home
to take over the family firm in preparation for, or on the death of, its
founder; and they obey the summons. One of the more spectacular
examples was Huang Shi-hui. In 1979, Dr. Huang, a Taiwanese, was
a neurosurgeon and a professor at an American medical school. He
had no business experience but, when his father died that year, he
fulfilled his duty as the eldest son and went home to Taipei to take
over Chinfon Global, the family's trading and carmaking firm. Dr.
Huang has since turned the company into a large conglomerate
that deals (among other things) in finance, construction, and management consulting.

The overriding aim of family control helps explain the autocratic
character of the classical overseas Chinese firm. Decision-making
powers are concentrated in one pair of hands, those of the firm's
founding father (who is the family's natural father). There is, in a
Chinese firm, none of the Japanese yearning for consensus. Papa
may be (and usually is) paternalistic about the welfare of his employees; but they are employees and he is the boss.

This sort of organization works better for some kinds of business
than for others. The overseas Chinese customarily started out as
traders, and the nimbleness and opportunism that make for a great
trader linger in the culture of their firms; which is why, for example,
Hong Kong Chinese firms found it so easy to make quicksilver
moves from textiles to clothes to toys to electronics as market demand shifted (see chapter 4). The overseas Chinese have been partial, too, to businesses such as property, commodities, and shipping.

As Mr. Redding points out, even when these businesses are conducted on a global scale, the instinct of one man at the top for
the right price, time, and place can count for more than complex
managerial or technical skills. Conversely, this system is ill suited
for industries that demand high levels of organization, professional
management, technology, or brand-name marketing.

Most overseas Chinese firms are small, and all tend to be hawk-
eyed about cost control and financial efficiency. This is a natural
result of the family-firm structure, but there is more to it than that.
Whether in the majority or the minority in a given country, the
Chinese rarely "enjoyed" the sort of access to subsidized bank credit
that was made available in other parts of Asia or to other ethnic
groups (see chapter 14). The Chinese lent and borrowed through a
single informal market for capital that stretched throughout their
diaspora, including North America and other remote outposts. The
market rates of interest at which they lent (together with low taxes)
encouraged their prodigious capital accumulation. The market
rates at which they borrowed encouraged the efficient use of capital
and the proliferation of small, labor-intensive firms.

Yet impressive though the Chinese family-owned firms are as individual businesses, they would not have had the aggregate impact
they did without something else: a method for tying the individual
firms, few of them extraordinary in their own right, into a powerful
business network. A peculiarity of the diaspora—its origins in just a
few regions of China—opened the way for the evolution of a global
web through which money, goods, ideas, and occasionally people
could flow unimpeded from one family's firm to those of others.

Many of today's overseas Chinese originated in Shanghai, notably
the textile makers who fled from communism to Hong Kong in
1949–50 and gave the British colony its first industrial boom. But
most have come from southern China—more than half, probably,
from just two provinces: Guangdong, next to Hong Kong, and Fujian, across the strait from Taiwan.

Wary of governments and laws and simply unable to deal at all
times within the reassuring confines of the immediate family, the
overseas Chinese found that dialect, kinship, or a common origin in
a clan, a village, or (at a pinch) a county gave a sure footing of trust
to a business deal conducted even at a great distance. However
widely separated in the diaspora, Hakka tended to deal with Hakka,
Chiu Chownese with Chiu Chownese. The certainty this gave and

the informality it allowed shaped the loftiest transactions as well as the most humble.

It also allowed a uniquely gifted business system to take root. A system based on a multitude of autocratic owner-managed firms with intimate and nearly instantaneous links to scores of others just like them has the great advantages of extremely fast decision-making ability and acute sensitivity to markets. When some of the firms grow big enough, and the capital that can be called upon through the network substantial enough, the system also has the capacity to play a significant role on the world business stage. By the late 1980s, with a big boost from the rise of China, that is exactly what had happened with the overseas Chinese.

MISTERS BIG

In 1987, Li Ka-shing, a billionaire Hong Kong Chinese businessman who eight years before had taken over Hutchison Whampoa, one of the colony's great British trading houses, decided to mount a bid for Hongkong Land, the property arm of the oldest British trading company in the colony, Jardine Matheson. The interesting part of the story is that Mr. Li is supposed to have put together the financing for the multi-billion-dollar takeover during an all-night session of no more than a dozen Chinese businessmen, many of them mahjong-playing chums of his: no papers, no lawyers, no consultants, no boards of directors; just a decision and a handshake and a commitment of billions of dollars.

Deals of like scale became increasingly possible as the wealth machine of the Chinese diaspora churned out growing piles of cash in the 1970s and 1980s. Although, as noted in the previous section, the average family firm of the overseas Chinese was small, not all were. Mr. Li's empire, which had famously begun in the 1950s with plastic flowers, had grown so large (mainly through property development and property holdings) that the inevitable press description or him for a decade or so in the 1980s and 1990s was "Hong Kong's richest man."

Yet Mr. Li was hardly alone in commanding huge wealth. In the early 1990s there were a dozen or so billionaire families in Hong Kong, and a like number in Taiwan, running large business groups. There was Robert Kuok from Malaysia (see chapter 10), a billionaire in Li Ka-shing's league; the Sophonpanich family in Thailand (the tip of their financial iceberg being a one-third share in Bangkok Bank, Southeast Asia's biggest bank); the Cheng family in Singapore; even a rising star in the Philippines, John Gokongwei, who was rudely elbowing aside some well-established non-Chinese families as he made his way forward. And there was Liem Sioe Leong, "Indonesia's richest man," whose stable of four hundred-odd companies accounted for roughly 5 percent of Indonesia's GDP and included such diverse overseas holdings as UIC, a big Singaporean property group, and Hagemeyer, a Dutch distribution company with sales of $2 billion a year in the early 1990s.

For Westerners, the frustrating thing about the great overseas Chinese business families is that no outsider can ever hope to understand their real business or significantly participate in it. For years investors and stock analysts have been grousing about the habit of every big family-owned Chinese firm to keep the best assets in private firms the family controls and shove the second-rate stuff into the public companies. This is, in fact, the norm, and it is unlikely to change; if public investors resent it, their only recourse is to shy away from the public companies. Joint-venture partners have a better chance of getting near the core of a Chinese business, but probably only if they use their clout in Western markets as a bargaining counter.

That is because the overseas Chinese have a pretty dismal record of doing business outside the Chinese orbit. Li Ka-shing's excursions, in the 1980s, into oil in Canada and, in the 1990s, into telecommunications in Britain were star-crossed (though both might yet turn out good). Such weakness raises broader questions about whether the Chinese family firm can really modernize, or ever become multinational beyond Asia. Some firms are beginning to break through: notably Acer, a Taiwanese computer firm that pulled itself back from catastrophe in the late 1980s and early 1990s to become a world-class competitor by the mid-1990s. More overseas Chinese firms, however, have decided to bet their future on China itself.

Such a strategy could be a dangerous one—and one that astute Westerners might profit from eventually—but it has its logic. China was growing enormously fast in the early 1990s, and nobody but the overseas Chinese had any idea how to deal with it. The top managers of President Enterprises, Taiwan's biggest food group and a would-be heavy investor in China, in private professed their amaze-

ment at how backward Western firms were in understanding and
dealing with China (a perhaps misleading comment in view of the
fact that President, although it had big ambitions for its China business by the year 2000, had probably invested no more than $150
million there by 1995). So, ran the reasoning, why should the overseas Chinese not grab this great opportunity that Westerners were
neglecting?

One of the most interesting firms to do so—in part because of its
global ambitions—is Thailand's Charoen Pokphand (CP). CP was
started as a seed company in Thailand in the 1920s by a Chinese
immigrant; agribusiness—especially animal feed and chickens—remains its main line. But over the years it has expanded its interests
to the point where, in 1994, it had ten divisions incorporating more
than two hundred companies with a diverse portfolio of businesses:
among them, motorcycles in China, retailing in Thailand and Taiwan, and (in a big joint venture with America's Nynex) telephones
in Thailand. In ownership as well as organization, CP hews closely
to the overseas Chinese line. Its chairman, Dhanin Chearavont, is
the son of CP's founder, and earns the usual helping of criticism
from foreign stockbrokers for shuffling the good assets into the
family firms in the group and the mediocre ones into the listed
companies.

Mr. Dhanin is one of the best-connected overseas-Chinese businessmen in China, where CP began operations in 1979, almost as
soon as Deng Xiaoping had thrown open the door to foreign investment. CP has never had a second thought about China. It is the
biggest single foreign investor in the mainland, and by the mid-
1990s its interests there had grown nearly as large as its non-
telecommunications businesses in Thailand.

The biggest of CP's mainland businesses are feed mills and
chicken farms. (By the mid-1990s, CP operated one or more of them
in twenty-six of China's thirty provinces and was opening five new
plants a year.) Tony Asvaintra, who in the early 1990s ran the mainland businesses out of Hong Kong, boasts that CP has had it easy in
China because the big Western firms with which it competes—notably Con-Agra and Cargill—do not understand the country and have
not adapted to the environment. (CP's Western competitors agree,
though they mean it in a different way, sniping that in contrast with
CP they have not been too cozy with Chinese officials.) Mr. Asvaintra
says that, whereas CP's competitors try simply to bring in modern

technology, CP modifies it to suit local conditions (a trick it began learning in then backward Thailand in the early 1960s). He also says that CP takes China's infrastructure failings in stride. It shuffles portable generators among its many plants. One reason the plants are dispersed so widely is so that their output can be sold in a relatively small radius, an important consideration in a country whose transport is as rickety as China's.

CP is using its China business as a lever to lift itself to a global scale. It is helped in this by being much sought after by Western firms as a joint-venture partner in China. However, in agribusiness anyway, considerably more is involved. By CP's reckoning, in the early 1990s, each Chinese on average consumed 3.2 kilos of chicken a year; that compared with 45 kilos per American and (a more realistic benchmark) 12 kilos for each Thai. Mr. Asvaintra thinks that by the early 1990s CP was already the world's fourth- or fifth-biggest animal-feed and chicken producer. He expects that, as the Chinese market swells (and CP's dominance of it remains more or less intact), CP will overtake Tyson, an Arkansas producer of chickens, to become the world's biggest chicken producer before 2000, and will follow a similar arc with animal feed.

And thanks to the skills honed and the scale economies achieved in China, the whole world will then beckon to CP. The company has no intention of competing with the likes of Cargill in commodities; it has no base for that. But by the mid-1990s, CP had chicken and animal-feed ventures in Turkey and was exploring the idea of entering Russia; in this sort of agribusiness it has ambitions to rule the world. Yet can the methods of the Chinese family firm really be employed by a globe-spanning multinational?

FATHERS AND SONS

The generational transition of the overseas-Chinese firm has, in many ways, already been set in motion. Although some of the firms were founded long ago, it was not until East Asia itself took off in the 1960s that any of the Chinese firms reached a size worth reckoning with on an international scale. The first generation, the men who presided over the spectacular rise in the fortunes of the Chinese firm, is near its end.

The sons (except in Thailand, very few daughters yet get involved in the family businesses) are a different breed. They are armed not with market instincts and personal connections alone but—almost universally—with MBAs from American universities as well. Already, says Victor Fung, the head of Prudential Asia Capital (and himself both an American Ph.D. and a scion of an old Hong Kong business family), the days are gone when big deals were done on the basis of nothing more than a common birthplace or ancestor. The old bonds of blood and village are no longer as tight, nor are they any longer exclusive. Another network, that of the second-generation American MBAs, is beginning to overlay the first. This, says Mr. Fung, has reduced the ironclad reliability of the old handshake deals with a local compatriot, though there are still traces enough of the former rules that "at least you know where [in the deal] to do due diligence."

The arrival of the second-generation MBAs has brought at least an awareness of more systematic management methods to the old family trading firms. So, too, has the hiring of professional, some-times expatriate, managers for high positions in the firms. In some cases the family has actually stood back and let the hired hands do the managing. One of the more successful examples of this is First Pacific, a Hong Kong-based miniconglomerate that is owned mostly by the family of Indonesia's Liem Sioe Leong. The family, whose Indonesian name is Salim, set up First Pacific in 1981 and put it in the hands of Manuel Pangiligan, then a thirty-three-year-old Philip-pine investment banker who had been introduced to the Liems by a Taiwanese friend of theirs. Mr. Pangiligan, who is close to the family's first son, has been left free since to run First Pacific as he—and his multicultural management team—thinks best. He was even able to override the Salims' objection to an audacious acquisition in 1988 that by the mid-1990s had turned the firm into one of the great successes of the Hong Kong stock market: buying a cellular telephone company to add to First Pacific's finance, property, and marketing businesses.

Yet a First Pacific is still the exception. After Li Ka-shing had taken over Hutchison Whampoa, he installed his own (mostly Western) managers but left the firm to run along Western lines. Even so, says Simon Murray, who ran Hutchison for Mr. Li until he left for Deutsche Bank in 1993, a traditionally managed Chinese firm—Cheung Kong Holdings—was overlaid on Hutchison as its parent: "They are just not sold on Western ways." Mr. Murray suggests that the overseas-Chinese firms are in roughly the same position that American firms were in a century ago, towards the end of the robber-baron era: in need of a shift to a more modern institutional and management structure.

Things may prove less tidy than that. Vincent Lo—another Hong Kong scion, an Australian degree holder, and the head of a property and construction company called Shui On—says that overseas-Chinese firms must change if only because the heirs are not willing to put in the sixteen-hour days the founder did. On the other hand, the family is never going to allow its holding in the core companies of the firm to be reduced below 35–40 percent. His view is that this floor under family ownership will stop overseas-Chinese firms from ever growing to the size of Western (or South Korean) multinationals.

As good a pointer as any to the fate of the Chinese firms will be what happens to Li Ka-shing's empire. By the early 1990s the elder Li had brought back to Hong Kong his two sons, Victor and Richard, then in their mid-twenties, after the requisite stay in North American universities and companies. Victor was installed in Cheung Kong; Richard was given permission to set up Star-TV, a satellite network that was thought to be a bauble for the boy but which he sold to Rupert Murdoch in 1993 at a profit of some $425 million. Victor is apparently the guardian of the family's patrimony; Richard, the experimenter with the future.

By early 1994, Richard had turned part of the profit from the sale of Star into a new (privately held) company called Pacific Century. In his office, with a bank of color televisions silently flickering entertainment programs above his desk, Richard explained that Chinese firms needed to preserve the entrepreneurial spirit while making operational adjustments: Property, for instance, needed different management structures from groceries or the media.

Richard's own company was going to concentrate on three lines throughout Asia—infrastructure, financial services, and technology in the service sector (which so far has turned out to be telecommunications). Mr. Li emphasized how important it was not to put all your eggs into one basket in terms of business (consumer lines are explosive but unsteady; technology and infrastructure, steady but unspectacular) or operating centers (Hong Kong is good for some purposes, Singapore for others) or markets (China's exhilarating fluctuations must be hedged by more stable places). This approach also requires a diversity of shareholders, because not all lines of business produce a gain immediately and "Asian shareholders want to see their profit yesterday."

Some observers think that the complex blend exemplified by what Richard Li seems to be trying to do bodes well for the overseas Chinese. Mike Morris, for instance, the Manila-based consultant introduced in chapter 10, thinks that the old network mixed with the new skills may produce a spectacular combination: a corporate model far more sophisticated than Japan's, in which firms are able to think with the depth of strategists but act with the speed of traders.

Others, among them Ronnie Chan, the head of Hong Kong's Hang Lung property group (see chapter 6), and Vincent Lo, are not so sure that overseas Chinese firms will be capable of making the transition to modernity in terms of size, institutional structure or diversity, and technological sophistication of business lines. Mr. Redding argues that since the conditions that created the overseas-Chinese firm in the first place—a low-tax, high-interest-rate, little-regulated business environment—are still in place, the decentralized Chinese industrial structure is unlikely to change.

Nor does he find this at all alarming. Individual firms may well flounder because they are constrained by an inability to grow beyond a certain size or to arrange a smooth succession. But as a system, with individual firms coming and going in quick response to market pressures, the overseas-Chinese network should still do fine.

There will be changes: adroit additions like the younger Mr. Li's or firms like Taiwan's Acer, whose management from the beginning followed a Western rather than a Chinese pattern. Another development—of particular interest to Western firms hoping to penetrate Asia and overseas-Chinese firms hoping to reach beyond their Asian or specialist (e.g., property) base—is the growth of joint ventures or less formal strategic alliances between overseas-Chinese and foreign firms. Paper companies in Indonesia, for instance, have already been looking to swap equity stakes with American counterparts to grow business in both markets. Yet for a long time such hybrids are likely to be confined to the exotic part of the business zoo.

What Western businessmen need to keep in mind, however, is that the distinctive feature of the overseas-Chinese model has never been the individual firm, however prominent, or the linkup in the future with a Western partner, however eminent. The strength of overseas-Chinese business has instead always resided, and will continue to do so, in the network—whose systemic power in Asia a lot of competitors have already tasted; more of them will do so as Asia's markets grow larger.

CHAPTER 12

A BILLION CONSUMERS

In every country private consumption accounts for the biggest single share of GNP—bigger than that of government, of investment, of exports. And in almost every country the share of GNP spent on consumption is more than half. In countries badly ground down by poverty, most of that consumption is of unprocessed food and barely processed textiles and is of little interest to any sizable or modern business. But practically every Asian country is now rich enough that the continent as a whole is in the early stages of the biggest consumer boom in history. It is beginning to create a modern middle class in cities throughout Asia that will eventually have deep implications for Asian societies and politics (see chapter 16). Well before that social transformation occurs, however, the rise of Asian consuming classes will transform world markets for almost every product and service.

The growing size of Asia's consumer markets is why an all-out trade war, or even a serious stab at managed trade, between Asia and the West is improbable. Important though exports are for the efficiency and development of Asia's economies (for the reasons explained in chapters 4 and 5), the new-wave Asian economies—especially China, India, and Indonesia—will not depend on exports to fuel their growth as much as did Japan and the four tigers (Hong Kong, Singapore, South Korea, and Taiwan). Even in Japan's case, the raw influence of exports on economic growth was not as great as most people assume. In the days when Japan was exporting most furiously, private domestic consumption contributed more than four times as much to Japan's GNP as exports did. Now that the fastest growth has moved from some islands on Asia's periphery to the Asian landmass itself, for Asia as a whole the ratio of domestic consumption to exports will be rising. And, despite considerable barriers to imports or FDI in some of these countries, their markets will be more open to foreign penetration than were many of those of the first-generation Asian success stories.

The size and pace of growth of these markets are staggering. As already mentioned in chapter 5, two-thirds of the worldwide growth in car sales in 1993–2000 will probably come in Asia outside Japan. Carmakers expect that in Southeast Asia alone, where a million cars were sold in 1993, more than 3 million a year will be sold before the decade is out.

Motorola, the world's biggest maker of telecommunications pagers, thinks that China will be the world's single biggest market for pagers by 1997. China is already the biggest single market for telephone switches, and if India's ambitious telecoms upgrading plans are realized, it will soon be installing as much switching capacity every year as China. By the early 1990s, Citicorp was signing up, net, more new Asian credit-card holders than American ones. And Boeing believes that, of the tripling in world air travel it expects between 1995 and 2005, 60 percent of the growth will be accounted for by travel involving Asia. Two-thirds of that Asia-related growth will come from increased travel between the rich world and Asia, the rest from increased travel within Asia itself (and no wonder, since more than half the world's people live within five hours' flying time of Hong Kong).

The rest of this book could consist of a list of further breathtaking numbers about Asian consumer markets, but the important question to address is not whether the opportunities in Asia are gigantic —in almost every line of business they are—the question is instead how they can be exploited. It is impossible for this chapter to answer that question comprehensively, because consumer markets depend so much on the kind of good or service being offered and where it is sold; this is why later sections of this chapter are filled with interesting examples rather than systematic theories. But even to begin to explain what goes into the running of a consumer business in Asia, we need to understand how Asia's consumer markets have developed over the past generation.

The Rise of the Many Haves

One of the greatest events of post-1945 Asia has been the break-through in one country after another of large numbers of people from poverty (and marginal consumption at best) into the lowest reaches of the middle class. It is the abrupt crossing of this line, rather than the subsequent and more continuous movement of people up through the various gradations of the middle class, that has had the most revolutionary impact on modern Asian societies. When masses of people cross the line and are able to begin consuming, almost everything about the population changes, including people's physical appearance and capacities. Calorie intake rises, diets become more varied and nutritious, the population becomes healthier and more robust, average height increases significantly, and so, too, according to studies by Wacoal, a Japanese lingerie maker, of changes in Japan's female population over the years, does the size of women's breasts.

The breakthrough of the mass of a country's people into the lower middle class has come at different times this century: in the West in the early decades of the century; in Japan between 1950 and 1970; and in coastal China, parts of Java and Sumatra, most of Malaysia, and much of Thailand in the late 1980s and early 1990s. The rise into low-level consumerism of a class—essentially the peasantry—that disappeared in the West some seventy-five years ago presents Western firms with an opportunity, but one that few of them have any institutional experience of. Ideally, they should be aiming both to capture the mass market at the bottom as the peasants enter the consumer society and also the deeper but narrower markets further up the income pyramid as people climb to higher levels.

How big are these new markets? Mike Morris of the Marketing Partnership in Manila has taken a stab at estimating their size. He reckons that the stupendous economic growth of the 1980s transformed the structure of Asian society, replacing the traditional division between a thin layer of "haves" and a thick layer of "have-nots" with something a bit more complicated.

Today there are, at the top, the "superhaves": the old elites—superstar overseas Chinese businessmen, corrupt politicians' and generals' families, and so on—plus those who made it big in the

1980s. These people, with annual household incomes above $30,000 (in early 1990s dollars), may account for 8 million of non-Japanese Asia's households in 1995; Mr. Morris expects their number at least to double by 2000 (in terms of income in constant dollars). They live much like their upper-middle-class and rich counterparts in the West, with perhaps a few variations in taste. These are, for instance, the people for whom some $5 billion was spent building golf courses in Asia, mostly in Southeast Asia, in the first half of the 1990s.

The second group, the "have-somes," with incomes above $18,000, have more typical middle-class tastes and hopes: They want houses, cars, consumer durables, travel and recreation, even private health care and education. Their numbers—15 million households in 1995—could reach 75 million in 2000. Yet there are signs that even these figures may be too small. A marketing man at Mercedes-Benz says that a study commissioned by the car firm in the early 1990s suggested that in China alone, if the government allowed a free car market to develop, there would be enough household purchasing power to support the sale of 8–10 million cars a year from 1995 to 2010—roughly as many as Americans buy each year.

Whatever the true size of Asia's world-standard middle class, Mr. Morris reckons that by 2000 there will also be at least 150 million "near-have" households: the people who have just crossed the line into a consumer society. They will have enough income for regular purchases of packaged household goods and occasional purchases even of consumer durables such as televisions, and will also have (thanks to their experience of more or less perpetual economic boom since 1980) every expectation of moving up smartly from there.

Assuming five people per household, you thus have 1.2 billion Asian consumers by 2000 and an embryonic middle class spread throughout the continent.

To Get and to Spend

Estimates vary widely about the nature of this incipient middle class and about just how many consumers there are worth trying to reach. For instance, Stephen Shaw and Jonathan Woetzel of McKinsey's Hong Kong office tried to calculate how much effective spending power is in the hands of Chinese consumers. Their answer: a lot more than the official figures for dollar GDP per capita would lead you to believe.

Among the many things that lead purchasing power to diverge sharply from the official figures in China (a conservative guess is that average purchasing-power-parity incomes are three to four times higher than dollar-based incomes) are an undervalued currency, a large black-market economy, big government subsidies for housing, health, and transport, and the wealth accumulation brought about by years of savings rates equal to more than a third of GDP. The effects of such items can be big. Messrs. Shaw and Woetzel reckoned the subsidies were so high that in 1988 the average Chinese household devoted only 5 percent of its spending to housing, transport, and education, compared with the 20–40 percent spent on such things by households in other East and Southeast Asian countries. The subsidies free a lot of Chinese income for spending on other consumer goods. The McKinsey study calculated that, after taking account of subsidies and past savings alone, average incomes in China's rich coastal provinces in 1992 were 28 percent higher than the official figures said.

The result is a surprisingly large number of Chinese consumers buying goods that on the face of it would seem to be out of their financial reach. The McKinsey consultants found that when average incomes in a city surpass an official $1,000 a year, ownership of color televisions suddenly shoots up from under 40 percent to more than 75 percent of households. This does not mean that an individual household starts buying color televisions when its income reaches $1,000 but that the pool of those households which can afford a TV suddenly deepens when a city's average hits that level (see the following section). The McKinsey study calculated that China already had 60 million consumers in this near-have pool in 1992, a figure that McKinsey concluded two years later had already risen to 100 million and will (if fast economic growth continues) reach 260–270 million by 2000—a bigger market for consumer durables than any other East or Southeast Asian country had in 1992.

A similar, though less convincing, story can be told about India. India subsidizes the same sorts of public-service consumption items, plus a few more (like electricity, which is often simply stolen from the power grid by enterprising middlemen). Indians do not save nearly as much as the Chinese (the rates as a percentage of GDP are in the low twenties rather than the mid-thirties), but India's underground economy, perhaps 30 percent as big as the official economy, may well be proportionally larger than China's. India's regional and income inequalities are also more extreme than China's, so the numbers who have broken through the near-have threshold are proportionally larger than in China.

However many near-haves actually exist, there are several crucial differences between these people, who have just enough money to be counted as consumers, and the have-somes and superhaves, who would be counted as middle class even by Western standards of income and outlook. Ken Ohmae, a former business consultant and now would-be political impresario in Japan, puts the fault line somewhere between Mike Morris's near-have and have-some thresholds. Mr. Ohmae says the big change starts when a country's annual per capita GNP passes $5,000 (in 1990 dollars). At that point enough people—maybe 20–30 percent in all—cross the threshold of a $10,000 annual household income that they make for a strong conservative middle class which becomes the dominant force in public opinion. By the time the country as a whole has broken through the barrier of $10,000-a-year per capita GNP, the transformation is complete. It has become, irrespective of where it is located geographically, a modern middle-class country.

Still deeper changes are at work. Beginning at the $5,000 barrier, by Mr. Ohmae's reckoning, religion, war, and central government become declining industries (more about that in part IV). The important point for now is that in most of Asia that $5,000 barrier has not been breached. For the most part, today's Asia is consumerist but not truly middle-class. The markets are huge, but they are local, rooted in ethnic, religious, or national identity. And the contours of these markets are dictated by an oddity in the relationship between economic growth and consumer-market growth.

THE WEALTH EFFECT

Bandai, a Japanese company, is one of the world's biggest toy makers. Makoto Yamashina, Bandai's president, says that in the early 1990s Japan was by far the company's biggest market, accounting for around 80 percent of profits; the rest was divided roughly equally among America, Europe, and the rest of Asia. Yet Mr. Yamashina thinks it is possible that China may overtake Japan as Bandai's biggest market between 2000 and 2005. This is a startling statement on two counts: first, the speed with which this change might happen; second, how it could happen at all in view of the income differences between Japan and China.

Mr. Yamashina says that in the early 1990s the average Japanese family spent some 30,000 yen (then equal to about $250) a year on toys for each of its children—or a little less than 1 percent of average household income. Bandai, which had been making and selling toys in China since the mid-1980s, found that in the early 1990s Chinese parents who bought toys—of whom there were very few—annually spent about 10,000 yen per child for toys. By Mr. Yamashina's reckoning, China in the early 1990s had 300 million children under the age of fifteen (by 1995 it was more like 325 million). He sees this as a potential toy market of 3 trillion yen a year, $35 billion at the mid-1995 exchange rate.

There are some sound social and marketing reasons to think that much of this potential might be realized. China's tightly policed one-child family policy has created "little emperors" of the precious sole child whom parents are allowed to have; and, unlike in Japan or the West, Chinese parents still have a relatively narrow range of items to spoil a child with. Even so, the 10,000 yen Mr. Yamashina assumes will be spent annually for each child was equivalent in the early 1990s to 20 percent of China's average household income in dollar terms and at least 5 percent even in PPP terms—which are improbably high shares of spending on a luxury like toys.

Yet Mr. Yamashina is probably not dreaming when he talks about China's toy market surpassing Japan's within ten years, and chart 6 shows why. It is drawn from an analysis by GT Management (Asia), a Hong Kong-based fund-management firm, of car sales in Malaysia, though the pattern of demand for any consumer good looks the same (e.g., color television sales in China; see the previous section). What lies behind the chart is the fact that consumer markets do not expand smoothly but instead grow in big leaps. Few households with incomes below a given level buy cars, but large numbers of households suddenly do when their incomes break through that level.

Because a country's incomes are unequally distributed, a smallish increase in average per capita income can lead to a sharp jump in the number of households with incomes above the threshold for buying the good in question. In the Malaysian car example a 40

CHART 6
THE WEALTH EFFECT

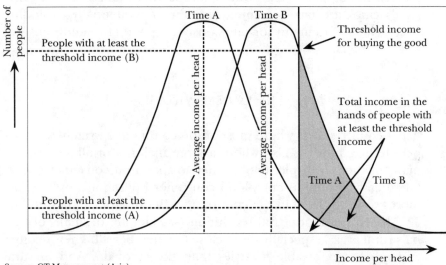

SOURCE: GT Management (Asia).

NOTE: The two curves represent the distribution of income in an economically expanding country at two different times: time A is earlier than time B. The rise in incomes between time A and time B causes the income to shift to the right, resulting in a modest increase in average income per head. But it causes a much bigger increase in the number of people who have incomes higher than the threshold at which consumers feel wealthy enough to buy the good in question. And it causes a huge increase in the amount of money in the hands of people with at least the threshold income (shown by the shaded areas under the curves).

percent rise in incomes between 1987 and 1991 was accompanied by a 290 percent rise in car sales, mostly in Kuala Lumpur, the capital.

Another example, somewhat more modest, comes from Bangkok. The average annual rise in Bangkok's personal incomes between 1986 and 1991 was 11 percent, but the yearly increase in the number of households with an annual income above $10,000 a year was 20 percent. That income seems to be the threshold for active department-store shopping; and sure enough, even though the rise over 1986–91 in average incomes in Bangkok would have warranted an increase of only half in the number of department stores, the threshold effect meant that market demand was able to support a doubling of department stores, from 49 to 102.

This process is not as cut-and-dried as the chart makes it look. For one thing, a substantially more inegalitarian income distribution than the one shown will muffle the effect of crossing the threshold; and Asia has plenty of unequal income distributions. Even so, the pattern has already been formed, and it will hold. As incomes rise, Asia's cities are fast becoming a chain of sequentially exploding firecrackers of demand for one consumer good after another. And not just the cities.

THE GLOBAL VILLAGES

Asia's countryside is where most of the continent's wretchedly poor people live, but it is also where a large majority of all Asians live, many of them with plenty of money to spend on consumer goods. Of India's 38 million entry-level consumer households in 1990, almost two-thirds lived in the countryside. Because of China's unique TVE-based rural industrial revolution (see chapter 6), many of China's rural areas, especially those close to cities, boast higher incomes and more comfortable lifestyles than the cities do. And in rural Indonesia, where small food shacks used to deal only in fresh foods like bean curd, rice, and fried bananas, by the early 1990s they were serving their customers packaged instant noodles. As anyone who has sampled both cuisines can testify, this change does not necessarily represent progress but it certainly represents profit. According to a well-connected Jakarta investment banker, in 1993 the Salim Group, the country's biggest conglomerate, was selling 450 million packets of instant noodles a month to rural consumers at a price of about sixty cents, on which it made a profit of twenty cents.

But, although for many consumer products, especially humble ones, the demand and financial wherewithal exist in rural Asia to support large markets, the constraints of distribution and marketing are much more binding there than in the cities. In some places— for example, large parts of Indonesia's main island, Java, which has a population of more than 115 million, and the Mekong delta in southern Vietnam—rural population densities are so high that distribution costs and methods are not much different from those in a city. But in most of rural Asia distribution is a nightmare.

Hindustan Lever, the Indian subsidiary of Unilever, has been one of the most adept marketers of consumer products in rural Asia. S. M. Datta, Hindustan Lever's chairman, explains that he realized as early as 1985 that the Indian countryside had a market demand worth meeting. At the time, Lever was looking for places to build fertilizer plants, and in the course of the search Mr. Datta visited the eastern states of Bihar and Orissa. These are two of the poorest states in India, yet even there, that long ago, it was obvious that many people had the money to buy packaged foods and even detergents and cosmetics—if only the stuff could be delivered to them cheaply enough.

As the company began investigating how it might pry open rural purchasing power, it collected data on incomes, village size, roads, and so on from each state and set up some test marketing and distribution programs. Among other things, it concluded that distribution channels in rural India were likely to remain splintered and fairly primitive for a long time. To take even a step towards the supermarket age requires three elements: at least a skeletal system of transport so that the customer can come to the store and take bulky goods back home; storage facilities (such as a refrigerator) to put the goods in once they are brought home; and levels of income high enough to finance a single "big" purchase—say, one kilogram of washing powder for use over two months—instead of a series of small purchases at more frequent intervals. India as yet has none of these elements in place.

This does not imply a lack of markets in rural India, but it does mean they must be exploited differently from the richer and more infrastructure-blessed rural markets in, for example, Thailand or Indonesia (where Unilever later successfully applied many of the techniques Hindustan Lever had developed for rural India). Hindustan Lever decided that its own outlets could be sustained only in villages with more than two thousand people that are served by all-weather roads: Some 60,000 Indian villages qualify (out of a total of 570,000 in the early 1990s), and by 1994 Lever had outlets in 34,000 of them. But that is only the beginning of Lever's reach into the Indian countryside. Store owners from smaller and less accessible villages come once a week to Lever's "big-village" outlets and are given a week's credit for goods that they buy and take deeper into the countryside for resale to final consumers.

The villagers are willing to pay a premium for Lever's packaged goods, which they trust not to be tainted. Lever made the goods more rural-friendly through the simple device of packaging shampoo and detergents in thirty-gram plastic sachets instead of one-kilogram boxes, which made them affordable even by those with only a few rupees and little storage space to spare. Lever ran distribution through several channels, even including little vans of its own that trundle down country roads and stop every so often—mainly to show promotional videos to the villagers but also to sell a few goods on the spot if the audience is interested.

On both sides of the supply chain, distribution in rural Asia (especially China and India) is often so rudimentary that a consumer-goods company has to build a system from scratch. With its first venture in China, a powdered-milk and baby-food plant in the far northeastern province of Heilongjiang, Nestlé decided to ignore the creaky government distribution channels entirely. It bought milk from farmers in dozens of villages near the plant, but rather than pick up the milk from the farms, it had the farmers bring their output themselves—on bicycles or even on foot—to scattered collection points. The farmers were willing to do this because Nestlé (unlike any other buyers the farmers had previously dealt with) paid on the spot.

Avon, an American beauty-products company, followed a similar path but had a built-in advantage when it set up operations in southern China: its longtime tradition everywhere of using "Avon ladies," part-time saleswomen on commission, as its main distribution channel to reach customers in their homes or workplaces. The difference in China is that the Avon ladies, of whom there were more than forty thousand scattered through southern, eastern, and central China by the mid-1990s, have to cycle to distribution centers to pick up their stock in trade. Such a solution is too small-scale for some companies. One reason McDonald's is building up so slowly in China is that it is likewise fashioning its own (nationwide) supply and distribution network.

As Hindustan Lever's video van suggests, rural marketing also has peculiarities of its own. Villagers throughout Asia have begun to watch a lot of television and, although this is undoubtedly turning them into consumers and changing their aspirations, rather different approaches appeal to them than to their city cousins. Hindustan Lever has found that, whereas television ads in the cities are most effective when they are thirty seconds long, the villagers watching its motorized video road show like the ads to run for a good two minutes.

Some advertising themes are misguided. This can, accidentally, sometimes help. One rural-market consultant in Delhi says that Coca-Cola first became popular with teenage village boys because they inferred from the television ads showing girls and boys together happily enjoying Cokes that a girl came with purchases of the beverage. (In rural India she would never otherwise be caught dead in public with a boy.) On the other hand, a shampoo marketer had a disastrous experience with footage showing the bounce in a luxurious head of female hair shampooed with its product. Its target audience, young married women, thought it bordered on the vulgar because in much of rural India a proper woman is still not supposed to show her hair in public.

MEGACITY LIGHTS

Although for fairly cheap personal products (such as packaged food and soap) rural Asia may prove the world's biggest market, it is in the rising megacities of Asia that the grand battles for the pricier consumer-durable trade are going to be fought. The cities are considerably richer than the countryside, for distribution and marketing reasons they are easier to tap, and they are the places where the sudden bursts of demand produced by the wealth effect make themselves felt most strongly.

One company whose Asian strategy is based almost entirely on the rise of megacities is Carrier, an American maker of air conditioners. Carrier, which is a subsidiary of United Technologies, began its serious Asian push in the mid-1980s. Between 1986 and 1993 its Asian sales tripled to $1 billion, about a quarter of the company's worldwide sales in the later year. Nicholas Pinchuk, the Singapore-based head of Carrier's Asian operations, expects its Asian sales to more than double by 2000. They will then be approaching half the company's worldwide sales, up from 5 percent in 1970.

From the beginning, Carrier has treated Asia not as a manufacturing base but as a market. By 1993 it had thirteen factories in the region; but ten of them were there to serve markets that would otherwise have remained closed, and the other three made only basic components or tinkered with models to adapt them to local conditions. The company has set up offices not because of cheap labor or other production advantages but at least in part because of the management talent available in the local workforce. This is why it has liked South Korea, Singapore, and looking to the future, India and Vietnam.

Carrier thinks the management question is crucial. Of the firm's

six-man executive committee in 1993, two were not Americans and
only one had never lived outside the United States. At the Asian
headquarters in Singapore, thirteen nationalities were represented
in management ranks in 1993, and Asians were heading all the
operations save the top one (and, says Mr. Pinchuk, his ambition is
for an Asian to succeed him). The pressure of building a good
management team is intense. In 1993, Carrier had sixty-five important management positions in Asia but expected that to grow to
140 by 2000.

The job of these people, says Mr. Pinchuk, is to address the particular needs of local markets but at the same time wring economies
of scale out of the operation by standardizing products and services
as much as possible across the region. One big economy of scale has
come with the cultivation of a good, consistent brand throughout
Asia. In providing service, Carrier has found it possible to develop a
basic package that is nonetheless substantially reshaped for each of
the twenty-three Asian countries where it does business. The variations depend on such things as building codes and consumer preferences; in Singapore, Carrier has had to wrestle with various
restrictions placed on the use of air conditioners in the public-
housing flats where most Singaporeans live.

In part because air conditioners are expensive—people start buying them well after they have acquired color televisions and refrigerators—and in part because of the dictates of distribution, Carrier is
focusing most of its effort on big cities in Asia. It is happy to sell
special orders in the countryside but has found that for a mass-
market consumer business—for, in essence, the drop-in customer
—securing market share in Asia's emerging megacities is the company's most pressing job. About three-quarters of Carrier's Asian
sales are already made in such cities, and Mr. Pinchuk expects that
share to rise.

In the early 1990s Carrier was trying to identify thirteen to fifteen
megacities which, over the following ten years, were likely to reach
half or more of Singapore's annual per capita spending on air conditioners (forty dollars then, compared with eighty dollars in Japan).
Demand for air conditioners explodes in the usual way at certain
income levels: When a city's average per capita income hits $2,000–
$3,000, small businesses start buying home air conditioners for their
offices; when it surpasses $10,000, people start buying them for their
homes. Markets then widen fast. In only five years in the late 1980s

and early 1990s, spending per person on air conditioning in Seoul jumped from four dollars a year to twelve dollars (and Bangkok is now at the point Seoul was at when it took off). Carrier's most-likely list includes, besides Bangkok, five cities in China (Beijing, Shanghai, Guangzhou, Tianjin, and Chongqing), three in India (Delhi, Bombay, and Calcutta), two each in Indonesia (Jakarta and Surabaya) and Vietnam (Hanoi and Saigon), and Manila.

The megacity strategy is particularly well suited to China. One reason is that the place is far too big to tackle as a whole. Second, its exceptionally fast and uneven economic growth magnifies the wealth effect, leading to bigger and more concentrated explosions of consumer demand (most conspicuously in the cities along the coast). Third, transport and distribution are among the worst in Asia, in some respects behind even India. This can cripple what should otherwise prove one of the biggest advantages of a foreign consumer-goods company in China: its ability to install centralized and computerized warehouse and inventory systems. The distribution problem is what mainly marred the entry into China in the early 1990s of Giordano, a Hong Kong–based casual-clothing retailer that had been extremely successful in Hong Kong and Taiwan largely thanks to such systems.

Yet a determined consumer-goods firm can often find a way to cope with the distribution headaches in a single city, usually by imitating the Nestlé example (see previous section) of setting up its own channels. Wall's, for instance, a Unilever subsidiary that makes ice cream, managed to create from scratch a retail-distribution network of more than twenty-five hundred outlets in Beijing in just four months during the summer of 1994.

For obvious reasons, distribution of ice cream during the summer has to be punctilious. The main methods Wall's used were to set up a factory fairly close to the city (because the transport system beyond the suburbs deteriorates so quickly), have large refrigerated trucks carry the ice cream from the factory to a half-dozen distribution centers scattered around Beijing, and from there to deliver it to the shops in small cars or even bicycles with little coolers of their own. The outlets had been carefully selected for location, opening hours, and so on, and Wall's made sure they were provided with—for China—innovative selling tools (a fancy little freezer, price lists) and a constant flow of product. *Business China,* a newsletter published by the Economist Intelligence Unit in Hong Kong, reckons that by the end of the four months in 1994 Wall's had the biggest ice-cream market share in Beijing.

China, a megacountry, has plenty of megacities where this kind of effort can pay. Up through 1995, a huge share of the non-overseas-Chinese FDI in China went into just three cities: Beijing, Shanghai, and Guangzhou. Most business consultants, including those from McKinsey mentioned above, recommend that consumer-goods firms aim for operations in fifteen to twenty Chinese cities by 2000. The McKinsey people identify sixteen target cities (including such household names as Urumqi, Taiyuan, and Changchun), which they say will by then have passed the magic threshold of $1,000 annual per capita income and thus contain a large enough pool of near-haves to be worth dipping into. Yet just how to dip into such pools throughout Asia is a task that will daunt even the best marketers.

NICHES RICHES

Except at the very highest levels of Asia's consuming classes, the internationalization of taste and lifestyle that Ken Ohmae describes as characteristic of the middle class has hardly happened (and may, thanks to the ever more discriminating powers of modern technology, never happen in Asia and may dwindle even in the rich world). So tailoring the marketing to the market matters as much as getting the distribution right.

Mike Morris sees this market-splintering as the greatest opportunity for consumer-products companies in Asia. Anybody who succeeds in pulling off what Carrier is trying to do with its Asian air-conditioner business—exploit scale economies while precisely adjusting to cultural niches in markets—will be onto a very good thing. Mr. Morris suggests some broad lines of cultural differentiation that can be followed: Greater China, a Malay-Muslim axis in Southeast Asia, the Hindi-language market of India. (He might have added the related though mutually hostile Japanese and Korean cultures of Northeast Asia.)

But for now most consumer-products firms face markets that are not even as broad or coherent as those. The market around Saigon, with its greater wealth, greater ethnic-Chinese influence, and recent acquaintance with capitalist ways and with Americans, is far racier and more sophisticated than that around Hanoi. China's markets, that is, the ones currently worth trying to reach, are shattered into as many as twenty to thirty pieces—which may not be entirely a bad thing, since distribution is so ramshackle that it would be hard to sell beyond their confines anyway. But it is still hard to deal simultaneously with, say, Guangzhou and Shanghai when their spoken (though not written) languages are entirely different and their consumer tastes largely so.

In environments of this sort it is no surprise that advertising, branding, and even shelf display become sensitive and—if wrongly handled—occasionally fatal matters. Rick Yan, a consultant with Bain and Company in Hong Kong, points to several instances in China where a simple name change has sharply boosted sales. Revlon made one of the happiest choices of name, calling itself in Mandarin *Lu Hua Nong*. These three characters mean, roughly, "the fragrance of the flowers that are covered with morning dew," which in itself sounds pretty good for a cosmetics firm but has far deeper resonances than that for Chinese: The three characters come from a line in a famous love poem about the affair between a Tang dynasty emperor and one of the four most beautiful women in Chinese history. Conversely, Mr. Yan points out, the Chinese have a suspicion of discounted or "free-trial" goods that dates back almost as far: to a time six centuries ago when the Han Chinese spread the word of what eventually became a successful rebellion against their Mongolian rulers by handing out gifts of little cakes in which were embedded slips of paper with messages about the planned uprising.

Things change so fast in Asia that marketers need to be aware of niches forming at both higher and lower points than they had become accustomed to. For example, by the early 1990s in Kuala Lumpur, Malaysia's capital, more than half of the households were already consumers of instant coffee—in other words, that market was already saturated. Variations quickly sprang up for decaffeinated instant coffee, freeze-dried coffee, and instant cappuccino—a differentiation of this product that is not much behind that of the West.

Meanwhile, in the travel business throughout Asia demand is shooting up for what would in America be the motel trade. The old pattern in Asian hotels was extraordinary luxury at the high end for expatriate business travelers in cities and expatriate holidaymakers at beach resorts; and squalor at the low end for the few locals who happened to be on the road and not staying with friends or relatives.

But by 1993 Malaysia had more tourist arrivals from China than it did from the United States, a shift that is coming to the rest of Southeast Asia as well. In India, ITC Hotels, a subsidiary of an Indian conglomerate hooked up with Britain's B.A.T. Industries, has found that its fastest-growing segment is in modest middle-class travel by Indians rather than pricier travel by expatriates. Several multinationals—among them America's Holiday Inn and Choice Hotels (Quality Inn and Comfort Inn) and France's Accor (Novotel)—have already begun expanding in Asia's budget-travel business, particularly in the suddenly booming Indian market.

IN ORBIT

It is, however, in entertainment generally and television in particular that the dimensions of Asia's market opening and the diversity of its audiences are most apparent. Before the 1990s satellite television was practically unknown in Asia outside Japan and the region's luxury hotels. Most TV broadcasting was in the hands of government-owned monopolies that dished up some of the most boring and politically tendentious rubbish seen outside the Soviet Union. One of the worst of these networks was India's Doordarshan, whose two channels did not broadcast for most of the day and then when they did come on in the evening were prone to broadcast nationwide such worthy prime-time fare as agricultural marketing tips.

By 1995 several satellites were beaming dozens of channels to dishes throughout Asia; forty more Asian satellites, with a total channel-carrying capacity running into the hundreds, are scheduled to be put into orbit in the years 1995–97 alone. Star-TV, a Hong Kong–based pan-Asian satellite broadcaster, was set up in 1990 by Li Ka-shing's Hutchison Whampoa, and 64 percent of it was taken over three years later, at a price of $525 million, by Rupert Murdoch's News Corp. (In 1995 News Corp. bought out the rest at roughly the same price per share.) Star had a tiny audience at the beginning of 1992, was broadcasting to around 60 million Asians by January 1993, and in October of that year had an audience of more than 200 million.

Cable networks, too, have been growing at telephone-digit rates. Cable TV was virtually unknown in India in 1992. Two years later, India had more than sixty thousand cable operators, who controlled the access of some 75 million viewers to the dozens of satellite channels being broadcast into India. By 1994, Shanghai had more than a million cable subscribers, Beijing close to a million, and in Sichuan Province a four-channel microwave pay-TV network served 22 million. In 1993 China awarded almost seven hundred cable-TV licenses, and more are on the way; plans have been made for subscription networks in almost all of China's twenty-nine cities.

In 1993, Taiwan legalized the hundreds of unauthorized cable operators that had made the island Asia's most comprehensively wired place, opening the market for programmers that had previously shunned it for fear of piracy; India followed suit the following year.

Most of the world's media companies are scrambling to get in on the act. Besides News Corp.'s Star-TV, America's CNN, ESPN, HBO, Time Warner, and Viacom (which owns rock-music MTV), and Japan's NHK are all involved in satellite broadcasting in Asia, in producing programs for Asian television, or both. Specialist broadcasting—such as the Asian business-news channels of Dow Jones and NBC—is also on the rise.

The multinationals are having to compete with, or form alliances with, local firms that have leaped from nonexistence to dominance in two or three years. The most spectacular such rise was that of Zee TV in India. Formed in 1992 by Subhash Chandra, a Bombay entrepreneur, Zee paid over the odds for space on Star's satellite and then used its own Hindi-language programming to outstrip Star in India's city markets and pull even with (a now-much-improved) Doordarshan. Television Broadcasts (TVB), one of Hong Kong's two local stations, has made an alliance in India, but its moves to enter broadcasting agreements in East Asia are the ones drawing serious attention. This is because TVB's real strength is its library of Mandarin and Cantonese programming, the biggest in the world, to which the company is adding the six thousand hours a year of new Chinese-language programs that it produces.

As Asia's television markets messily sort themselves out over the next few years, the sorting principle is likely to be opposite to the one with which Star opened the Asian television race at the beginning of the decade. Star began with a single set of programs (mostly sports, music videos, and ancient American soap operas), almost all of them in English, and broadcast simultaneously throughout the continent along with the advertising that was supposed to pay for it.

This may not have been a bad way to start in view of the audience size Star has managed to build up, but by 1994 it was already clear that program localization and narrowcasting were the way forward for Asian television.

It took only two years for American soap operas to begin paling on Asian viewers, who turned in preference to programs in their own languages and cultural idioms. Star never really cracked Southeast Asia, partly because governments like Malaysia's and Singapore's refused to let it in but also because the Malay fare available in Indonesia off its Palapa satellite went down well with the audience. Zee TV's startling success had much to do with its being programmed in Hindi rather than English. The success of more recent start-ups (and upstarts) such as Jain-TV, also in India, is likewise due to their narrowcasting in such exotic languages as Tamil, Telugu, and Malayalam.

The localization of programming should not necessarily warm the hearts of Southeast Asian autocrats who worry that Western programs will undermine such "Asian values" as respect for authority and for the family. A new Indian network owned by Zee, called EL TV, promptly produced shows featuring illegitimate pregnancies and the like, though with familiar Indian settings instead of glamorous Californian ones.

But the success of dialect-based programs does suggest the extent to which the TV business (and other media businesses) in Asia will have to be localized. Combining local content with pan-Asian or even global operations leads into a thicket of complications about production, distribution (how can viewers be organized to pay, since advertising alone will not cover the costs?), and relations with suspicious and interventionist governments. A good summary, all in all, of the challenge of consumer markets in Asia.

CHAPTER 13

BRICKS AND MORTAR

All that delicious consumption cannot continue without a huge amount of investment to support it. Much of Asia has been diligent about supplying the needed capital. In 1965, investment rates in East and Southeast Asia equaled about 20 percent of GDP, only a shade above the figure in Latin America. By 1990 the East Asian investment rate was 35 percent, more than twice the Latin American investment rate; even the Indian subcontinent was investing 19 percent of its GDP by then, appreciably ahead of Latin America. By the mid-1990s, East and Southeast Asia were still investing about a third of their GDPs, and the Indian figure had risen to the low twenties, still a little ahead of Latin America. As explained in chapters 2 and 3, these high rates of investment are responsible more than any other single thing for East Asia's high rates of economic growth. They are also behind the second vast business opportunity in Asia in the coming decade: property development, capital goods, and infrastructure.

The bigger market is in private-sector investment, which means mostly property development and capital goods. For the past quarter century East Asia has had substantially more private capital formation than other regions at its income levels, both in absolute terms and as a share of total investment (see chapter 2). This is likely to continue. It has already lured Western architects, engineers, designers, and builders to cities throughout Asia, most recently to Shanghai for a building spree there. And it is behind much of the keen interest in Asia being shown by construction companies such

as America's Bechtel and Fluor Daniel, France's Dragages, and a
clutch of Japanese and Korean competitors.

By 1994, Fluor alone had built factories for thirty different kinds
of industries in Asia, in lines almost as diverse as the company's
American business (and for many of the same customers it serves in
America). Among the factories it had built were car-assembly plants,
baby-food and other consumer-products factories, oil refineries, pet-
rochemical plants, and high-tech electronics factories. And Fluor
expects, in common with others, that Asia will have accounted for
fully half of the worldwide growth in heavy-construction projects
this decade.

Those new factories have to be filled with equipment, and here,
too, Asian demand is jumping. Whole assembly lines, some new and
some used, are being shipped to Asian factories, sometimes from
the West and sometimes from elsewhere in Asia (most recently in
large volumes from Japan to China). Sales of this sort of capital
equipment are quickly reaching Western levels. In 1994 one Chinese paper-making factory imported advanced production machinery from Velmat, a Finnish firm, capable of turning out 120,000 tons
of high-quality paper a year. Before that shipment, China's entire
high-quality paper capacity had been 200,000 tons, with the biggest
factory having a capacity of 20,000 tons. Likewise, in 1991 all of
China had only two glass-coating machines; three years later it had
about twenty of the machines (which sell for $5 million apiece),
already half as many as the United States had.

As for another sort of capital equipment, Boeing has predicted
that by 2015 China alone will have become the world's third-biggest
buyer of commercial jet aircraft (behind only America and Japan).
It is no wonder the trade statistics show that in the late 1980s exports
of capital goods from Japan to Southeast Asia began rising by as
much as 40 percent a year. The countries of Southeast Asia have
reached a stage of development where capital goods, at first from
the West and then from leading Asian producers, should be their
fastest-growing imports for the next several years.

Significant though Asia's appetite for capital goods is—among
other things because it indicates Asia is taking a big step up the
industrial ladder—the growth of its infrastructure spending matters
more. The dividing line between infrastructure investment and
other kinds of capital spending is not a straight and sharp one.
Infrastructure projects tend to be gigantic, and more of them are

paid for with public money (though the public share is going to have to decline if Asia is to have any hope of meeting its building plans; see the last section of this chapter). The important difference, though, is that whereas, say, a paper-making plant, heavily capitalized though it undoubtedly is, obeys market signals in the same way a toy shop does, an infrastructure project is both enormously swayed by economies of scale and has a strong effect not just on those who directly use its services but on non-users and on the economy as a whole.

Infrastructure has a large element of what some economists call such "social overhead capital." This is why roads, railways, water-supply and sewage-treatment systems, ports, airports, power plants, and telecommunications networks are in a class of their own. They can do good (or harm) out of all proportion to their cost.

It is also why Asia's infrastructure spending—or rather, so far, the lack of it—is so much a part of the continent's general institutional weakness. Infrastructure is the physical equivalent of good management or fairly transparent politics, a social good that is needed only (and is indeed much preferable) in relatively small quantities but in the right dose has immensely beneficial effects on private-sector productivity. Infrastructure also has special funding needs, described in the last section of this chapter and in much of chapter 14, that will help to revolutionize Asian finance. No wonder both governments and private firms are eyeing it so carefully.

THE POTENTIAL

The cost of Asia's needed infrastructure is not niggling. Modern power plants can easily cost $3 billion apiece to put up. By the time Hong Kong's new airport is completed in 1997 or 1998, it and the bridges, ports, and railway lines associated with it will probably have devoured some $25 billion (in what are called current dollars, i.e., ones that, because of inflation, buy less in real terms the later they are spent during a project's construction). And if China's Three Gorges dam project on the Yangzi River is ever actually completed (which would happen around 2010), it should prove to be at least nominally the costliest infrastructure project in history: $50–$70 billion in current dollars.

Yet, overall, infrastructure spending has accounted for only a modest share of Asia's total capital investment—less than 15 percent —and an even more modest share of GDP: less than 5 percent. The spending bulks large and needs special handling financially and otherwise because it is so "lumpy": enormous projects, few of them.

Well placed, these lumps can smooth the passage of whole economies. The dense network of paved roads laid down, with American help, in Taiwan in the 1950s as part of a national-security plan to make it easier to ward off a mainland Chinese invasion were crucial for raising rural incomes and equalizing wealth on the island. Farmers could get higher-value produce such as fruit to city markets before it spoiled; their children could live at home and commute to small factories nearby instead of flocking to the slums of one or two metropolises. Some of the same benefits came, similarly unintentionally, to Thailand in 1965–75, when America built roads and ports there to help in the war it was fighting against North Vietnam.

In the United States itself infrastructure spending has had at times surprisingly large economic benefits. The toll-free interstate highway system, built at then extravagant expense in the 1950s and 1960s (and, again, justified at the time on grounds of national security) did so much good for the economy as a whole that one study found that three-quarters of its cost was recouped by reductions in trucking rates alone. Gordon Wu, a Hong Kong–based construction entrepreneur who has become something of an Asian "King of Infrastructure," was so impressed by the effects of the interstate system he saw being built while he was a student at Princeton in the 1950s that he has called for Asia to undertake a similar project. It would knit together China and India through a Mekong River superhighway running from southwestern China into Indochina and Southeast Asia and thence through Burma into India. A branch through the Malay Peninsula would hook up the Asian landmass with Indonesia's large islands of Sumatra and Java.

This sounds visionary (and Mr. Wu is one). But an intercontinental superhighway system is probably the best gigantic project for catapulting much of Asia into the ranks of rich twenty-first-century countries as the Interstate Highway System was for intertwining and strengthening modern America in the 1950s. Such a scheme is already taking shape in Asia, willy-nilly, but it could do with a bit more of the strategic vision that Mr. Wu has for it. A pan-Asian road network, as absurd as it sounds, could be—as it was on a small scale for Taiwan and Thailand—the biggest single stimulus for the modernization of continental Asia.

Yet at the moment Asia faces more mundane and pressing problems than whether it can make the last great leap to continental unity via a modern system of highways. Practically everywhere in Asia, save Singapore, a quarter-century of fast industrial growth has left the region's already primitive local systems of roads, railroads, airports, telecommunications networks and power plants unable to cope with the demands being put on them. In the early 1990s each American consumed 11,000 kilowatt-hours of electricity a year; each Briton, Japanese, Hong Konger, and Singaporean, around 5,000 a year. Every poor Asian country save Malaysia (at 1,000 a year) had a per capita consumption of around 600 or less.

Electricity in Asia is so scarce that in most places industrial output is significantly reduced by power bottlenecks. The most extreme case was the Philippines in the late 1980s and early 1990s. Until the government reorganized the national power company and threw the business of power generation open to private firms in 1993–94, blackouts were the rule. In the first quarter of 1993 industrial users were deprived of power an average of four to six hours a day. Their direct production losses alone were some 6.2 billion pesos (more than $200 million) over the quarter, equal on an annual basis to 2 percent of GDP. Indirect losses—for example, in foreign direct investment that shied away from the Philippines—may have been even more damaging. A year later, the problem had been solved, for the moment, anyway, and FDI had started pouring in for the first time in years.

The story is similar for telecommunications and transport. In 1992, China had barely 2 telephone lines for every 100 people; Pakistan and the Philippines, barely one. Indonesia and India had only 0.8 lines per 100 people. Rich countries had 50 lines or more per 100 people, and even middle-income Asian countries like Taiwan and South Korea had 35 or so lines.

A visit to almost any booming Asian city brings the traveler into immediate personal contact with what may be the continent's biggest single infrastructure failing: woeful transport. Among Asian cities only Singapore, which imposes extremely high taxes on cars and has begun to charge for road use, has a less than horrific traffic problem. The most horrific of all belongs to Bangkok, where in 1994 some 550 new cars and 700 new motorbikes were registered every day in a city only 7 percent of whose area is devoted to roads (compared with 15–20 percent in most cities) and whose average traffic speed had by then reached four miles an hour, the pace of a brisk walk, and was falling from there. Work on mass-transit systems for the city, planning for which was done in the early 1970s, had hardly even begun by 1995.

Transport is so inadequate in most of Asia that the economies of whole countries are being dented. The country most in trouble is China. In the 1980s, when the Chinese economy was growing faster than that of any other big country, China invested only 1.4 percent of GDP in a transport system that was under strain even before fast economic growth began; South Korea, Brazil, and even India were spending 2–3 percent of GDP on transport during that decade. And in the early 1990s, China was investing only 1 percent of GDP in transport. By then, according to the World Bank, China had only 0.05 kilometers of railway track per person, about half the rail density of India, a quarter the density of Brazil, and a tenth the density of Russia. Worse yet, China had just under 1 kilometer of roadway per person, less than half as much as India, a quarter as much as Russia, and one-twelfth as much as Brazil.

By the early 1990s, China's freight-moving capacity was groaning under the strain: China was shipping more than twice as much freight as Brazil per kilometer of rail track, three times as much as the United States, and five times as much as India. And it was paying for this overwork. Some three-quarters of China's energy comes from burning coal, and coal is the heaviest user of transport and the commodity most affected by its inadequacies. Counting electricity and other losses, a World Bank estimate suggests that the economic cost to China of its lousy transport systems has been running at more than 1 percent of GDP for years.

THE BONANZA

The first thing needed to fix Asia's infrastructural weaknesses is not spending but saving. The World Bank has calculated that in the early 1990s the poor world spent about $200 billion a year on infrastructure. (A little less than half of that was spent in Asia.) But it also wasted almost $180 billion each year by running existing infrastructure badly.

Almost $125 billion of that waste came in the form of government subsidies for infrastructure services: cheap electricity (which accounts for the vast majority of subsidies by value), cheap or even free water, and underpriced rail fares and utility tariffs. This not only imposes a direct drain on state coffers (which is all that the $125 billion counts) but also artificially increases the use of scarce infrastructure. The other $55 billion in waste came from technical inefficiency: water lost through leaky pipes that had not been properly maintained; electricity stolen from the national grid.

Asia has plenty of examples of both sorts of vice. Electricity is habitually underpriced throughout the continent. For instance, Indian farmers in the early 1990s were paying an electricity tariff equal to about one-sixth the cost of supplying the power, and that was on paper. In fact, they rarely paid their bills: The average electricity account for farmers in Uttar Pradesh, a big agricultural state, was three years' past due. Inefficient operations are also rife, whether in the form of electricity theft in India or extravagant overmanning on both Indian and Chinese railways.

Then, too, infrastructure projects frequently offer some of the choicest examples of bad government in Asia. The colossal sums they require, spent in one chunk, are an invitation to proportionally colossal bribes. In Japan, so far advanced in many ways, government-run construction projects were a notorious source of personal reward and party fund-raising well into the 1990s.

Even in the rare cases where that sort of corruption is absent, infrastructure projects are frequently of a size and complexity to test severely the not always impressive organizational skills of Asian governments. One reason ground has barely been broken in grid-locked Bangkok for any of the mass-transit projects that have been under discussion there for the past quarter-century is that sixteen distinct government agencies have had a say in the city's traffic "planning" and three big government authorities had enough standing to proceed with rival plans of their own for the biggest projects—to the extent of signing contracts with rival bidders. (The wonderfully named Office of Megaprojects was created in 1994 to try to tidy up this mess.) Similarly, Taiwan's much-trumpeted six-year development plan of 1991–96, which at one time was supposed to spend $325 billion modernizing the island's infrastructure, had fallen into serious disrepute by 1994 because the government had had such a project-management failure on the $17-billion Taipei mass-transit system that fires had broken out, and elevated-rail supporting pillars had cracked, even while the system was still being built.

Yet even if Asian governments went a long way towards correcting these failings, the continent's need for new infrastructure would still be immense. China alone plans to add 17,000 megawatts of electricity-generating capacity every year for the rest of the century —although unless China's economic growth slowed drastically, even that gigantic building program, which would cost around $10 billion a year to carry out, would not stop capacity from slipping further behind demand than it already is. Almost every other Asian country has electricity plans that are proportionally even more ambitious than China's. Whereas China is aiming to increase its capacity by no more than two-thirds in the years 1994–2000, India wants to raise its capacity by some 170 percent, from 59,000 megawatts to 160,000 megawatts (even then it would still be only about 55 percent of China's intended level); the Philippines, by 150 percent; Pakistan, by 135 percent; and Indonesia and Malaysia, by some 120 percent each.

The story is much the same in telecommunications. China wants almost to triple its switching capacity from less than 40 million lines in 1995 to 100 million lines in 2000, at a cost of $10 billion or more a year. India hopes at least to match China's expansion, at a like cost, though in India's case that would mean increasing capacity sixfold in the years 1995–2000. Lastly, there is transport, the biggest gobbler of capital. In China alone spending on transport infrastructure (mainly roads and railroads but also ports and airports) is expected to account for some $115 billion of the $235 billion that China intends to spend on infrastructure in the years 1994–2000.

Seers who have added up the numbers Asia-wide predict that the continent's total infrastructure spending in the seven years 1994–2000 will run anywhere from $700 billion (in current dollars) to $1 trillion (the guesstimate of the Asian Development Bank (ADB) and the generally quoted figure) to a preposterous $2 trillion (courtesy of the Long-Term Credit Bank of Japan). The highest of those figures is preposterous not because Asia couldn't do with that much extra infrastructure but because it implies that the continent would be spending more than two and one-half times as much each year (in nominal terms) on infrastructure in the last half of the 1990s as it did in the early 1990s and 25 percent more each year than was spent in the entire developing world in the early 1990s.

Even $143 billion a year (the ADB estimate), with power and

transport each accounting for $48 billion and telecommunications for $24 billion, would be a very steep climb. Taiwan's experience with its six-year development plan suggests that, even if the financing could be found (see the last section of this chapter), the managerial resources of both the companies doing the work and the governments trying to orchestrate them are just not up to a task this vast. In Taiwan the plan has fallen far short of its heady intentions, and the work has often been shoddily done. The implications for Asia as a whole are more interesting.

In coming up with the $1 trillion figure—which would roughly equal 7 percent of Asia's GDP over the seven years—the ADB reckoned that if anything less were spent it would start to eat into the continent's economic growth rates. By 1994–95 the conventional view was that most of Asia's economies (save those of the Indian subcontinent), growing as they were by around 7–8 percent a year on average, were performing as well as they ever could. In other words, for much of Asia a growth slowdown is probably in the works anyway; and Asia's likely failure to build infrastructure as furiously as it needs to for the rest of this decade will accelerate that deceleration of economic growth.

At the same time, Asia's surplus of investable capital may well evaporate. Since the early 1980s, when fast growth and rising wealth allowed savings rates in most East Asian countries to vault into the low thirties as a share of GDP, they have been saving one or two percentage points more each year than they have been investing. Movements in savings rates are notoriously hard to predict, depending as they do on so many things, but it is possible that for the next several years Asia will be investing one or two percentage points more than it saves. It will need, net, an import of capital to help pay for its projected huge infrastructure building.

Fascinating though it will be to watch how East and Southeast Asia cope with something they have not known for a long time—a step down rather than up to a new trend line of growth and an insufficiency of domestic savings (if this is indeed what happens)—this is still unlikely to alter radically the business facts about Asia's infrastructure boom. However they look at Asia, most providers of infrastructure—whether of power plants, telephone switches, or construction services—see a similar share of the whole world's growth in demand for their product or service for the rest of this decade coming from Asia: about half. If, that is, someone can work out how to enlarge significantly the role of private companies and finance in providing and running the new infrastructure.

BUILD-OPERATE-LITIGATE

Understandably, the race to build the new Asia is attracting world-class entrants from everywhere. The rights to build power plants are being fought over by such heavyweights as General Electric, Westinghouse, ABB Asea Brown Boveri, Mitsubishi, Hitachi, and Hong Kong's Gordon Wu (via a company called Consolidated Electric Power Asia, or CEPA). Every telephone-switch maker in the world is beating a path to various Asian doors, especially China's. Alcatel, Siemens, Ericsson, AT&T, and NEC are among those authorized to sell switches in China; Motorola dominates the cellular-phone market there. And in construction Bechtel and Fluor vie with a dozen big European, Japanese, and South Korean firms for shares in the world's biggest building projects.

Yet however juicy the pickings, these ventures are increasingly fraught for the companies in more than just a logistical sense. Before Asian governments began waking up to the scale of the demands that would be placed on all sorts of resources by their ambitious building programs, they tended to assume that infrastructure was a public affair, to be financed by public money and run by public agencies. Reality is forcing them to change their minds, but the process of adjustment is hard on everyone.

Gordon Wu has been ahead of most in trying to convince governments that they must be imaginative about regulation, ownership, and finance if these huge projects are actually to get built. Mr. Wu, who had started out as a property developer and had no experience whatever in the power-plant business, decided to build power plants in China during a visit to Guangzhou in the 1980s. He got stuck for a while in an elevator in a luxury hotel because of a power blackout and, after discovering that blackouts happened all the time in Guangdong province, espied an unmet need. He convinced the Chinese that he could build power plants, and get foreign financing for them, on the basis of a ''build-operate-transfer'' (BOT) contract. This allowed his company to build a plant, run it, and then transfer ownership to a Chinese authority. The contract also set a floor under the return to the developer.

Mr. Wu's road, bridge, and mass-transit rail projects are designed to solve a different problem. Mr. Wu is convinced that these projects normally cannot pay for themselves. If the tolls or fares are set low enough to allow a large number of users onto the system, the revenues will not be high enough to generate a profit; yet if they are set high enough to generate a profit, they will in practice drive down usage to the point where, again, revenues will be too low.

The solution ("started by the nineteenth-century railway robber barons in America," Mr. Wu notes with satisfaction) is to combine property development with infrastructure and use the profits from property to subsidize the (inevitable) losses from running a transport system. The unfortunate historical conclusion from nineteenth-century American railways is that this sort of solution often ends in defaults on the obligations to its initial (normally foreign) investors. It is only when locals get involved in a big way that the obligations (usually bonds) tend to get paid.

Mr. Wu's expressway from the Hong Kong border to Guangzhou, which opened late in 1993, was designed to allow huge shopping centers to be built at certain interchanges. A bridge he has agreed to build in the northern Chinese city of Qingdao will never turn a profit, but property development on the 660 hectares of land next door that he acquired "for a song" will more than make up for that. He has applied the same thinking to his proposals for a mass-transit rail project in Bangkok (which he got interested in when, again, he got stuck, only this time in Bangkok traffic rather than in an elevator).

Governments are not always impressed by such cleverness. Through much of 1994 China tried to impose a 12 percent ceiling on new power-project returns (18 percent is what most builders reckon is needed in view of the risks involved), only when Mr. Wu, among others, threatened not to do any more deals did the Chinese begin reconsidering. Too much law can be as bad as too little. One Philippine BOT toll-road operator saw its toll increase held up for six months by a court that had been petitioned by a single disgruntled driver.

By the mid-1990s, however, the most alarming infrastructure incident from a foreign investor's viewpoint was a dispute in 1993–94 over an expressway in Bangkok. The Japanese-led consortium that built and was to operate the project had a contract with the Bangkok authorities that specified a certain structure of tolls to provide an

agreed rate of return on the consortium's investment. But when the
time came for the road to open, the authorities unilaterally set a
politically more palatable, that is, lower, toll. Following this example
of what one banker called the new "build-operate-steal" concept,
the original foreign partners in the consortium were bought out by
Thais; but the incident made investors wonder just how secure their
investments would prove to be in politically sensitive projects.

Perhaps the best way to remove politics from the business of
running infrastructure projects is to privatize the provision of infrastructure services. There is a much broader potential scope for privatization in Asia than infrastructure projects alone. In Indonesia in
1993, for instance, one investment banker reckoned that, whereas
the whole of the Jakarta stock market had a market capitalization of
some $30 billion, the country's state-owned firms were capitalized at
$100 billion. Yet most state-owned firms throughout Asia are in the
infrastructure business, and these are the outfits that will dominate
any privatization program.

Some of the efforts to bring private investors into existing firms,
or to let new projects be developed from the start by private entrepreneurs, have worked well. The usual procedure with existing state-
owned operations is for the business to be "corporatized"—
government departments are turned into government enterprises,
and those into regular corporations, with a board of directors supervising the firm's execution of mainly commercial goals. Only later
(in the case of Indonesia's ports the process has taken ten years) is
the outfit turned into a for-profit firm some or all of whose equity is
sold to private investors. If the business is a monopoly, the government retains regulatory power over tariffs and fees; if competition
can be introduced (as it often can be in, e.g., some kinds of telecommunications services), even the regulation can be dispensed with.

Malaysia has led the privatization pack in Asia. After a heavy
round of nationalizations in the late 1970s and early 1980s, the
government suddenly reversed course in the mid-1980s and drew
up a program that aimed at the privatization of more than two
hundred government enterprises. By 1994 around eighty-five enterprises had been sold off in part or in whole, among them the country's biggest container port and the national telecommunications
company. The government also put new projects in private hands to
develop. The biggest set of these businesses consists of five private
power projects that are to cost roughly $4 billion to build between

1995 and 1997 (compared with $7 billion that the government-owned national utility is to invest in its own plant). Other private projects include a $2.4 billion 900-kilometer toll road that runs the whole length of the country (this was finished in 1994) and a $500 million light-rail system for Kuala Lumpur.

The Malaysian highway shows how mixed the motives of politics and business can remain even in private infrastructure projects. The problem is not efficiency or incentives. The operator (which has a thirty-year BOT concession for the road) completed the project more than a year ahead of schedule and on budget; and the contract has reasonable provisions for toll increases and puts no limit on the operating firm's profits. Even so, the firm's main shareholder companies are owned by the Renong Group, which is closely tied to the United Malays National Organization, the country's long-ruling party. These excellent connections were presumably of some help in getting a concessional government loan to finance the project, a government guarantee about traffic levels on the road for ten years, and an enthusiastic response from Malaysia's capital markets to calls for private finance.

Other Asian countries have taken more halting steps towards opening infrastructure to private development. Singapore has sold only a small slice of its telecommunications company. Thailand has been bold in allowing private provision of electric power and tele-communications—even basic local telephone service in Bangkok—but (as explained above) very backward on transport. Indonesia has been cautious about both roads and power, although agreements on power projects began coming through more quickly in 1994–95. In all, the World Bank reckons that of the $23.5 billion which developing countries received from selling off infrastructure in 1988–92, Asia collected only about $6.5 billion, compared with Latin America's $16 billion. And almost all of the financing for Asia's privatizations (98 percent to be precise) came from domestic investors, compared with 44 percent in Latin America.

Asia's slowness to privatize seems odd. Every study shows that the economic savings from privatization are extremely large. In the case of Chile's telecoms privatization they equaled more than 150 percent of the firm's annual revenues, and in the case of America's airlines deregulation, a recurrent $15 billion (in 1990 dollars) a year. And many of the Asian countries that have (apparently) so fervently rejected foreign participation in infrastructure investment are more than happy to welcome FDI in other kinds of business. Why is Asia reluctant to privatize infrastructure?

The main reason is political. Even governments that, like Malaysia's, recognize the economic efficiencies of privately run infrastructure want to preserve their influence over projects that always bulk large in the public view and are occasionally quite lucrative to their promoters and others. Other governments, like Thailand's in the case of the Bangkok toll road, are swayed by populist considerations.

Dictatorships like China's have the power, at least in theory, to ignore popular resentment of high (i.e., market-based) tolls and fares, but they have other worries. Despite its urgent determination to build up China's telecoms services at breakneck speed, the Chinese government has said flatly that foreign investors will not be allowed to help provide telecoms services (as distinct from equipment such as switches, where foreigners already dominate the business). Bureaucratic politicking in Beijing, and perhaps even concerns about state security if foreigners were allowed to help run a telecoms network, may be to blame.

Yet the Chinese government's resolution is already beginning to buckle. By 1995, Hongkong Telecom had signed a contract that seems to give it a role in running a cellular-phone network in Beijing and will certainly give it a cut of the revenues; and another Hong Kong firm, Champion Technology Holdings, was already involved in an up-and-running cellular-phone network in Chengdu, the capital of Sichuan Province. Moreover, the Chinese government is busily undercutting its own position by allowing foreign investment in China's flourishing cable-TV networks. It is doing this presumably with the idea of using the cash flow that cable-TV franchises generate to help finance telecoms development; yet it seems to be ignoring the technological likelihood that soon in China, as elsewhere in the world, cable will be able to carry telephone services, too. But it is not politics or technology but instead the staggering financial burden of Asia's new building programs that may force the continent's governments to loosen their infrastructural grip.

CASH ON THE NAIL

It should come as no surprise that financing $1 trillion of infrastructure spending over seven years—if that is really what it amounts to

—will not be a cinch. In the past some 80–90 percent of the money for infrastructure came from government spending of one kind or another: from the host government's tax revenues (75–80 percent) and from international institutions, such as the World Bank or Asian Development Bank, or from country-to-country aid or cheap government-to-government loans (together 10–12 percent). This may have worked when Asia was spending $100 billion a year on infrastructure, but a financial chasm opens if you assume the figure is $140 billion a year instead. The usual sources of government money are unlikely to cough up more than $100–$105 billion of this. That means $35–$40 billion a year has to be found in private (or unusual government) pockets—up from no more than $10 billion a year in the late 1980s and early 1990s.

Asia's (and the world's) capital markets do not seem obviously ready to cope with this demand. Most private infrastructure financing in the past has come from bank loans and syndications; these sources still account, for example, for 80 percent of the financing for infrastructure projects built by Gordon Wu's CEPA. But the trouble with banks, as Mr. Wu points out, is that they are nervous creatures which need to be cashed out of a project within a few years. That poses problems for the smooth financing of projects that by their nature do not pay for themselves in less than ten to twenty years.

Banks (and other investors) can sometimes be pacified by government guarantees for project financing. The backing of India's central government for the obligations of India's notoriously feckless state electricity boards, for instance, was the price India had to pay to induce Western power-plant builders and operators to start coming into the country in 1993–94. Yet sovereign guarantees have their limits. By late 1994 alarm among foreign lenders to China about the government's willingness to stand behind the debts of state-owned firms and lower-tier governments was common enough that international credit-rating services began looking into whether the ratings of some Chinese debt should be lowered. Then, too, once governments begin to understand that putting their name willy-nilly behind infrastructure projects limits their ability to borrow for themselves (or raises the cost of doing so), their enthusiasm for providing guarantees cools.

Equity ought, in theory, to be able to plug much of Asia's infrastructural financing gap; this is why privatization is so logical an option. Another growing source of capital is foreign-equity-investment funds. The bluest chip of the Asian infrastructure funds set up in 1993–94 were the AIG Asian Infrastructure Fund, established by AIG, the American insurer, and including the Singapore government as the other big investor; the Asia Infrastructure Fund, sponsored by Peregrine Investments in Hong Kong, with contributions from the Soros Group in New York, the Asian Development Bank, and the World Bank's International Finance Corporation (IFC); and the Global Power Investment Fund, intended to finance Asian power plants, which includes GE Capital and the IFC as big investors.

The pedigrees of all of these, and no doubt of others, is impeccable, but look at their initial funding: $1 billion each for the first two, $500 million for the third. In at least one case the fund is supposed to be invested over five years, which, if true of all of them, would imply investments worth $500 million a year, or a not-so-handsome 1.25 percent of Asia's annual infrastructure financing needs from private sources. These are welcome contributors, but they are not saviors.

What makes the most sense for investments like infrastructure, which have long-term payouts, is investors with long-term obligations—like pension funds. Singapore's vast Central Provident Fund, which collects compulsory savings from virtually all of the city-state's workers and employers, has long invested in Singaporean government corporations, most of which have an infrastructural slant to them. And the Philippine social-security fund has set aside 4 billion pesos (some $1.8 billion at the end-1994 exchange rate) for fifteen-year loans for power-plant investments via Philippine banks.

Yet for the moment Asia has a dearth of pension funds, save for the government-mandated schemes in Singapore and Malaysia. The logical financing vehicle for the infrastructure explosion is therefore long-term bonds placed with a wide variety of investors. The trouble is that most Asian investors, unlike their Western counterparts, are uncomfortable with the idea of a long-term investment (which may be a useful caution to foreigners about the risks involved in putting money into large, immovable, and politically sensitive projects whose streams of revenue begin flowing only slowly, and then in a currency different from the one in which the borrowing is done). Lastly, the markets for trading and evaluating Asian bonds are still fairly primitive. Although Asian bond markets will undoubtedly now grow fast (see next chapter), they are unlikely to grow fast enough to take up all of the financing slack that Asia's infrastructure ambitions are sure to create.

Something therefore has to give. For many Asian infrastructure projects, the first thing giving way is any resistance on the part of Western governments' export-financing agencies to extending cheap credit to Asian borrowers. Every European telecoms-equipment firm in China mentions the role of cheap credit in making possible the sale of switches from European factories to the Chinese. The same holds for commercial aircraft, both American and European. And one of the most important elements in GEC-Alsthom's winning bid for the rolling-stock contract (worth $2.1 billion) for South Korea's $13 billion high-speed train (Asia's first outside Japan) was the French government's efforts to arrange financing so cheap that it cut some 10 percent off the contract price.

My own guess is that Asia's infrastructure-finance gap will be filled by a combination of (a) lots more government-subsidized export finance from the West; (b) a forced acceleration of Asian privatization, including a big growth in the capitalization of some Asian stockmarkets; (c) a blossoming of Asian bond markets, which, as it occurs, will raise returns on bonds relative to those on equities, and returns on infrastructure relative to returns on private investment (see end of chapter 14); and (d) not as much infrastructure being built as everyone says should be, which will then lower Asia's economic growth rates slightly. However all this works out in practice, one sure result will be a big shake-up in Asian finance. None too soon.

CHAPTER 14

THE MONEY MACHINE

Anyone who hopes to come to grips with finance in Asia needs a wide-ranging mind. The only fairly consistent financial fact about Asia is the continent's high rates of savings and investment. What institutions have been created and what rules put into effect to channel the savings to the investments vary greatly from country to country. As Asia modernizes, old restrictions will have to go; but that is no reason to expect a uniform set of new structures to take their place across the continent anytime soon. The differences from one Asian country to another are liable to be as big as those from one European country to the next in the early 1990s.

Despite this complexity of detail, the structure of Asia's present-day financial markets has grown out of a simple split—one with huge consequences for Asian economies and societies—between two kinds of financial institution: those in the informal sector and those in the formal sector. The informal financial institutions—credit clubs, curb markets, extended families—function without government regulation and entirely along free-market lines. Their purpose is to deliver credit to the emerging parts of an economy, and one of Asia's greatest strengths (especially in the Chinese parts of Asia) has been the ability of these informal financial bodies to channel capital to small entrepreneurial manufacturing firms. As economies grow, the informal financial sector fades in significance.

The formal sector tends to be highly regulated and has been widely used as an instrument of government policy. Some of its policy functions are direct: Banks in much of Asia are required to make "policy loans" to certain kinds of industries or even (as in the case of bank lending to South Korea's *chaebol*) to particular borrowers. The more significant policy purpose of the formal sector has been to act as the linchpin of the trade, exchange-rate and inflation-fighting strategies that almost all East and Southeast Asian governments have pursued.

One of the biggest mistakes of most of the poor world's failed economies, particularly those of Africa and (until recently) Latin America, has been to keep their exchange rates overvalued against rich-world currencies (especially the U.S. dollar, in which most foreign trade is invoiced). Among other things, this discourages the developing country's manufacturers from exporting and hence muffles the important price signals and even more important marketing and technological information that the world market can deliver.

East Asia's countries took the opposite tack to that of most of Africa and Latin America. They have striven to keep their exchange rates slightly undervalued against the dollar as a way of promoting exports and economic growth. The East Asian model of export-led growth through an undervalued exchange rate—which, in one of the most amusing ironies of modern economic history, originated in the "Dodge plan" that the American occupation authorities imposed on Japan in 1949—has many benefits for a developing economy but one serious problem. It tends to promote inflation (because if the developing country's exchange rate cannot fall to equalize the prices of traded goods there and in, say, the United States, then the price level in the developing country must rise instead). The inflationary impact has usually been strengthened by the relatively high liquidity introduced into most of these countries by capital inflows from abroad and high savings rates at home.

The single most significant use that Asian governments have made of the formal financial system has been to contain the chronic inflation fever caused by an undervalued exchange rate. Different countries used their formal financial systems to this end in different ways. South Korea's government used "monetary stabilization bonds" that it forced the state-owned banks to hold. Taiwan did it through tight controls on bank lending. Singapore's government did it through its control of most of its citizens' savings, which to this day are compulsorily taken from salaries and put into the Central Provident Fund.

Hong Kong's government, free-market in most other respects, has tried to control inflation by interfering extensively in the colony's property market. Real estate used as loan collateral has been the most important source of long-term finance for Hong Kong companies (they have issued few bonds), and the government's manipulation of the property market affects the credit available to the corporate sector. Lastly, and perhaps most cleverly of all, Indonesia has tried to control inflation and the inflow of foreign capital for investment in stocks and bonds by depreciating its currency at a steady 4–5 percent a year. For foreign investors, this acts in effect as a 5 percent tax on speculative portfolio investment in Indonesia—since the money will be worth 5 percent less in the foreigner's own currency—while encouraging long-term foreign direct investment in export industries.

The first serious blow to this system, from which none of Asia has yet recovered, was delivered in 1985, when the dollar fell sharply as a result of the colossal budget deficits that the American government began running. The resulting huge flow of investment capital into the East Asian countries was too big for their inflation-containment systems to cope with. The outcome was fast and steep rises in the prices of Asian assets, especially real estate and stock-market shares.

But the system is breaking down for other reasons, too, among them the gradual financial liberalization and deregulation that most Asian countries (including Japan) have been introducing. As the old methods in both the informal and formal financial sectors disappear, East Asia's countries are going to face the same sort of problems of institution-building for the financial system as those they face in the cases of infrastructure and government. With no tradition of credit-risk assessment by banks (they lent against land as security or simply to whom the government told them) or of objective credit assessment in the informal sector, Asian finance lacks the tools for running a more modern and transparent financial system. To develop them will take time and cost money. But Asia will have plenty of foreigners ready to help with the task, drawn to the region by the vast amount of capital that has already been built up there.

FLUSH WITH MONEY

Asia's high savings rates, combined with some of the world's lowest effective tax rates, are creating an extraordinarily deep pool of liquid capital. This makes Asia probably the world's most-sought after market for private bankers (the suitably hushed phrase for banks taking deposits from, and investing on behalf of, very rich people). In 1993 there were seventy banks in Hong Kong offering private-banking services, forty-five in Singapore, thirty-seven in Malaysia, more than thirty in the Philippines, and twenty-five or so each in Indonesia, Taiwan, and Thailand.

No wonder. America has the world's highest concentration of American dollar millionaires—almost 0.9 percent of the population, or around 2.5 million people, in 1993—but you would expect that from the world's richest country. The Boston Consulting Group, an American business consultancy, reckons that Hong Kong, with a per capita GDP equal to only about three-quarters that of the United States, has the world's second-highest density of millionaires: around 0.5 percent in 1993, or 30,000–35,000 in a population of 6 million. Thailand had more than 20,000 millionaires in 1993; Malaysia and Taiwan, some 15,000 each; the Philippines, somewhat fewer; Indonesia, 10,000–12,000; and little Singapore, with 3 million people, perhaps 5,000 millionaires, or 0.3 percent of the population. One Hong Kong–based private banker says that every one of her firm's South Korean clients (of whom there are perhaps six) has at least $20 million on deposit with the bank. It is no surprise that Hong Kong's two biggest private bankers—Wardley, a subsidiary of Hongkong and Shanghai Bank, and Citibank—each had $10 billion of private-banking assets under management in 1993.

Asia's private-banking clients are only the glamorous tip-top of a gigantic iceberg. In 1993, Asians (outside Japan) saved around $650 billion, compared with savings of $900 billion by Americans and $1.2 trillion by Japanese. The difference between Japan and the rest of Asia, on one side, and America, on the other, is that whereas the Americans have probably the world's most sophisticated and transparent mechanism for transmitting savings, their own and other people's, to investments that deliver the highest returns, Asians in general have a creaky mechanism that was originally designed to serve government policies rather than respond to market signals. The rapidly increasing size of Asia's annual savings and investment flows, combined with the needed sprucing up of the transmission mechanism between them, will decide how financial modernization takes shape in each market.

INFORMALITY

An American economist, Jeffrey Frankel of the University of California at Berkeley, has sketched a three-step process for the emergence of a modern financial market. In the first stage, a firm (or a country) takes care of its financing needs internally through family or corporate savings or government-directed credit. The second stage involves bank finance: Banks, at first under the orders of bureaucrats and later with merely their nudges, try to make judgments about the creditworthiness of borrowers and supervise their use of the credit. In the third stage, those seeking money turn directly to the anonymous securities markets, where readily transferable equity or debt instruments, such as stocks and bonds, create an objective auction-based system for the pricing of credit and risk.

All three stages overlap in every economy. And, in fact, internal financing for firms—just like national savings for national investment—accounts for by far the biggest share of investable funds no matter how advanced the banking system and capital markets are. Figures compiled by Joseph Stiglitz, an economist at Stanford University, show that in the two decades after 1970 no less than two-thirds and as much as 98 percent of the net financing of companies in America, Japan, Germany, France, and Britain came from the companies' own retained earnings. Bank lending was second, bond finance third, and equity finance a distant fourth—so distant that in three of the countries it provided companies with negative financial support over the twenty years; and in the other two a trivial positive share of their total financing.

In developing Asia these internal capital flows account for an even bigger share of corporate finance than elsewhere. The most extreme example is the overseas Chinese firms described in chapter 11. Family owned, for the most part small, and operating in often hostile environments, these firms have put a premium on keeping the corporate reins in family hands; the family owners have been particularly reluctant to part with equity in the firm.

Nor are these firms overly fond of debt. They will turn to banks for financing—until recently debt securities were almost unheard of—but only under carefully defined conditions that limit any exposure of the firm's own equity to its creditors. Hong Kong property companies have refined these principles to a high art. In an ideal

Hong Kong property development, almost none of the developer's own money is ever at risk. The initial stages of the project are financed with bank loans, but these are quickly liquidated as the developer "presells" space in the development to end users even before construction of the project is complete. In a rising market, it is not unusual for all of the project loans to be paid in full and for there already to be a return on the developer's equity before the first occupant has even moved in.

Even in the overseas-Chinese network, however, family savings and cash flow cannot cover all the financing needs of the corporate sector. Among the overseas Chinese, capital pooling for big deals has been carried out through personal and clan contacts that often reach back for a generation or two. Almost everywhere in East Asia smaller loans have traditionally been handled through "credit clubs," or *huis,* as the Chinese call them. These are groups of twenty or so people who pool their money for business loans that are extended through a bidding process to members of the club.

In Taiwan, whose *huis* are fairly typical of clubs throughout East Asia, there is a monthly auction of the club's available capital to all the members who want to bid for it, with the offer of the highest interest rate winning the loan. The leader of the *hui,* who guarantees the loan in exchange for a commission, understandably keeps a careful eye on how the proceeds are being used. When the term of the loan is up, the repaid capital becomes available for further bidding and lending. It is a popular form of investment for Taiwan's savings. The average household keeps about half its money in the bank, secure but earning low interest, and half in a *hui,* which generally charges interest rates of 18–20 percent. (Interestingly, a rate in this range—typical for loans on the informal market throughout East Asia—is almost identical to the rates charged in the United States for loans against credit cards, which increasingly are used for start-up capital by very small American businesses.)

The credit-club arrangement, seemingly humble in the individual case, is mighty in aggregate. A survey in the mid-1980s found that almost half of all loans in Taiwan were made through credit clubs or on the black market rather than through formal financial institutions. The story in South Korea was probably even more extreme. Most bank lending was at the mercy of government directives. Between 1962, when Korea's banks were nationalized, and 1980, just before a limited program of financial liberalization was introduced,

70 percent of Korean bank lending to manufacturing firms was at the behest of government, with the aim of promoting its industrial policies. For any but the handful of favored bank borrowers—invariably they were *chaebol* (see chapter 10) until, in the late 1980s, the government switched course and ordered a certain share of bank loans to be made to small firms—financing had to come from family savings, cash flow and retained earnings, credit clubs, or the informal "curb market" of street-side moneylenders.

Such informal financing arrangements have attained a grander scale with the rise of China's township and village enterprises (TVEs; see chapter 6). The TVEs, which by the mid-1990s accounted for almost a third of China's industrial output, have some access to bank credit, but most of the TVE financing that cannot be supported by cash flow has come from China's recognized "non-bank financial institutions" (market-based financial firms that do not themselves take deposits but often do illicitly recycle the deposits and loans of true banks), or from larger and more intricate versions of Korea's and Taiwan's credit clubs.

DROIT DE SEIGNOR

In only two places in Asia—Hong Kong and Thailand—have companies been free to work out their internal financing needs pretty much independently of government wishes. The one direct (and large) exception to this in Hong Kong was the government's sanctioning of a bank interest-rate cartel that guaranteed fat spreads in the banks' favor between borrowing and lending rates. The indirect intervention, as mentioned in the first section of this chapter, was through the government's control of the property market and hence of the availability of long-term credit through property-collateralized loans.

Thailand's robustly independent financial system stretches a century or more into the past. Daniel Unger, an American economist who is an expert on Thailand, has described how nineteenth-century Siam's fear of European colonialism—all its Southeast Asian neighbors were subjugated, though it never was—led it early on to recoil from becoming indebted to foreign powers, a process that had been the downfall of several Asian states. This gave it an entrenched legacy of fiscal conservatism. Thailand also early on (in

1942) developed a strong-willed central bank dedicated to maintaining the value of the currency and spawned several big private banks that were allied with Chinese commercial interests which had a lot to gain from free trade and not much from force-fed industrialization. The state satisfied its own revenue needs mostly through fiscal measures—excise and export taxes—rather than through ownership or control of the banks. As a result, Thailand's government has mostly stayed away from intervention in the financial system.

Not so the rest of Asia's governments. As mentioned in the first section, most Asian countries have run a two-track financial system along one line of which scooted the nimble credit clubs and other wholly market-based financial intermediaries; and along the other line lumbered the massive money locomotives stoked and directed by the state. In many countries many or all of the banks were owned outright by the state. China, Indonesia, Vietnam, South Korea (until the early 1980s), and India (since the mid-1970s) are examples. Even where banks were in private hands, as in Malaysia and in South Korea following the denationalization of the banks there, they were under tight government control and were often directed to make policy loans, at below-market rates, to classes of borrowers favored by the government.

Such systems drew their financial power from the fact that, in the early days of Asia's rise from poverty, household savings shot up much faster than the availability of financial instruments to invest them in. (This is still overwhelmingly the case in China.) People therefore kept by far the greatest share of their rapidly expanding savings in bank deposits. These yielded, in general, a small but positive return at rates regulated by the government. Lending rates were controlled along with deposit rates, in part to keep spreads narrow and ensure that as much of the savings as possible went into investment.

Loan-rate regulation also worked to deliver mildly negative real interest rates to government-favored borrowers such as exporters. Such "financial repression" is frowned upon by economists—for the good reason that pricing anything, including money, below its market rate is an excellent way to create excess demand for it and cause it to be used inefficiently—but in much of East Asia (though not China or India) governments avoided most of the harmful effects by keeping the interest-rate subsidy within strict limits.

Governments intervened in lending decisions in other ways too. Most Asian countries created development banks to make loans to specific classes of borrowers, such as farmers or industrialists, or for social purposes like housing. In the case of deposits under its own banks' control, governments simply ordered development loans to be made. In the early days of Japan's industrialization, for example, as much as 20–40 percent of household savings were deposited with the postal-savings system, which redeposited them with bodies whose express purpose was to make development loans in line with government policy. Taiwan, hyperconservative on financial matters, made use of its own postal-savings network to immobilize rather than deploy savings (for the purpose, mentioned earlier, of controlling the asset-price inflation that its undervalued currency would otherwise have pushed it straight into). As recently as the early 1990s, more than four-fifths of Taiwan's postal savings were idly on deposit with the central bank.

The influence of banks on the running of big industrial firms has been enhanced by the fact that most outside finance for these firms has come from bank loans rather than the capital markets. In the East Asian countries for which figures are available, in the two decades after 1970 debt and equity issues each provided less than 10 percent of total financing for industrial firms, compared with 40–50 percent from bank loans.

Yet even though most Asian countries are united in having built their financial systems around a core of tightly regulated (and often government-owned) banks, they otherwise show a splendid variety in their financial structures. Taiwan and South Korea maintain extensive controls on capital flows into and out of their countries, though these barriers are now being gradually dismantled. So does China, though the efficient black market there, firmly plugged into the overseas-Chinese network, makes a mockery of much of the apparatus of control.

India used to have one of Asia's most watertight barriers against the sloshing of capital into and out of its closely regulated economy. But within two years of the start of its reform program in 1991, the rupee had been made freely convertible for foreign-trade transactions; and within another year or two it is likely to be made convertible for all transactions (including the buying and selling of stocks and bonds).

Indonesia defied conventional wisdom about the right order of economic liberalization and thus now ranks with Malaysia, Thailand, and Hong Kong in being among the most open Asian economies to international capital flows. Indonesia did this by making the rupiah freely convertible even on the capital account as early as the 1970s and by starting to liberalize the rest of its financial markets in the late 1980s and early 1990s, even though the freeing of the real economy has proceeded much more slowly than either of these financial openings. Singapore, meanwhile, has been cordial to FDI but sharply restricts retail banking by foreign banks and foreign-bank dealings in Singapore dollars.

The differences are just as pronounced in domestic financial structures. South Korea, much of whose economic development was financed by borrowing, has one of Asia's best developed corporate-bond markets. Taiwan, which abhors debt, has long had a market in commercial paper for short-term corporate borrowings but virtually no corporate bonds and—until its grandiose infrastructure plans of the early 1990s—no government-bond market to speak of either. (By the mid-1990s, however, the government had quickly built up a large amount of debt.)

Yet Asian finance stands to be revolutionized—that is, made more like that of the rich world—over the next decade. The pressures for this transformation are coming in part from American badgering (e.g., of the Koreans over currency and financial-market reforms). The more intense, and more useful, pressures are coming from the strains on balance sheets and on efficiency that decades of acting as government tools have imposed on Asian banks. China admitted in late 1994 that bad debts to state-owned industrial firms amounted to 40 percent of the Chinese banking system's total outstanding credits. And South Korean and Taiwanese banks, imbued with the civil-service mentality, would be cut to ribbons if they had to compete directly with multinational banks.

The coming transformation in Asian finance will present many chances for making fortunes (and losing one or two as well). The perhaps discouraging fact for now, however, is that, because practically the whole of Asia is still deep in the stage of internal finance, where useful information about companies is rarely available to the public, some of the best investments for the rest of this decade will be those that involve taking direct stakes in Asian companies rather than lending to them or trading in the publicly listed stocks and bonds issued by them. Representatives of several rich investors, usually families, have spent the 1990s combing Asia for investments, and by 1995 perhaps two dozen direct-investment funds had been set up to take stakes in mainland Chinese companies alone.

Many direct-investment outfits are backed mostly by institutions (pension funds and the like) and make investments throughout Asia. One of these is Prudential Asia, run out of Hong Kong by Victor Fung. Mr. Fung says that his firm looks for investment targets in ten to fifteen high-income cities, which serve as sophisticated growth centers, with a large low-wage hinterland to support them. The associated hinterland is important because the cities alone, in Mr. Fung's view, cannot sustain high-margin output growth for long. Sometimes the hinterland is nearby—as southern China is to Hong Kong—and sometimes farther away. Mr. Fung says northeastern China is now fulfilling this role for Seoul. The concentration in these "pressure points" of people with fast-rising incomes is "a marketer's dream." But for investment purposes, Mr. Fung thinks that what still counts most is not the consumer or infrastructure demand building up in these cities but rather their ability to generate export earnings. For fast returns, cash flow rather than sales or assets is the main engine, and export growth delivers a lot of cash (and in hard currency) more reliably than anything else.

By 1993, Prudential Asia had made investments in fifty companies, at least three-quarters of them run by overseas Chinese. That should be warning enough to eager but not well-connected Western investors. Asia's growing ranks of direct-investment firms have by no means begun exhausting the lode of direct-investment opportunities in the continent, but the sad truth for the world at large is that direct investment is a game that only the biggest and savviest investors can play.

INTERMEDIARIES . . .

The second stage of financial development is commercial bank lending—that is, lending by banks on commercial grounds instead of government-induced policy grounds. Japan reached this stage early, with the rise of its "main-bank" system after the end of the Pacific war in 1945. Policy loans were confined to specialized government-owned development banks. Commercial banks, by contrast, were usually attached to industrial groups and would lend to companies within the group while keeping a close watch on what the borrower was doing with the money. In this they were more akin to nineteenth-century British banks than to modern American banks. The lending officers of Japanese main banks had enough expertise in the businesses of the people to whom they lent that they could make informed judgments about what was likely to be done with the money and even intervene with advice if things seemed to be going wrong.

Elsewhere in Asia governments are beginning the process of bringing policy-influenced banks closer to the marketplace through competition and deregulation. Foreign banks, completely free to operate in Hong Kong and mostly free in Thailand and Indonesia, have some leeway in India and even in Taiwan. Private banks have been allowed to spring up in Indonesia, Taiwan, and India. Even South Korea, beginning in 1993, started deregulating interest rates, dragging management out from under bureaucrats' thumbs and allowing would-be banks more freedom to enter the market.

Liberalization and deregulation may hold terrors for the worst of Asia's civil-service-era banks, but even for many of them (and for all upstart competitors and all bank customers) the loosening up holds much promise instead. For one thing, the example of Japan's extremely slow decompression of its financial system suggests that other Asian governments are not suddenly about to expose their long-protected banks to the blast of full competition. In most places —South Korea, Indonesia, China, and India—state-owned (or, in Korea, state-guided) banks carry too many bad loans on their books to be able to survive untempered competition. Yet even a gradual market opening can have dramatic effects. Despite the Indonesian government's sharp awareness of bad-debt problems at the country's banks (mostly at state banks but at several private ones as well); entry has been free enough that between 1988 and 1993 the state banks' share of bank assets fell from 70 percent to half, even while almost tripling in absolute terms; the share of private banks rose from a quarter to more than 40 percent; that of foreign banks, from 5 percent to almost 10 percent.

Sharp shifts of market share can happen even in a controlled liberalization because Asia's financial markets are growing so fast. There will be plenty of chances to make good money despite the increased competition of banks among themselves and with other financial institutions. In the years 1990–94 non-Japanese Asian bank assets (mostly loans) almost doubled, to more than \$3 trillion; there is a lot of lending, and of savings, to go around.

The competition among banks for this business is beginning to cross national borders. The normal first step is for banks to follow their corporate customers into overseas markets. With Asian firms investing and trading more within Asia itself, this sort of activity is growing fast; it accounts for the recent venturesomeness of Taiwanese and South Korean banks. Other Asian banks have avowedly regional ambitions, often running through the lines of the overseas-Chinese business network: Indonesia's Lippo Bank, Hong Kong's (Indonesian-owned) First Pacific, and Thailand's Bangkok Bank are examples. One Asian bank with great strength throughout the region, Hongkong and Shanghai Bank, has already catapulted itself into the global league by acquiring Britain's Midland Bank in 1993.

Foreign banks are attracted to a wide range of banking activities in Asia, especially unsexy-sounding ones like trade finance, foreign-exchange transactions, and custody services, all of which offer much higher spreads than they do in the West. Several European contenders are fighting for shares of the Asian corporate and project-finance market, including Deutsche Bank, Holland's ABN-Amro, and Britain's Barclays Bank. Japanese banks are making their presence felt in the usual way, through their massive capitalization and aggressive pricing. A big balance sheet comes in especially handy for infrastructure-project finance, which so far is being done almost entirely through bank-loan syndications rather than bonds (see previous chapter). Japanese banks have been swift to pounce on the project to build Hong Kong's new airport, which may cost nearly \$25 billion in all. That will be paid for in a variety of ways, but Japanese banks will end up accounting for the biggest single share of the bank loans, perhaps as much as two-thirds. (Japanese construction firms, probably not incidentally, have also won the biggest share of the building contracts for the airport, though that slice amounts by contrast to just over a quarter.)

America's big banks are in the strongest position of anyone (save Hongkong Bank) to mount an Asia-wide campaign to win a significant place in a broad range of banking markets. Their balance sheets are not as hefty as those of their biggest Japanese competitors, but they have in the United States a deeper pool of institutional savings to draw on for recycling in Asia; they also have far more sophisticated technological and management systems. The Americans also have no doubt about how important Asia's markets are. In 1994, Citicorp's revenues and net profits from Asia surpassed those from Europe for the first time.

Much of that handsome Asian performance came from consumer banking, in which Citicorp has the leading pan-Asian position (its only plausible—though still distant—rival through the breadth of Asia for the rest of the 1990s being Hongkong Bank). In 1986, Asia accounted for just over 20 percent of Citicorp's consumer-banking revenues outside the United States. By 1995 it was half.

Citicorp got an early start in Asia and has been more skillful than most foreign banks at localizing its staff and managers while maintaining global standards of management and service (see chapter 10). With all due credit for that, Asia is a pleasant place for any consumer banker to do business. High disposable incomes are concentrated in the hands of a few people who treat financial services as a badge of success and are willing to pay accordingly. In the early 1990s, Citicorp was able to charge its "gold" credit-card holders in every Asian market except India a higher annual fee than it did in America. Product innovations—such as the early 1990s ideas of selling mutual funds through bank accounts—are easy to carry out in Asia because regulators do not fuss over them. Regulators do, however, guarantee unusually high spreads in almost every market (including Hong Kong, at least until some mid-1990s reforms threatened to spoil the fun). In a good year in the early 1990s, Citicorp's Asian consumer business had a return on assets of 2.3 percent—an amazingly high figure compared with the 0.8 percent return on assets earned by the bank in a like good year from its worldwide consumer business.

Corporate banking in Asia cannot match the charms of the consumer market: In the corporate line, spreads are narrower, regulators less of a help, and the competition is much more ferocious. True, American and Japanese banks do not have to worry in Asia about the regulations that stop them from most investment-banking activities back home. But in seeking corporate-banking business, they have to look over their shoulders not just at other local and multinational commercial banks but also at the hordes of American investment bankers who began to mount a major invasion of Asia in the early 1990s. It is not a pretty sight, coming as it does just as emerging capital markets are challenging commercial banks for the attention of corporate customers.

...AND DISINTERMEDIARIES

The third and last stage in the evolution of finance is the rise of
capital markets—of stocks, bonds, and related securities, including,
most recently, derivatives—as alternatives to bank loans. (The process of banks losing out to capital markets goes by the fantastically
ungainly name of "disintermediation.") This stage normally begins
when a government starts freeing interest rates and relieving banks
of the obligation to buy and stockpile government debt. The first
result is the growth of a money market, meaning a market in short-
term corporate obligations like notes and bills. This has already
happened throughout Southeast Asia, though not yet in India or
China. Next in the usual sequence comes the development of a
government-bond market, followed by a corporate-bond market and
lastly a thriving stock market. Asia has mostly reversed these latter
steps: Its equity markets have leaped ahead of bond markets.

Asia's stock markets are a predictable hodgepodge of the advanced and retarded, open and closed, and regulated and freewheeling. China has an up-to-date, screen-based system of
computerized trading, though it also has a small number of listed
companies, little corporate disclosure, and a tiny shareholding public. India, by contrast has century-old stock markets, a wealth of
listed companies (around seven thousand by the end of 1994, compared with some two hundred in China), and a broad shareholding
base: More than 20 million Indians were mutual-fund shareholders
in 1994, when the funds had $20 billion under management. Any-
body can buy any amount of shares in Hong Kong's listed companies, whereas South Korea and Taiwan have had strict (though now
loosening) rules on foreign ownership of listed shares, and Indonesia has had a limit of 49 percent on foreign shareholdings of any
listed company.

For the most part, regulation and disclosure standards are not at
rich-world levels; even when they look good on paper, the standards
are not enforced with the same zeal that they are in the West.
And the markets are often distorted in odd ways. On the Jakarta
stockmarket in 1994, for instance, foreigners owned less than a third
of the shares but accounted for more than three-quarters of the
trading: locals tend to think, rightly, that the corporate action is
elsewhere than in publicly traded shares. A taste for risk, as well as

for uncertainty and lack of information, also helps if you are investing in Asian equities. The stock markets are notoriously volatile. Taipei's stock-market index rocketed from 850 in 1986 to over 12,000 in February 1990 and then crashed to 2,600 by October 1990. (By June 1995 it had modestly recovered to 5,600, before falling again to 4,500 two months later.)

None of these failings has done much to contain the explosion of Asian stock-market capitalization. In 1987, Asia's stock markets (minus those of Japan) were capitalized at $200 billion; at the end of 1994, after a year of falling prices had knocked perhaps a quarter off the value of total capitalization at its high in January, Asia's market capitalization was $1.1 trillion. This represents a nominal growth rate of more than 25 percent a year. It is a fair bet that, depending on the exact point market cycles have reached at the time, by 2000 Asia's markets could be worth $3-$5 trillion, or in total, bigger than Japan's stock-market capitalization by then.

The continued fast growth of Asia's equity markets is not inevitable, but it is likely. The first reason is that there is a rough correlation between the size of an economy and the size of its stock market. By 1995, Asia's stock-market capitalization was equal to less than 10 percent of the world's; by 2000, Asia's economies may well, on a purchasing-power basis, account for 20 percent of world output.

Even giving due regard to the rather introverted financing habits of Asian companies and the relative insignificance of equity in corporate finance everywhere, it seems improbable that, as Asian firms modernize and their financing needs grow, a two-to-one gap will be maintained between Asia's economic weight and its stock-market size. For at least the last half of this century, stocks have been better than any other financial instrument at capturing the gains from improved economic and corporate performance. A deep shift (e.g., a long-term worldwide fall in the prices of just about everything) may change that, but short of such a monumental turnaround, the value of Asian equities should keep growing until the size of Asia's markets more closely reflects the size of Asia's economies.

A second reason for expecting Asia's equity markets to go on expanding at a fast clip is more specific. Asia has badly lagged Latin America in selling off its state-owned firms. This seems sure to change in most of Southeast Asia, especially Indonesia (which has drawn up a long list of candidates for privatization), and even in more cautious countries like China and India. The needs of infra-

structure financing in particular—most state firms have an infrastructural bent to them—will help push Asia's belated privatization
along (see previous chapter).

Foreigners are a third reason for expecting the Asian equity boom
to continue. Rich-world portfolio flows to poor countries (which
means money going into securities like stocks and bonds rather than
directly into the building of factories) jumped from $28 billion in
1991 to $51 billion in 1992 and to more than $90 billion in 1993.
Asian stock markets alone received $40 billion in 1993, up from $11
billion in 1992. And even this understates matters, since some Asian
companies (especially Chinese firms) have begun listing themselves
on foreign stock markets. More significantly, many others have been
listing themselves overseas through American depositary receipts
(ADRs) and global depositary receipts (GDRs), which effectively
allow indirect equity trading abroad when markets are restricted or
closed to foreigners at home. Indian firms are especially fond of
GDRs, having been responsible for $4 billion of the $11 billion
worth issued worldwide in 1992–94.

When securities markets worldwide began wobbling in 1994, people started muttering that the days of heavy foreign investment in
Asian equity markets would be short-lived. That is highly improbable. Returns are a lot higher in Asian markets than in Western ones,
though you would naturally expect that from riskier markets. Far
more important, a portfolio that mixes stocks from markets that do
not move synchronously and have different volatilities will deliver a
higher return with less risk than a portfolio made up of stocks from
one market only (see chart 7). Since at least the mid-1980s, American and Asian stock markets have tended to move independently of
each other, and their tenuous correlation has recently been weaken-
ing. This a powerful long-term argument for American investors to
put more rather than less money into Asia.

Some Asian markets offer more of such "portfolio diversification" than others. Those that have strong ties to the dollar, such as
Hong Kong, Singapore, Malaysia, Indonesia, and Thailand, will be
more exposed to movements in American interest rates and markets. But, overall, Asian stockmarkets offer, in the right proportions
(which in some portfolios may be as high as 50 percent each of
Asian and American stocks), a virtuous counterweight to American
equity investments. America's institutional investors are aware of
this even if its mutual-fund investors are not, and Asian stock mar-

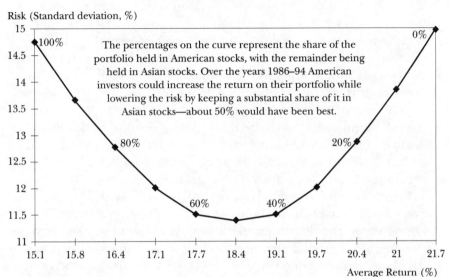

CHART 7
RISK AND RETURN (1986–94)

Risk (Standard deviation, %)

The percentages on the curve represent the share of the portfolio held in American stocks, with the remainder being held in Asian stocks. Over the years 1986–94 American investors could increase the return on their portfolio while lowering the risk by keeping a substantial share of it in Asian stocks—about 50% would have been best.

Average Return (%)

SOURCE: CS First Boston, Asia Equity Research, "Diversification Pays—Always Has, Always Will," July 27, 1994.

kets should remain a good bet for attracting foreign money despite their greater ups and downs than markets in the rich world.

BONDAGE AND DENOMINATION

Asian bond markets remain a mystery by their absence. At the end of 1994 there were around $17 trillion worth of bonds outstanding in the world (compared with about $10 trillion worth of listed equities). Of these bonds, a mere 2 percent had been issued in Asia. And of the $1.6 trillion worth of bonds issued worldwide in 1993, only about 1 percent were issued in Asia. This suggests that Asia is either on the edge of one of the biggest bond binges in history or that is is going to avoid bondage altogether.

Bond avoidance does happen—in Britain for example, the value of outstanding bonds is equal to 35 percent of GDP, compared with 110 percent in America and 74 percent in Japan—but it would be a pity if Asia followed this route. Bonds are a cheaper way than equities (or bank loans) to raise money for long-term investments, and in some ways they pose less risk of outside interference in the management of a firm. Yet issuing bonds in appreciable numbers will force a big change—bigger than going to the stock market has required—in the way Asian companies and governments behave. A lot more will have to be disclosed about the inner workings of companies that issue bonds; and if a bond market is really to take hold, governments will have to help create it.

One sign of how far Asian bond markets have to go is that the overwhelming majority of the fairly trifling sums of bonds issued by Asians up through 1994 were issued on international markets. The issuers have been almost exclusively governments and big banks; the buyers have been mostly non-Asian—even, absurdly, for the "Dragon bonds" promoted since 1991 by the Asian Development Bank and Lehman Brothers, an American investment bank. Dragon bonds were intended to jump-start an Asian bond market through the development of instruments issued in a non-Asian currency by Asian companies, listed on at least two Asian exchanges and bought mostly by Asians. As it turned out, they have mostly been Eurobonds in dragon's clothing: usually bought by non-Asians, traded on Eurobond markets, and often issued by Western companies. Even the international debt issues, Dragon or not, that undoubtedly have a strong Asian tinge are often equities at heart. Some 40 percent of those issued in 1994 were convertible bonds. This means they could be swapped on certain terms for stock in the issuing company, and in almost all cases they were bought for this equity entree, not because they were appealing debt insruments.

Except for South Korea—which for now is of limited interest to non-Koreans, since that market is almost entirely closed to foreigners—local markets for corporate bonds are tiny in Asia. In 1994 corporate bonds accounted for only 23 percent (or $77 billion) of the total bonds outstanding in East Asia (excluding Japan). By contrast, in 1993 net *issues* (never mind the oustanding stock) of corporate bonds in America added up to $104 billion.

Although the base is small, Asia's bond markets have been growing fast: The value of outstanding bonds doubled between 1989 and 1994. The value of outstanding corporate bonds in Hong Kong surpassed 5 percent of the territory's GDP in the early 1990s (although turnover as a share of GDP remains extremely low, a sign that there is still no secondary market to speak of; see below). In the right circumstances, though, bond markets can quickly spring to life. In 1992, Malaysia decreed that every debt issuer had to get a credit rating from an approved agency before issuing bonds. A year later $6 billion worth of Malaysian bonds were issued, up from a small fraction of that in previous years. The reason was that, with ratings, foreign fund managers were able to invest much more freely in Malaysian paper.

The World Bank, for one, believes that the Malaysian experience is going to spread throughout Asia over the next decade. In a study published in mid-1995, the Bank predicted that, whereas at the moment bank lending and stock markets are far more advanced in Asia than debt markets (see table 8), the use of bonds to finance Asia's economic growth will sharply increase in the next several years. The Bank guesses that the outstanding issues of bonds in six East Asian countries (China, Indonesia, Malaysia, the Philippines, South Korea, and Thailand) will grow from $282 billion at the end of 1994 to $533 billion at the end of 1999 to $1.1 trillion at the end of 2004 (all in constant 1994 dollars). The Bank expects the fastest growth to come in corporate bonds. In 1994 they accounted for

TABLE 8
BANKS, STOCKS, AND BONDS (1994)

	Bank Assets		Stock Market Cap		Bond Market	
	U.S. Dollars	% of GDP	U.S. Dollars	% of GDP	U.S. Dollars	% of GDP
China	388	76	44	9	33	7
Hong Kong *	257	195	270	205	11	9
Indonesia	90	57	47	30	9	6
Korea	283	75	192	51	161	43
Malaysia	70	100	199	283	40	56
Philippines	34	54	56	87	25	39
Singapore	115	186	135	217	45	72
Thailand	153	110	132	94	14	10
TOTAL	1,390	92	1,073	71	338	22
Germany	3,255	169	471	25	1,719	90
Japan	7,106	152	3,720	80	3,443	74
United Kingdom	2,257	216	1,210	116	366	35
United States	3,620	54	5,082	75	7,429	110

* Includes only assets denominated in Hong Kong dollars.
SOURCE: World Bank, *The Emerging Asian Bond Market* (June 1995).

only 23 percent of Asia's outstanding bonds (compared with 45 percent for government bonds), a figure the Bank guesses will zoom to 42 percent by 2004 (when government bonds will represent a modest 23 percent of the total).

The World Bank study reckons that this explosion of Asia's bond markets will be ignited by several things. The first is the need for gigantic quantities of long-term capital to finance investments in infrastructure, housing, and factories. The Bank estimates that the six countries listed in the previous paragraph will be spending $7.8 trillion (in constant 1994 dollars) in the decade 1995–2004 on gross fixed investment, $5 trillion of which will be private investment.

Some of the money will go for the upgrading of Asia's woefully inadequate infrastructure (see previous chapter). The Bank estimates that East Asia alone (i.e., leaving out the Indian subcontinent) will need to spend about $1.5 trillion on infrastructure between 1995 and 2004 and that an increasing share of the investment will come from private sources (hence one push for the growth in corporate bonds). But the lion's share of the investment will be devoted to factory-building as Asia undergoes a structural shift in manufacturing from labor-intensive to capital-intensive industries.

With banks unable or unwilling to provide long-term money on such a scale and regional stock markets growing but not that fast, bonds are the natural vehicle for financing Asia's coming boom in capital investment. They are also going to be much in demand on the part of Asia's (and the world's) savers. The World Bank study reckons that the assets of East Asia's institutional investment funds —compulsory plans such as Singapore's and Malaysia's government-run provident funds, the embryonic government-run pension funds in the Philippines, Thailand, and Indonesia, private pension funds, and mutual funds—will rise from $109 billion in 1994 to $400 billion in 2004. Most of these funds have long-term liabilities (mostly to pensioners), and as Asia's populations age the funds are increasingly going to want long-term assets to match the liabilities.

It all sounds logical, but a lot will have to change if an Asian bond boom is to come off. The first need is for ratings from reliable credit agencies. This is a very new game everywhere in Asia. Japan's first independent credit-rating agency, Mikuni & Co, was set up only in the mid-1980s, and India got two independent agencies only in the late 1980s. Even so, the habit is spreading. In the early 1990s, Indonesia and Thailand as well as Malaysia set up credit-rating agencies and started requiring companies to get a rating before they issued debt. Big American agencies such as Moody's and Standard & Poor are also regularly rating Asian issuers. To get even this far, however, requires something of a change of culture at many Asian firms: They have to be more willing than in the past to disclose information about their business if they are to be rated accurately. Many, particularly the family-owned firms of the overseas Chinese will be tempted to decline the honor.

Second, governments must also start behaving differently. With a couple of exceptions, Asia's thrifty governments have rarely seen the need to borrow by issuing bonds. That may be praiseworthy from a fiscal point of view, but it causes a technical problem for the smooth development of a bond market. Investors normally evaluate corporate bonds by comparing them with bonds issued by the government of the country where the corporate issuer is located. Without a government-bond market—preferably boasting issues with a wide variety of maturities—the process of evaluating other bonds becomes much harder. If Asian governments do start issuing bonds, even if only to set such "benchmarks" for corporate bonds, they will find a receptive international audience. Asian governments, often flush with foreign-currency reserves and fiscally conservative, have much better credit ratings than other poor-country governments. If bond markets do take shape in Asia, the sturdy credit umbrella hoisted by their governments will help Asian corporate borrowers in the competition for global savings: They will often have emerging-market growth potential combined with asset quality closer to rich-world levels.

Provided, that is, Asian governments can also adjust to the idea that the development of bond markets will require them to be less bossy about movements of capital across their borders. In 1993, Malaysia gave a good example of what not to do. After whipping up foreign enthusiasm for the corporate-bond market, the Malaysian central bank then put severe restrictions on foreign deposit-holders in Malaysia because it felt they were driving up the value of the currency.

The third necessary element for Asian bond markets is an active secondary market—that is, a liquid market in the buying and selling of bonds after they have been issued. If Asia's governments and corporate issuers continue to rely for their bond customers on people and institutions that are happy to buy a bond and then keep it in a safe-deposit box until it matures, the market will not be growing at breakneck speed.

Thailand, which is carrying out Asia's most comprehensive program of financial liberalization and modernization, is likely to have the continent's best developed bond market by the end of the 1990s. Thai companies were allowed to begin issuing debt only in 1992; but the next year, new issues of bonds in Thailand were considerably larger than new issues of equities. In 1994 secondary trading began on an exchange in Bangkok. The market started slowly, but both turnover and capitalization are expected to increase quickly. Thai companies have grown tired of expensive bank loans and equity-issuing exercises; infrastructure spending is shooting up and needs a new source of finance; and foreign investors, reassured by the stability of the Thai currency, its free convertibility to other currencies, and the managerial skills of the central bank, are likely to be eager to buy a piece of some of the fastest economic growth in Southeast Asia. Thailand's big banks are also backing the development of the bond market, setting up bond-underwriting and bond-trading subsidiaries to recapture some of the corporate clients that have been drifting away from commercial-bank loans. With Thailand deregulating and liberalizing so quickly, the pressure will be on other Southeast Asian markets (particularly Malaysia's and Indonesia's) to follow suit if they want to keep up in the competition for international flows of debt capital.

On balance it is a good bet that the World Bank is right and bonds will for the next decade be Asia's fastest-growing financial market. This would have three important consequences. The first is a convergence of returns on equities and bonds, with bond returns rising and equity returns falling. Among the many reasons bond markets have been so slow to develop in Asia is that returns on equities have been relatively so high. As the appetite of investors for long-term instruments rises, they will bid up the prices of bonds relative to those of equities. In addition, as Asia's economic growth inevitably slows during the period when the continent's infrastructure deficit is being redressed, equities will become somewhat less attractive than they were during the torrid growth years of 1970–95.

The second consequence should be a sharp cut in margins on traditional banking business, since bonds are a much more direct substitute for bank loans than stocks are. This may not be bad for all commercial banks, many of which can (as Thai banks intend to)

compete for old customers in new markets, but it will be bad for
banks that are not good at anything more sophisticated than deploying masses of capital and simply lending it (meaning Japanese and
Korean banks had better watch out).

The third result is that, if bond markets really get going in Asia, so
should investment in Asian currencies. Far-sighted investors should
welcome a reliable vehicle for betting on rises in Asian currencies.
In the same way that decades of faster economic growth and large
current-account surpluses made it inevitable that the Japanese yen
and Singapore dollar would appreciate against the American dollar
(see chart 8), the currencies of most countries in Southeast Asia and
of China and India will appreciate against the dollar and even the
yen in the long run unless economic and productivity growth in
these emerging economies falls drastically. That should not happen,
provided Asia does not go to war.

CHART 8
SINGAPORE DOLLAR AND JAPANESE YEN VERSUS U.S. DOLLAR

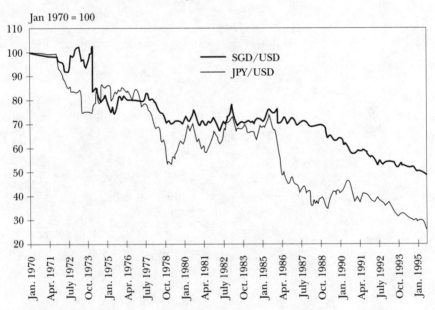

SOURCE: Datastream.

PART IV

POLITICS AND GEOPOLITICS

CHAPTER 15

WAR AND PEACE

If you think this book has been far too optimistic about Asia's prospects, you will like this chapter. It is about the darkest storm clouds gathering over the Asian miracle.

In the quarter century after 1950, Asia was the world's most warring place. But in the two decades since 1975 almost all of Asia has been peaceful and stable, with the notable exceptions of Cambodia and Afghanistan, which suffered both invasion and civil war, and civil-war-plagued Sri Lanka. Twenty years is plenty of time for people to grow accustomed to thinking that what they themselves have experienced is an intrinsic condition. This is an especially dangerous delusion in Asia, or at any rate East and Southeast Asia, where the post-1975 period of blessed quiet has been ensured by a geopolitical aberration: an unusual coincidence, which has disappeared probably for good, of three factors that made for a stable balance of power in a complex and inherently unstable neighborhood.

The first of these elements was the mutual hostility of Russia and China, which set the two great continental powers of Asia against one another. This balance of hostility on the Asian landmass was reinforced by the attitude of East Asia's maritime and economic power, Japan, which had bad relations with the Soviet Union and hesitant and suspicious ones with China. Lastly, that triangular combination of mutually antagonistic powers enabled intelligent American leadership to hold the balance among them and to restrain each from attempting to grab an advantage over the others.

History is not replete with examples of such improbable elements of great-power balance coming together happily for very long. Indeed, Asia's own period of unrepeatable stability is over. Russia is in eclipse as a great power, Russia and China are more cooperative than at any time in the past century, and Japan, though still deeply wary of China, is becoming increasingly entangled with it economically. And the power that actively and skillfully held the Cold War balance among these three, the United States, is questioning whether its role in Asia has much point any more, forgetting or misunderstanding how much good its military presence in Asia has done both for that continent and for its own national interests.

What Vietnam Meant

Most Americans think their country lost the war in Vietnam. This is, of course, true in the narrow sense that South Vietnam itself fell to the North, and with it the rest of Indochina to Communists of one sort or another. But the broader aims of America's effort in Vietnam were to keep the capitalist semi-democracies of Southeast Asia from falling to communism in their turn and to shore up the continent-wide balance of power between America and its regional allies, on one side, and the Soviet Union and its friends on the other.

With Singapore now richer than almost all of Europe, Malaysia booming, Thailand thriving, and Indonesia moving steadily and surely up, it is easy to forget what peril Southeast Asia was in just thirty years ago. All these countries were poor and their governments all at risk of violent overthrow by invasion or Communist insurgency. Malaysia had been fighting a guerrilla war for a decade against China-backed Communist rebels; Singapore's ruling party was still struggling to vanquish the Communists with whom it had made a tactical alliance in the 1950s to win independence from Britain; Indonesia was on the edge of civil war after a decade of demagogic leadership; and Thailand faced both armed internal rebellions backed by China, Vietnam, and the Laotian Communists and the longer-range threat of a direct invasion from Vietnam.

America's intervention in the Vietnam war bought these countries roughly a decade's breathing space, and that was enough to save them. In economic terms, by the mid-1970s all these countries had entrenched the policies which over the following generation were to bring them such extraordinary success. They were given an immense fiscal boost to start with by the heavy spending that America's Vietnam War effort brought to the whole region; Thailand, on the front line, enjoyed the more direct contribution of America's construction of extensive road and communications networks in the countryside, which quickly raised rural incomes and brought previously isolated peasants into the money economy. The decade of American shelter also gave Southeast Asian governments time to stabilize their countries' politics and to strengthen their armies to the point where they could adequately resist armed subversion.

In the rest of East Asia, too, America's broader war aims were realized, though in a less dramatic way. By 1971 the Nixon administration had begun the overture to China that was to lead in Northeast Asia to a rebalancing among that region's three great military powers—the United States (with Japan under its nuclear umbrella), China, and the Soviet Union—so that China conspicuously became a counterweight to the Soviet Union. The uneasy peace in Northeast Asia that had followed the end of the Korean War in 1953 became a stable one instead. Geopolitical stability was brought to Southeast Asia, too, as Vietnam was left with the Soviet Union as its sole ally and China began to wind down its support for the Communist insurgents fighting America's Southeast Asian allies.

In other words, and notwithstanding the almost universal view of Americans themselves to the contrary, America was not only right about Vietnam, but the sacrifices it made there, far from being in vain, accomplished in a spectacular way the broader aims of Asian stability and prosperity that the intervention was intended to secure. Anybody who remains unconvinced by the abstract argument for this need only set foot in both Vietnam and Thailand today to realize with a jolt which side prevailed in the fight for Asia's future. The United States made a terrible mistake in Vietnam—in Lee Kuan Yew's words, it "did not understand the history and drew the line in the wrong place"—and the price has been paid ever since in the coin of American self-confidence and willingness to exert its military might. But the idea behind the war was right; and East Asia, with what is now a full generation of peace and stability behind it, is one place where the cost of America's tactical mistake has been small compared with the benefits of its strategic commitment.

That, however, is history. Much of Asia is getting rich, and its rising powers—China above all—are getting ambitious. An arms race has already begun in Asia. Are the days of quiet numbered?

The Spending Spree

In Europe and America the collapse of the Soviet Union brought five years of shrinking defense budgets, a process that may be ending as Russia risks turning again to authoritarianism and nationalism. In East and Southeast Asia the end of the Cold War gave a further prop to the stability the continent has enjoyed since the late 1970s. Yet in the first half of the 1990s, Asia has had the world's fastest growth in arsenals and the arms trade.

Accurate figures for military spending are hard to come by and even harder to interpret. Governments do not always make a clean breast of their defense spending (China's generals make a career of publishing misleadingly modest figures for their spending), exchange rates distort the picture (there is no purchasing-power-parity index for military hardware), and efficiency under fire is correlated in no predictable way with the cost and sophistication of an armed force. It does not become clear until after the guns have been blazing for a while just how good an army has been bought.

Yet the general pattern is plain enough. Asia's defense spending was fairly modest in the early 1980s, rose sharply in the mid-1980s, leveled off towards the end of that decade, and has been rising quickly throughout the first half of the 1990s. According to figures compiled by the Stockholm International Peace Research Institute, Asia accounted for around 25 percent of the world's military spending in the early 1990s (leaving aside what was spent by America and Russia, whose budgets were so much larger than everyone else's). That does not sound extravagant in light of Asia's size, population, and strategic complexity. But the comparable figure for the early 1980s was 15 percent, implying a near doubling in Asia's share in just over a decade.

And Asia's share keeps rising. Alone among the world's rich countries, which otherwise spent the early 1990s slashing their military budgets in real terms, Japan increased its defense spending every year through 1994 (though at gradually declining rates of growth). By some measures Japan is now the world's second-biggest military spender after the United States. China's defense spending has grown at double-digit rates throughout the 1990s, with the increases in Indonesia, Malaysia, South Korea, and Taiwan not far behind. Only India has substantially cut back in real terms, reducing military spending by a quarter between the late 1980s and early 1990s.

Yet this military buildup is far from being as menacing as it sounds. In an unstable neighborhood, a fast buildup of arms often portends or accompanies war; this is why the arms race in the Middle East (the only part of the poor world to have outspent Asia) was alarming. But, to paraphrase a slogan from a different field of endeavor, guns do not start wars; people do. Wars break out because of unstable security structures or imbalances of power, not because neighboring armies have acquired new toys they want to use. Britain, France, and West Germany spent large sums on weapons from 1960 to 1990 (including nuclear arsenals in the case of Britain and France), but nobody seriously suggested that they were therefore about to go to war with each other. Asia today is closer to the West European model than to that of the Middle East. Its arms buildup has little to do with any imminent threat to the peace.

The first reason for the Asian arms race is merely cyclical. Many Asian countries, such as Malaysia and China, spent comparatively little on defense in the late 1980s; it was inevitable that spending would bounce back as equipment aged and had to be replaced. The replacement has been speeded up by a shift in the uses to which armies are likely to be put. The military energies of most Southeast Asian countries, particularly Malaysia and Indonesia, were long concentrated on defeating domestic insurgencies; different equipment (especially modern ships and aircraft) is needed for armed forces that must be prepared to fight a conventional war instead. Likewise, China for three decades had based its military preparations on the threat of an invasion from the Soviet Union. With that threat in abeyance, China's generals have turned their attention from deploying a massive land army to building up smaller but technologically more sophisticated quick-strike forces that can support a beefed-up navy (see below).

Second, Asia is spending a lot more because its economies are growing fast. Military spending that makes up a constant or even declining share of a country's GDP can nonetheless be rising quickly in absolute terms when the economy is bounding ahead. And as Andrew Mack, a professor at the Australian National University, has pointed out, it is true everywhere that no factor seems better correlated with rises in a country's military spending than its economic growth.

Third, with the end of the Cold War the world's arms bazaar has become very much a buyer's market. Western defense suppliers, squeezed by declining military budgets at home, were quick to seek outlets abroad, and no outlet was more flush with cash than Asia. America's military exports to the poor world rose by a third, to some $13 billion, between 1988 and 1992; French exports doubled to almost $4 billion, and Britain's tripled to $2.4 billion. Russia, which had been the world's biggest seller of arms in the late 1980s, suffered a 90 percent fall in the value of its military exports, to just $1.5 billion (or only 10 percent of the world market) by 1992.

Russia, as well as many former Soviet allies in Eastern Europe, has been fighting hard to recapture market share ever since, concentrating most of its attention on Asia. In 1994, Malaysia bought eighteen advanced MIG-29 jet fighters and started looking into the purchase of sixty T-72 main battle tanks. East German patrol boats have been sold to Indonesia, and Russia has proposed joint-venture defense factories to India. By the mid-1990s even South Korea had begun examining Russian wares for possible purchase.

But it is China that has become Russia's biggest market for military sales. Despite decades of hostility, the Russian and Chinese armed forces share a common heritage of technology and design for much of their hardware. In the early 1990s, China began buying Su-27 attack aircraft, S-300 surface-to-air missiles, and T-72 tanks. By the mid-1990s, China was talking with Russia about tripling its stock of Su-27s, buying more T-72 tanks, and acquiring Russia's most advanced fighter jets, versions of the MIG-29 and MIG-31.

Most significant of all, Russia has begun transferring advanced military technology to Asia, especially to China. By the early 1990s technology exchanges between China and Russia had started sending Chinese engineers to Russian military factories to advise on the conversion of the factories to the production of civilian goods (something that China's soldiers, who get a lot of their income from commercial manufacturing and sales, have considerable experience with); and Russian technicians to China to advise on the updating of defense factories the Russians helped the Chinese build in the 1950s. Many defense analysts think the wholesale transfer of advanced Soviet-bloc technology is the most important part of the arms trade with Asia—and the most dangerous. It could, in five or ten years, give Asian countries enough of a home-grown defense industry that Western suppliers such as the United States would have little influence over their behavior. But, again, whether that is really a danger depends on the Asian balance of power.

From Threat to Uncertainty

Asians are also putting on military muscle because of a geopolitical shift brought on by the end of the Cold War. Asia has moved from what Jonathan Pollack, a researcher at RAND, a think tank in Santa Monica, has called a "threat-driven" defense calculation to one that is "uncertainty-based." The clean lines of the Cold War, when everyone knew where the threat was coming from and what needed to be done about it, have been smudged.

Russia could, at any time, re-emerge as a wonderful concentrator of minds. It still has the world's second-biggest defense establishment, with a huge nuclear arsenal and, in the Pacific in the early 1990s, almost two dozen ballistic-missile submarines, almost 100 attack submarines, almost 50 main surface warships, and 150 land-based strike aircraft. For now, however, this equipment is decaying, its management in as much disarray as that of the country that nominally commands it. Vietnam, another of the old threats, has far more interest in learning from its capitalist neighbors than in subjugating them.

North Korea remains what it has been since 1950, the most unpredictable threat to peace in Asia. By mid-1995 it was impossible to say whether the North would honor the nuclear-weapons deal it made in 1994 with the United States or even whether the deal would continue to exist. Although during the agreement's first six months the North appeared to be abiding by its promise to freeze its nuclear program, it also tried weaseling out of other parts of the deal. It is possible that the North will be the possessor of a nuclear arsenal before 2000—a state of affairs that could lead Japan to acquire nuclear weapons of its own and would pose a serious risk to the stability of East Asia. It is even possible (nobody has any idea what goes on at the top of the North Korean government) that the North will prove as reckless as it sometimes appears and launch a full-scale invasion of the South.

That seems improbable. It was not craziness that led Kim Il Sung to order the invasion of the South in 1950. It was instead his conviction that America would not fight to defend the South (American troops had been withdrawn from the South the year before, and American officials had made ambiguous statements about the importance of the South to America's vital interests); and that he would have the backing of the two great Communist powers if he got into a fix. Today America still has soldiers stationed in the South, and it has repeatedly made clear its intention to fight if the North attacks. And these days any such attack would have the backing of no outside power. So the greater likelihood is that the North will by 2000 have collapsed into the South's unwilling arms or be on its way to a China-like economic modernization that (temporarily at least) precludes military adventurism.

However welcome in principle, the fading of these threats has left Asian geopolitics in an unsettled state that is even more worrying than the confusion elsewhere in the world. Life may seem precarious in Europe, with the crackle of gunfire on its eastern edges and the menacing thunder of potential and possibly hostile Islamic regimes to its south. But Western Europe has a set of more or less long-standing multilateral institutions—NATO, the European Union, and even the Organization for Security and Co-operation in Europe—that can absorb some of the shocks of adjustment to the new world disorder. Asia has almost nothing of this sort.

For half a century Asian security has depended mostly on a set of bilateral relationships between Asian countries and an outside power (usually America). Asia's own powers, mindful of history both ancient and modern, think that despite the present lack of obvious tension among them almost any of them could quickly become an outright enemy of any of the others. With the overriding discipline of the Cold War now gone, Asia's era of uncertainty and army building has begun.

RATING THE BIG POWERS

Apart from the incalculable risk that North Korea might madly launch an attack against the South, the chances of serious fighting breaking out in Asia in the next two decades depend mainly on the behavior of three powers: India, Japan, and China.

India has fought three wars with Pakistan since 1947, a border war with China in 1962 and an ill-fated campaign against Tamil rebels in Sri Lanka in 1987–90; for good measure, it invaded and gobbled up the Portuguese colony of Goa in 1961 and easily suppressed a coup attempt in the Maldives in 1988. India is plainly determined to keep a favorable geopolitical balance in its subcontinental neighborhood, a fact it underlined throughout the 1980s by siding against America, China, and Pakistan and firmly backing the Russians in their attempted subjugation of Afghanistan. Indian and Pakistani troops still face each other across cease-fire lines in northern India, and both countries could produce a nuclear bomb in fairly short order. The chance of conflict between them remains uncomfortably high, and if a fourth India-Pakistan war broke out, it would have repercussions throughout Central Asia and into the Middle East (though China, which has recently become more even-handed between the two subcontinental rivals, would probably stay aloof).

Even so, India's geopolitical ambitions are likely to be muted for a long time to come. It faces a formidable job in trying to rehabilitate its economy after forty-five years of misrule (see chapters 8 and 9). The collapse of the Soviet Union deprived India of the ally on which it had anchored its foreign policy since the early 1970s. This may not have been a wise alliance, but at least it gave Indian policy some coherence. The Indians have not thought through what might take its place, particularly in light of their fears about some sort of Muslim uprising in the Middle East or in ex-Soviet Central Asia and the possible impact of this on Pakistan and on their own minority Muslim population (unless you think of India's mid-1990s political and military flirtation with Israel as the kernel of a serious policy on this subject). The odds are, therefore, that despite its crack army and formidable navy, much more modern than China's, India is unlikely to make its weight felt beyond the subcontinent anytime soon (unless Burma, the natural geographic and cultural link between the Indian and Chinese spheres of Asia, becomes a bone of contention between the two giants; see below).

Japan is the reverse image of India: it has not fought at all since 1945. But what it did to Asia in the fifteen years before that, and its failure to make a clear atonement since, still haunt Asian views of Japan and sharply divide Japan's own politics. If Japan did shake off its own self-doubts, it could become a major military power very quickly. Its equipment is superb, second only to America's in quality and technological sophistication. It has the wealth to support a far larger standing army than it does today and the industrial capacity to equip it with advanced weapons. And few people doubt that, if push came to shove, Japan could develop a nuclear bomb within months, if not weeks.

Yet it is highly improbable that any of this will happen unless East Asia is plunged into a security crisis of catastrophic proportions and then left on its own by America to deal with it. Despite two years of attempted political reform, Japan in 1995 was only partway towards a system in which such highly charged questions as its proper role in the world could even be effectively debated, let alone resolved. Some of the country's leading political reformers are also in favor of a more assertive international role for Japan, though still in harness with the United States, but they are far from winning the argument. Meanwhile, Japan's continuing nuclear and geopolitical dependence on America, and the two allies' inextricable involvement in one another's economies, make it even less plausible that Japan will steel itself to make the fairly radical political and diplomatic changes that would be needed before it could even think of staking out an Asian policy of its own.

CHINA ON THE RISE

This means that all Asian eyes are, or should be, focused on China. In one sense China is already a great power. It is big enough to be beholden to no one, in terms either of alliances or values, and is ruthless in the pursuit of its own self-interest. Probably more than any other country today, it measures up to de Gaulle's description of great powers as "cold monsters."

For a long time it was possible to shove disturbing observations about China's essential amorality to the back of the mind. During the Cold War, China was every bit as useful to the West in its mortal contest with the Soviet Union as the West was to China in its own mortal contest with the Soviet Union. Then, too, there was the comfort of knowing throughout the 1980s that the modernization of China's armed forces, proclaimed by Deng Xiaoping in 1979 as one of the "four modernizations" China must achieve, in fact meant no modernization at all. The number of men in uniform was cut by a quarter during the 1980s, and nowhere near enough money was spent to upgrade military equipment that was pretty awful to begin with.

China has now begun remedying the weaknesses of its armed forces. The Chinese economy has reached a size where it can support a burden of military spending that is significant by regional if not global standards. China's government is willing to spend the money, as the steep increases in military budgets (and off-budget spending) throughout the first half of the 1990s have shown. And China's military thinking took a sharp turn in the early 1990s after the collapse of the Soviet Union.

The appointment in 1992 of Liu Huaqing, a septuagenarian admiral, to the Communist party Politburo's Standing Committee was a sign, little noticed at the time, of the country's new military priorities. Admiral Liu, China's highest ranking military officer, is a modernizer. Moreover, he represents the first ascendancy of champions of naval and air power in modern China. As China's arms purchases and its officers' surprisingly frank talks with visiting American generals make clear, the Chinese want to build up their quick-strike air and naval capabilities.

What does this mean for China's behavior? One of the most worrying questions about China is that nobody knows. China deliberately kicks up clouds of dust not only about its military spending and force structure but about its intentions as well. The long-term aims of India and Japan are also shrouded, but at least they disclose through defense "white papers" and the like the drift of their military thinking. China is a blank.

On the reassuring side of the ledger, the first entry must be the poor quality of much of the Chinese armed forces. In 1979, the first year of Deng's modernization drive, the Chinese decided to teach Vietnam a lesson in a border war and themselves got a bloody nose instead. Fifteen years later, not many experts would give a high rating to China's fighter aircraft or submarines. So a measure of bluster is involved.

Second, China has a huge amount of work to do at home before it goes looking for quarrels abroad. However phenomenal the performance of the Chinese economy since the late 1970s, China would have a hard time supporting a predatory military machine even if it wanted to.

Third, China has been reaching out to its neighbors rather than spurning them. In quick succession in the late 1980s and early 1990s it established full diplomatic relations with Singapore, Indonesia, and South Korea and in the mid-1990s sent high-level visitors to Russia, Vietnam, South Korea, and Indonesia. India and China agreed in 1993 to patch up their border dispute peacefully, and in the summer of 1995 the two neighbors held joint war games in the

Himalayan border region of Ladakh, a sensitive spot between India and Pakistan.

China has not recently been an expansionist power (the glaring exception being its grab of Tibet in 1950), but a long history of being invaded has made it obsessed with protecting its borders. The Chinese seem to have concluded that the main requirement for border protection these days is an ability to launch quick air and sea strikes with smallish but technologically sophisticated forces— hence, the shift of strategy and spending since the early 1990s. The term border, however, has grown worryingly elastic. In the early 1990s, China's military thinkers began talking about the importance of being able to defend the country's "strategic borders," which would often be found a couple of hundred miles beyond the real thing. In light of all this, China's unbending assertion of sovereignty over the Spratly Islands, some dots of rock in the South China Sea that are claimed by six countries and may sit on top of rich oil reserves, and its occasional growls at Taiwan must be taken seriously.

There are signs, too, that China is attempting to create a sphere of influence in Southeast Asia, not with any wish to attack it but with the intention of establishing itself as the dominant power in the neighborhood. By the mid-1990s it had formed a loose alliance with Burma's military leaders and apparently been given a couple of listening posts in Burmese territory on the Bay of Bengal and the Andaman Sea—sensitive spots near the Strait of Malacca and athwart the main tanker route between the oil fields of the Middle East and the thirsty industries of East Asia.

For the next decade, at least, it is improbable that China will risk any serious military clashes with its neighbors—with one exception. The exception is Taiwan. One Hong Kong businessman, well connected in China thinks there is a fairly high risk that, as Taiwan moves towards full democracy, it will be more and more prone to put forward stubborn demands for formal independence from China, being no longer content with the independence-in-fact that it now enjoys. Taiwan's voters have so far shown themselves more practical minded than that, but it is hard to see the momentum of pro-independence sentiment on the island being reduced or deflected as the years go by. The Chinese have said repeatedly that, if Taiwan declares independence, it will invade the island. The Hong Kong businessman is convinced they mean it, and so, for the most part, do Taiwan's military planners. The pessimistic view of cross-straits relations gained strength in the summer of 1995, when America authorized a "private" visit by Taiwan's President Lee Teng-hui to Cornell University and China responded with military exercises near Taiwan that included the repeated "testing" of ballistic missiles.

Apart from the possibility of war between Taiwan and China, which is a likelier threat to the peace in Asia than that posed by North Korea, China will probably concentrate for a decade or more on building its military strength, establishing its geopolitical authority, and manipulating as best it can Asia's complicated balance of power. Yet although some of China's neighbors, especially in Southeast Asia, take comfort from this line of thought, others are more frankly worried.

In 1994, Australia issued a defense white paper in which it said flatly that Indonesia was its most important strategic partner, virtually its front line of defense. This was an arresting change: The previous white paper, released in 1987, had more or less said that Indonesia, whose annexation of East Timor deeply angered Australian public opinion, was a threat rather than a defense partner. The (unstated) explanation for the switch is Australia's growing anxiety about the long-term intentions of China, which is the only conceivable power against which Indonesia might act as a comforting front line.

Japan, too, is increasingly worried about China. China's actions in Northeast Asia are necessarily more circumspect than its behavior in Southeast Asia. There is too much firepower in the north—large Russian, Korean, American, and Japanese forces, as well as China's own—for the Chinese to show any swagger. But China can still make its weight felt. It is likely, for example, that during the negotiations over North Korea's would-be nuclear weapons program in 1992–94, China was concerned less with pressing the North to make a deal with America and South Korea than it was with using the North to make an indirect point to Japan about security in their corner of the world: South Korea felt much less threatened by the North's nuclear program and missile tests than Japan did, and the slow-motion deal eventually agreed on will leave that threat hanging over Japan's head at least for the rest of the 1990s. The point was taken. Japan's military anxieties, concentrated for decades on the Soviet Union, are now dominated by reflections on China.

THE POLICEMAN ON THE BEAT

Lee Kuan Yew, Asia's most strategic-minded leader, says two things are needed if war in Asia is to be avoided. The first is free trade:

> It is the only way in which you can keep the world peaceful, where people cooperate and compete with each other economically without going to war. If I cannot export my goods and if goods and services cannot go across borders and I have an excess of energy, then I must capture territory and population with it and control and integrate it into a bigger economic unit, an empire. Then you get a large land-mass or an overseas empire, which you control as one trading bloc. That is the time-honored way, the traditional way, of growth. That's what we moved away from after the end of World War II in 1945 with GATT, the IMF, and the World Bank.
>
> That made possible a Germany where large numbers of Germans were cramped into a smaller area. And large numbers of Japanese left the Asian mainland and were cramped into a few Japanese islands. The Japanese and the Germans were told, you stay behind your boundaries and we will exchange goods and services. You can invest in me; I can invest in you. We will cooperate; we will compete. And the Japanese and the Germans were able to flourish and grow without causing wars in the world.
>
> The other way you are saying, let's go to war and see who runs the place. Every Chinese schoolboy knows how China's civilization began: through the unification, over 2000 years ago, of the seven warring states. If you say you can't grow except by controlling people and territory, then the Chinese will carry on doing what they've always done, grow bigger.

But free trade alone is not enough:

> The peace would be kept in Asia provided there is a balancer to help make aggression unprofitable. And that balancer will be helped if there is a system through which the exchange of goods and services can release the pressures and tensions, which would otherwise build up between societies some of which are more dynamic than the others. But that alone is not good enough.
>
> Although you can export goods and services and live a peaceful life, if there is no policeman on the beat and you see a chance to drive away a Mercedes car, I will drive off with it. So you need the two:

one, the policeman who makes that unprofitable; two, not such dire
economic straits where you say to hell with it, you've got to do it.

The problem of the policeman is more acute just now. Free trade
is constantly under political attack, particularly (and perversely) in
the rich democracies, but its adherents, mainly the businesses whose
profits increasingly depend on fairly free access to the global marketplace, are also strong—especially where the free-trade debate
counts most, in America. But in post–Cold War Asia, far more than
in Europe, the identity and even the duties of the policeman on the
beat are already being called into question.

The complexity of the power balance in Asia aggravates the uncertainty caused by the almost complete absence of any institutions
for handling security disputes. In Northeast Asia, where the great
geopolitical plates grind against each other hardest, there are no
multilateral institutions at all, just a series of bilateral arrangements,
some of them shifting, between America, Japan, Russia, China, and
the two Koreas. Southeast Asia, with ASEAN and its informal
postsummit conferences to which outsiders such as China and Japan
are invited, is a bit farther along but not much.

The truth is that probably for another generation the United
States will remain the only power with the resources, the strategic
and economic reach, and the trust (or at least the tolerance) of
enough Asians to be capable of maintaining a balance of power in
the region. But America is ambivalent about continuing to do the
job, and several Asian voices, the loudest among them Malaysia's,
are urging it not to.

In the dying days of the Cold War the Philippine Senate voted to
eject the United States from the Subic Bay Naval Base, its main
military base in East Asia. America pieced together an inadequate
substitute from increased use of its bases in Japan and Guam and
port calls at various Southeast Asian spots, particularly Singapore.
The Bush administration, in what was to be its last year, drew up a
plan for cuts in American deployments that were intended to preempt expected calls in Congress for a more extreme pullback from
Asia. By the end of 1995, American troop strength in the region will
have been reduced by about 30 percent from its level in 1992. Are
more cuts to come?

The Clinton administration has said no, and spokesmen for it,
such as Joseph Nye at the Department of Defense, have strongly

argued the case for continued American engagement in Asia. But this is an especially difficult time for American internationalists to make such a case. The collapse of the Soviet Union and twenty years' worth of peace in Asia naturally raise the question of why the United States should go on shouldering the burden of helping to keep a difficult neighborhood quiet, particularly when the residents of the neighborhood are getting richer fast and so many of them (though by no means all) share so few of America's political values. The difficulty of offering a convincing answer is compounded because what America will most be needed for in Asia over the next decade is so uncongenial to the American temperament. It will be needed not to respond to a crisis or to right a wrong, but instead to prevent the possibility of far-off disorder by even-handedly maintaining a balance of power among countries some of which run their societies in ways that are deeply distasteful to Americans.

There is a noble reason for America to do this: Continued peace and economic growth in Asia offer the best hope in the long run that billions of people will live happier and freer lives than they do now. But the main reason for America's active involvement is that so many of its own national interests, economic and strategic, are now bound up in East Asia's future that it would be only a bit less unsettling for the United States than it would be for Asia if that future turned bloody.

If America does stay the course in Asia, its biggest job will be to keep its strategic (particularly its nuclear) umbrella open over Japan —which is vital for preventing a destabilizing all-out arms race throughout Asia—while simultaneously trying to balance China's growing might without driving it into enmity. Japan, with its troubled Asian history, its domestic-policy paralysis, and its security fears about all its close neighbors (Russia, China, and a probably soon to be reunified Korea), will be a handful. China will be more than that.

The biggest problem in knowing how to handle China is that, unlike the Soviet Union (or a revivified nationalistic Russia), China does not pose an immediate and obvious security threat either to its neighbors or to the West—but it might well come to do so. There is no reason now to assume the immense burden of trying to contain China, as the West contained the Soviet Union for decades, and a great risk that a policy of antagonism would provoke China into posing exactly the kind of threat that everyone fears. Yet there are good grounds for a policy of firmness that leads China to expect that if it oversteps itself some resistance will be offered—in other words, for a policy of maintaining a stable balance among Asia's many jostling powers and making sure that the nature of this balance will not be dictated by China.

These aims argue for a policy of, first, trying to draw China into regional arrangements, such as defense talks and information exchanges, that will gradually make it less of a maverick country (though it is always going to be special because of its size). Second, it makes sense to build lines of quiet resistance against any temptation the Chinese might feel to assert themselves too enthusiastically. American patrols of the South China Sea are one example of such a line. Recent bridge building between Japan and Taiwan on one side and Vietnam on the other is another example. It might not be a bad idea at all, and would be suitably ironic, for the Vietnamese to give America base rights at its old haunt of Cam Ranh Bay on the South China Sea.

All this is a tall order for what will probably be at least a twenty-year transition to a new order of security in Asia. The rise of great powers rarely happens smoothly and peacefully. A century ago Europe was enjoying a more modest version of the economic miracle that has recently swept East Asia, in the framework of free trade and investment flows and a level of global economic integration that equaled those of today. Yet that European golden age soon came to a horrific end in the years 1914–45 with the two worst wars in history and a global economic balkanization that took the world another half century to recover from. A like unhappy end for Asia's golden age can be prevented. But that will require the exercise, preeminently on the part of the United States, of great diligence and patience in highly complicated circumstances. One of history's lessons is that it is rare for so many things to go right for so long.

CHAPTER 16

POLITICS AND SOCIETY: ASIA'S NEW MILLENNIUM

A democracy cannot exist as a permanent form of government. It can only exist until a majority of voters discover that they can vote themselves largesse out of the public treasury.

—ALEXANDER TYTLER

I realized after living in Asia for a few years that probably the world's biggest intellectual gulf among highly educated people lay between Westerners and Asians on the subject of democracy. In the West democracy is generally thought to be the only form of government by which a civilized society should consider running itself. A few diplomats and academics will muse quietly, and in private, about the failures of representative democracy and the availability of alternatives, but the topic is essentially taboo.

This is understandable. In the West's experience for the whole of this century, the only alternative to democracy has seemed a horrible dictatorship that looted countries and brought war. In fact, this black-and-white perception is wrong. Some of the best-working political institutions in the West are deeply undemocratic: the most important being the central banks, some of which (notably Germany's) are also deeply popular with ordinary people. But the general assumption is, the more democratic the better. After the fall of the Soviet Union, the certitude in the West about democracy had reached the stage where some Americans were arguing that democracy should be considered a "fundamental human right" whose promotion was hence a proper ground for American military intervention abroad. The Clinton administration, while not putting the matter quite that strongly, was edging in the same direction both in its general pronouncements and in the specific matter of sending soldiers to Haiti to restore an elected government there.

By contrast, many thoughtful people living in Asia—including a lot who, unlike, say, Lee Kuan Yew, do not have a personal interest in making the case for authoritarian government—are open to the idea, and sometimes argue it vigorously, that a certain kind of authoritarianism is better than a freewheeling democracy. This, too, is understandable. In modern Asia, unlike modern Europe, authoritarian government has often brought not hardship and war but instead peace, prosperity, and equality. How the successful authoritarians managed to do this is one of the most significant questions about the rise of Asia.

THE DOLLAR-BILL GAME

To answer that question adequately, it is best to begin with the biggest flaw in the advanced democracies of the rich world. The defect is simple to understand, as shown by the quote from a minor eighteenth-century Scottish historian with which this chapter opened. But in practice the flaw has proven very hard to eradicate. Something economists call the dollar-bill game helps explain why.

Suppose there is a dollar and three people who by majority vote can split it among themselves. The logical answer is equal shares for each. But it makes sense for A to say to B, since they have a majority between them, "I'll split it with you fifty-fifty if you vote with me." C can then counterbid to B: "I'll give you fifty-five and keep only forty-five for myself if you vote with me instead." A reacts with a proposal to C: "I'll take only fifty-two and give you forty-eight, three more than you would get under your proposal to B." C tries a bold stroke, arguing to B, "You're now in danger of getting nothing, but I'm willing to give you forty if you vote with me now." And so on. It turns out that the game has no stable solution. In fact, the only thing the players can ever agree on is that there should be more than just one dollar in play. This is the world of lobby-based, special-interest democratic politics.

The problem is hardly unique to modern democracies, but it has become endemic in them. In democracies, government interventions in the economy create lobbies that politicians have trouble antagonizing; and once a dollar passes into the public domain, it is almost never taken away. Even democratic politicians as ideologically committed as Margaret Thatcher and Ronald Reagan were to reducing the reach and appetite of the state found that the most they could accomplish was to slow or stop the growth of government spending, not cut it back.

On the face of it, this does not make sense. One of the reasons people voted for President Reagan or Mrs. Thatcher was presumably because they believed what they said about the need to shrink government. The trouble with representative democracy is that the link between the broad wishes the voters express when they elect their rulers and the forces that actually shape the decisions of the rulers once they are in office has been stretched to the point where it has almost snapped. One especially painful example is India. It is exhilarating to watch that country's great mass of people freely voting to decide who will rule them. It is dejecting in the extreme to realize, after some acquaintance with how the Indian government runs, that the interests of the broad sweep of the electorate count for little in government decision-making, whereas the desires (and money) of rich, powerful, and well-organized special-interest groups —who almost always want what is bad for the interests of Indians as a whole—carry great weight.

In general, lobby-based democracy has two awful consequences. The first is bad government. An analogy is often drawn between consumer choice in a free market and voter choice in a democracy, but it is false. There can be no such thing as a "bad" consumer choice in a free market. You can almost always bet that if not enough people are prepared to buy a product or service to make it profitable for someone to produce it, then it is better for the economy as a whole that the product or service should cease to exist.

But in a lobby-based democracy, elections necessarily give only a vague indication of what policies the voters are after; unlike in a consumer market, the specific decisions get made not by the "buyers" (voters) but by other people later. Bad government is commonplace because no obvious mechanism exists for making these decisions conform to the interests of the nation as a whole instead of to the interests of those organized and rich enough to have lobbies. Not many people would be prepared to argue that it is good for the American government to be adding $200–$300 billion a year to the $3 trillion in debt it ran up in 1980–94. Nor will anyone except a politician claim that it is about to stop doing so anytime this century and probably well into the next.

The second bad result of lobby-based democracy is the increasing frustration of the voters, who see their collective general wishes defied at every turn in the detailed operation of government. This is behind much of the anti-incumbent sourness that began seeping into all the advanced democracies in the early 1990s, especially America's. It will not change until the politicians of the advanced democracies begin once more to act more in the national interest and less in the sectional interest.

Encouragingly, this is starting to happen in some countries. The most spectacular example is New Zealand, which until 1984 had run one of the world's most protectionist and lobby-friendly governments. In the years since, under governments of both the "left" and right, New Zealand's laws and policies have become among the least economically distorting in the world. And this reversal of dollar-bill-game politics came through a system as democratic as any in the West. New Zealand's success provides an excellent retort to the Asian authoritarians who argue that the West can never rescue itself from the welfare-state policies of the past. But it is a small example, and most of the rich democracies have a very long way to go if they are to emulate it.

TRANSITIONS . . .

The reason why Asia has so far escaped the special-interest trap is that the successful authoritarian governments—in the forefront of which are South Korea, Taiwan, Hong Kong (though it was less authoritarian than just totally undemocratic), and Singapore—had the laserlike aim of modernizing their countries by getting their economies to grow very fast. In practice this meant that they outlawed the dollar-bill game. They largely refused to accommodate the claims of special interests over those of the economy as a whole; this in turn made possible low government spending and low taxes.

In all these places, the refusal to bend to special pleading freed a competent and mostly uncorrupt bureaucracy to set economic policy according to the national interest. But the ability to override narrow interests had a considerable price: For almost thirty years Taiwan and South Korea were run by rather nasty military dictatorships. Yet there, and in Hong Kong and Singapore too, the authoritarian approach was not only more efficient economically than democratic decision-making; it proved to be more egalitarian as well —for the simple reason that it is the rare lobby in a democracy that wins government benefits for the poor rather than the privileged.

The fairly lobby-proof character of these governments also explains at least part of the mystery why some of them were able to make occasionally successful forays into industrial policy. As chapter 3 argued, such interventions do good only if they are made on behalf not of the individual firms involved but of the economy as a whole and if they can quickly be reversed when circumstances change. Once an industrial favor has been granted in Europe (or, more rarely, America), it becomes very hard to withdraw. Authoritarian Asia has been better able to shrug off the protests of those deprived of a favor by a shift of policy.

While some thinkers, such as Mancur Olson, an American sociologist, have acknowledged the theoretical advantages of enlightened despotism in economic policymaking, particularly its ability to squash special interests, they have also concluded that it is not worth the risks. One undoubted superiority of a democratic system is that it settles the crucial question of succession briskly and peacefully. Under authoritarianism there is always a doubt about who is going to come next and how he will be chosen. Is it going to be a wise philosopher-king like Lee Kuan Yew or instead the thugs who run Burma? The question matters a lot more in an authoritarian state because the power of the ruler ranges more widely than it does in a democracy. No matter how incompetent or awful an American president is, he will be in no position to seize your property or throw you in jail. Some say that only democracy can offer people the security of person and property that will let an economy flourish in the long run.

Yet the destabilizing effects of arbitrary rule have also been avoided in Asia's successful authoritarian countries. Singapore is a highly disciplined place, but it also has a rule of law that leaves people in no doubt their property will be protected. Taiwan and South Korea did not have Singapore's common-law tradition or its ferocious impartiality in stamping out corruption; but there was no sign even during Taiwan's or Korea's days of military rule that businessmen or ordinary people in either country lacked confidence that the fruits of their labor would remain theirs.

One key to the secret of Asia's successful instances of authoritarianism may lie in history. Lucian Pye, an American authority on Asian politics first mentioned in chapter 1, has pointed out that in the best Asian traditions the subservience of the people had a counterpart in the obligation of the ruler to act on behalf of the community. This was reinforced by the rather disdainful refusal of the ruler to be identified with any particular interest or party or point of view. These were useful legacies for authoritarian regimes gripped by the fervor of modernization after 1960 and for the anti-special-interest and growth-promoting policies they adopted.

Yet these legacies had also existed throughout the hundreds of years of Asian disorder, squalor, and corruption that preceded the continent's reemergence in this half century. What really turned the key may never be known, but the combination of circumstances was unique. A booming world economy, America's great-power beneficence, and the threat of annihilation (which all of East Asia, including Japan, shared in the middle decades of the twentieth century) all helped to make possible two generations' worth of focused authoritarian achievement in East Asia. Asia's unusually successful experience with authoritarianism may therefore hold no lessons for the rest of the world beyond the following two. The first is that, in the right circumstances, a country in the early stages of economic takeoff will benefit from a government that has the power to override special interests, and that it is quite likely in a poor country with weak institutions that an enlightened despotism will have a better chance of doing this than a democratically elected government. The more banal, but also more general lesson, is that all governments, whatever their form, will perform better the less heed they pay to special interests.

In any event, the ability of an enlightened authoritarian government to pull off the kind of economic feat that several East Asian countries did in the decades after 1950 is transitory. Successful authoritarianism breeds the economic and social changes that make for its own destruction. With the rise of a middle class and the wider availability of all kinds of information, the forms of government throughout Asia will over the next generation inexorably take on a more democratic cast. How Asia's countries make the transition will depend on their past, especially on their societies.

... AND TRADITIONS

One of the best hints that the form of politics in Asian countries may be a lot less important than the nature of the societies that underpin it comes not from Asia but from Italy. Robert Putnam, a professor at Harvard, studied what happened when an entirely new set of governing institutions—more modern, democratic, and accountable—was introduced in Italy's various regions during the period 1970–90. Did the regional voters' faith in government and their participation rates rise? Did patronage and corruption decline? Did interest in civic affairs rise? Did economic performance improve?

The answer after twenty years' experience was, in essence, that nothing had changed. Regional differences that had persisted in some cases for centuries continued unperturbed. Previously happy, prosperous, and well governed regions remained so, and their negative counterparts also stayed as depressingly stuck as they had always been. Politics, or at least the institutional form of politics, seemed nothing more than froth on the ancient, powerful waves of Italian society.

This result would not surprise Lee Kuan Yew, who is the most articulate and intellectually coherent exponent of a certain set of assumptions and beliefs that have had the label "Asian values" pasted on them. Mr. Lee is an unapologetic proponent of the view that, as one of his interviewers put it, "culture is destiny"—or, to make things a little more controversial, that "genetics and history interact," as he once told me. On pages 329–331 is reprinted the transcript of part of an interview of Mr. Lee that I did for *The Economist* in 1991. In addition to talking about democracy and economic growth, Mr. Lee strongly made the point that the political forms which develop in a country depend very much on how that country's culture and society run—and that these deeper traits, often immutable, are the ones that make for success or failure.

DEMOCRACY AND ECONOMIC GROWTH:
A TALK WITH LEE KUAN YEW

Is being a democracy a help, a hindrance, or irrelevant to how fast Asian countries can grow?

I would say that democracy is not conducive to rapid growth when you are in an agricultural society. Take Korea, Japan, Taiwan. In their early stages they needed and had discipline, order, and effort. They must create that agricultural surplus to get their industrial sector going. Without military rule or dictatorship or authoritarian government in Korea and Taiwan, I doubt whether they could have transformed themselves so quickly.

As against that, take the Philippines. They had democracy from the word go in 1945. They never got going; it was too chaotic. It became a parlor game—who takes power, then who gets what spoils. Or take India and Ceylon. For the first three elections after independence, they went through the mechanics of democracy. But the lack of discipline made growth slow and sluggish.

But once you reach a certain level of industrial progress, you've got an educated workforce, an urban population, you have managers and engineers. Then you must have participation, because these are educated, rational people. If you carry on with an authoritarian system, you will run into all kinds of logjams. You must devise some representative system.

That will ease the next stage to becoming industrialized. Then you may get the beginnings of a civic society, with people forming their own groups: professionals, engineers, Methodists, Presbyterians. Almost spontaneously, these will form, because being educated, knowing of the wider world, will bring like-minded people together. Then only do you have the beginnings of what I would call an active grassroots democracy.

So the disparity between country and town matters a lot?

That's the big problem China faces. It's so vast. The countryside has 80 percent of the people. But the towns are 20 percent and cannot be ignored if they want to industrialize. That's their dilemma. They can govern the country as a whole, just depending on support from the countryside, where they recruit their soldiers, and they can keep the towns in check. But that means constant tension. They will not get the lifting of the spirits which carries a people on to the next stage: They will not take off like Korea and Taiwan. They cannot

continued

enthuse their urban population, the intelligentsia especially. Somehow these people have to be drawn into the system, not just in running enterprises but in running their cities, their towns, their districts.

China's key problem is to find a twin-track approach, one for the towns, one for the countryside. They're really two different populations, two different levels of education, cultural levels, aspirations.

Aren't Japan's electoral system and civil liberties really indistinguishable from those in the West?

It's just the forms. Their loyalties, their motivations, their norms, are different. The faction leaders in the ruling Liberal Democratic party are like samurai chiefs. Each has his samurais; he provides them with their needs. He's got to find $1.5 million a year for each of his Dietmen, and at elections he has to find $3 million each. So they're in a bind.

This sprang from Japan's Meiji Restoration system. Elections were made deliberately expensive from the start; the court did it to keep Dietmen in check. After the war, it slipped back to the old system. Even if there had not been the brutal interruption of militarism in the 1930s, Japan would not have become like Westminster or the Assemblée Nationale in Paris. It's a different culture.

What other parliament would have 150 out of 600 Dietmen as sons of Dietmen? Kaifu [Toshiki Kaifu, Japan's prime minister in 1991] has just been in Singapore. Before dinner, the wife introduced her son to me. Young Kaifu, thirty, thirty-one, is his father's secretary. I've also been introduced to young Fukuda, young Nakasone, several other Japanese prime ministers' sons. It's an inheritance, like their golf-club memberships.

As development takes place in Asia, will it lead on to Western freedoms?

Not necessarily like the West, but comparable ways of life and ways of doing things. Put it this way. Regardless of American pressure, Korea and Taiwan could not have gone on the way they were, because they had produced a very thick layer of well-educated engineers and managers and an educated workforce. If you want this educated workforce to make its full contribution, you cannot carry on with the old patriarchal system of management.

But to have the kind of democracy Britain or America has developed, you need certain cultural impulses in a people. I think it was workable because there was a certain culture in a people, a certain tolerance of different views, and a certain willingness to accept that for the time being the opposite view prevails and their orders will be

continued

obeyed, but that does not prevent me from trying to win over a majority next time around.

India is slightly different. But China has always had an autocratic center. The king emerges; he makes himself emperor by knocking out all the other chieftains and all the other kings. Then he sends you his magistrate, a superior being: He's sat through the imperial examinations. He sends the magistrate to look after this village in this prefecture. And if you disobey the magistrate, that's damn foolish.

It's a very different cultural tradition. Democracy will now come as a result of the needs of industrial society. I'm the boss; you run this steel mill my way. Well, the steel mill will go bankrupt. It's not possible to run a modern steel mill that way. The system requires participation.

That participation of the workforce inevitably spills over into government, into society. This is reinforced by the media, plus travel and so on. There's no going back to the old days. But at the same time the old patterns, old habits of looking to the magistrate to solve problems, remain.

They say I am authoritarian. But if I did not take the initiative, nobody would. Who's going to stop people smoking in public places? Is there an anti-smoking movement?

There's a very strong anti-smoking movement in America now.

That's right. I wish we had that.

Why don't you?

I tell you that it goes back to culture. People feel strongly about it, but nobody feels strong enough to take the lead and say, let's form an anti-smoking league, we have the right to fresh air. No. They wait for the government.

At what point do you start developing these small groups that make up a civic society in Singapore, for instance?

I have no idea whether it will come, because the culture is the other way. It may never come.

You cannot break out of your culture altogether. You can take individuals and scatter them into another culture. If you take a Japanese or a Chinese and you dump him in America, over one or two generations he'll become an American. But if you introduce American values into Japan or China, the results are very different.

Culture is very deep rooted; it's not tangible, but it's very real. The values and perceptions, attitudes, reference points, a map up here, in the mind.

Two years after that conversation, Mr. Lee was willing to countenance the idea that Asian countries could evolve—very slowly. Pooh-poohing the suggestion that the end in 1993 of almost forty years' rule by the Liberal Democratic party in Japan was a momentous event, he said:

> I do not see them becoming a fractious, contentious society like America, always debating and knocking each other down. That is not in their culture. They want growth and they want to get on with life. They are not interested in ideology as such, or in the theory of good government. They just know a good government and want a good government.

The reason for the slowness with which Asian politics changes, in Mr. Lee's view, is that Asia's societies are still far from becoming middle-class in the Western sense. Technology now makes it possible to raise incomes very fast to rich-world levels: thirty or forty years, compared with the hundred years it took for a country to modernize beginning in the nineteenth century. But it takes as long as ever to train a whole society to modernity, to educate people "until they are capable of critical judgment, absorbing information from the written word and applying a critical eye to it." Even Japan, with more than a century of modernization behind it, is not quite there yet. South Korea, Taiwan, and Singapore, Mr. Lee reckons, will need another twenty to thirty years to get to that stage.

And the most populous societies of Asia—China, India, and Indonesia?

> It takes a very long time. In China 20–30 percent are semi-literate. When you talk about that, you are talking about 300–400 million semi-literate people. They can't read newspapers or even notices. Where are they going to produce the millions of teachers to spread into these outlying provinces? The teachers will have to come from the towns. Given a choice, they will not want to go into the country-side, where there are no social and recreational amenities, doctors, medicines, or modern sanitation.

> India may take even longer. Indonesia, they have made considerable progress. But look at the number of islands they have. Communications between islands are difficult. They have to think in terms of eighty-ninety years before Indonesians can reach a Japanese-style spread of knowledge and critical thinking.

It is not that Asians live in ignorance. There are lively discussions aplenty in Asia—I have found them more adventurous on the whole than those I have run across in places like London—but these debates are conducted in private. One of China's most intriguing paradoxes is how open its rulers are to intellectual give-and-take so long as the discussions take place behind closed doors. I have experienced this myself. And Communist party officials who have joined foreign firms say that, like a Japanese company, China's Communist party, behind its impassive façade, is surprisingly good at collecting broad and accurate information from the grass roots, sending it up to the top, debating it, and sending the conclusions back down. Within the walls, challenge and criticism are not only allowed but encouraged. Yet not a peep of public protest is allowed from outside.

"Americans," says Lee Kuan Yew, "believe that out of contention, out of the clash of different ideas and ideals, you get good government. That view is not shared in Asia." That sounds, and to some extent surely is, self-serving. Yet anybody who has spoken in public to Asian audiences as well as Western ones is struck by how relatively unwilling the Asians are to engage in open debate. The tendency to look upon public confrontation with distaste runs to the most sophisticated and Westernized reaches of Asian societies. In 1993, Takashi Inoguchi, a youngish professor at Tokyo University who is one of Japan's best political scientists and is well acquainted with both Europe and America, asked me with amused puzzlement, "Why do Americans put so much emphasis on being able to say what you want in public?"

This may point to the biggest single gap between the undeniably consumerist, but still unindividualistic, societies of Asia and the middle-class societies of the West. There is a good reason why most of Asia is yet today governed by what Robert Scalapino, a professor at the University of California at Berkeley, has called a system of "authoritarian pluralism," or "soft authoritarianism." Asians crave freedom but are not yet ready to swallow individualism whole—and democracy is an individualist creed. Even so, Asia's small-government bent may make it easier than it now seems for the continent to marry its relentless move to democratic forms with the social traditions that it would like to preserve but which are so at odds with post-1950s Western democracy.

Politics on the Wane

The real destroyer of the liberties of the people is he who spreads among them bounties, donations and benefits.

—Plutarch

The way to square the circle—how modern Asia can preserve its strong family-based societies against the atomizing ravages of democratic individualism without forsaking the advantages of modernity —is best described by Jimmy Lai. Mr. Lai, a Hong Kong clothing entrepreneur turned publisher who was first introduced in chapter 7, says stoutly that history is moving Asia's way. He means that governments are becoming less powerful at so fast a pace that they soon will become irrelevant to most decision-making. Mr. Lai is no friend of authoritarians such as Lee Kuan Yew or China's rulers; indeed, he is now making a career out of deriding them in his publications (and he thinks China's Communists have no more than ten years of life left in them). He believes that democracy, combined with civil liberties, is the right form of government but—and this is the crucial point—that government should have little power; it should spend no more than 10–15 percent of a country's GDP (around a third of the current level of government spending in most rich countries in the West). The private institutions of the economy and society, mainly business and the family, would take care of the rest.

A government that puny, reasons Mr. Lai, cannot do much damage. He thinks democracy is needlessly slow—it has taken American voters sixty years, he remarks incredulously, to discover how damaging government-sponsored benefit programs can be—but unlike authoritarian systems, at least it does not offer would-be usurpers of liberty the scope to abuse power. He reasons that if government spending is as sharply curtailed as he suggests, the barriers that democracy erects against arbitrary power (especially arbitrary succession) can be maintained while the special-interest lobbying that plagues modern Western democracies will evaporate of its own accord: Nobody will find it worthwhile arguing over a slice of government benefits that small. Mr. Lai's answer to the protests of Western liberals that tiny government would make the burden of life crushing for the poor is simple. When deprived of the crutch of modern government, people will instead form strong families to protect themselves—which, as Mr. Lai says with no more than tenfold exaggeration, "they have naturally done for millions of years."

Yet, though Mr. Lai describes a sensible goal, it is hard to imagine Asia making the transition from small-authoritarian to small-democratic government so easily. Since rising wealth leads to middle-class aspirations, and those in turn to an increase in freedom and democracy, both the special-interest consequences of democracy and the socially corrosive effects of wealth and individualism on the family do not seem far behind. The problem lies in the tension between individual freedom, which is the greatest blessing that modernization confers, and social order. Left on their own, people frequently make choices that suit them as individuals (to leave an unhappy marriage, for instance), which, when added together, nonetheless do severe damage to society.

On politics alone, most East Asian countries seem unlikely to slip too far into the special-interest bog. True, the previously unthinkable has begun happening in Asia. In 1994, Hong Kong's government toyed with the idea of introducing a modest Social Security-like retirement scheme (meaning that it would be financed out of current tax revenues instead of paying for itself, as Singapore's, Malaysia's, and Chile's pension schemes do). At about the same time, foreign investors calling on upper-echelon Taiwanese bureaucrats reported that the put-upon civil servants refused to make decisions that they would have made in a snap in the old days. The bureaucrats complained that almost any contact with foreign investors would earn them a legislative investigation, simply because it made for juicy publicity for the legislators.

It is therefore possible that greater democracy will reduce the economic efficiency of some countries such as Taiwan, where the expansion of democracy in the early 1990s contributed to a steep rise in government spending on social welfare and in the previously small government debt, and to turning the government budget surplus sharply into deficit. Likewise in South Korea, which plans to increase welfare spending sharply by 2000, and in Hong Kong, where, in its dying days, the British colonial administration introduced, in 1993–95, a 26 percent (in real terms) increase in the social-welfare budget. This led to a 44 percent rise in cash handouts; by 1995 a family of four could receive HK$8,200 a month in government payments, while a laborer imported from China for construction work got HK$8,000 a month. It is no surprise that Hong Kong's unemployment rate around this time began suddenly rising even though the territory's economy was just beginning to revive.

Even so, the drift towards welfarism in Hong Kong is likely to prove a curiosity of the twilight of colonial rule; overall, the democratization of Asia is unlikely to do any appreciable damage to economic growth. The successes of post-1950 Asia have been built on a foundation of small, pro-business government, and not many Asian politicians have been tempted to stray far from it even as their societies have begun maturing economically and aging demographically. In contrast to America and the countries of Western Europe, for instance, Japan has decided to confront the challenge of its population's rapid aging in 2010–20 by starting to pay for it now through budget surpluses in most years—not, as in Europe and America, by putting it off for others to deal with through taxation at the time. Besides, the currents of change that are beginning to carry Western societies towards smaller government will only reinforce Asia's natural political bent. Preserving Asia's societies, however, may prove harder than keeping its governments small.

ASIAN VALUES

Because of Asia's history, its people have learned over the centuries to count on their governments for nothing much except trouble. This attitude has an unfortunate side but also a good one: Very few Asians (and no Chinese) think they can rely on anything but their personal ties to see them through hard times.

The need for self-sufficiency has been the greatest single spur to the creation, and retention, of what have come to be called "Asian values": the family rather than the individual as the paramount unit of society; a preference for order over freedom and the common good over individual fulfillment; hence, considerable deference to authority; frugality; and a belief in the virtues of education and hard work. These values are sometimes called "Confucian." But that is a misnomer, and not only because these values permeate all of Asia, not just the Chinese part of it.

Confucianism does entail respect for authority, for education, and for the family, but it was founded on a deep contempt for commercial life and an assumption that an unchanging society was the natural sort. The values that sustain modern Asia's societies work in some of the world's most commerce-minded countries in the midst of the fastest social and economic change in history. Nor are the values even peculiarly "Asian." They may not be the values by which life in America is conducted today, but they are not radically different from the values by which American life was conducted in the 1950s.

The reason why such values have been on the decline in the rich countries of the West is a matter of much dispute. One view, held by what might be called "the ruthless school" (of which Jimmy Lai is a pupil), contends that it is only when a government leaves people for the most part to fend for themselves that they turn, in large measure out of fear, to the only other institution capable of shielding them to a degree from life's hazards: the family. The rest of "Asian values" follow naturally from that.

But there is also a view—supported among others by Kim Dae Jung, a South Korean who was a longtime dissident and then a presidential candidate in 1994—that it is not government policies, and certainly not political liberalism, that undermine stable and community-minded social institutions but instead the effects of growing wealth and industrialization. This view was persuasively argued in 1942 by Joseph Schumpeter, the Austrian economist, who wrote that rising wealth will jeopardize the family because "as soon as men and women learn the utilitarian lesson . . . and introduce into their private life a sort of inarticulate system of cost accounting, they cannot fail to be aware of the heavy personal sacrifices that family ties and especially parenthood entail under modern conditions."

It is true that the same signs of social decay that have so eaten away at America and Europe in recent decades are beginning to make themselves felt in middle-class Asia, too. Family life is coming under strain in much of Asia as wealth increases. Japan's divorce rate rose by half during the 1980s; Singapore's, by half between 1982 and 1992. South Korea's doubled in 1982–92. The better-off countries of Asia are producing fewer and fewer children. South Korea's fertility rate halved during the 1980s, and Japan's population is expected to have begun falling in absolute terms by 2010. Filial piety is also not what it once was. In the rich cities of Southeast Asia middle-class kids often while away their hours hanging out in the shopping malls rather than remaining glued, Confucian-like, to their textbooks. They sometimes get into more mischief than that.

In 1994, Kuala Lumpur was in a tizzy over the *boh sia* girls, bored young teenagers who spent their evenings waiting by the roadside to be picked up by passing motorists for paid sex. (The name, which roughly means "no sound," refers to the quiet compliance with which they submit.)

Drug use in Asia has grown alarmingly. Figures compiled by the *Asian Wall Street Journal* show that in 1994, when America was thought to have around 600,000 heroin addicts, Thailand had that many in its northern Chiang Mai and Chiang Rai provinces alone, Malaysia had 100,000 addicts (or about twice as many per capita as America), and Taiwan had 50,000 (or roughly America's per capita share). Even Singapore, which is second to none in the ferocity with which it attacks drug use, had 7,000 heroin addicts under treatment in 1994, up from 5,700 in 1990; this implies probably a higher incidence of addiction than the United States suffers.

Crime in many Asian countries is rising as well. Even orderly Singapore, which exacts swift, sure, and often painful punishment through the liberal use of caning, suffered a rise in juvenile crime of some 25 percent between 1992 and 1993.

The tendency of rising wealth to weaken social bonds has some obvious causes. Cities are more anonymous, and hence less socially regulated, than the villages from which the fast-rising populations of Asia's cities have mostly been drawn. The temptations of the good life are stronger, and the recollections of the insecurities (or even horrors) of the past fainter, for the younger generation than for their parents. Perhaps most of all, universal education and a booming job market have given far more women sufficient economic independence to leave an unhappy marriage if they wish.

Yet however inescapable the debilitating effects of modern life on social stability everywhere, it is important to keep some perspective. Except perhaps in the case of drug use, Asia's indicators of social decay remain far below their counterparts in the West. Nowhere are divorce rates more than a third of the American level, and the incidence of violent crime in every prosperous Asian city is much lower than in any American or European city of comparable size. Everyone concedes that Asia's growing wealth will put the same sorts of strain on its societies that America and Europe have experienced. The issue is whether the damage can be contained.

Those in Asia with an authoritarian bent think that, with a combination of small government and disciplinarian government, the

Schumpeterian logic can be resisted. Small government is important for the reasons Jimmy Lai explains. If people feel their only social security is going to come from their family, they will tend to stick with the family despite the expansion of individual freedom that rising incomes would otherwise bring; it is too scary not to (which is why this method of social control is ruthless).

The authoritarians believe discipline is also needed—for a fundamental reason, in Lee Kuan Yew's view:

> Certain basics about human nature do not change. Man needs a certain moral sense of right and wrong. There is such a thing called evil, and it is not the result of being a victim of society. You are just an evil man, prone to do evil things, and you have to be stopped from doing them.

Mr. Lee himself admits that it will be a fight every step of the way to preserve what he thinks of as the basics of the Asian way: the family ("governments will come, governments will go, but this endures"), self-reliance, and enough freedom for people to make the best use of their talents but enough order to ensure that in exercising that freedom they do not deprive others of their rights to peace and security. But how can you preserve this? Mr. Lee answers:

> In the 1950s, Americans already had a different society [from Asian ones]. But it had not loosened or unraveled as it has today, where single parenthood is considered quite normal. That's a disaster for society.

> *I agree it is a disaster.*

> Then you've got to stop it. You have made no serious effort to stop it.

> *I'm skeptical about the ability of anybody in the world to stop it.*

> No, I disagree. Look at the Japanese. Our divorce rates have gone up, too, but what is the total? We are slowing down the process at every stage. And people don't shack up together; it's unacceptable. And we can't have single mothers. It's totally unacceptable, and we keep it unacceptable.

> We reinforce it with social sanctions and economic sanctions. It is disapproved of. If you want to have a quiet affair, that's your business; it's always going on. But this flagrant disregard of social norms is unacceptable because we think it will lead to the disintegration of the family, which supports and nurtures the children.

I am not saying that we are unchanging and unchangeable. But I do say that we will do everything possible not to allow this building brick of society to disintegrate. Without this we are no different from animals. You cannot bring up children in institutions, whether day school or boarding school or whatever. It is not possible. They can supplement what values are transmitted in the home, but they cannot be a substitute for the home.

We should not substitute the state for the parents or the family. If you bring a child into the world in the West, the state caters for him. That's dangerous. If you bring a child into Asia, that's your personal responsibility.

The disciplinarian side of this argument has its logic, but it also has a problem. The boxed interview with Mr. Lee earlier in this chapter contains a line where he says that, if he had not made the decision to ban smoking from certain places in Singapore, ordinary Singaporeans would not have banded together to do that obviously sensible thing. The problem is that if ordinary Singaporeans do not learn to make their own decisions about such matters by being given the freedom to, the effect is to protect them little less than a social-welfare system would do.

That is why Singapore could face problems competing with less tightly controlled parts of Asia early next century. It also explains why, in general, building modern institutions of all kinds is now Asia's biggest job. Even with a desirable end in view, directives from the top cannot keep order in a modern society or company, so something else has to. Few Asian companies or countries have yet worked out just what, in their own cultural and historical circumstances, that something else is.

EPILOGUE:
ASIA ON THE BRINK

By mid-summer 1995, Deng Xiaoping was out of sight but not yet dead, the dollar had rallied significantly from its springtime lows against the yen, and foreign money was again pouring into Asia after a brief wintertime absence caused by Mexico's financial collapse in December 1994 and January 1995. It was a good time to reflect on where Asia stood in the world.

The economic rise of East and Southeast Asia in the half-century since the end of World War II has been, if perhaps not precisely miraculous, nonetheless astounding. In 1945 most of these countries were at one of the lowest points in their long histories. Many of them were among the poorest countries in the world. For a century many had sufferd colonization at the hands of various European powers, the Americans, and (in the cases of Taiwan and Korea) the Japanese. Almost all had endured the ravages of nearly two decades of probably the most destructive warfare in Asian history. A few, conspicuously Korea and Vietnam, were about to face yet more war; or, in China's case, civil war, followed a decade later by mass starvation and a few years after that by a decade-long bout of near anarchy.

East Asia appeared to have almost no advantages as it began its struggle to enter the modern world. Its countries were generally poor in natural resources and seemed oversupplied with people who, to make matters worse, were largely illiterate (except in Japan, which had been modernizing for a century). Large numbers of East Asians had nothing. Millions were refugees, homeless and uprooted by war and civil war; many more millions were landless peasants, ground down by centuries of feudalism and decades of colonialism.

Out of these ashes rose the biggest and fastest economic improvement the world has ever seen. It took Britain, then the world's fastest-growing economy, almost sixty years to double per capita incomes after its economic takeoff in 1780. It took America almost fifty years to repeat that performance after 1840. Japan's per capita incomes doubled in thirty-three years after 1880. Then, after the war-torn first half of the twentieth century had ended, came the great East Asian miracle. Indonesia's per capita incomes doubled in seventeen years after 1965; South Korea's, in eleven years after 1970; and China's, in ten years after 1978.

As that downward cascade of numbers suggests, modern Asia's breathtaking success has happened in part simply because it took advantage of changes in the world economy which over the past two hundred years have made fast economic growth progressively easier to achieve. The world's stock of technology and economically productive ideas has been growing exponentially, both in size and in quality and sophistication. And the speed with which that stock of technology and ideas is added to and diffused throughout the world has constantly been accelerating.

These advantages of the modern economy are there to be seized by anyone; yet almost no other countries have pounced on them as quickly, comprehensively, and successfully as the rising economies of East and Southeast Asia. For decades these economies have vastly outstripped any others in successfully putting together the four elements of economic growth: labor, capital, human capital, and productivity. The reasons why Asia was able to do this are among the most complicated questions about human society in the second half of this century. But the complexities can be boiled down to a set of attributes widely shared by the East Asian success stories—attributes which, moreover, reinforce each other and reflect a consistent view of how a society and economy should be run.

The nub of the Asian idea of public policy is that governments should not do much to temper the hazards of life, particularly the often harsh consequences of fast technological and economic change. Asia's governments have tended to offer little social protection, such as pay-as-you-go pensions, unemployment insurance, or state-provided health care. Government spending in Asia accounts for an unusually small share of economic activity; and, in comparison with Western countries, very little of Asian government spending goes for transfer payments from the pockets of one class of taxpayers into those of another class. Except in such places as India and the Philippines, even less of Asian governments' money goes for current spending on such things as civil servants' salaries. Conversely, Asian governments devote proportionally more of their more modest spending to investment, especially in education.

Although Asia's governments have been pro-business as well as small—meaning they leave much economic (and even social) decision-making to the competitive interplay of businesses in marketplaces—these governments have in general been as reluctant to safeguard individual companies as they have been to protect individual people. It is true that whole industries in Asia, such as Japan's agriculture and its retail distribution system, sometimes receive impregnable protection from foreign competition. The more common practice is to force participants in the economy to live up to world standards of performance.

The Asian approach confuses many Westerners, who see (often rightly) a great deal of trade and other protection for Asian companies and therefore infer (usually wrongly) that the companies are being allowed an easy life. Some countries, such as Hong Kong, Taiwan, and (to a lesser degree) Thailand, allow competition to rage as unchecked as it does anywhere on earth. Yet even the countries that pursue industrial policies and invoke the protectionism usually associated with them—South Korea is Exhibit No. 1—do so in ways that force the discipline of world competition on their firms even if world competitors are absent from the home market. When Korea's technocrats got some industrial policy wrong, as they often did, they quickly reversed themselves: The companies concerned were unhesitatingly stripped of whatever privileges they had been granted and told to fend for themselves. Throughout East Asia companies have tended to run scared.

So have people. In Hong Kong, the world's most free-market territory, few people have ever been shielded from the gusts of technological and market change that blow in from the whole world. From the days in the 1950s when industries like wigmaking rose and fell with extraordinary speed, Hong Kongers have come to expect to change jobs and even careers as matter-of-factly as they do clothes or cars. Yet even in as corporatist a country as Japan, where company loyalty and lifetime employment have traditionally gone together at the big firms, most workers toil in establishments that boast nothing of that kind of job security.

Few people can cope on their own with unbridled change. But most of Asia has thrown the shock-absorbing that an individual is bound to need onto the family, and the community and neighborhood networks associated with families, rather than onto public institutions. This is a policy that makes it extremely risky in Asian society to function as a maverick: nobody, certainly not the government, will catch you if you fall.

A hands-off policy has deep consequences. If the family rather than the individual is the main unit of society, individual freedom is undoubtedly reduced. Nobody, to take the principal example, however unhappy he or she is, ducks out of the obligations of marriage and children as readily in Asia as spouses do in the West. People are encouraged to work harder and save more; insecurity is a great spur to effort. Education is an even more worthwhile investment than it would otherwise be, since the parents providing it stand to gain from it almost as much as the children receiving it.

This sort of policy makes for a harsh world; people without a social connection of some sort tend to be lost when they stumble. A society organized along these lines is utterly contrary to the spirit of modern Western Europe and mostly at odds with the assumptions introduced into America's public life during the New Deal and pushed far forward in the 1960s. Yet the refusal of Asia's governments to protect people is, I think, the main explanation of why Asian economies have grown so fast and why Asian social institutions are still so strong. It also is one of Asia's biggest advantages in a world of accelerating technological and economic change. A society organized along Asian lines is far better equipped than the average Western society to embrace and absorb change: If a powerful government will not conserve the patterns of the past on your behalf (and it is, eventually, futile to try), you learn quickly that you must cope with the future.

It stands to reason that Asia should have done well by its system of small government and strong society. Society, after all, is sunk a lot deeper in human nature than government is, and it is a more efficient regulator of people's behavior. The question now is whether Asia can continue to build on the substantial advantage of its social strengths.

THE NEXT STEP

Asia's trajectory over the next twenty-five years is unlikely to be a smooth continuation of the curve it has traced over the past twenty-five. For one thing, the world's geopolitical structure has been completely transformed—especially the complicated Cold War balance among the Soviet Union, China, and Japan that allowed the United States to maintain a long period of unusual stability in Northeast Asia. Second, the pace of technological change is accelerating, and with it the speed of transmission of new technologies throughout the world; like every other region, Asia is going to have much more change to absorb in the next quarter century than it did in 1970–95. Third, Asia's relative economic weight in the world has grown so large that its further development cannot take place in the obscurity that it enjoyed during its fast ascent of 1970–95. China's rise has already provoked more controversy and more conflict with the United States than Japan's growth did until the Japanese were ten times richer than the Chinese now are. Asia as a whole, and China in particular, will henceforth bulk much larger in the world both as an economic force and as a policy question, and this will change the character of its interaction with the West.

Asia is therefore about to enter a period when its long-term fate will be settled much more decisively than it was during its youthful and exuberant successes of the past quarter century. Asia is on the brink. Within another quarter-century it will have become clear whether two-fifths of mankind was in 1995 on the brink of greatness, of world-changing (indeed history-changing) dimensions, or of failed early promise, failure in the worst case meaning the appalling destruction of large wars.

My view is that it will turn out to have been greatness. Whether I am right depends mainly on two things: on Asia's own success at strengthening its weak institutions; and on the willingness of the West in general (and of America in particular) to maintain a relatively free and open system of world trade, and of the United States to exert the role of global great-power leadership that it alone is capable of playing.

The next section deals with the West's attitude. As for Asia itself, this book has been full of examples of the continent's institutional weaknesses. They run the gamut from opacity of company governance to lack of political accountability to paucity of infrastructure to the historic inability of Asian countries to maintain the peace among themselves through their own balance of power.

These weaknesses have done Asia very little damage so far—so little, indeed, that it could be argued they have been strengths. Modern Asia was a lot smarter than other parts of the poor world: Asia let its societies and economies run away with themselves at first rather than smothering them under government directives. Yet the imbalance in Asia between private strength and public weakness cannot last. If Asian firms are ever to function outside Asia—or, eventually, even to compete successfully with Western firms in a modernized Asian economy—they will have to learn how to appraise and appease public concerns as well as they do private ones.

The same is true for Asian societies as a whole. There is very little that governments need to do, but within their narrow scope of proper concern it is crucial that they act efficiently and thoroughly. It is well documented that in a modern economy public investments of the right sort can not only deliver a big boost to economic growth generally but also sharply raise the returns to private capital investment. This is why America's interstate highway system, built in the 1950s, was one of the most productive uses of public money this century. In only one aspect—albeit a crucial one, education—has most of East and Southeast Asia been good at providing public investment (and education has been well looked after in part because its benefits are so closely tied to the fortunes of an individual family). Save only for Singapore, which has made a habit of investing heavily and prospectively in infrastructure, Asia has been slow to provide the institutions a modern economy needs: accountable governments, accountable (to minority or non-family shareholders) corporate management, and adequate (in Asia's case meaning huge) amounts of physical infrastructure.

It will not be easy for Asia to rebalance itself this way. The rise of modern Asia has overwhelmingly depended on judgments (business and otherwise) based on personal trust and connections. Such a system, which is at its most intense and refined in the Chinese part of Asia, has many advantages, the greatest being speed and informality of decision-making. But it makes transactions with those you do not personally know almost impossible. Moving to a more modern and objective institutional structure will be hard: There is an inherent conflict between loyalties based on personal ties and loyalties based on institutions.

The transition that Asia needs to make in this respect will have as deep and wide-ranging consequences for its future as its strong societies will. Although Asian countries have in general been brilliant at pricing private assets and risk, they have had no idea how to do so with public ones. As they learn, companies and public institutions will be transformed, and the prices of all sorts of things will shift. This is one reason why interest rates should rise and returns on bonds (which will account for a great deal of new corporate finance and for much of Asia's infrastructure financing) should rise relative to those on equities. It is also why Asia's economic growth must soon slow from its recent astonishing levels. Public investment —including bringing companies up to international scratch in terms of management and accounting—is expensive, and for an individual company, at first unprofitable.

Yet although Asia's growth seems bound to slow down a bit as its institution-building gets under way, it is unlikely to plunge dangerously. It had better not. Asia still has to absorb another generation's worth of young people into its workforce—and remember that that twenty-year bulge of workers will total 1.7 billion people, almost twice as many workers in their prime years as the 1 billion people Asia had to absorb during the miraculous years of 1975–95. I think Asia will succeed in growing fast enough to accomplish this. None of its countries has America's strengths; likewise, however, little of the continent has the sort of weaknesses that doom people to perpetual poverty. Their governments, even when harsh, believe in growth and try to promote it. Their societies are attuned to effort and progress, and this is unlikely to change over the next generation even as Asia begins to erect the institutions of a modern economy.

BUD-GRAFTING

If things go reasonably well, during the first decade of the new millennium a belt of mostly middle class societies—concentrated in a couple of dozen huge metropolises and their hinterlands—will run from South Korea (which by then could well include the whole of the Korean peninsula and, in an economic sense at least, a fair chunk of Russia's Far East), through Japan, all of coastal China, Java and Sumatra in Indonesia, the urban parts of Indochina, and the whole of the rest of Southeast Asia: a zone boasting a consumer class of about a billion people. To this should be added consumerist pockets in the Indian subcontinent including another 200 million people. The people of this zone will be enjoying, in material terms, roughly the lives of average people in North America and Western Europe in the 1950s. They will make up the biggest middle class in history.

The spending power of this middle class will offer the West, and especially America, some of the most extraordinary business and financial opportunities ever. The rich world will probably account for half the worldwide growth of demand for most products and services in the next five to ten years; but it is extremely hard in the rich world to grab much market share from rivals unless you are in a brand-new industry. The lion's share of the other half of worldwide demand growth will come from Asia, much of it from China. And, because Asia's markets are so new, most of that chunk of extra demand will be up for grabs by anybody. That is why Asian markets should prove so vital to any Western company that wants to grow fast.

Among Western companies, those of the United States are best positioned to profit from the rise of Asia and to compete on reasonably even terms with Japanese firms in their own backyard; and in the most advanced industries, where America is most competitive, American firms are in a position to do better even than that in the struggle for Asia's huge markets. This is one big reason why the American government should be unstinting in its support of the open world trading system and unhesitant about maintaining its role as the holder of Asia's balance of power. That America is today neither unstinting nor unhesitant poses the biggest single threat to Asia's continued prosperity.

In the case of trade, some American thinking about Asia is colored by America's experience with Japan. Leave aside the question whether that experience has been good or bad for the American economy and American business; the economic development of the great Asian landmass will not follow that of Japan. Even when Asia's fast-growing domestic markets have barriers to imports—and these vary widely across the continent—Asian countries are generally more receptive to foreign direct investment than Japan (or South Korea) has ever been. For American firms, Asia's booming markets are an almost unalloyed blessing.

What about American workers? For the large majority of them, rising incomes and demand in Asia have either no effect or a bene-

ficial one. It is true that free trade and free flows of capital speed up
the impact of technological change and that some American workers are harmed by such change. But the solution to this problem is
not to be found in resisting trade or capital flows (still less in resisting technological progress, which is responsible for most of the
dislocation that today's economies are undergoing). One of the
biggest lessons of Asia's rise is that accepting change and adapting
to it lifts up whole societies, whereas trying to protect a society and
economy from change makes for both individual and social disaster.

The world's open trading and investment system has so powerful
(and growing) a business and economic logic that the political struggle against it in the rich countries of Europe and America is likely
to prove only a rear-guard action. Yet even if walls are foolishly built
in the West against the freeish flow of goods, services, and capital,
this will only slow Asia's rise, not stop it: By 1994, trade of Asian
countries among themselves (excluding Japan) already accounted
for 18 percent of world trade, compared with the 13 percent share
that belonged to America. It would be better for everyone if the
world trading regime stays open, but it would not plunge Asia into
disaster if it did not.

So optimistic a conclusion cannot with confidence be drawn
about a possible breakdown in Asia's balance of power. The rise of
China and—above all—its increasingly tense relationship with
Japan have the potential to turn Asia back into what it was before
the past miraculous quarter-century: a huge battlefield. America,
the only power with a global reach and of sufficient importance to
every major Asian country to serve as an anchor of stability in the
region, can prevent this. Will it?

It ought to: not for Asia's sake (though a resurgence of the generosity of spirit that made the United States of 1950–90 the most
benevolent great power in history would not go amiss) but for the
sake of America's own interests. In part these interests are economic, but they also involve American security. Every time since
1930 that America has allowed geopolitical power in Asia to get
badly out of kilter, the United States has been drawn into an Asian
war. None would be bigger and more destructive than a conflict
that pitted China against Japan. It is worth a lot of America's foresight, and a modest but appreciable amount of its defense spending,
to guard against such a catastrophic event.

If catastrophe does not strike, by 2020 Asia and the West—homes to the greatest of human civilizations—will be in a very different relationship from any they have had before. When China was strong and Europe weak, there was little contact between the two. Then, when the West grew strong, it subjugated Asia. In another generation the two could well be closely entangled but also treat with each other on an equal footing. They have plenty to teach one another: Asia needs to imbibe more of the West's knowledge of technology and institution-building, and the West can learn from the successes of Asia's small governments and strong societies.

Westerners need not fear this process of intermingling, or (as Asia's Moses, Lee Kuan Yew, puts it) "grafting of buds from different trees, as each strives to improve." Asia's successes in the past forty years have come through optimism, hard work, openness, a passion to learn, a willingness to change, and a conviction that there are no free rides. Its successes in the next twenty-five years will come from the same things. These qualities are not a threat to the West. They are what made the West in the first place, and will now help to remake it.

ACKNOWLEDGMENTS

Anybody arrogant enough to write a book generalizing about the fate of three-fifths of mankind living in the world's most ancient and complex and now fastest-changing civilizations deserves all the criticism that I will now probably get. All I can say is that what has been happening in Asia since 1950 is of extraordinary and happy significance, and justifies a broad description, however simplified; and that this is a work of journalism rather than scholarship. Anyone who thinks this book has been worth reading should know that what I have been able to learn about Asia owes much more to the insight and generosity of other people than it does to me.

Asia, from the angles both mental and physical that I saw it, was made possible to me first and foremost by *The Economist*. I spent twelve years at *The Economist*, years that I suspect will turn out to have been intellectually the most influential for my life. I learned there how important it is to think clearly, write plainly, and keep an open mind. As an institution, the editorial department of *The Economist* is a place whose equal I expect never to see again, where nothing generates more respect and excitement than people successfully pursuing ideas and then vigorously explaining them. I was lucky enough to absorb this spirit while the two leading lights of the modern *Economist*, Norman Macrae and Brian Beedham, were still burning brightly there. Neither ever became editor, though I doubt that any of the men who did in their place would think I was wrong to put Norman and Brian ahead of them.

To the editors, too, under whom I served I owe thanks: Andrew Knight for hiring and promoting me against the counsel of others; Rupert Pennant-Rea for sending me to Asia when I was too ignorant to realize that I had yet to discover it; and Bill Emmott, my best friend on the magazine, for giving me the time to research this book in Asia when by all rights I should have been called back to new duties in London. From another almost-editor, and another close friend, Clive Crook, now *The Economist*'s deputy editor, I learned the power of crystal-clear logic and the breadth of social vision that can be generated by thinking like an economist.

I am grateful, too, that the people at CS First Boston, the investment bank that hired me away from *The Economist* to be its economist for Asia, had enough faith in me to give me the time to finish this book before they really knew me or I had done any work for them. Deirdre Ang, the statistician who works with me at CS First Boston in Hong Kong, ably put together the tables and charts that dot the book, and Caron Fan, my longtime secretary, made the whole thing possible through her ever bulldozerlike logistical efforts.

Several people were kind enough to read parts of the manuscript: Paul Romer in Palo Alto, Jim McGregor in Beijing, Mohan Guruswamy in Delhi, Spencer Hyman in Tokyo, Gordon Redding and Sarah Sargent in Hong Kong, and Brian Beedham in London. Each knows far more about his or her subject than I do, and I am grateful to all for their comments. It is my fault that I stubbornly refused to take all their solicited advice on board.

Toby Brown, also in Hong Kong, deserves special thanks for his advice on the book. Toby devoted almost as much care to commenting on the manuscript as I did to preparing it, giving more generously of his time and more deeply of his perceptive and well-informed thoughts about Asia—many of which I pinched without acknowledgment—than I could have expected of anyone.

I also owe a lot to the efforts and advice of two fine pairs, agents Andrew Wylie and Sarah Chalfant of Wylie, Aitken and Stone, and editors Alice Mayhew and Roger Labrie of Simon & Schuster. Books are a business, but for people like these they are still something more than that.

I spent a decade picking the brains of people all over the world for the ideas that form this book, and it is from the sum of these conversations that I profited most of all. The sources of a lot of these ideas should be obvious from the mentions (usually numerous) of their names in the text. Among those who do not happen to have been mentioned prominently enough otherwise but who have nonetheless strongly influenced my thinking are:

In Hong Kong, David Akers-Jones, Jack Cater, Alex Chan, Anson Chan, Ronnie Chan, Gary Coull, Marc Faber, Kevin Jones, Martin Lee, C. Y. Leung, Vincent Lo, Jim Mellon, Chris Patten, Patrick Thomas, James Wong, and Francis Yuen.

In China, Bob Ching, Tommy Hu, Cherry Li, David Mahon, Stapleton Roy, Wang Daohan, Wu Jinglian, Zhao Yu Jiang, and Zhou Xiaochuan.

In Taiwan, Jaw Shau-kong, Steve Kwiatkowski, Lee Kao Chao, Liang Kuo-shu, and Ma Ying-jeou.

In Korea, Han Sung Joo, Hwang Young Key, Kim Seok Ki, Lee Hong Koo, Suh Sang Mok, and Young Soo Gil.

In Japan, Kazuo Chiba, Ken Courtis, Takashi Inoguchi, Akio Mikuni, Kazuo Nukazawa, and Ken Ohmae.

In the Philippines, Jesus Estanislao, John Gokongwei, and Peter Wallace.

In Indonesia, Barry Desker, Eugene Galbraith, Mari Pangestu, and Teddy Rachmat.

In Singapore, Chan Heng Chee, Derek da Cunha, and Walter Woon.

In Thailand, Anand Panyarachun.

In Vietnam, Dan de Mirmont and Do Duc Dinh.

In India, Montek Ahluwalia, Udayan Bose, Uday Kotak, Hemendra Kothari, Amit Mitra, and Pradip Shah.

In Pakistan, Babar Ayaz.

In Britain, Cyril Lin and George Robinson.

In America, John Greenwood, Peter Harrold, Karl Jackson, Gerry Manolovici, Deryck Maughan, and Ron McKinnon.

There comes a paragraph in every acknowledgment where the author says how wonderful his or her spouse was for putting up with the trials of authorship, etc. I could never see why this was so big a deal that it deserved much thanks. That was before I had written a book.

Book-writing, I found, is a crushing, consuming, and miserable process. It was far worse for my wife, Julia Mart, who got her full share of most of the troubles of writing this book without enjoying any of its satisfactions. She bore my moods, tantrums, and absences (come to think of it, she probably appreciated those) with more patience than I deserved, especially since she was engaged at the time in the even more punishing task of starting a company of her own from scratch.

Yet I owe Julia thanks not just for forbearance but for inspiration: She evoked the spirit behind the book. She encouraged me to get out of my London rut and come to Asia in the first place. Julia is a great and infectious believer in action, movement, and new things —which, as I have learned, are what Asia is all about.

Jim Rohwer
Hong Kong, September 1995

PUBLISHED SOURCES

I have never run across a satisfactory solution to the puzzle of how sources should be cited in books of general interest. Footnotes are maddening to anyone who wants to get on with the story. On the other hand, why should you believe all the "facts" an author cites unless you are told where they come from?

In the text of this book, which I think of as an extended piece of journalism, I have pretty much adopted the practice followed at *The Economist* when I was there. This was to give a general but fairly clear idea of the sources from which the information for an article came so that readers who were interested could track them down, but not to specify the origin of every single fact or quote.

Following *Economist* practice, this book's human sources are mentioned by name, or quoted directly, only when they have some idea that is original or some way of putting it that is memorable. Anything directly quoted in this book was actually said in my hearing or has been published. Much of the information in the book came from interviews I did and other observations I made on my travels in Asia in the years 1990–95. It should, I think, almost always be obvious when I am referring to something I heard or saw firsthand.

As for the rest, this list of sources, organized by chapter and section, will tell you whence I got almost all of the published information relied upon in the book. It will not tell you exactly from where, within each of those sources, I got the information. It also will not necessarily (though it will usually) tell you from which of the cited sources a given piece of information in the text came. And a tiny number of facts came from sources I do not mention at all, such as the occasional newspaper snippet.

Whatever mistakes may have crept into the text—and I believe them to be very few—are, as any journalist would admit to you in a bar, far less significant than those that crop up as a matter of course in a normal piece of reporting, and no more rectifiable by being shoved off via citation onto someone else. So blame me if you come across something wrong.

REPEATED STATISTICAL SOURCES

Bank for International Settlements, *Annual Reports* (1991–95).
International Monetary Fund, *World Economic Outlook* (1991–95).
Asian Development Bank, *Asian Development Outlook* (1991–95).
World Bank, *World Development Report* (1987–95).
World Bank, *Global Economic Prospects and the Developing Countries* (various, 1991–95).

PROLOGUE

Robert Ford and Douglas Laxton, "World Public Debt and Real Interest Rates," IMF Working Paper WP/95/30 (March 1995).
IMF, *World Economic Outlook* (May 1995).
Christopher Tremewan, *The Political Economy of Social Control in Singapore* (Macmillan, 1994).

CHAPTER 1 *(The Miracle)*

In general

Norman Macrae, "Two Billion People," *The Economist* (May 7, 1977).
Jim Rohwer, "A Billion Consumers," *The Economist* (October 30, 1993).

Section 1

Takashi Inoguchi, *Japan's Foreign Policy in an Era of Global Change* (Pinter, 1993).
Gunnar Myrdal, *An Asian Drama* (20th Century Fund, 1968).
Frida Johansen, "Poverty Reduction in East Asia" (World Bank, 1993).

Section 2 (The Carping)

Paul Krugman, "Does Third World Growth Hurt First World Prosperity?" *Harvard Business Review* (July-August 1994).
Angus Maddison, *The World Economy in the 20th Century* (OECD, 1989).
Samuel P. Huntington, "The Clash of Civilizations," *Foreign Affairs* (November/December 1993).

Section 5 (Old and New . . .)

J. G. Farrell, *The Singapore Grip* (Weidenfeld & Nicolson, 1978).
Lucian Pye, *Asian Power and Politics* (Harvard, 1985).
World Bank, *World Population Projections* (1992–93).

CHAPTER 2 *(How East Asia Did It: The Basics)*

Section 2 (The Elements of Growth)

Angus Maddison, *Dynamic Forces in Capitalist Development* (Oxford, 1991).
World Bank, *The East Asian Miracle* (1993).

Section 3 (Labor)

Andrew Mason and Minja Kim Choe, "An Overview of Critical Population Trends and Issues" (East-West Center, 1991).
Ronald Findlay and Stanislaw Wellisz (eds.), *Five Small Open Economies* (Oxford, 1993).

Section 5 (Human Capital)

Estelle James and Gail Benjamin, *Public Policy and Private Education in Japan* (Macmillan, 1988).
Nancy Birdsall and Richard Sabot, "Growth with Equity in East Asia" (unpublished paper, World Bank, 1993).

Section 6 (That Certain Something)

Alwyn Young, "A Tale of Two Cities: Factor Accumulation and Technical Change in Hong Kong and Singapore," *NBER Macroeconomics Annual,* 1992.
Alwyn Young, "Lessons from the East Asian NICs: A Contrarian View," *European Economic Review* (1994).
Alwyn Young, "The Tyranny of Numbers: Confronting the Statistical Realities of the East Asian Growth Experience" (unpublished paper, 1993).

CHAPTER 3 *(How East Asia Did It: The Advanced Course)*

Section 1

"Taiwan and Korea: Two Paths to Prosperity," *The Economist* (July 14, 1990).

Section 2 (Two Stars in Different Orbits)

Mark Clifford, *Troubled Tiger: Businessmen, Bureaucrats, and Generals in South Korea* (Sharpe, 1994).

Section 3 (Small and Large)

Alice Amsden, *Asia's Next Giant* (Oxford, 1989).
Robert Wade, *Governing the Market* (Princeton, 1990).

Kim Kihwan and Danny Leipziger, "Korea: the Case for Effective Government-Led Development" (unpublished paper, World Bank, 1992).

Section 4 (Where Credit Was Due)

Tibor Scitovsky, "Economic Development in Taiwan and South Korea: 1965–81," *Food Research Institute Studies* (1985).
Mark Clifford (see Section 2 above).
Kim Seok Ki, "Business Concentration and Government Policy in Korea, 1945–85" (Harvard MBA thesis, 1987).

Section 5 (Governments and Their Place)

Lawrence Lau and Kim Jing Il, "The Sources of Growth of the East Asian NICs," *Journal of the Japanese and International Economies* (1994).
Amar Bhattacharya and Mari Pangestu, "Indonesia: Development Transformation Since 1965 and the Role of Public Policy" (unpublished paper, World Bank, 1992).
Ismail Salleh, Yeah Kim Leng, and Sahathevan Meyanathan, "Growth, Equity and Structural Transformation in Malaysia" (unpublished paper, World Bank, 1992).
David Friedman, *The Misunderstood Miracle* (Cornell, 1988).

Section 6 (The Idea of Ideas)

Jane Jacobs, *Cities and the Wealth of Nations* (Random House, 1984).
Paul Romer, "Two Strategies for Economic Development: Using Ideas and Producing Ideas," *World Bank Conference on Development* (1993).
Paul Romer, "Idea Gaps and Object Gaps in Economic Development" (unpublished paper, World Bank, 1993).
Paul Romer, "New Goods, Old Theory, and the Welfare Costs of Trade Restrictions," *Journal of Development Economics* (1994).

CHAPTER 4 *(How Long Can This Keep Going On?)*

Section 1

Joseph Schumpeter, *The Theory of Economic Development* (Harvard, 1934).
Alwyn Young (see Chapter 2, Section 6).
Monetary Authority of Singapore, *Annual Report* (1993/94).

Section 2 (In Brass, Muck)

Vaclav Smil, *China's Environmental Crisis* (Sharpe, 1993).

Section 3 (The Parable of Hong Kong)

Ronald Findlay and Stanislaw Wellisz, "Hong Kong," in Findlay and Wellisz (see Chapter 2, Section 3).

Section 4 (A Gamble on Democracy)

Robert Cottrell, *The End of Hong Kong* (John Murray, 1993).

CHAPTER 5 *(One Asia, Not Too Divisible)*

Section 1

P. Drysdale and R. Garnaut, "The Pacific: an Application of a General Theory of Economic Integration," in F. Bergsten and M. Noland, *Pacific Dynamism and the International Economic System* (Institute for International Economics, 1993).

Yeung Yue-man (ed.), *Pacific Asia in the 21st Century* (Chinese University Press, 1993).

Bank for International Settlements (see repeated statistical sources).

Section 2 (The Pacific Century)

C. H. Kwan, *Economic Interdependence in the Asia-Pacific Region* (Routledge, 1994).

"Economic Growth in East Asia and the Role of Foreign Direct Investment," *Bank of Japan Quarterly Bulletin* (February 1994).

Jeffrey Frankel Wei Shang-Jin, "Yen Bloc or Dollar Bloc?" in T. Ito and A. Krueger, eds., *Macroeconomic Linkage: Savings, Exchange Rates and Capital Flows* (University of Chicago, 1994).

Section 3 (Factories on the Move)

Shojiro Tokunaga (ed.), *Japan's Foreign Investment and Asian Economic Interdependence* (University of Tokyo, 1992).

Section 4 *(Primi Inter Pares)*

E. Graham and N. Anzai, "Is Japanese Direct Investment Creating an Asian Economic Bloc?" *Columbia Journal of World Business* (Fall 1994).

CHAPTER 6 *(China's Triumphs . . .)*

In general

Michael Bell, Hoe Ee Khor, and Kalpana Kochhar, *China at the Threshold of a Market Economy* (IMF, 1993).

Barry Naughton, *Growing out of the Plan: Chinese Economic Reform, 1978–1993* (Cambridge, 1994).

Dwight Perkins, *China: Asia's Next Economic Giant?* (University of Washington, 1986).

Dwight Perkins, "Reforming China's Economic System," *Journal of Economic Literature* (June 1988).

Jim Rohwer, "When China Wakes," *The Economist* (November 28, 1992).

Section 1

David Shambaugh, "The Cash and Caches of China's Brass," *Asian Wall Street Journal* (September 22, 1994).

Section 2 (What Deng Wrought)

Harrison Salisbury, *The New Emperors* (Little, Brown, 1992).
Li Zhisui, *The Private Life of Chairman Mao* (Random House, 1994).
Ross Garnaut and Ma Guonan, *Grain in China* (Australian Government Publishing Service, 1992).

Section 3 (Crossing the River by Feeling the Stones Underfoot)

Ronald McKinnon, "Gradual versus Rapid Liberalization in Socialist Economies" (International Center for Economic Growth, 1994).
John Kenneth Galbraith, *A China Passage* (Paragon, reprinted 1989).

Section 5 (Down Off the Farm)

William Byrd and Lin Qingsong, *China's Rural Industry* (Oxford, 1990).
Qian Yingyi and Xu Chenggang, "Why China's Economic Reforms Differ" (Center for Economic Policy Research, Stanford University, 1992).

Section 6 (The Bracing Wind Through the Open Door)

Nicholas Lardy, *Foreign Trade and Economic Reform in China, 1978–1990* (Cambridge, 1992).
Nicholas Lardy, *China in the World Economy* (Institute for International Economics, 1994).

Section 7 (Southern Belle)

Ezra Vogel, *One Step Ahead in China* (Harvard, 1989).

CHAPTER 7 (. . . and China's Problems)

Section 2 (Dances with Dinosaurs)

William Byrd, *Chinese Industrial Firms under Reform* (Oxford, 1992).
Gene Tidrick and Chen Jiyuan, *China's Industrial Reform* (Oxford, 1987).
Harry Broadman, "Meeting the Challenge of Chinese Enterprise Reform" (World Bank Discussion Paper 283, 1995).
Janos Kornai, *The Socialist System* (Princeton, 1992).

Section 3 (Straws of Hope)

Thomas Rawski, "Implications of China's Reform Experience" (unpublished paper, February 1995).

Gary Jefferson and Thomas Rawski, "Enterprise Reform in Chinese Industry," *Journal of Economic Perspectives* (Spring 1994).

Gary Jefferson, Thomas Rawski, Chen Kuan, Wang Hongchang, and Zheng Yuxin, "Productivity Change in Chinese Industry: 1953–1985," *Journal of Comparative Economics* (Vol. 12, 1988).

Gary Jefferson, Thomas Rawski and Yuxin Zheng, "Growth, Efficiency, and Convergence in China's State and Collective Industry," *Economic Development and Cultural Change* (Vol. 40, No. 2, 1992).

John McMillan and Barry Naughton, "How to Reform a Planned Economy: Lessons from China," *Oxford Review of Economic Policy* (Vol. 8, No. 1, 1992).

Dwight Perkins, "China's Gradual Approach to Market Reforms" (unpublished paper, 1992).

Lawrence Lau, "Growth Versus Privatization—an Alternative Strategy to Reduce the Public Sector" (unpublished paper, 1991).

Section 4 (In the Balance)

World Bank, "China Country Economic Memorandum: Macroeconomic Stability in a Decentralized Economy" (October 26, 1994).

Ronald I. McKinnon, *The Order of Economic Liberalization* (Johns Hopkins, 1993).

Section 5 (Banking on Trouble)

Qian Yingyi, "Lessons and Relevance of the Japanese Main-Bank System for Financial Reform in China" (unpublished paper, 1993).

World Bank (see Section 4).

Central Committee of the Chinese Communist Party, "The Decision on Issues Concerning the Establishment of a Socialist Market Economic Structure" (November 1993).

Section 6 (Peasants Under Heel)

Keith Griffin and Zhao Renwei, "The Distribution of Income in China" (unpublished paper, 1992).

Carl Riskin, "Rural Poverty in Post-Reform China" (unpublished paper, 1991).

Section 7 (The Non-Dangers of Disintegration)

Susan Shirk, *How China Opened Its Door* (Brookings, 1994).

Section 8 (The Party on the Precipice)

Yan Huai, "A Survey of Political Organization in China," *China Report* (August 1991).

Section 9 (Trust and Competence)

Huang Yasheng, "Why China Will Not Collapse," *Foreign Policy* (Summer 1995).

Chapter 8 *(India: The Tortoise in Its Shell)*

Section 2 (The Lost Decades and Their Consequences)

Economist Intelligence Unit, *Business China Special Report: China and India* (Summer 1995).
Isher Ahluwalia, *Productivity and Growth in Indian Manufacturing* (Oxford, 1991).

Section 3 (Planned in Hell)

Jagdish Bhagwati, *India in Transition* (Oxford, 1993).
Clive Crook, "A Tiger Caged," *The Economist* (May 4, 1991).
P. N. Dhar, "Constraints on Growth" (Oxford, 1990).

Chapter 9 *(India: The Tortoise Sets Out)*

Section 3 *(Trahison des Clercs)*

Amit Mitra, "Industrial Reforms in India" (unpublished paper, 1992).

Section 4 (Where the Roadblocks Lie)

Bhagwati (see Chapter 8, Section 3).

Section 5 (Financial Follies)

Center for Monitoring Indian Economy, *Basic Statistics Relating to the Indian Economy* (annual, 1991–95).
Philip Wyatt, "India: Testing Times Ahead for State Funding," *Asian Monetary Monitor* (May/June 1995).

Section 6 (Profane and Sacred)

F. R. Faridi and M. M. Siddiqi (eds.), *The Social Structure of Indian Muslims* (Institute of Objective Studies, 1992).

Section 8 (Percolating Up)

Economist Intelligence Unit, "Consumer Marketing in India" (1993).

Section 9 (Country Matters)

Social and Rural Research Institute, "Villages of India" (1991).

National Council of Applied Economic Research, *Consumer Market Demographics in India* (1994).

CHAPTER 10 *(The Business Roster: The West, Japan, and Korea)*

Section 3 (Eurosclerosis East)

Philippe Lasserre, "Why Europeans Are Weak in Asia," *Long Range Planning* (1988).
Philippe Lasserre and Charlotte Butler, "The European Presence in Asia: Problems and Prospects" (unpublished paper, 1992).
Harris Research, "UPS Europe Business Monitor IV" (November 1994).

Section 5 (The Hunt for Allies)

Stephen Shaw and Johannes Meier, " 'Second Generation' MNCs in China," *McKinsey Quarterly* (1993).

Section 6 (Japan, Leading but Worried)

Kazuo Wada, *Yaohan's Global Strategy* (Capital Communications, 1992).

CHAPTER 11 *(The Business Roster: The* Hua Ch'iao*)*

Section 1

Sterling Seagrave, *Lords of the Rim* (Bantam, 1995).
"The Overseas Chinese: a Driving Force," The *Economist* (July 18, 1992).
World Bank, *Global Economic Prospects and the Developing Countries* (1993).

Section 2 (The Sojourners' Life)

Gordon Redding, *The Spirit of Chinese Capitalism* (Walter de Gruyter, 1990).
Gordon Redding, "Determinants of the Competitive Power of Small Business Networking" (unpublished paper, 1991).
Gordon Redding, "Beyond Bureaucracy: Towards a Comparative Analysis of Forms of Economic Resource Coordination and Control," in D. Wong-Rieger and F. Rieger (eds.), *International Management Research* (Walter de Gruyter, 1993).

Section 3 (Misters Big)

Takuya Shikatani, "Corporate Finances of Overseas Chinese Financial Groups," *NRI Quarterly* (Spring 1995).

CHAPTER 12 *(A Billion Consumers)*

Section 2 (The Rise of the Many Haves)

Stephen Shaw and Jonathan Woetzel, "A Fresh Look at China," *McKinsey Quarterly* (1992).
DRI/McGraw Hill, *China's Consumer Market* (August 1994).
Kito de Boer and Gordon Fell, "A Fresh Look at India," *The McKinsey Quarterly* (1993).

Section 6 (Megacity Lights)

Kate Newman, *Asian Retailing* (Kleinwort Benson Research, 1993).
"Avoiding Meltdown," *Business China* (October 17, 1994).

Section 7 (Niches Riches)

Rick Yan, "To Reach China's Consumers, Adapt to Guo Qing," *Harvard Business Review* (September/October 1994).

CHAPTER 13 *(Bricks and Mortar)*

In General

World Bank, *World Development Report: Infrastructure and Development* (1994).

Section 2 (The Potential)

World Bank, "China Country Economic Memorandum: Reform and the Role of the Plan in the 1990s" (June 19, 1992).

Section 3 (The Bonanza)

World Bank, *The Emerging Asian Bond Market* (June 1995).

CHAPTER 14 *(The Money Machine)*

In General

Gideon Rachman, "Insatiable: A Survey of Asian Finance," *The Economist* (November 12, 1994).
Ronald I. McKinnon, *The Order of Economic Liberalization* (see Chapter 7, Section 4)

Section 3 (Informality)

Jeffrey Frankel, "Recent Changes in the Financial Systems of Asian and Pacific Countries" (University of California, Berkeley, Center for International and Development Economics Research, December 1993).

Joseph Stiglitz, "The Role of the State in Financial Markets," *Annual Conference on Development Economics* (World Bank, 1993).

Section 4 *(Droit de Seignor)*

Richard Doner and Daniel Unger, "The Politics of Finance in Thai Economic Development" (unpublished paper, 1993).
Yoshio Suzuki (ed.), *The Japanese Financial System* (Oxford, 1992).
Amar Bhattacharya and Mari Pangestu (see Chapter 3, Section 5).

Section 5 (Intermediaries . . .)

"Citicorp in Asia," *The Economist* (October 24, 1992).

Section 7 (Bondage and Denomination)

Organization for Economic Co-operation and Development, *Emerging Bond Markets in the Dynamic Asian Economies* (1993)
World Bank, *The Emerging Asian Bond Market* (June 1995)

CHAPTER 15 *(War and Peace)*

Section 2 (What Vietnam Meant)

Robert McNamara, *In Retrospect: The Tragedy and Lessons of Vietnam* (Random House, 1995).

Section 3 (The Spending Spree)

Stockholm International Peace Research Institute, *Yearbooks* (1989–95).
International Institute for Strategic Studies, *The Military Balance* (1989–95).
"Asia's Arms Race," *The Economist* (February 20, 1993).
Andrew Mack, "Arms Proliferation in the Asia-Pacific" (unpublished paper, 1993).

Section 4 (From Threat to Uncertainty)

Jonathan Pollack, "The United States in East Asia: Holding the Ring" (unpublished, 1993).

Section 6 (China on the Rise)

David Shambaugh (see Chapter 6, Section 1).

Section 7 (The Policeman on the Beat)

Joseph Nye, "The Case for Deep Engagement," *Foreign Affairs* (July/August 1995).

CHAPTER 16 *(Politics and Society: Asia's New Millennium)*

Section 3 (Transitions . . .)

Mancur Olson, *The Logic of Collective Action* (Harvard, 1965).

Section 4 (. . . and Traditions)

Robert Putnam, *Making Democracy Work* (Princeton, 1993).
Fareed Zakaria, "Culture Is Destiny: A Conversation with Lee Kuan Yew," *Foreign Affairs* (March/April 1994).
Surjit S. Bhalla, "Free Societies, Free Markets and Social Welfare" (unpublished paper, 1994).

Section 6 (Asian Values)

Kim Dae Jung, "Is Culture Destiny?" *Foreign Affairs* (November/December 1994).
Joseph Schumpeter, *Capitalism, Socialism and Democracy* (1942).
Asian Wall Street Journal editorial (January 10, 1995).
Eric Jones, "Asia's Fate: A Response to the Singapore School," *The National Interest* (Spring 1994).

EPILOGUE

Section 1

Kishore Mahbubani, "The Pacific Way," *Foreign Affairs* (January/February 1995).

Section 3 (Bud-Grafting)

"Some Aspects of the Dollar/Yen Disequilibrium," *The China Analyst* (May 1995).

INDEX